# SHARED LEADERSHIP

*Dedicated to*
*Clayton L. "Bud" Pearce*
*Wilma "Sally" Pearce*
*and*
*Nathaniel Alden Conger*
*Zoe Elise Conger*

# SHARED LEADERSHIP

## Reframing the Hows and Whys of Leadership

### Editors

## Craig L. Pearce
Claremont Graduate University

## Jay A. Conger
University of Southern California

**SAGE Publications**
*International Educational and Professional Publisher*
Thousand Oaks ▪ London ▪ New Delhi

*For information:*

Sage Publications, Inc.
2455 Teller Road
Thousand Oaks, California 91320
E-mail: order@sagepub.com

Sage Publications Ltd.
6 Bonhill Street
London EC2A 4PU
United Kingdom

Sage Publications India Pvt. Ltd.
B-42 Panchsheel Enclave
Post Box 4109
New Delhi 110 017 India

Printed in the United States of America

*Library of Congress Cataloging-in-Publication Data*

Shared leadership: Reframing the how's and why's of leadership / [edited by] Craig L. Pearce, Jay A. Conger.
    p. cm.
Includes bibliographical references and index.
ISBN 0-7619-2623-2 © — ISBN 0-7619-2624-0 (P)
    1. Leadership. 2. Teams in the workplace. I. Pearce, Craig L. II. Conger, Jay Alden.
HM1261 .S53 2003
303.3´4—dc211

                          2002010085

02  03  04  10  9  8  7  6  5  4  3  2  1

| | |
|---|---|
| *Acquiring Editor:* | Al Bruckner |
| *Editorial Assistant:* | MaryAnn Vail |
| *Production Editor:* | Diana E. Axelsen |
| *Typesetter:* | C&M Digitals (P) Ltd. |
| *Indexer:* | Jeanne Busemeyer |
| *Cover Designer:* | Janet Foulger |

# Contents

# Preface

Leadership has historically been conceived around an individual and his or her relationship to subordinates or followers. As a result, the leadership field has focused its attention on the behaviors, mindsets, and actions of *the leader* in a team or organization. This paradigm has dominated our thinking in the organizational behavior field for decades. In recent years, however, a few scholars have challenged this notion, arguing that leadership is an *activity* that is shared or distributed among members of a group or organization. For example, depending on the demands of the moment, individuals can rise to the occasion to exhibit leadership and then step back at other times to allow others to lead. This line of thinking is gaining attention among leadership scholars. Yet our understanding of the dynamics and opportunities for shared leadership is still quite primitive. Given the infancy of the field, it is timely to introduce a volume on the subject that would significantly "jumpstart" our knowledge. *Shared Leadership* is designed to do just that. It brings together in one resource the foremost thinkers on the subject. Its aim is to advance our understanding along the many dimensions of the shared leadership phenomenon: its dynamics, moderators, appropriate settings, facilitating factors, contingencies, measurement, practice implications, and directions for future research.

## Why Is Shared Leadership an Important Topic?

Today, the fastest growing organizational unit is the team, specifically cross-functional teams. What distinguishes these groups from traditional organizational forms is often the absence of hierarchical authority. Although a cross-functional team may have a formally appointed leader, this individual is more commonly treated as a peer—opening the door to shared leadership. Leadership is therefore not determined by positions of authority but rather by an individual's capacity to influence peers and by the needs of the team in any given moment. In addition, each member of the team brings unique perspectives, knowledge, and capabilities to the team. At different junctures in the team's life, there are moments when these differing background characteristics provide a platform for leadership to be distributed among the team.

Moreover, it is important to remember that teamwork and its implications for shared leadership are not limited to junior levels of the organizations. For example, at the very peak of corporations, there have been a growing number of experiments in which leadership is being shared. At Dell, for instance, there is an "office of the CEO" where the responsibilities of the chief executive are distributed among several executives. As organizations and their worlds grow more and more complex, it is increasingly difficult for a single individual holding the position of chief executive officer to lead. In many ways, organizations are today ripe for shared leadership across all levels.

Although the need for shared leadership has grown, our knowledge of it lags seriously behind. Mentioned in our introductory chapter is the fact that the leadership field has focused almost entirely on conceptions of *the leader* as a single individual to the neglect of distributed forms of leadership. As a result, there have only been a small number of published studies to examine distributed forms of leadership. It seems timely in light of the growing demand and opportunities for shared leadership that a volume that pushes the boundaries of our current knowledge be produced.

## Audience for the Book

This book will be attractive for a number of audiences. First, there is a large community of academics in the leadership, management, organizational behavior, industrial/organizational psychology, and social psychology fields who are concerned about team effectiveness, leadership, executive behavior, and organizational performance. They will find this volume full of new findings, theoretical advances, and future research directions. Second, *Shared Leadership* would be very appropriate as a text in an organizational behavior or general management course or as a principal text in a seminar devoted to teamwork or leadership. Finally, practitioners will have an interest in the book—specifically, individuals engaged in leadership and team development either as consultants or internal company resources. Managers who have a keen interest in building more effective teams and in their own approaches to leadership will find important lessons as well.

## Acknowledgments

Many people deserve acknowledgement for their roles in helping this book become a reality. First, we are both thankful for the colleagues we have around us at our respective institutions. We would specifically like to thank Mihaly Csikszentmihalyi and Jean Lipman-Blumen for their helpful comments on our introductory chapter. Also, the administrative assistance of Tamer Awad and Sandra Dirks was indispensable in bringing together the final copy.

The authors of the chapters deserve special recognition. Not only did they agree to contribute chapters, but also they produced outstanding contributions that provide the foundations for advancing future scholarship in the realm of shared leadership. We would also like to thank Henry P. Sims, Jr., for his continued encouragement on this project. Finally, as the coeditors of a volume on shared leadership, we would like to recognize each other for mastering the sharing of leadership roles on this volume. We can say from our own experience that leadership can indeed be shared.

— *Craig L. Pearce*
— *Jay A. Conger*

# CHAPTER 1

# All Those Years Ago

## *The Historical Underpinnings of Shared Leadership*

*Craig L. Pearce*

*Jay A. Conger*

The purpose of this book is to articulate a model of a particular form of leadership—shared leadership—and to stimulate future research on this poorly understood form of leadership. We define shared leadership as a dynamic, interactive influence process among individuals in groups for which the objective is to lead one another to the achievement of group or organizational goals or both. This influence process often involves peer, or lateral, influence and at other times involves upward or downward hierarchical influence. The key distinction between shared leadership and traditional models of leadership is that the influence process involves more than just downward influence on subordinates by an appointed or elected leader (see Pearce & Sims, 2000, 2002). Rather, leadership is broadly distributed among a set of individuals instead of centralized in hands of a single individual who acts in the role of a superior.

This conceptualization of leadership stands in stark contrast to traditional notions. Historically, leadership has been conceived around a single individual—*the leader*—and the relationship of that individual to subordinates or followers (see Chapter 1, Conger & Kanungo, 1998). This relationship between the leader and the led has been a vertical one of top-down influence. As a result, the leadership field has focused its attention on the behaviors, mind-sets, and actions of "the leader" in a team or organization. This paradigm has been the dominant one in the leadership field for many decades. In recent years, however, a few scholars have challenged this conception, arguing that leadership is an *activity* that can be shared or distributed among members of a group or organization. For example, depending on the demands of the moment, individuals who are not formally appointed as leaders can rise to the occasion to exhibit leadership and then step back at other times to allow others to lead. This line of thinking is gaining attention among leadership scholars. Yet our understanding of the dynamics and opportunities for shared leadership remains quite primitive. At the same time, there is a sense of urgency to understand the dynamics of this phenomenon given growing demands for shared leadership within the world of organizations.

These demands have largely to do with shifts in how work is performed. For example, today the fastest growing organizational unit is the team and, specifically, cross-functional teams. What distinguishes these units from traditional organizational forms is the absence of hierarchical authority. Although a cross-functional team may have a formally appointed leader, this individual is more commonly treated as a peer. For example, outside the team, they often do not possess line authority over the individual members. Moreover, the formal leader is usually at a knowledge disadvantage. After all, the purpose of the cross-functional team is to bring a very diverse set of functional backgrounds together. The formal leader's expertise represents only one of the numerous functional specialties at the table. The leader is therefore highly dependent on the expertise of team members. Leadership in these settings is not determined by positions of authority or depth of expertise but rather by an individual's capacity to influence peers and by the leadership needs of the team in a given moment. In addition, each member of the team brings unique perspectives, knowledge, and capabilities to the team. At various junctures in the team's life, there are moments when these differing backgrounds and characteristics provide a platform for leadership to be distributed across the team.

In addition to organizational demands for team-based work arrangements, there is a parallel demand for leadership to be more equally distributed up and down the hierarchy. This need is being driven by a number of forces. The first is the realization that seniormost leaders may not possess sufficient and relevant information to make highly effective decisions in a fast-changing and complex world. In reality, managers down the line may be more highly informed and in a far better position to provide leadership. Second, speed of response is an organizational imperative given a faster-paced environment. Many companies, for example, have actually incorporated speed as one of their core values (General Electric being the most commonly cited example). This demand suggests that organizations cannot wait for leadership decisions to be pushed up to the top for action. Instead, leadership has to be distributed or shared across the organization to ensure speedier response times. The final force driving the need for shared leadership has to do with the complexity of the job held by the seniormost leader in an organization—the chief executive officer. Increasingly, this individual is hard-pressed to possess all the leadership skills and knowledge necessary to guide complex organizations in a dynamic and global marketplace. In response to this dilemma, there have been a growing number of experiments in which leadership is being shared at the very top. At Dell, for example, there is an office of the CEO where the responsibilities of the chief executive are distributed among several executives. In summary, a powerful set of forces within organizations is fostering greater demand for shared leadership across all levels.

Although the need and appreciation for shared leadership has been growing, our understanding of it lags seriously behind. In large part, this shortcoming is due to the leadership field's singular focus on the conception of an individual leader to the neglect of distributed forms of leadership. As a result, there have only been a small number of published studies examining shared forms of leadership. For example, until very recently, only two publications have indicated a clear interest in shared leadership as a potential mechanism for constructively engaging in integrated human effort. The first was in the 1920s, and the second occurred more than 40 years later in the mid-1960s. Shortly, we will describe in some detail these two instances.

The purpose of this introductory chapter is to provide a historical backdrop for shared leadership. As Bass and Avolio (1993) have astutely noted, the field of leadership often reinvents itself without regard to previous theory. We hope to avoid falling into this selective memory trap and, rather, hope to illuminate the extensive historical underpinnings of the concept of shared leadership. Specifically, we wish to illustrate how our current conceptions of the phenomenon have been shaped by other contributions in the fields of leadership, organizational behavior, psychology, and teamwork (see Table 1.1). In so doing, we intend to craft the proper space for future research on the topic to be well-grounded and to advance the understanding and practice of teamwork and leadership in a deeper, more meaningful way.

## The Emergence of the Scientific Study of Leadership: The Leader in a Command Role

Not until the Industrial Revolution was the task of leadership formally studied and documented in a scientific manner: At the beginning of the 1800s, leadership and management was formally recognized as a factor of production when Jean Baptiste Say (1803/1964), a French economist, claimed that entrepreneurs "must possess the art of superintendence and administration" (p. 330). Prior to this time, economists were primarily occupied with two factors of production—land and labor—and, to a lesser extent, capital. During the Industrial Revolution, however, the concept of leadership as important to economic endeavor was recognized. Nonetheless, the predominant role of leadership was command and control. It was not until much later that we observed slight acknowledgment of concepts related to the notion of shared leadership.

The emphasis on leadership centered on control or oversight—in other words, the "vertical model" of leading. For example, James Montgomery (1840) is credited as the first author to scientifically study industrial management and leadership. In 1840, he published a book that compared and contrasted cotton manufacturing in the United States and Great Britain. He concluded that the British organizations were more effective based on their enhanced level of managerial expertise. This expertise was largely focused on the establishment of control systems (Wren, 1994).

Throughout the 1800s, the literature on management focused primarily on organizational forms, structures, and manufacturing processes shaped in large part by the advent of the Industrial Age and the needs of an emerging new industry—the railroads. The advent of the railroads, the first of the large-scale American corporations, necessitated more systematic organizational and leadership approaches to coordinate and control these vast organizations that were geographically dispersed, capital intensive, and employing large numbers of people (Chandler, 1965).

**Table 1.1**    Historical Bases of Shared Leadership

| Theory/Research | Key Issues | Representative Authors |
|---|---|---|
| Law of the situation | Let the situation, not the individual, determine the "orders." | Follett (1924) |
| Human relations and social systems perspective | One should pay attention to the social and psychological needs of employees. | Turner (1933) Mayo (1933) Barnard (1938) |
| Role differentiation in groups | Members of groups typically assume different types of roles. | Benne and Sheats (1948) |
| Co-leadership | Concerns the division of the leadership role between two people—primarily research examines mentor and protégé relationships. | Solomon, Loeffer, and Frank (1953) Hennan and Bennis (1998) |
| Social exchange theory | People exchange punishments and rewards in their social interactions. | Festinger (1954) Homans (1958) |
| Management by objectives and participative goal setting | Subordinates and superiors jointly set performance expectations. | Drucker (1954) Erez and Arad (1986) Locke and Latham (1990) |
| Emergent leadership | Leaders can "emerge" from a leaderless group. | Hollander (1961) |
| Mutual leadership | Leadership can come from peers. | Bowers and Seashore (1966) |
| Expectation states Theory and team member exchange | Team members develop models of status differential between various team members. | Berger, Cohen, and Zelditch (1972) Seers (1989) |
| Participative decision making | Under certain circumstances, it is advisable to elicit more involvement by subordinates in the decision-making process. | Vroom and Yetton (1973) |
| Vertical dyad linkage/leader member exchange | Examines the process between leaders and followers and the creation of in-groups and out-groups. | Graen (1976) |
| Substitutes for leadership | Situation characteristics (e.g., highly routinized work) diminish the need for leadership. | Kerr and Jermier (1978) |
| Self-leadership | Employees, given certain conditions, are capable of leading themselves. | Manz and Sims (1980) |
| Self-managing work teams | Team members can take on roles that were formerly reserved for managers. | Manz and Sims (1987, 1993) |

| Theory/Research | Key Issues | Representative Authors |
|---|---|---|
| Followership | Examines the characteristics of good followers. | Kelly (1988) |
| Empowerment | Examines power sharing with subordinates. | Conger and Kanungo (1988) |
| Shared cognition | Examines the extent to which team members hold similar mental models about key internal and external environmental issues. | Klimoski and Mohammed (1994) Cannon-Bowers and Salas (1993) Ensley and Pearce (2001) |
| Connective leadership | Examines how well leaders are able to make connections to others both inside and outside the team. | Lipman-Blumen (1996) |

One of the early management thinkers in this arena was Daniel C. McCallum. He developed six principles of management, and this was perhaps the first articulation of management principles that could apply across industrial lines. One of McCallum's principles dealt specifically with the notion of leadership. Although this principle did not indicate what was appropriate leadership, it indicated that the organization should not interfere with supervisors' "influence with their subordinates" (Wren, 1994, p. 77). Thus, during the mid-1800s, we observe the beginnings of interest in the scientific study of leadership.

By the turn of the century, thinking on management and leadership had crystallized into what was ultimately termed "scientific management" (Gantt, 1916; Gilbreth, 1912; Gilbreth & Gilbreth, 1917; Taylor, 1903, 1911). The fundamental principle of scientific management was that all work could be studied scientifically and optimal procedures could be developed to ensure maximum productivity. An important component of scientific management was the separation of managerial and worker responsibilities, with managerial ranks having responsibility for identifying precise work procedures and workers following the dictates of management to the letter. Thus, scientific management perhaps went the furthest in clearly articulating a command-and-control perspective on the role of leaders in organizational life. The formally appointed leader was to oversee and direct those below. Subordinates were to follow instructions to the letter. The notion that leaders and their subordinates might mutually influence one another was largely unthinkable at the time.

During the period of the development of scientific management in the United States, two Europeans also made particularly noteworthy intellectual contributions to the formal study of leadership. Henri Fayol from France derived 14 flexible principles of management (Fayol, 1916/1949). Thus, one could credit him with early developments in contingency theory. The second, Max Weber from Germany, developed both a theory of organizational structure—bureaucracy (Weber, 1924/1947)—and a theory of authority or leadership (Weber, 1905/1958). Both individuals clearly articulated influence or leadership processes centered on an individual leader whose authority was top-down and based on command and control. Thus, by the end of the Industrial Revolution, management and leadership had come to be scientifically studied. The consensus was one that emphasized a distinction between leaders and followers and rested on the principle of the unity of command. Orders should come from above and be followed by those below. In addition, these early thinkers on management also spent considerable time trying to figure out ways to prevent followers from shirking responsibilities and thus designed more and more elaborate methods for controlling the behavior of followers. The absolute control of worker behavior—down to the smallest detail—was defined as the prerogative of management.

# The Management Field's Brief Flirtations With Concepts Related to Shared Leadership

Despite this strong historical emphasis on a command-and-control approach to leadership, alternative perspectives did appear in the 20th century—albeit briefly. In fact, in two instances, management thinkers pointed to the possibility of shared leadership processes augmenting the strictly command and control orientation to leadership. These are reviewed below.

## Flirtation Number One

Mary Parker Follett (1924) introduced the concept of the *law of the situation.* The law of the situation stated that rather than simply following the lead of the person with the formal authority in a situation, one should follow the lead of the person with the most knowledge regarding the situation at hand. Thus, Follett proposed a radically different leadership process in contrast to her contemporaries—one closely aligned with the concept of shared leadership.

Follett was a popular speaker and management consultant during the 1920s and was regarded as "the brightest star in the management firmament" of the times (Drucker, 1995, p. 2). Many of her ideas, however, were discounted and discarded by business leaders due to the socioeconomic realities of the late 1920s, 1930s, and 1940s. This period erased any notion that workers might actively shape the thinking and actions of management. Peter Drucker recalls a conversation he had with a member of the National Labor Relations Board (NLRB) in the late 1940s that powerfully illustrates the attitudes of the times. Drucker (1995) explains that

> when I said something about both management and workers having "a common interest in the survival and prosperity of the company" (also one of Follett's arguments, although I did not know that at the time), my friend cut me short: "Any company that asserts such a common interest," he said, "is prima facie in violation of the law and guilty of a grossly unfair labor practice." (p. 5)

Thus, the common wisdom following the stock market crash and depression years was very much one of command and control: Leaders and subordinates in the modern industrial complex were to have separate roles and conflicting goals. Influence was to remain vertical and unidirectional—downward.

## Flirtation Number Two

The second instance of historical interest in shared leadership-type concepts came with the Bowers and Seashore (1966) study of insurance offices. Interestingly enough, Bowers and Seashore did not cite Follett in their theoretical development of a concept they termed "mutual leadership."

What Bowers and Seashore (1966) empirically documented was that leadership influence processes could come from peers and that this source of leadership could positively affect organizational outcomes. As with Follett over 40 years earlier, however, the Bowers and Seashore study was a mere blip on the radar screen of scientific thought regarding leadership processes. Their concept of mutual leadership came and went much the same as did Follett's concept of the law of the situation.

Not until the late 1990s did scholars return to an examination of shared leadership in organizations. In reality, although the majority of scholars have not explicitly conceived of leadership as a shared phenomenon, there have been implicit links for some time. Important theoretical developments from the 1930s through the 1960s in the fields of leadership, psychology, and organizational behavior laid historical roots that today inform the study of shared leadership.

# Laying the Theoretical Groundwork for Shared Leadership: Organizational Research From the 1930s Through the 1960s

Between Follett's (1924) book and the Bowers and Seashore (1966) paper, the interest in topics related to shared leadership was not completely absent. At least six theoretical contributions have informed our current understanding of the concept of shared leadership. These are (a) the human relations and social systems perspective, (b) role differentiation in groups, (c) co-leadership, (d) social exchange theory, (e) management by objectives and later research on participative goal setting, and (f) emergent leadership theory (see Table 1.1).

## Human Relations and Social Systems Perspectives

The major advance in the 1930s regarding the management of organizations was the adoption of a *social* view of organizational life. The relations between leaders and those led took on new significance with a newfound emphasis on interpersonal dynamics in the workplace (e.g., Barnard, 1938; Mayo, 1933; Roethlisberger & Dickson, 1939; Turner, 1933). This viewpoint did not characterize workers as shirkers who primarily required direction and control but, rather, suggested that leaders needed to understand the psychological bases of human motivation in order to more fully integrate employees into a productive system. Accordingly, this major advance—paying attention to the psychological needs of employees—was an important step toward the ultimate articulation of shared leadership as an organizational possibility. It opened the possibility that the act of leadership was not simply a unidirectional process of "leader to led" but, rather, a more complex one in which subordinates and their needs might influence the leader as well.

## Role Differentiation in Groups

By articulating 19 distinct roles that members of a working group could serve, Benne and Sheats (1948) raised the possibility that group members played roles as critical as that of the group's leader. In addition, several of these roles could be considered leadership roles. Leadership was no longer unidirectional but was now a reciprocal process. Benne and Sheats subdivided their roles under two broad categories: task roles and socioemotional roles. Task roles included initiator/contributor, information seeker, opinion seeker, opinion giver, elaborator, coordinator, orienter, evaluator/critic, energizer, procedural technician, and recorder. Socioemotional roles included encourager, harmonizer, compromiser, gatekeeper/expediter, standard setter, group observer/commentator, and follower. The important contribution of this early work on role differentiation was that it identified the potential for different types of influence originating from different members of the group beyond the formally appointed leader. There was a growing realization that members of a group could be playing roles as influential as the leader him or herself. Many of these types of influence that Benne and Sheats describe fall squarely into the realm of the modern-day purview of leader behavior research (see Pearce & Sims, 2000, 2002). Thus, they opened the door to the study of shared leadership dynamics within groups through the notion of multiple roles.

## Co-Leadership

Early writings on co-leadership research appeared in the early 1950s (Solomon, Loeffer, & Frank, 1953). This work focused primarily on situations in which two individuals simultaneously shared one leadership position. The literature, however, has been dominated by research in *group therapy settings* where co-leaders occupy mentor-protégé relationships (e.g., Mintz, 1963; Rittner & Hammons, 1992; Solomon et al., 1953; Winter, 1976). Much of it examines how co-leadership develops (e.g., Winter, 1976) and the tactics for improving co-leadership effectiveness in these settings (e.g., Greene, Morrison, & Tischler, 1981; Herzog, 1981). Since this literature is primarily concerned with mentor-protégé relationships, it might be viewed as a special case of vertical leadership. In last few years, there have also been explorations of co-leadership in the executive suite—most notably between the CEO and COO or between a company founder and his or her "right hand man," or woman, as the case may be (e.g., Heenan & Bennis, 1999). Under these circumstances, co-leadership can be considered a special case of shared leadership—the two-person case. Nonetheless, co-leadership, although a distinct concept, is clearly related to the concept of shared leadership.

## Social Exchange Theory

Originating in the 1950s, social exchange theory (Festinger, 1954; Homans, 1958; Thibaut & Kelly, 1959) extends theories of economic exchange by claiming that people enter into social relationships expecting some type of social "gain" and some type of social "cost." This body of work is concerned with "the exchange of rewards and punishments that take place when people interact" (Berscheid, 1985,

p. 429). Much of the work in social exchange theory has dealt with friendship groups and interpersonal attractiveness (Byrne, Ervin, & Lamberth, 1970; Festinger, 1954; Newcomb, 1960). The essence of this theory, as it relates to shared leadership, is that it suggests that influence processes are embedded in most, if not all, social interactions and, by extension, influence is not limited to appointed leaders but widely distributed among others.

## Management by Objectives and Participative Goal Setting

Drucker (1954) identified management by objectives (MBO) as a useful technique for engaging individuals by tying their objectives to the larger organizational purpose. The essence of MBO is that subordinates and superiors actively engage in a process of articulating the objectives toward which subordinates will work and subsequently the ones they will be held accountable for achieving. Extensions to MBO followed under the rubric of participative goal-setting research (see Erez & Arad, 1986; Locke & Latham, 1990), in which subordinates participate in defining their objectives. The leader is no longer the sole source for defining the objectives of their subordinates; rather, this becomes a *shared* activity. MBO and participative goal setting therefore identify a role for subordinates in the articulation of performance expectations and thus inch us closer toward a model of shared leadership in organizations.

## Emergent Leadership

Developed by Hollander (1961), the concept of emergent leadership refers to the phenomenon of leader selection by the members of a leaderless group (e.g., Bartol & Martin, 1986; Hollander, 1978; Stein & Heller, 1979). Whereas emergent leadership is typically concerned with the ultimate selection of an appointed leader, the concept of shared leadership is linked to the "serial emergence" of multiple leaders over the life of the team (Pearce, 1997, 2002). Thus, emergent leadership provides yet another theoretical base for shared leadership.

# Building the Case for Shared Leadership: Organizational Research From the 1970s Through the Turn of the Millennium

As the preceding section suggests, the period of the 1930s through the 1960s witnessed several interesting developments in the scientific study of management and leadership. These developments culminated in the Bowers and Seashore (1966) study of mutual leadership. Following their study of mutual leadership, however, the field once again lost sight of shared leadership. Instead, scholars began work on several other theoretical concepts that help to provide a rich theoretical foundation for the emergence of the study of shared leadership today and in the future. The period of the 1970s through the turn of the millennium, not counting participative goal-setting research (which was discussed earlier), witnessed the development of at least 10 conceptual foundations related to the conceptualization of shared leadership: (a) expectation states theory, which later led to research on team member exchange; (b) participative decision making; (c) vertical dyad linkage theory (later termed leader-member exchange); (d) substitutes for leadership; (e) self-leadership; (f) self-managing work teams; (g) followership; (h) empowerment; (i) shared cognition; and (j) connective leadership (see Table 1.1). We review each of these, in turn, below.

## Expectation States Theory and Team Member Exchange

Building on social exchange theory, Berger, Cohen, and Zelditch (1972) developed expectation states theory. Expectation states theory suggests that team members intuitively develop ideas regarding one another's status in the team. Later, elaborating on and integrating expectation states theory and leader member exchange, Seers (1989) introduced the team member exchange construct. Whereas leader member exchange focuses on the quality of the relationships between leaders and their followers, team member exchange focuses on the quality of the exchange relationships between the team members. Seers theorized that the quality of the exchange attributed to individuals was positively related to their respective status in the team. Thus, from a shared leadership perspective, this idea translates into the possibility of individual members (beyond the leader) gaining status to the point at which they are able to influence the team themselves. More important, this perspective suggests that different individuals may acquire high levels of status depending on the specific function or task being addressed, thereby permitting the transference of the influence process from one team member to the next.

## Participative Decision Making

Vroom and Yetton (1973) articulated a model that prescribed when and how leaders should involve their subordinates in the decision-making process. Generally speaking, their model suggests that greater involvement is required under the following conditions: when there is a higher need for quality decision making; when subordinates have knowledge that augments the leader's knowledge; when subordinate acceptance of the decision is important; and when there is low potential conflict among subordinates regarding the potential decision. Thus, Vroom and Yetton's model identifies certain circumstances under which shared leadership is likely to be more or less efficacious than directive forms of vertical leadership.

## Vertical Dyad Linkage/Leader-Member Exchange

Building on social network theory, Graen and colleagues (e.g., Graen, 1976; Graen & Scandura, 1987; Graen & Schiemann, 1978) introduced vertical dyad linkage/leader-member exchange (LMX) into the formal lexicon of leadership studies. These authors have discussed the importance of the leader-follower dyad in their work on leadership process. The theory suggests that leaders will need to vary their styles depending on different subordinates. In other words, subordinates influence how the leader behaves. Their work suggests that followers have a role in the leadership process, but do not go so far as to say that the source of leadership can be from the followers, as is the case with shared leadership.

## Substitutes for Leadership

The substitutes for leadership literature (e.g., Kerr & Jermier, 1978) also provides a useful framework for understanding the concept of shared leadership. The literature on substitutes for leadership suggests that certain conditions, such as highly routinized work or professional standards, may serve as substitutes for social sources of leadership. In this sense, shared leadership may serve as a substitute for more formal appointed leadership. For example, if team members are actively involved in developing the vision for their team, it may be possible that a strong visionary leader is not necessary for the team to focus on its distal goals. Therefore, the substitutes for leadership concept serves as another theoretical base of shared leadership.

## Self-Leadership

Building on the substitutes for leadership framework, Manz and Sims (1980) identified self-management, or self-leadership, as a potential substitute for more formal leadership. To the extent that subordinates were knowledgeable about organizational needs, had appropriate skills for the tasks at hand, and were motivated to engage in productive activity, self-leadership could alleviate the need for close supervision, direction, and control. If we take their argument to the group level of analysis, we might see how shared leadership could operate in a similar manner. In fact, Pearce and Sims (2002) identified shared leadership as accounting for more variance in team performance than the leadership displayed by the appointed leaders of the teams in their study of 71 change management teams.

## Self-Managing Work Teams

Recent work on self-managing work teams (SMWTs) has taken the boldest steps toward articulating the concept of shared leadership (e.g., Manz, Keating, & Donnellon, 1990; Manz & Sims 1987, 1993; Stewart & Manz, 1995). Although recognizing that team members can, and do, take on roles that were previously reserved for management, this literature focuses more on the role of the appointed leader and less on the role of the team members in the leadership process (see Stewart & Manz, 1995). Thus, although the self-managing work teams literature does acknowledge the role of team members in the leadership process, it does not go so far as to suggest a systematic approach to the examination of how, and to what effect, the process of leadership can be shared by the team as a whole.

## Followership

Although followers have not been of central interest in leadership research, several scholars and practitioners from widely disparate fields have emphasized the role that followers play in the leadership process (e.g., Campbell & Kinion, 1993; Cooper, Higgott, & Nossal, 1991; Kelly 1988; Lundin & Lancaster, 1990; Nakamura, 1980; Nishigaki, Vavrin, Kano, Haga, Kunz, & Law, 1994; Rippy, 1990; R. Smith, 1991; W. Smith, 1994). The primary emphasis of this line of research is around the definition of what constitutes "good" followership. Kelly (1988) defined good followers as those who

> have the vision to see both the forest and the trees, the social capacity to work well with others, the strength of character to flourish without heroic status, the moral and psychological balance to pursue personal and corporate goals at no cost to either, and, above all, the desire to participate in a team effort for the accomplishment of some greater purpose. (p. 107)

Under conditions of shared leadership, followership is dynamically determined. Thus, the need for good followership skills in all team members is heightened: Team members need to be able to clearly recognize when they should be leading and when they should be following.

## Empowerment

The topic of empowerment has received considerable attention in recent years (e.g., Blau & Alba, 1982; Conger & Kanungo, 1988; Manz, 1986; Manz & Sims, 1989, 1990; Mohrman, Cohen, & Mohrman, 1995; Pearce & Sims, 2000, 2002; Cox, Pearce, & Sims, in press). The central issue in the empowerment literature is that of power (e.g., Conger & Kanungo, 1988). Whereas traditional models of management emphasize power emanating from the top of an organization, the empowerment concept emphasizes the decentralization of power. The rationale behind empowering individual workers is that those dealing with situations on a daily basis are the most qualified to make decisions regarding those situations.

Although the vast majority of the empowerment literature focuses on the impact on the individual (e.g., Conger & Kanungo, 1988), some researchers have expanded the concept to the group level of analysis (e.g., Mohrman et al., 1995). To empower, or share power with, members of a team, however, is not the same as observing shared leadership emanating from a group. Shared leadership only exists to the extent that the team actively engages in the leadership process. As such, empowerment is a necessary, but not sufficient, condition for shared leadership to be developed and displayed by teams.

## Shared Cognition

Shared cognition in teams primarily refers to the extent to which the team members have similar "mental maps" regarding important aspects of their internal and external environment. As recently as 1991, shared cognition was viewed as "almost a contradiction in terms" (Resnick, 1991, p. 1). As more and more organizations are turning to team-based approaches to organizing (Aldag & Fuller, 1993), however, the study of teams has become increasingly important in recent years. With the focus on teams, organizational researchers have taken a strong interest in the role shared cognition may play in teams in an effort to develop a deeper understanding of team dynamics and team effectiveness (e.g., Cannon-Bowers, Salas, & Converse, 1993; Ensley & Pearce, 2001; Klimoski & Mohammed, 1994; Knight et al., 1999). Shared cognition theory advances our understanding of shared leadership by providing a cognitive framework through which leadership might be shared: Without similar mental models, it seems unlikely that team members would be able to accurately interpret influence attempts within the team, and the potential effectiveness of shared leadership would be seriously limited. Thus, shared cognition provides yet another conceptual foundation for shared leadership.

## Connective Leadership

Lipman-Blumen (1996) introduced the concept of connective leadership. Connective leadership focuses on the ability of leaders to develop interpersonal connections both internal to the team and in external networks. Although most of the discussion of shared leadership is focused on the internal leadership dynamics within teams, connective leadership helps in further developing the external focus of leadership activity by the team. For example, it explores the necessity of leaders to connect their own visions with the visions of their constituents.

# The "Arrival" of Shared Leadership and the Way Forward

From the 1970s to the mid-1990s, we have witnessed a multitude of theoretical and research developments that provide conceptual grounding for the concept of shared leadership. By the mid-1990s, several scholars began mining this fertile intellectual soil. These scholars, independently and simultaneously, developed models that directly addressed shared leadership (Avolio, Jung, Murry, & Sivasubramaniam, 1996; Pearce, 1997; Seers, 1996). Conditions were finally right for the acceptance of this seemingly radical departure from the traditional view of leadership as something imparted to followers by a leader from above. Additional publications on shared leadership have followed. For example, Pearce and colleagues have refined the articulation of a theory of shared leadership by developing a general theoretical model (Pearce & Sims, 2000) and context-specific models that address unique organizational contexts, such as sales teams (Perry, Pearce, & Sims, 1999), nonprofit organizations (Pearce, Perry, & Sims, 2001), entrepreneurial top management teams (Ensley, Pearson, & Pearce, in press), and cross-cultural implications for shared leadership (Pearce, in press).

At the same time, the empirical examination of this alternate source of leadership has remained relatively unexplored. There are four notable exceptions. First, Bowers and Seashore (1966) found what they termed "mutual leadership" between life insurance agents to be predictive of the types of insurance sold and the cost per unit of new policies. Second, Avolio et al. (1996) found shared leadership in teams of undergraduate students to be positively correlated with self-reported ratings of effectiveness. Third, Pearce and Sims (2002) found shared leadership to be a more useful predictor of change management team effectiveness than the leadership of the appointed team leader. Fourth, Pearce, Yoo, and Alavi (in press), in a study of virtual teams, found shared leadership to be a more useful predictor of team dynamics and perceived effectiveness than vertical leadership. Nonetheless, very few empirical studies of shared leadership have appeared in the literature. Thus, we can confidently state the field is clearly still in its infancy.

Therefore, the purpose of the chapters that follow is to more fully articulate the way forward for future research on shared leadership. We do this in three specific ways. In the first section, five chapters delve into the conceptual issues surrounding shared leadership. Fletcher and Käufer open this section by exploring the paradoxes surrounding the idea of shared leadership. Cox, Pearce, and Perry subsequently develop a model of the role of shared leadership in innovation and new product development. Next, Seers, Keller, and Wilkerson theoretically ground the concept of shared leadership in role differentiation theory, social exchange theory, and expectation states theory. This is followed by Burke, Fiore, and Salas, who explore the role of shared cognition in the development of shared leadership. Finally, Houghton, Neck, and Manz articulate a model that focuses on the roles of vertical leadership and self-leadership in the enactment of shared leadership in teams.

In the second section, three chapters illuminate methodological issues surrounding the study of shared leadership. Avolio, Sivasubramaniam, Murry, Jung, and Garger open this section by articulating an approach to studying shared leadership based on rewording the MLQ with the group as a whole as the agents of leadership behavior. Subsequently, Seibert, Sparrowe, and Liden articulate an approach to studying shared leadership that is also based in social network analysis. They, however, focus more on the structure of the group in understanding shared leadership dynamics. Finally, Mayo, Meindl, and Pastor articulate an approach to studying shared leadership, based on social network analysis that focuses on the dispersion of influence as a metric for the level of shared leadership.

In the third section, four chapters investigate shared leadership in applied settings. Hooker and Csikszentmihalyi open this section by conducting an in-depth, qualitative study of shared leadership in a research lab and linking shared leadership to creativity and the experience of flow. Next, Shamir and Lapidot report an in-depth, qualitative study of shared leadership in the Israeli military and demonstrate the vulnerability of vertical leaders when they do not provide the organizational space for leadership from below. O'Toole, Galbraith, and Lawler examine shared leadership at the very top of organizations—the office of the CEO.

In our final section, Locke begins by providing a counterpoint to shared leadership. His chapter outlines the limits to shared leadership, especially as it concerns leadership at the top of organizations. In our concluding chapter, we will synthesize the various contributions to date and explicate the most pressing issues for the advancement of shared leadership theory. We also take the important step of providing guidance on the most fruitful avenues for future research. Our hope is that this final chapter will serve as a springboard for researchers to undertake broader and deeper explorations into this largely overlooked form of leadership. A more serious effort at investigation is sorely needed given the fact that our traditional models of leadership must change in an age of teamwork and knowledge work (Avolio et al., 1996; Drucker, 2001; Hollenbeck, Ilgen, & Sego, 1994; Pearce, 1997; Pearce & Sims, 2000, 2002; Seers, 1996; Yukl, 1998).

This volume is but a beginning for research on shared leadership. One thing that is clear is that shared leadership will not merely be another blip on the radar screen of organizational science. Its time has arrived.

# References

Aldag, R. J., & Fuller, S. R. (1993). Beyond fiasco: A reappraisal of the groupthink phenomenon and a new model of group decision processes. *Psychological Bulletin, 113*(3), 533-552.

Avolio, B. J., Jung, D., Murry, W., & Sivasubramaniam, N. (1996). Building highly developed teams: Focusing on shared leadership process, efficacy, trust, and performance. In M. M. Beyerlein, D. A. Johnson, & S. T. Beyerlein (Eds.), *Advances in interdisciplinary studies of work teams* (pp. 173-209). Greenwich, CT: JAI Press.

Barnard, C. I. (1938). *The functions of the executive.* Cambridge, MA: Harvard University Press.

Bartol, K. M., & Martin, D. C. (1986). Women and men in task groups. In R. D. Ashmore & F. K. Del Boca (Eds.), *The social psychology of female-male relations* (pp. 259-310). New York: Academic Press.

Bass, B. M., & Avolio, B. J. (1993). Transformational leadership: A response to critiques. In J. G. Hunt, B. R. Baliga, H. P. Dachler, & C. A. Schriesheim (Eds.), *Emerging leadership vistas* (pp. 29-40). Lexington, MA: D. C. Health.

Benne, K. D., & Sheats, P. (1948). Functional roles of group members. *Journal of Social Issues, 4,* 41-49.

Berger, J., Cohen, B. P., & Zelditch, M. (1972). Status characteristics and social interaction. *American Sociological Review, 37,* 241-255.

Berscheid, E. (1985). Interpersonal attraction. In G. Lindzey & E. Aronson (Eds.), *Handbook of social psychology* (3rd ed., Vol. 2, pp. 413-484). New York: Random House.

Blau, J. R., & Alba, R. D. (1982). Empowering nets of participation. *Administrative Science Quarterly, 27,* 363-379.

Bowers, D. G., & Seashore, S. E. (1966). Predicting organizational effectiveness with a four factor theory of leadership. *Administrative Science Quarterly, 11,* 238-263.

Byrne, D., Ervin, C. R., & Lamberth, J. (1970). Continuity between the experimental study of attraction and real-life computer dating. *Journal of Personality and Social Psychology, 16,* 157-165.

Campbell, J. M., & Kinion, S. (1993). Teaching leadership/followership to RN-to-MSN students. *Journal of Nursing Education, 32*(3), 138-140.

Cannon-Bowers, J. A., Salas, E., & Converse, S. (1993). Shared mental models in expert team decision making. In N. J. Castellan Jr. (Ed.), *Individual and group decision making* (pp. 221-243). Hillside, NJ: Erlbaum.

Chandler, A. D., Jr., (Ed.). (1965). *The railroads: The nation's first big business, sources and readings.* New York: Harcourt Brace Jovanovich.

Conger, J. A., & Kanungo, R. N. (1988). The empowerment process: Integrating theory and practice. *The Academy of Management Review, 13,* 639-652.

Conger, J. A., & Kanungo, R. N. (1998). Charismatic leadership in organizations. Thousand Oaks, CA: Sage.

Cooper, A. F., Higgott, R. A., & Nossal, K. R. (1991). Bound to follow? Leadership and followership in the gulf conflict. *Political Science Quarterly, 106*(3), 391-410.

Cox, J. F., Pearce, C. L., & Sims, H. P., Jr. (in press). Toward a broader agenda for leadership development: Extending the transactional-transformational duality by development directive, empowering and shared leadership skills. In R. E. Riggio & S. Murphy (Eds.), *The Future of Leadership Development.* Mahwah, NJ: Lawrence Erlbaum.

Drucker, P. F. (1954). *The practice of management.* New York: Harper.

Drucker, P. F. (1995). *Management in a time of great change.* New York: Penguin Putnam.

Drucker, P. F. (2001). *The essential Drucker.* New York: Harper Collins.

Ensley, M. D., & Pearce, C. L. (2001). Shared cognition in top management teams: Implications for new venture performance. *Journal of Organizational Behavior, 22,* 145-160.

Ensley, M. D., Pearson, A., & Pearce, C. L. (in press). Top management team process, shared leadership and new venture performance: A theoretical model and research agenda. *Human Resource Management Review.*

Erez, M., & Arad, R. (1986). Participative goal-setting: Social, motivational, and cognitive factors. *Journal of Applied Psychology, 71,* 591-597.

Fayol, H. (1916/1949). *Administration industrielle et generale.* Storrs, London: Sir Isaac Pitman and Sons.

Festinger, L. (1954). A theory of social comparison processes. *Human Relations, 7,* 117-140.

Follett, M. P. (1924). *Creative experience.* New York: Longmans Green.

Gantt, H. L. (1916). *Industrial leadership.* New Haven, CT: Yale University Press.

Gilbreth, F. B. (1912). *Primer of scientific management.* New York: Van Nostrand Reinhold.

Gilbreth, F. B., & Gilbreth, L. M. (1917). *Applied motion study.* New York: Sturgis & Walton Co.

Graen, G. B. (1976). Role making processes within complex organizations. In M. D. Dunnette (Ed.), *Handbook of industrial and organizational psychology* (pp. 1201-1245). Chicago: Rand McNally.

Graen, G. B., & Scandura, T. A. (1987). Toward a psychology of dyadic organizing. In L. L. Cummings & B. M. Staw (Eds.), *Research in organizational behavior* (pp. 175-208). Greenwich, CT: JAI Press.

Graen, G. B., & Schiemann, W. (1978). Leader-member agreement: A vertical dyad linkage approach. *Journal of Applied Psychology, 63,* 206-212.

Greene, L. R., Morrison, T. L., & Tischler, N. G. (1981). Gender and authority: Effects on perceptions of small group co-leaders. *Small Group Behavior, 12*(4), 401-413.

Hennan, D.A., & Bennis, W. (1999). *Co-leadership: The power of great partnerships.* New York: Wiley.

Herzog, J. (1981). Communication between co-leaders: Fact or myth: A student's perspective. *Social Work with Groups, 3*(4), 19-29.

Hollander, E. P. (1961). Some effects of perceived status on responses to innovative behavior. *Journal of Abnormal and Social Psychology, 63,* 247-250.

Hollander, E. P. (1978). *Leadership dynamics: A practical guide to effective relationships.* New York: Free Press.

Hollenbeck, J. R., Ilgen, D. R., & Sego, D. J. (1994). Repeated measures regression and mediational tests: Enhancing the power of leadership research. *Leadership Quarterly, 5,* 3-23.

Homans, G. C. (1958). Social behavior as exchange. *American Journal of Sociology, 63,* 597-606.

Kelly, R. E. (1988). In praise of followers. *Harvard Business Review, 66*(6), 141-148.

Kerr, S., & Jermier, J. (1978). Substitutes for leadership: Their meaning and measurement. *Organizational Behavior and Human Performance, 22,* 374-403.

Klimoski, R., & Mohammed, S. (1994). Team mental model: Construct or metaphor. *Journal of Management, 20,* 403-437.

Knight, D., Pearce, C. L., Smith, K. G., Sims, H. P., Jr., Olian, J. D., Smith, K. A., et al. (1999). Top management team diversity, group dynamics, and strategic consensus: An empirical investigation. *Strategic Management Journal, 20*(5), 445-466.

Lipman-Blumen, J. (1996). *The connective edge.* San Francisco: Jossey-Bass.

Locke, E. A., & Latham, G. P. (1990). *A theory of goal setting and task performance.* Englewood Cliffs, NJ: Prentice Hall.

Lundin, S. C., & Lancaster, L. C. (1990, May-June). Beyond leadership: The importance of followership. *The Futurist,* 19-22.

Manz, C. C. (1986). Self-leadership: Toward an expanded theory of self-influence processes in organizations. *Academy of Management Review, 11,* 585-600.

Manz, C. C., Keating, D., & Donnellon, A. (1990). Preparing for organizational changes in employee self management: The managerial transition. *Organizational Dynamics, 19,* 15-26.

Manz, C. C., & Sims, H. P., Jr. (1980). Self-management as a substitute for leadership: A social learning perspective. *Academy of Management Review, 5,* 361-367.

Manz, C. C., & Sims, H. P., Jr. (1987, March). Leading workers to lead themselves: The external leadership of self-managing work teams. *Administrative Science Quarterly, 32,* 106-128.

Manz, C. C., & Sims, H. P., Jr. (1989). *Super leadership: Leading others to lead themselves.* New York: Prentice Hall.

Manz, C. C., & Sims, H. P., Jr. (1990). *Superleadership: Leading others to lead themselves.* New York: Berkley Books.

Manz, C. C., & Sims, H. P., Jr. (1993). Businesses without bosses: How self-managing teams are building high performance companies. New York: Wiley.

Manz, C. C., & Sims, H. P., Jr. (2001). *The new superleadership: Leading others to lead themselves.* San Francisco: Berrett Koehler.

Mayo, E. (1933). The human problems of an industrial civilization. New York: Macmillan.

Mintz, E. (1963). Special value of co-therapists in group psychotherapy. *International Journal of Group Psychotherapy, 13,* 127-132.

Mohrman, S. A., Cohen, S. G., & Mohrman, A. M. (1995). *Designing team-based organizations: New forms for knowledge work.* San Francisco: Jossey-Bass.

Montgomery, J. (1840). The cotton manufacture of the United States of America contrasted and compared with that of Great Britain (p. 138). London: John N. Van.

Nakamura, R. T. (1980). Beyond purism and professionalism: Styles of convention delegate followership. *American Journal of Political Science, 24*(2), 207-232.

Newcomb, T. M. (1960). Varieties of inter-personal attraction. In D. Cartwright & A. Zander (Eds.), *Groupdynamics: Research and theory* (2nd ed., pp. 104-119). Evanston, IL: Row, Peterson.

Nishigaki, S., Vavrin, J., Kano, N., Haga, T., Kunz, J., & Law, K. (1994). Humanware, human error, and hiyari-hat: A template of unsafe symptoms. *Journal of Construction Engineering and Management, 120*(2), 421-432.

Pearce, C. L. (1997). The determinants of change management team effectiveness: A longitudinal investigation. Unpublished doctoral dissertation, University of Maryland.

Pearce, C. L. (in press). *Mas allá del liderazco heroico: Como el buen vino, el liderazco es algo para ser compartido.* Revista de empresa.

Pearce, C. L., Perry, M. L., & Sims, H. P., Jr. (2001). Shared leadership: Relationship management to improve NPO effectiveness. In T. D. Connors (Ed.), *The nonprofit handbook: Management* (pp. 624-641). New York: Wiley.

Pearce, C. L., & Sims, H. P., Jr. (2000). Shared leadership: Toward a multi-level theory of leadership. In M. M. Beyerlein, D. A. Johnson, & S. T. Beyerlein (Eds.), *Advances in interdisciplinary studies of work teams* (pp. 115-139). Greenwich, CT: JAI Press.

Pearce, C. L., & Sims, H. P., Jr. (2002). The relative influence of vertical vs. shared leadership on the longitudinal effectiveness of change management teams. *Group Dynamics: Theory, Research, and Practice, 6*(2), 172-197.

Pearce, C. L., Yoo, Y., & Alavi, M. (in press). Leadership, social work and virtual teams: The relative influence of vertical vs. shared leadership in the nonprofit section. In R. E. Riggio & S. Smith Orr (Eds.), *Nonprofit leadership.* San Francisco: Jossey-Bass.

Perry, M. L., Pearce, C. L., & Sims, H. P., Jr. (1999). Empowered selling teams: How shared leadership can contribute to selling team outcomes. *Journal of Personal Selling and Sales Management, 19,* 33-52.

Resnick, L. A. (1991). Shared cognition: Thinking as social practice. In L. B. Resnick, J. M. Levine, & S. D. Teasley (Eds.), *Perspectives on socially shared cognition* (pp. 1-19). Washington, DC: American Psychological Association.

Rippy, K. M. (1990, September). Effective followership. *The Police Chief,* 22-24.

Rittner, B., & Hammons, K. (1992). Telephone group work with people with end stage AIDS. *Social Work With Groups, 15*(4), 59-72.

Roethlisberger, F. J., & Dickson, W. J. (1939). *Management and the worker.* Cambridge, MA: Harvard University Press.

Say, J. B. (1803/1964). *A treatise on political economy* (pp. 330-331). New York: Augustus M. Kelley.

Seers, A. (1989). Team-member exchange quality: A new construct for role-making research. *Organizational Behavior and Human Decision Processes, 43,* 118-135.

Seers, A. (1996). Better leadership through chemistry: Toward a model of shared team leadership. In M. Beyerlein (Ed.), *Advances in interdisciplinary studies of work teams* (pp. 145-172). Greenwich, CT: JAI Press.

Smith, R. (1991, October/November). Principals need to be good followers. *High School Journal,* 24-27.

Smith, W. (1994). Followership: The art of working together. *Principal, 74*(2), 22-24.

Solomon, A., Loeffer, F. J., & Frank, G. H. (1953). An analysis of co-therapist interaction in group psychotherapy. *International Journal of Group Psychotherapy, 3,* 171-180.

Stein, R. T., & Heller, T. (1979). An empirical analysis of the correlations between leadership status and participation rates reported in the literature. *Journal of Personality and Social Psychology, 37,* 1993-2002.

Stewart, G. L., & Manz, C. C. (1995). Leadership for self-managing work teams: A typology and integrative model. *Human Relations, 48,* 347-370.

Taylor, F. W. (1903). *Shop management.* New York: Harper & Row.

Taylor, F. W. (1911). *Principles of scientific management.* New York: Harper & Brothers.

Thibaut, J., & Kelley, H. H. (1959). *The social psychology of groups.* New York: Wiley.

Turner, C. E. (1933, June). Test room studies in employee effectiveness. *American Journal of Pubic Health, 23,* 577-584

Vroom, V. H., & Yetton, P. W. (1973). *Leadership and decision-making.* (Rev. ed.). New York: Wiley.

Weber, M. (1905/1958). The Protestant ethic and the spirit of capitalism. New York: Scribner's.

Weber, M. (1924/1947). *The theory of social and economic organization.* (T. Parsons, Trans.). New York: Free Press.

Winter, S. (1976). Developmental stages in the roles and concerns of group co-leaders. *Small Group Behavior, 7*(3), 349-362.

Wren, D. A. (1994). *The evolution of management thought* (4th ed.). New York: John Wiley.

Yukl, G. A. (1998). *Leadership in organizations* (4th ed.). Englewood Cliffs, NJ: Prentice Hall.

# PART I

# CONCEPTUAL MODELS OF SHARED LEADERSHIP

# CHAPTER 2

# Shared Leadership

*Paradox and Possibility*

*Joyce K. Fletcher*
*Katrin Käufer*

## New Leadership Practices

Over the past two decades, a shift has occurred in how we think about, understand, and theorize organizational phenomenon. Gone are images of the organization as machine, a black box that can be understood by an analysis of inputs and outputs with leaders at the top who direct and control the process. In its stead is the image of organization as a living, dynamic system of interconnected relationships and networks of influence. This paradigm shift in the image of what an organization is has been accompanied by a corresponding shift in the notion of leadership itself.

New models of leadership recognize that effectiveness in living systems of relationships does not depend on individual, heroic leaders but rather on leadership practices embedded in a system of interdependencies at different levels within the organization. This has ushered in an era of what is often called "post-heroic" or shared leadership, a new approach intended to transform organizational practices, structures, and working relationships. New models conceptualize leadership as a more relational process, a shared or distributed phenomenon occurring at different levels and dependent on social interactions and networks of influence.

In this chapter we offer a way of thinking about the relational concepts and assumptions embedded—either explicitly or implicitly—in new models of leadership. We suggest that there are three powerful relational shifts that underlie models of shared leadership and we link these shifts to a number of paradoxes and dilemmas that arise in practice. Finally, we apply what we argue is a particularly useful theory of social interactions—Stone Center Relational Theory (Jordan, Kaplan, Miller, Stiver, & Surrey, 1991) —to inform the interactional nature of dialogue, one of the key coordinating practices of shared leadership (Yukl, 1998).

# Shared Leadership: What Is It?

Traditionally, leadership research has focused on individual leaders and, by extension, on vertical approaches to organizing work tasks. The work of leadership in this view is to make strategic decisions and then to influence and align the rest of the organization to implement these decisions effectively (Northouse, 2001).

Shared approaches to leadership question this individual level perspective, arguing that it focuses excessively on top leaders and says little about informal leadership or larger situational factors. In contrast, shared leadership offers a concept of leadership practice as a group-level phenomenon (Bryman, 1996; Spillane, Halverson, & Diamond, 1999; Pearce & Sims, 2000; Scully & Segal, 1997; Senge, 1997; Yukl, 1998.) Interestingly, although this recognition of leadership as a group phenomenon would seem to suggest an important theoretical and practical link between leadership research and research on group processes and teamwork, this connection is rarely made. Ilgen (1999), for example, notes that research on teams and small groups has actually decreased in recent years despite the fact that during the same period the importance and use of teams has increased. He argues that rather than looking at the microprocesses within groups, current research focuses on the macrolevel phenomenon of teams and groups embedded in organizational structures.

We agree that the theory and practice of shared leadership would benefit from a closer examination of the relational microprocesses that embody the group-level phenomenon noted in concepts of shared leadership. Toward this end, we offer three shifts that have been identified elsewhere (Fletcher, 2002) as characteristic of the paradigm shift in relational interactions inherent in shared leadership.

## Shift I: Distributed and Interdependent

Models of shared leadership conceptualize leadership as a set of practices that can and should be enacted by people at all levels rather than a set of personal characteristics and attributes located in people at the top (Badaracco, 2001; Kouzes and Posner, 2002.) We might see—and even need to see—figureheads at the top. But models of shared leadership recognize that these visible "heroes" are supported by a network of leadership practices distributed throughout the organization. There are many different images and metaphors that have been used to describe this phenomenon. Peggy McIntosh (1989) talks about the iceberg—the individual achievement we acknowledge and celebrate is but the tip of the iceberg, she notes. Underneath is the collaborative subtext of life, the numerous acts of enabling, supporting, facilitating, and creating conditions under which the tip of an iceberg can break through the surface. Wilfred Draft (2001) uses another, equally compelling image from the sea. He notes that although we might see the white caps in the ocean as leading, it is actually the deep blue sea that determines the direction and capabilities of the ocean. Others (Pearce & Sims, 2000; Senge, 1997; Senge & Käufer, 2001) develop multilevel frameworks to explain how leadership is distributed in organizations and describe the interdependencies among these levels.

Frameworks and images such as these evoke images of a relational "whole" rather than parts. They implicitly acknowledge the interdependent nature of leadership and signal a significant shift away from individual achievement and meritocracy toward a focus on collective achievement, shared responsibility, and the importance of teamwork (Conger, 1989; Heenan & Bennis, 1999; Hosking, Dachler, & Gergen, 1995; Lipnack & Stamps, 2000; Manz & Sims, 1987; Pearce & Sims, 2000; Seely Brown & Duguid, 2000; Thompson, 2000; Yukl, 1998).

## Shift II: Embedded in Social Interaction

Another key relational aspect of shared leadership is its emphasis on leadership as a social process. Shared leadership is portrayed as a dynamic, multidirectional, collective activity that, like all human action and cognitive sense-making, is embedded in the context in which it occurs (Lave & Wenger, 1991; Suchman, 1987). Social interactions are key in this concept, as leadership is seen as something that occurs in and through relationships and networks of influence (Fletcher et al., 1997; Hosking et al., 1995; Jordan et al., 1991; McNamee & Gergen, 1999.) But instead of describing an individual leader as the social integrator (Alvesson, 1992), shared leadership focuses on the whole, looking at social interactions as a group phenomenon. There are many images used to describe these leadership interactions, from bottom-up images of influence such as *Power Up* (Bradford & Cohen, 1998) and *Leading Up* (Useem, 2001) to "servant" (Block, 1993; Greenleaf, 1977) or "connective" (Lipman-Blumen, 1996) leadership. What these images have in common is their focus on the egalitarian, collaborative, more mutual, less hierarchical nature of leader-follower interactions. In other words, the relational interactions that make up shared leadership are understood to be more fluid and multidirectional and less individual, one-directional, and static than more traditionally individualistic models. Rather than a focus on the leader's effect on followers, the followers are understood as playing a role in influencing and creating leadership (Aaltio-Marjosola, 2001; Harrington, 2000).

## Shift III: Leadership As Learning

A third important relational shift underlying shared leadership has to do with the particular quality and characteristics of the social processes in which leadership occurs. Models of shared leadership focus on specific kinds of relational interactions: those that lead to learning for the individuals involved as well as the organization (Argyris & Schon, 1978; Beer, 1999; Heifitz, 1994; Isaacs, 1999; Marsick & Watkins, 1999; Palmer, 1993; Senge, 1990). In other words, the kinds of social interactions that comprise the ideal of shared leadership are differentiated from other, less positive social interactions by virtue of their outcomes: mutual learning, greater shared understanding, and eventually, positive action.

Most importantly, there is a growing recognition that leadership depends not only on an individual's ability to learn, question assumptions, and understand concepts such as the "ladder of inference" (Argyris, 1992) for oneself, but also on the ability to create conditions—such as Bill Isaacs's (1999) notion of a "safe container"—where collective learning can occur and things that undermine it, such as organizational silence (Morrison & Milliken, 2000), are less likely to occur. For example, Scharmer and Käufer (Käufer & Scharmer, 2002; Scharmer, 2001) note that collective learning occurs when individuals within a group are able to move the dialogue through different stages. The first stage, "talking nice," is a rule-repeating phase in which people keep within the bounds of what is expected. The second stage is "talking tough," during which people begin to speak their minds, advocate for their own perspectives, and engage debate. The third phase is "reflective dialogue," when listeners develop an inner voice that helps them reflect on their own perspective in order to be influenced by the perspectives of others. The fourth phase is something they call "generative dialogue," when the group loses its individual level focus and generates truly co-created ideas. They suggest that in order to move the group from one phase to another, someone within the group must make a relational move, for example from talking nice to talking tough, or from talking tough to reflective dialogue. Although one individual's action does not ensure that the group as a whole moves, it creates an invitation to which others might respond and can therefore be thought of as leadership practice.

The shift toward collective learning is particularly significant because it highlights the need to expand the individual level skills and characteristics that are related to learning (such as self-awareness) in order to include other more group-level focused relational practices and skills such as authenticity, openness, vulnerability, and the ability to anticipate the responses and learning needs of others (Fletcher, 1994, 1999).

In summary, models of shared leadership reenvision the *who* and *where* of leadership by focusing on the need to distribute the tasks and responsibilities of leadership up, down, and across the hierarchy. They reenvision the *what* of leadership by articulating leadership as a social process that occurs in and through social interactions, and they articulate the *how* of leadership by focusing on the skills and ability required to create conditions in which collective learning can occur.

# Paradoxes of Shared Leadership

Despite a widespread recognition of the need for new, more relational models of leadership, many note that there are a number of paradoxes and contradictions associated with it in practice.

## Paradox I: Hierarchical Leaders Are Charged With Creating Less Hierarchical Organizations

As new models of leadership indicate, the skills it takes to engage in learning and leading need to be shared throughout the organization, creating leadership communities that move the enterprise forward. Creating these flatter, more adaptive organizational paradigms in which organizational learning and reflection can occur often requires deep corporate cultural change and strong leadership. To engage this type of change, organizations tend to turn to "hero CEOs" who, paradoxically, are asked to distribute authority and business accountability (Senge, 1996). As many have noted, however, it is difficult to create less hierarchical systems by relying solely on better hierarchical leaders (Bradford & Cohen, 1998; Day, 2001; Gary, 2001; Manz & Sims, 1987.) For example, Bartunek, Walsh, and Lacey (2000) highlight the dilemmas that arise when positional leaders have expertise in how to create empowering conditions, but the initiating behavior they would have to use to create these conditions violates the shared leadership principles the group embraces. They note that this paradox is a variation on the self versus group dilemma commonly referred to as the paradox of group life (Smith & Berg, 1987). It creates contradictory demands of leaders who are expected both to set themselves apart—and above—the group, while at the same time interact as an integral part of the group, even as coequals with other members. These conflicting demands and expectations can have a negative effect on the group, not only leading to the demise of individual leaders but causing the group itself to doubt its own principles of shared leadership.

## Paradox 2: Shared Leadership Practices "Get Disappeared"

Although at the macro level the rhetoric about leadership focuses on teamwork, collaboration, and collective learning, the everyday narratives about leadership and leadership practices—the stories people tell about leadership, the mythical legends that get passed on as exemplars of leadership behavior—often remain stuck in old images of heroic individualism.

Heifitz and Laurie (1999), for example, note that despite all the data supporting the need for new leadership practices, "managers and leaders rarely receive promotions for providing the leadership required to do adaptive work" and enhance organizational learning (p. 65). Furthermore, Michael Beer (1999) notes that in recounting the story of their success, leaders themselves tend to ignore the relational practices that accounted for that success and instead focus almost exclusively on individual actions and decision points (p. 133).

Beer suggests that because of the nature of identity and ego, once we have achieved a goal and some prominence for having achieved it, it is natural to dismiss the help we have been given and reconstruct our behavior—in our own minds as well as in the perception of others—as individual action. Others suggest causality in the other direction: that followers' need for heroes exerts pressure on both formal and informal leaders to comply and retell their stories to meet this implicit expectation and need (Hirschorn, 1990). Others offer a related but more benign explanation, what Meindl, Ehrlich, and Dukerich (1985) call the "romanticizing" of leadership that happens when a series of causally unrelated, ambiguous events are reconstructed in retrospect as intentional action and then described as "leadership."

Fletcher (1999, 2002) offers a more postmodern framing of the issue, relating it to gender and power dynamics in the workplace. She observed and chronicled a number of specific relational practices related to collective learning, mutual empowerment, and shared leadership. Her findings suggest that relational leadership in practice is acted on by the dominant discourse in a way that disappears it as "real" work or competence. For example, she found that many of the specific actions that enact principles of relational leadership—such as taking time from one's own deliverables to share information, sending notes of appreciation, or asking for help, input, or both—appeared so routine, mundane, and "nonheroic" in practice that they were hard to recognize as acts of leadership. Moreover, the intention and effect were difficult to describe as leadership because there is no commonly accepted "language of competence" in organizational discourse to link these seemingly mundane, relational actions to more grandiose images and narratives of leadership. Instead, these practices were often linked to interpersonal attributes and noted as personality characteristics rather than leadership skills. Thus people—and this was especially true for women—who practiced relational leadership were often described not as leaders but as "nice" or "thoughtful" people who "cared about others' feelings."

### Paradox III: The Skills It Takes to Get the Job Are Different From the Skills It Takes to Do the Job, or the "That's Not How I Got Here" Paradox

Organizations have a training and development regimen that is premised on what some have called the tournament model (Hall & Mirvis, 1997; Rosenbaum, 1989). Early career opportunities for fast-trackers are intense, competitive assignments in which it is assumed that the cream will rise to the top. This encourages tremendous attention and energy on differentiating yourself from others, distinguishing your individual accomplishments and level of commitment. The result is that jobs and careers are organized around principles of individual achievement and meritocracy (Hall & Mirvis, 1997; Kram, 1997). This developmental path is prevalent in many organizational contexts, from law firms and investment banks where new associates are under pressure to put in long hours with grueling schedules to prove themselves and make partner, to tenure track systems in which heavy investment in time and output is required in the early years to distinguish oneself from others (Bailyn, 1993; Fletcher, 1997; Rapoport, Bailyn, Fletcher, & Pruitt, 2002; Williams, 2000.)

The paradox this creates for the practice of relational leadership is reflected in the words of one CEO we interviewed (Käufer and Fletcher, 2001) He spoke passionately about his belief in the power of collaborative action, how no one can "do it alone," and how the most important attribute he brings to the table is the ability to listen and learn from others. As we nodded in understanding, he suddenly grew silent and, after a long pause and with a little smile, said, "But frankly, I have to tell you, that is not how I got here."

## Possibility: Rethinking Shared Leadership From a Relational Perspective

The paradoxes noted above suggest that the paradigm shift in leadership is more complex in practice than the rhetoric implies. We suggest that what lies at the heart of many of these paradoxical situations are some underlying dynamics that have to do with the shift from individual-level conceptualizations of leadership to concepts that are more relational and interactional in nature. We use a theory of relational interactions, Stone Center Relational Theory, which we believe is uniquely suited to highlighting some of the deeper implications of this shift and why it engages paradox as well as possibility.

## Stone Center Relational Theory: What Is It?

Stone Center Relational Theory is a model of human growth developed by feminist psychologists and psychiatrists at the Stone Center for Developmental Services and Studies at Wellesley College in Wellesley, Massachusetts. Its tenets, articulated throughout the 1970s and 1980s, detail a process of human development the authors call growth-in-connection (Jordan, 1986; 1991; Jordan et al., 1991; Miller, 1976; Miller & Stiver, 1997; Surrey, 1985). The theory's hallmark is that it privileges connection as the primary site of human growth and carefully delineates the relational processes that account for this growth.

We believe there are two unique contributions Stone Center Relational Theory can make to the theory and practice of shared leadership. First, its carefully nuanced delineation of the processes, outcomes, characteristics, and skills associated with relational interactions highlight the microprocesses *within* social interactions that have been largely ignored in the shared leadership literature (Ilgen, 1999.) Its second, and perhaps even more important, contribution is that unlike other relational ideologies that differentiate themselves from individualistic conceptualizations of human development (e.g., Draft, 2001; Hosking et al., 1995; McNamee & Gergen, 1999) Stone Center Relational Theory situates these microlevel concepts within the larger, societal contexts of gender and power in which they occur. This dual contribution is embodied in the tenets of Stone Center Relational Theory listed below.

### Tenets of Stone Center Relational Theory

*Self-in-Relation.* The concept of self that underlies most theories of human interaction—especially human interaction in the doing of work—is rooted in traditional, Western models of adult development. These models emphasize independence, autonomy, and individuation, envisioning human development as a process of separation in which independence and self-sufficiency are the hallmarks of maturity (Kegan, 1994; Marsick & Watkins, 1999; Miller, 1976; Miller & Stiver, 1997.) In other words, traditional theories of human development conceptualize growth as a process of getting increasingly proficient at separating and individuating oneself from others in an implicit move from dependence to independence.

Stone Center relational theorists take issue with these models of development and assert that they are inadequate in capturing the growth process They argue that growth, rather than occurring primarily through processes of separation, occurs primarily through processes of connection. The hallmark of growth they suggest is not increased ability to separate oneself from others but increased ability to connect oneself to others in ways that foster mutual development and learning.

While transactional models of growth include the importance of human connection, relational theory recasts the nature of these interactions. For example, Miller and her colleagues (Miller, 1976; Surrey, 1985; Miller & Stiver, 1997) claim that the notion of "self" is too static and discrete a concept to describe what happens in an interactional field because it does not adequately capture the more fluid, two-directional flow of mutual influence, learning, and co-creation that characterize these interactions. They cite several studies (e.g., Beebe & Lachman, 1988; Tronick, 1989) indicating that even in the earliest days of life an infant influences the emotional field between self and caretaker and begins to develop an interacting sense of self. They assert that a different, more relational conceptualization of self is needed to better capture the human developmental process and offer such a concept: self-in-relation (Surrey, 1985).

This more fluid, dynamic notion of self as a relational entity (as differentiated from self as an autonomous entity) has important implications for notions of dependence and independence, subtly recasting these concepts. For example, the concept of self-in-relation emphasizes *inter*dependence as the basic—or ideal—human condition, and conceptualizes dependence and independence as more temporary, fluid states. In contrast, self as separate entity leads to the opposite emphasis, with *in*dependence implicitly cast as the "ideal" state and interdependence as a temporary condition. This is an important distinction: Separate self is on a journey toward independence; self-in-relation is on a journey toward interdependence.

*Characteristics.* Another important aspect of relational theory is its identification of the specific conditions, characteristics, and outcomes that characterize growth-fostering interactions. Relational theory does not simply assert that growth and learning are dependent on social interactions. Rather than casting *all* relational and dialogic interactions as occasions when human agency can be accomplished interactively (e.g., Della Noce, 1999: McNamee & Gergen, 1999; Hosking et al., 1995), relational theory differentiates these growth fostering interactions from non-growth-fostering interactions. More specifically, it identifies the *conditions*, set of beliefs, and stance toward others that underlie the motivation to create opportunities for collective growth, the relational *skills* this requires, and the expected *outcomes*.

*Conditions.* Growth-in-connection is characterized by the construct of mutuality in which the boundary between self and other is more fluid and multidirectional (Jordon, 1986; Jordon et al., 1991). The process is one that moves from mutual authenticity (we bring our authentic selves to the interaction); to mutual empathy (in which we hold onto self but also experience the other's reality); and finally to mutual empowerment (in which each is in some way influenced or affected by the other, so that something new is created). The theory posits that this kind of mutuality depends on parties operating from a self-in-relation stance in which both (or all) parties recognize vulnerability as part of the human condition, approach the interaction expecting to grow from it, and feel a responsibility to contribute to the growth of the other.

*Skills.* Growth fostering interactions require that participants approach the interaction expecting to grow, learn, and be changed by it and feel a responsibility—and a desire—to contribute to the growth of the other. Putting these beliefs into practice, however, requires relational skills such as empathy, listening, and emotional competence as well as skills in relational inquiry and the ability to tolerate ambiguity and uncertainty (Fletcher, 1999). In other words, relational theory asserts that growth-fostering social interactions do not occur "naturally" but depend on the exercise of certain strengths, abilities, and relational skills.

As Miller (1976) notes, however, the characterization of these attributes as strengths is a challenge to conventional wisdom, which has pathologized attributes like vulnerability, often characterizing them as weaknesses or psychological defi- ciencies, often coding them as signs of personal inadequacy rather than as part of the human condition.

*Outcomes.* Relational theory offers evaluative criteria with which to differentiate growth-fostering interactions from other types of social interactions. When mutual learning and growth have occurred, parties in the interaction achieve "five good things": zest, empowered action, increased self-esteem, new knowledge, and (particularly important for this discussion of shared leadership) a desire for more connection (Miller & Stiver, 1997). They define the five good things as: (1) zest: connection with the other that gives both or all a sense of increased energy and vitality; (2) empowered action: motivation and ability to put into practice some of what was learned or experienced in the relational interaction; (3) increased self (-in-relation) esteem: increased feelings of worth that come from the experience of having used one's "self-in-relation" to achieve mutual growth-in-connection; (4) new knowledge: learning that comes from the ability to engage in "fluid expertise," fully contributing one's own thoughts and perspective while at the same time being open to others; and (5) desire for more connection: a desire to continue this particular connection, establish other growth fostering connections, or both, leading to a spiral of growth that extends outward, beyond the initial participants.

Importantly, all five of these outcomes must be mutual in order for the connec- tion, learning, and growth to continue and begin to spiral outward in any transfor- mational sense. This means it is not enough for only one party to experience the five good things. For example, if one party is not moved to empowered action but instead wants to avoid future connection or feels disempowered or exploited, or if one party does not achieve new knowledge or does not desire more connection, this is an indi- cation that the ideal of generative or transformative growth has not occurred.

*Systemic Power.* Stone Center Relational Theory highlights how traditional concepts of self as an independent entity and growth as a process of separation from others contribute to what Jean Baker Miller calls the "myth of individual achievement." She asserts that the belief that independence is a state that can be achieved belies the essentially interdependent nature of the human condition. Moreover, it is a discursive exercise of power whereby some in society are expected to provide the collaborative subtext of life invisibly so others can enact the "myth of individual achievement" without acknowledging that this collaborative subtext of support is needed and important. Growth-in-connection depends on a belief that inter- dependence is an essential part of human nature. But the myth of individual achievement that permeates Western society precludes that belief and makes growth-in-connection hard to achieve except by accident or sporadically. The theory points out that both a gender/patriarchical power and a more general power dynamic are involved in sustaining these so-called myths of independence and individual achievement.

**Table 2.1**  Tenets of Relational Theory

| Tenet | Definition |
|---|---|
| Self-in-relation | Conceptualize self as a relational as opposed to an individuated entity. |
| Conditions | Mutual authenticity, mutual empathy, mutual empowerment. |
| Skills | Empathy, vulnerability, emotional competence, ability to contribute to the development of another with no loss to self-esteem, ability to operate in context of interdependence. Two-directional relational stance where interactions are approached as opportunities for *mutual* growth. |
| Outcomes | Five good things: zest, empowered action, increased self-esteem, new knowledge, desire for more connection. |
| Systemic Power | Women expected to be the "carriers" of relational activity invisibly, enabling the "myth of individualism" to endure and associating a relational stance with *femininity*<br>Unequal power relations (gender, race, class) leads to distortion of growth-in-connection principles, where parties with less power have more highly developed relational skills, thereby associating these skills with *powerlessness*. |

*Gender.* Relational theory places the construct of relationality within the discourse on the social construction of gender, highlighting the fact that relationality is not a gender-neutral concept. On the contrary, gender socialization, especially in Western society, assigns to women the task of creating the relational conditions under which human growth in connection can occur (Chodorow, 1978; Fairbairn, 1952; Miller, 1976; Miller & Stiver, 1997; Smith, Simmons, & Thames, 1989; Winnicott, 1958). The result is that women become the "carriers" of relational strengths, not only expected to provide the collaborative subtext of life that supports and enables human agency and achievement, but also expected to do it invisibly, so the need for it is not acknowledged nor is the recognition that something important was done.[1] The fact that—at a societal level—women are the carriers of relational skills and expected to provide conditions of growth invisibly means that using relational skills and enacting the ideology of self-in-relation is, at some deep, perhaps even unconscious level, associated with femininity.

*Power.* In systems of unequal power (inequities based, for example, on race, class, gender, or organizational level), those with less power are required to develop relational skills in order to be attuned to and anticipate the needs, desires, and implicit requests of the more powerful. This means that at some deep, perhaps unconscious, level, most of us associate these skills with powerlessness. In other words, what marks one as powerful in Western culture is the entitlement of having others adopt a self-in-relation stance, which allows them to anticipate your needs and respond to them without your even asking; what marks one as less powerful is being the one to do the anticipating and responding.

The tenets of relational theory, summarized in Table 2.1, offer some new ways of thinking about the paradoxes that organizations experience in putting new models of leadership into practice.

# Revisiting the Paradoxes of Shared Leadership

The tenets of Stone Center Relational Theory not only can help us understand some of the deeper dynamics underlying the paradoxes associated with the practice of shared leadership but also can suggest some ways of addressing those underlying dynamics in future research. Below, we suggest four aspects of shared leadership that we believe must be revisited—and ultimately rewritten—from a relational perspective to address the paradoxes associated with this new model of leadership and capture its transformational potential.

## Rewriting the Image of Self

The more fluid, dynamic entity of self-in-relation, as differentiated from a self that is discrete and separate from others, provides an opportunity to reconceptualize many of the concepts underlying shared leadership. Indeed, substituting the concept of self-in-relation for self subtly but significantly changes the entities of the participants in leadership interactions. This makes visible some interesting distinctions that might otherwise go unnoticed and offers the possibility of rethinking some of the basic assumptions underlying notions and images of leadership. How might concepts like self-esteem, self-efficacy, and self-interest change if they were explored from the perspective of self-in-relation and its corollary of interdependence as the basic or ideal state? What, for example, would a concept of self-in-relation efficacy or self-in-relation interest look like, and how might it change leadership tasks and processes such as relational dialogue, inquiry, or adaptive change?

The first paradox of shared leadership—expecting hierarchical leaders to create and foster less hierarchical systems—is an interesting example of how the concept of self-in-relation might inform models of shared leadership. As Bartunek et al. (2000) note, this paradox is related to the basic paradox of group life and the desire to both stand out as an individual and be a part of the group (Smith & Berg, 1987). Rethinking the dimensions of this dilemma by substituting the concept of self-in-relation could help theorists rethink the tasks and challenges inherent in it. Interestingly, Bartunek et al. (2000) suggest that efforts to resolve the contradiction between the demands of "facilitating" and "initiating" leadership practices are less helpful than acknowledging and finding a way to work with the tension. Self-in-relation is a concept that holds within it *both* self and other and offers a more fluid image of the leadership relationship. Using this concept could help theorists and ultimately practitioners think more creatively about how to respond to the challenge to "work with" rather than resolve such dilemmas.

For example, the concept of self-in-relation affords the possibility of challenging and perhaps decoupling the link between leader and static expertise—the notion that leaders "know best." Furthermore, it makes visible and discussable an underlying assumption about human development that may account for the resiliency of this assumption that leaders know more than others: the belief that increasing levels of independence is the hallmark of adult growth. Positional leaders of a group who are operating from a self-in-relation stance—and the corollary belief that increased proficiency in mutuality and interdependence is the hallmark of adult growth—belie the notion of a static state of knowledge in which one member of a group, by virtue of her position, is less open to influence on *all* topics.

The concept of self-in-relation makes visible and discussable the contradiction inherent in models of shared leadership, which relies on principles of interdependence but does not address the way independence as an ideal or achievable state underlies traditional theories of human development on which organizational practices are founded. The shift in privileging interdependence over independence is neither trivial nor benign. Indeed, we suggest that it is linked in powerful ways to deeply rooted beliefs about individual achievement and meritocracy that underlie many organizational practices and norms (Scully & Donnellon, 1994). This suggests that new models of leadership, at the very least, need to acknowledge the profound nature of this shift and begin to theorize its implications.

## Rewriting the Language of Leadership

The concept of self-in-relation also offers the possibility of identifying additional leadership skills and competencies. Adopting a self-in-relation stance and putting into practice principles of a belief in interdependence and mutuality as ideal states require relational skills. Relational theory's concept of self-in-relation suggests that relational competence (Fletcher, 1999) requires more than the individual level attributes such as self-awareness popularized by books on emotional intelligence (Goleman, 1998). In addition, it requires skills and abilities in creating the conditions under which relational growth and learning can occur in the collective: self-in-relation awareness, if you will. This raises the possibility of identifying in concrete terms what these skills, attributes, and abilities entail and what specific behaviors exemplify them. What, for example, does it take to operate effectively in an atmosphere of "fluid expertise," where expertise shifts and spirals around the collective, regardless of hierarchical position and authority? What specific practices create the conditions in which the group can enact "fluid expertise" and achieve the five good things?

Relational theory sheds light on yet another aspect of the paradoxes associated with shared leadership: the way people who practice shared or relational leadership often "disappear" it in their own narratives of leadership success. What the relational model helps us see is that because the skills needed to establish conditions for mutual growth, development, and achievement have been understood historically as deficiencies in processes of separation rather than as strengths in processes of connection, the language describing them is inadequate. The lack of a strong language of competence to describe relational skills or behavior makes it very difficult to claim these practices as leadership. Often those who do relational work rely on words like "help," "nurture," or being "polite" to describe what it is they are doing. For example, Fletcher (1999) notes that one engineer, describing what went on in a meeting, said that those who yelled and spoke forcefully in advocating for their perspective were the ones whose ideas were taken up. She said that she liked to understand why someone thought the way they thought, and she liked to ask questions to help her connect to the ideas and understand them. But—and these were her words—"If you tried to be 'polite' and ask someone 'why do you think that' you were likely to just get steamrolled and the meeting would go on as if you hadn't said anything" (p. 102).

"Polite" is an odd choice to describe action that is contributing to the collective effort. But that is just what adopting an attitude of inquiry in the face of disagreement is. It is a contribution to collective learning, a way of making sure that diverse perspectives are heard and considered, and a way of creating an environment where people can understand and perhaps build on each others ideas. Calling this kind of behavior "polite" obscures not only the intention but also the skill and competence it takes to do it well. Other common descriptors of relational work such as "nurturing," "empathy," or "sensitivity" have the same effect, linking the behavior to personal attributes rather than skilled, intentional action, thereby obscuring the value of this work and its contribution to effectiveness.

## Rewriting Leadership Development

Identifying the need for a language of competence to describe relational practice highlights yet another aspect of the paradoxical nature of shared leadership. More specifically, it identifies some of the underlying issues in the paradox of "that's not how I got here" and suggests interesting ways to develop relational competence more broadly in today's workforce. Developmental programs, built on a notion of self as independent entity and maturity as a process of outgrowing dependence, tend to foster skills in achieving and demonstrating independence. Shared leadership requires a different set of skills, and, perhaps more importantly, a different kind of developmental experience. As noted earlier, career paths within organizations are built on tournament models of competition based on images of autonomy, self-promotion, and the goal of differentiating oneself from others. When people get to the top, they are, inexplicably, expected to have developed the relational skills it takes to enable, empower, and contribute to the development of others. But where would they have gotten these skills?

Stone Center Relational Theory is not the only place where the lack of these skills in the general population is noted. Certainly, the new emphasis on emotional intelligence suggests that competence requires—at a minimum—if not a two-directional notion of self-in-relation, then at least an emotional awareness of one's impact on others (Goleman, 1998). What relational theory helps us see, however, is that one fertile but overlooked area for developing these skills is the private sphere of family and community. In other words, what relational theory helps us see is that one way of getting these skills is to experience the responsibility for "growing people." Since "growing people" is the basic intent of family life (as opposed to an add-on in the list of managerial requirements), it is fertile ground for developing relational competence. Some of the relational skills recently associated with involvement in family and community life, for example, include a welcoming stance toward change; an ability to focus on long-term versus short-term goals; and an ability to integrate thinking, feeling, and acting into practice (Erkut, 2001; Fletcher & Jacques, 2000; Held, 1990; Ruddick, 1989; Ruderman, Ohlott, Panzer, & Kim, 2002.)

Interestingly, new empirical research—although it does not delineate the reasons or the causality of the link—indicates that having multiple roles combining work and personal life is correlated with high performance (Ruderman & Ohrlott). The challenge for organizations, however, is that to be a leader in today's competitive, fast-paced workplace you don't have any *time* for outside responsibilities related to personal life. Indeed, images of leadership, commitment, and competence assume single-minded attention and focus on one's work life, with a personal life (family, community, etc.), that is either nonexistent or taken care of by someone else (Rapoport et al., 2002; Williams, 2000). Relational theory calls attention to the inadequacy of that model and the *costs* of continuing to assume that work and personal life are separate, gendered spheres of life that do not, or cannot, benefit from integration. Relational theory, in other words, calls us to rethink the strict boundary organizations place on work life and personal life if we are serious about moving to new models of shared leadership.

## Rewriting the Language of Power

Stone Center Relational Theory points to a unique gender/power dynamic underlying new models of leadership. Many have noted that the traits associated with new models of leadership are feminine (Calvert & Ramsey, 1992; Fletcher, 1994; Fondas, 1997). That is, men or women can display them, but the traits themselves—such as empathy, community, vulnerability, and skills of inquiry and collaboration—are socially ascribed to women in our culture and generally understood as feminine. Similarly, the traits associated with traditional, heroic leadership are masculine. Again, men or women can display them, but the traits themselves—such as individualism, control, assertiveness, and domination—are socially ascribed to men in our culture and generally understood as masculine (Acker, 1990; Calàs & Smircich, 1993; Collinson & Hearn, 1996).[2]

Although this association of new leadership practices with stereotypically feminine traits is generally accepted and increasingly noted even in the popular press (e.g., Helgeson, 1990; Peters, 1990; Rosener, 1995; Sharpe, 2000), relational theory takes the analysis a step further. More specifically, it situates relational interactions within the larger societal contexts of power and privilege in which all human interactions occur. Stone Center Relational Theory asserts that although most relational ideologies are described as if they were gender and, to a lesser degree, power neutral concepts, they are not. On the contrary, a strong gender/power dynamic underlies relational practices because of the way society devalues and distorts relational skills and abilities, inappropriately aligning them with femininity and powerlessness. Making this gender/power dynamic visible and discussible offers a different lens through which to view and understand the challenges and paradoxes inherent in putting relational leadership into practice.

For example, the gender/power lens inherent in Stone Center Relational Theory offers a deeper understanding of the paradox of the disappearing of new leadership practices. It suggests that any theory positioning leadership as a social process must include an analysis of how the practice—like all human interactions—is an occasion to enact ones' self image and identity. Two salient (and related) aspects of identity are gender and power. Thus, the social interactions that make up leadership are opportunities not only to "do gender" (West and Zimmerman, 1991) but to "do power." Because the skills, beliefs, and self-in-relation stance needed are inappropriately associated with femininity and powerlessness, however, when people enact new leadership practices they may be perceived by others as "doing femininity" and "doing powerlessness." "Doing femininity" and "doing powerlessness" are not, to put it mildly, traditional routes to leadership. So, is it any wonder that leaders avoid describing these practices when telling the story of their own effectiveness? Or that listeners, even if they heard leaders describe these behaviors, might trivialize or dismiss the description and leave it out of their own version of the story in the retelling?

This suggests that it is not enough for organizational theorists to call for new types of leadership. Deeply embedded gender- and power-linked aspects of self-identity are highly charged, emotional issues. Cognitive attempts to change behavior, for example by writing leadership books about the need for change (Breit & Stroh, 1999) without a recognition of the deeply embedded, emotional nature of the identity issues involved, are unlikely to have much effect. For example, in a study of a global company, Käufer and Pruyne (in press) found that although there was widespread *cognitive* agreement on the need to decentralize and distribute leadership practices and responsibilities, when the routine practices, behaviors, and structural changes needed to accomplish this shift became apparent, management and nonmanagement alike were unprepared to deal with the power issues involved. The rhetoric and theory in books about new models of leadership were inadequate in preparing the organization to anticipate and work with these issues. As a result, the initiative—although it was implemented at the level of rhetoric—failed to change basic structures, norms, and patters of behavior.

We argue that this situation is not unique and that it is the hidden, under-explored nature of these gender/power dynamics that may account for the failure of these models to achieve the transformational potential they profess. Theorizing leadership as a social process embedded in networks of influence requires an acknowledgement of these effects and an understanding of their implications. Failure to do so is likely to result in theories that are inadequate to the transformational task and promise of the new models.

# Possibility: Dialogue and Stone Center Relational Theory

In the following section, we explore the implications of using the tenets of Stone Center Relational Theory to understand dialogue, a process of communicating that Yukl (1998) argues is a prerequisite for shared leadership. Based on the work of Bohm (1990) and Buber (1970), dialogue is defined as the "art of thinking together" or as a conversation without a center (Isaacs, 1999). It is a type of learning conversation that requires a mix of advocacy and inquiry, and can result in learning across differences and in the co-creation of new knowledge (Heifitz, 1994; Draft, 2001; Argyris, 1992; Senge, 1990). As such, it is an important arena in which one of the key tasks of leadership—fostering organizational learning and adaptive change—can be accomplished.

To explore how principles of relational theory and growth-in-connection can inform the practice of shared leadership, we analyze one of the frameworks for this type of learning conversations used earlier (Scharmer, 2001). This framework is particularly suited to our use because it identifies phases within the dialogue process and highlights the importance of understanding the quality of communication and interaction in each phase.

## Dialogue: Four Phases of Learning Conversations

Scharmer (2001) expands the research on dialogue by suggesting a framework that describes the process of dialogue (see Figure 2.1). He argues that when groups

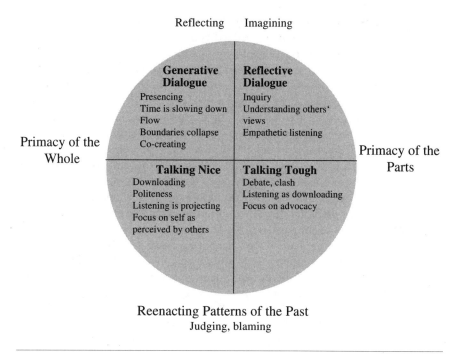

Reflecting    Imagining

**Generative Dialogue**
Presencing
Time is slowing down
Flow
Boundaries collapse
Co-creating

**Reflective Dialogue**
Inquiry
Understanding others'
views
Empathetic listening

Primacy of the Whole

Primacy of the Parts

**Talking Nice**
Downloading
Politeness
Listening is projecting
Focus on self as
perceived by others

**Talking Tough**
Debate, clash
Listening as downloading
Focus on advocacy

Reenacting Patterns of the Past
Judging, blaming

**Figure 2.1**    Enacting Emerging Futures

engage in a conversation, the quality of the interaction falls into four phases, each of which has distinctive characteristics. This framework allows teams and groups to evaluate the quality of their social interaction. The model of four dialogue phases is different from the notion of active listening because it conceptualizes dialogue as a group-level phenomenon rather than as individual behavior that simply occurs in a group setting

### Talking Nice

Most conversational interaction starts off with what Scharmer calls "talking nice." In this phase, participants in a group interact according to a given set of rules: "How are you? I am fine." Everybody knows what to say, nothing is a surprise. No one, for example, stands up and says: "This is nonsense." Because individuals do not speak up or say what they really think, conversation devolves to a rule-repeating interaction. An example is the following quote from a workshop participant: "At the beginning it was a little hard, there is much mistrust in the first meetings. No one wants to talk, everyone limits him/herself and says the minimum of what he has to say, but little by little that environment starts breaking down and you are able to have all sorts of things come out, and obviously they must be worked on" (De Leon & Diez Pinto, 2001). This mode of conversation is common in organizations: No one shares with the CEO what is discussed in the hallways. Although this mode of conversation may be a necessary first step in creating a shared understanding of the rules of interaction within a group, it does not allow for shared leadership because the responsibility for the common task has not been shared.

## Talking Tough

In this same meeting, the mode of conversation changes and moves the group to the next phase, "talking tough." As another participant in the meeting notes: "The first round of the first session was extremely negative because we were all looking back to the events of recent years, which had left a deep imprint on us. Thus, a first moment full of pessimism was generated. Suddenly, a young man stood up and questioned our pessimism in a very direct manner. This moment marked the beginning of a very important change, and we continually referred to it afterwards" (Diez Pinto, 2001).

The young man broke away from the rule of repeating norms in the first phase. He introduced a new quality into the interactional field by saying what he thought rather than what was expected of him. When participants start saying what they think, the level of authenticity increases. What distinguishes this type of talk from the first phase is that the interactions shift from rule repeating to rule producing. Once these new rules are introduced, others may follow. This is the moment that often sparks debate or conflict, during which participants in the conversational interactions "talk tough" across the divide.

Scharmer notes that groups often spend most of their interactional time moving back and forth between Phase I, "talking nice," and Phase II, "talking tough." Although important aspects of conversations occur in these phases, he suggests that they are not learning conversations. Rather than learning, the focus is on listening. Listening in these two phases means listening to and evaluating different opinions. Individuals want to make their perspectives understood and exert influence over the group rather than learn from others.

Scharmer notes that this step of "talking tough" is a prerequisite for shared understanding because it allows groups to articulate opposing views and to talk with authenticity. We suggest that if the group as a whole does not move into the next phase, reflective dialogue, the group will not be able to engage in an essential aspect of shared leadership: the ability to co-create and share responsibility for outcomes.

## Reflective Dialogue

The next phase is characterized by a new level of listening and mutual understanding. Scharmer calls this phase "reflective dialogue." As one workshop participant described it: "We were capable of understanding each other, of talking to each other; we were capable of respecting each other, of doing this." (Diez Pinto, 2001).

Reflective dialogue differs from the earlier phases of conversation in that shared leadership occurs for the first time. The participants of the conversation start to develop a quality of social interaction that includes self-reflection and a perception of the common task and the group as a whole.

One interviewee described the difference between Phase II, talking tough, and Phase III, reflective dialogue: "So I try to make an effort not to answer but to actually listen, not to be thinking mentally of how am I going to respond but rather 'What is this guy trying to tell me?' To think beyond what this person is trying to tell me, to go even deeper and say, 'Why is he saying it the way he is saying it?' . . . Just the exercise of saying 'Is this what you are trying to say? Am I understanding it correctly?' . . . So this is something that was very powerful and something that is part of my baggage. I take it with me, I go with it, I exercise it, I engage it, and it is good" (Diez Pinto, 2001).

The difference between reflective dialogue and the debate mode of conversation is that the listener adopts the perspective of the person talking. He or she tries to understand the other person's perspective. Participants often describe a special bond that evolves from the common effort to get to this level of understanding. In this phase of conversation, the individual participants begin to share the leadership task of creating the conditions in which learning and understanding can take place. We argue that without the ability to move into a reflective dialogue, shared leadership cannot occur. Groups that use shared leadership as their coordination mechanism need first to gain this level of communication.

### Generative Dialogue

Two interviewees described the next phase of dialogue. This quote is taken from recent research on dialogue conducted under the auspices of the United Nations (Gillespie, 2001; Käufer, 2000): "[One participant] witnessed an exhumation. It was a large field and he was suddenly called . . . to see what they had found . . . evidence of the skeleton of an unborn baby who had been buried, perhaps alive or still in its mother's womb, and the mother had been probably buried alive. That is the history. . . . But we were aware of it. I was. I was a politician. . . . It is one thing to know about something and know it as statistical data, and another to actually feel it. . . . And I think that all of us had to go through this process. . . . I think that, after understanding this, everyone is committed to preventing it from happening again. In giving this testimony, he was sincere, calm and serene, without a trace of hate in his voice. This gave way to the moment of silence that, I would say, lasted at least one minute. It was horrible. . . . If you ask any of us, we would say that this moment was like a large communion. No one dared to break the silence" (Diez Pinto, 2001).

Participants of this workshop referred to this moment of silence as a transformational moment among representatives of the military, civilians, politicians, guerillas, and paramilitaries. Participants described it as a moment when their communication reached a level of connection that transcended individual interests. Scharmer calls this level of communication "generative dialogue." Generative dialogue allows the participants to experience the group as a whole. What distinguishes reflective dialogue from generative dialogue is the level of trust and openness between its participants. We suggest that this high level of connectedness is a necessary condition for the type of co-created understanding—and group level ownership—of issues, problems, and solutions on which shared leadership depends. The quote we used describes an extreme example, not typical of issues discussed in most organizational settings. There are, however, lessons to be learned from it because it exemplifies what can happen when individuals experience the team or group as a connected web rather than as a set of individuals. In cases when the differences and history between the individuals are not as difficult as in this workshop in Guatemala, the process of finding the common ground would, of course, be easier. But the task of moving the group to a place where its participants experience the whole is the same. A generative dialogue is by definition shared leadership. It is a form of social interaction in which the whole team or group shares the responsibility of the process itself and improves their ability to cooperate (Käufer, 2000). The quality of social interaction—in other words, the high level of trust and mutual engagement—allows the group as a whole to explore new ideas and ways of thinking and to coordinate itself easily. Thus, we suggest that generative dialogue is by definition shared leadership

Scharmer notes that, although there are exceptions, groups rarely move into a reflective or generative dialogue without having moved through the two earlier quadrants. Neither do groups move through these phases automatically. Many groups get stuck in Phase II, talking tough, and then regress to Phase I, talking nice. Käufer (2000) observes that although reflective and generative dialogue are especially important for groups that have designated themselves as sharing the leadership task of coordination or for those times when any group faces challenging or crisis situations, moving to these quadrants should not be seen as a routine requirement. Rather, it is a requirement that demands process preparation on the part of some members of the group, to allow the time and space for this type of interaction to be established. She argues that in order to introduce shared leadership to a group in an organizational setting, that group must possess the ability to raise its quality of dialogue to a reflective or generative level.

## Using Relational Theory to Inform Dialogue

Stone Center Relational Theory can inform each of the four phases of Scharmer's model, highlighting certain microprocesses and conditions within each and suggesting directions for future research on the interactional principles inherent in such models.

### The Four Phases

When the notion of self-in-relation—and its corollary beliefs about interdependence, mutuality, and connection as the route to growth—are added to the model, it highlights why an expanded concept of self is needed to more fully understand the kinds of social interactions that exemplify shared leadership practices that enable learning. In the first two phases, talking nice and talking tough, individualistic notions of self dominate. Talking nice is an interaction characterized by a "self" who sees the "other" as a threat. This is a situation Jean Baker Miller and Irene Stiver (1997) refer to as the "relational paradox": keeping oneself out of growth-fostering connection in order to maintain connection. In other words, talking nice, or not representing one's experience or perspective, is often motivated by a desire to avoid disconnection in the belief that disconnection will ultimately be harmful. But, as notions of mutuality and interdependence suggest, the paradox is that *not* representing one's own experience or position actually inhibits mutual growth in connection and limits the possibility of achieving the "five good things," including new knowledge and learning. This underscores that shared leadership is not present in a talking nice mode of communication, which is more characteristic of traditional forms of leadership when the leader at the top sets the rules and conversations become rule-repeating interactions.

The next phase, talking tough, is also characterized by discrete images of "self" and "other." In this case, belief in the power of connection to foster growth and learning is largely absent. Instead, persuasion or strong advocacy is the norm. Differentiating oneself from others—even at the risk of disconnection—takes the form of advocacy and debate. Because one is speaking one's mind, however, the possibility of deeper connection and learning are more present than in Phase I. In this mode of communication, the person who speaks up takes on a leadership role or challenges other leaders. The result of this form of social interaction is a win or lose debate. It does not allow for shared leadership because the individual does not connect to the overall task. But, as noted earlier, this mode of conversation is often an essential precondition for shared leadership because it moves away from the rule-repeating interaction toward an authentic intervention, which allows individuals to begin to take on leadership responsibilities.

What the stance inherent in enacting a "self-in-relation" highlights is that what is needed to move from Phase II to Phase III is not only that someone speak his or her mind, but that it be done in a particular way. When advocacy is presented not from a stance of "self" (and "what is it I want to say") but from one of "self-in-relation" (that is, "what is it I want to say and how can it best be heard by the particular others with whom I am about to interact"), it opens up the interactional field and enhances the possibility of moving from talking tough to reflective dialogue. That is, someone who "talks tough" from a self-in-relation stance and authentically represents his or her own experience and perspective actually invites the possibility of movement to a place of deeper connection where the five good things might be achieved.

Moving to this place, however, is not guaranteed. It not only requires that the person introducing the topic present it from a self-in-relation stance so that others might hear, but also that the receiver be open to listening. In other words, movement to the next phase requires that someone else in the interactional field also be operating from a self-in-relation stance. For this action to engage reflective dialogue, a listener has to move to a place where he or she is not resisting the idea, but instead thinks, "I have something to learn from this." When at least two people are operating from this self-in-relation stance, the possibility for mutuality and mutual learning exists. The self-in-relation is aware of his or her effect on others *and* believes there is something to learn from others. In this instance, advocacy and inquiry are more fluid and two-directional, less hierarchical. That is, just listening to another's perspective is not enough to move the group—or even one person in the group—to real reflective dialogue. To move to reflective dialogue requires that at least the first step in a spiral of growth be engaged, in which each party moves in fluid fashion from "knowing" to "not knowing," from advocacy and speaking strongly in one's own voice, to inquiry and a stance of openness to influence.

Generative dialogue is, by definition, shared leadership because its participants are fully engaged with one another and are leading the process. It is a phase that is very similar to the type of interaction relational theorists describe as a fully engaged "spiral of growth," in which mutuality, learning, and the creative activity of co-creating solutions and shared understandings are shared by the collective. Multiple "selves-in-relation" would be interacting in a way that holds the whole, focused on the common good. It would require being comfortable with fluidity, especially with fluid power dynamics in which expertise was continually being shifted and redefined to include other perspectives. Rather than just one or two people having adopted a self-in-relation stance, the collective would need to have developed this stance. Only when this fluid, more egalitarian quality of interaction is present can a dialogue occur in which its participants start to take on leadership responsibilities. Therefore, we argue that this particular type of shared—or more fluid—power is a prerequisite for shared leadership. This is not to say that reflective and even generative dialogues do not occur in organizational settings that follow traditional hierarchical leadership models. But, we argue, the less democratic and less egalitarian, the less likely is the appearance of either reflective or generative dialogue.

### Possibilities

Substituting the concept of self-in-relation helps us see important aspects of individual interactions within the group and highlights the need to explicate the relational skills, competence, and intelligence that would need to be developed in people who are part of these learning conversations. As others have noted (Ely & Thomas, 2001; Palmer, 1993), simply calling for interactions that result in learning across difference belies how difficult it is to create conditions in which people can question underlying assumptions and begin to consider new possibilities. Relational theory offers ways of thinking about what this type of relational competence would look like in concrete practice and what skills it would take. It highlights the fact not only that adopting a self-in-relation stance is important, but what skills it takes to enact this stance and what, in more nuanced terms, those skills entail. For example, the mutual empathy or empathic competence needed to move from the bottom quadrants to the top would include the ability to anticipate another's reaction and modify one's input without silencing its impact or challenge. The notion of fluid expertise highlights the ability to move easily between expert and non-expert, teacher and learner with no loss to self-esteem but, rather, with some gain in self-in-relation esteem. Additional research that unpacks the specific practices needed to move along the phases of a framework, such as the one Scharmer offers, could help theorists—and ultimately practitioners—develop a language of competence to describe these practices more accurately, so the skills, intentions, and effects are visible. Only then will moving to the next challenge—rewriting leadership development—become a real possibility.

The power and identity issues associated with adopting a self-in-relation stance suggest other interesting research questions about establishing the conditions in which learning conversations can happen and makes visible some otherwise hidden aspects of the model. If adopting a self-in-relation stance is critical to learning conversations but is inappropriately associated with femininity and powerlessness, what would it take—at the individual as well as organizational levels—for people to adopt this stance? What happens to people who do? For example, Fletcher (2002) notes that the paradox of the disappearing of shared leadership practices is something that is experienced in a unique way by women. She calls attention to the fact that because women are expected to provide conditions of growth invisibly, it is very difficult for them to communicate the reciprocity and expectation of mutuality that is a precondition for the type of learning conversations described in the last two phases of dialogue. When women enact a self-in-relation stance, she suggests, they are at risk of being perceived not only as inappropriately "doing femininity" (something that might also happen to men), but also as "doing mothering" or "selfless giving" (something less likely to happen to men).

Although the particulars of the form of disappearing that Fletcher describes in her paper go beyond the scope of this chapter, the general principle of "differential impact" she describes opens up a space where new issues can be considered. Indeed, these questions raise a new set of problems and issues that learning conversation advocates and theorists need to consider in developing theory useful to practitioners:

What role does power—hierarchical power from organizational position as well as power that derives from other aspects of social identity such as race, class, gender, and sexual orientation—play in these interactions, and how can this explanatory variable be added to the model? Considering these questions makes visible the fact that movement through the phases of dialogue is not a gender- or power-neutral process and may even require a different conceptualization of power itself—perhaps something similar to Mary Parker Follett's (1924) notion of "power with" as opposed to "power over"—to make the model actionable.

This discussion of how tenets and principles of Stone Center Relational Theory can inform one aspect of shared leadership—the ability and felt responsibility to create conditions in which learning conversations can take place—serves as a model for how the theory might inform other aspects of shared leadership. It suggests that the tasks of rewriting self, rewriting the language of leadership, rewriting leadership development, and rewriting power from a relational perspective can yield significant new insights when used to unpack the specific actions and concrete practices within theoretical frameworks such as these.

# Conclusion

We suggest that the concept of shared leadership can be informed by Stone Center Relational Theory in three specific ways. First, it offers a concept of self-in-relation that is more fluid and multidirectional than notions of self as an independent entity. This relational notion of self carries with it some corollary shifts—such as a move from privileging independence as the basic human condition to privileging interdependence as the basic human condition—that can inform many aspects of shared leadership. As indicated in the example of dialogue, substituting self-in-relation for self opens up new discursive space where new questions—such as the skills it takes to enact a self-in-relation stance—can be explored.

Second, relational theory calls attention to the way in which the relational competence it takes to enact a self-in-relation stance is often dismissed and/or devalued by its association with femininity and powerlessness. Not only does this help us understand the phenomenon of the "disappearing" of relational leadership practices, it suggests we need a new language of competence to describe these skills and practices accurately, capturing nuances in the skills themselves, as well as the underlying beliefs about human growth and development that motivate people to use them.

Third, it offers a way of putting social interactions related to leadership in the broader societal context of power differences in which they occur. Rather than abstracting these concepts from the power and politics of social identity (e.g., race, class, and gender), relational theory makes these power dynamics visible and discussable.

Shared leadership is assumed to have transformational potential. We argue that achieving this potential requires more than a cognitive awareness of the need for change because the paradoxes embedded in the concept are rooted in a complex set of dynamics that underlie workplace interaction. Transformational change requires a process that would engage this profound shift not only in behavior and structure but also in some basic assumptions and mental models that underlie organizational life. These basic assumptions—about self as a discrete entity, about independence as an ideal state, about meritocracy and competition in developmental programs—are not benign concepts readily open to reexamination. On the contrary, they engage important identity issues that make it difficult to address on a cognitive level alone.

We believe that future research on shared leadership must begin to integrate theories of group and team processes at the microlevel of social interaction in order to understand and address the paradoxes inherent in shared leadership. Without such an integration, we fear that the concept of shared leadership will stall at the level of rhetoric, or worse, be coopted into the mainstream in ways that undermine its transformational potential. More specifically, we argue that it is important in exploring these microlevel interactions to use a theory of relational interactions that acknowledges the larger, societal-level gender and power dynamics at play. We offer Stone Center Relational Theory—and its related corollaries and tenets—as a particularly powerful tool in uncovering these processes and laying out the conceptual landscape needed to explore them.

# Notes

1. For a fuller explanation of this aspect of gender socialization, its psychological roots, and its effects on society, see *Toward a New Psychology of Women*, 1976, by Jean Baker Miller (Boston: Beacon); and *The Healing Connection*, 1997, by Jean Baker Miller and Irene Stiver (Boston: Beacon).

2. The terms "masculine" and "feminine" are used here to refer to a set of traits, skills, and abilities socially ascribed to men and women. These traits are not essential aspects of masculinity or femininity and indeed may not reflect the experiences of most men and women. Nonetheless these idealized images exist and exert subtle but very real pressure on women and men to "do gender" by defining themselves in relation to these stereotypes.

# References

Aaltio-Marjosola, I. (2001, June). *Charismatic leadership, manipulation and the complexity of organizational life.* Paper presented at the MIT Sloan School of Management Organizational Studies Seminar Series, Cambridge, MA.

Acker, J. (1990). Hierarchies, jobs, bodies: A theory of gendered organizations. *Gender & Society, 4*, 139-158.

Alvesson, M. (1992). Leadership as social integrative action. A study of a computer consultancy company. *Organization Studies, 13*(2), 185-209.

Argyris, C. (1992). *On organizational learning.* Cambridge, MA: Blackwell.

Argyris, C., & Schon, D. (1978). *Organizational learning.* Reading, MA: Addison Wesley.

Badaracco, J. (2001). We don't need another hero. *Harvard Business Review, 79*(8), 120-126.

Bailyn, L. (1993). *Breaking the mold.* New York: Free Press.

Bartunek, J., Walsh, K., & Lacey, C. (2000). Dynamics and dilemmas of women leading women. *Organization Science, 11*(6), 589-610.

Beebe, B., & Lachman, F. (1988). The contribution of mother-infant mutual influence to the origins of self and object representation. *Psychoanalytic Psychology, 5*, 305-337.

Beer, M. (1999). Leading learning and learning to lead. In J. Conger, G. Spreitzer, & E. Lawler (Eds.), *The leader's change handbook* (pp. 127-161). San Francisco, CA: Jossey-Bass.

Block, P. (1993). *Stewardship: Choosing service over self-interest.* San Francisco, CA: Berrett-Koehler.

Bohm, D. (1990). *On dialogue.* Transcription of a meeting edited by D. Bohm, Ojai, CA.

Bradford, D., & Cohen, A. (1998). *Power Up.* New York: Wiley.

Breit, J. M., & Stroh, L. K. (1999). Women in management. How far have we come and what needs to be done as we approach 2000. *Journal of Management Inquiry, 8*(4), 392-398.

Bryman, A. (1996). Leadership in organization. In S. R. Clegg, C. Hardy, & W. R. Nord (Eds.), *Handbook of organization studies* (pp. 276-292). Thousand Oaks, CA: Sage.

Buber, M. (1970). *I and thou.* New York: Touchstone.

Calàs, M. B., & Smircich, L. (1993, March/April). Dangerous liaisons: The "feminine-in-management" meets "globalization." *Business Horizons,*, 73-83.

Calvert, L., & Ramsey, V. J. (1992). Bringing women's voice to research on women in management: A feminist perspective. *Journal of Management Inquiry, 1*(1), 79-88.

Chodorow, N. (1978). *The reproduction of mothering.* Berkeley: University of California Press.

Collinson, D., & Hearn, J. (1996). *Men as managers, managers as men.* London: Sage.

Conger, J. (1989). Leadership: The art of empowering others. *Academy of Management Executive, 3,* 17-24.

Day, C. (2001). The salty line manager and organizational learning. *Reflections, 3*(1), 35-40.

De Leon, A., & Diez Pinto, E. (2001). *Destino Colombia 1997-2000: A treasure to be revealed.* New York: United Nation Development Program Work Report.

Della Noce, D. (1999). Seeing theory in practice: An analysis of empathy in mediation. *Negotiation Journal, 15*(3), 271-301.

Diez Pinto, E. (2001). *Vision Guatemala 1998-2000: Building bridges of trust.* New York: United Nation Development Program Work Report.

Draft, W. (2001). *The deep blue sea.* San Francisco, CA: Jossey-Bass.

Ely, R., & Thomas, D. (2001). Cultural diversity at work: The effects of diversity perspectives on work group processes and outcomes. *Administrative Science Quarterly, 46,* 229-273.

Erkut, S. (2001). *Inside women's power: Learning from leaders.* Wellesley, MA: Wellesley College Centers for Women, for the Winds of Change Foundation.

Fairbairn, W. D. R. (1952). *An object relations theory of personality.* New York: Basic.

Fletcher, J. K. (1994). Castrating the female advantage. *Journal of Management Inquiry, 3*(1), 74-82.

Fletcher, J. K. (1997). A relational approach to developing the protean worker. In D. T. Hall & Associates (Eds.), *The career is dead—long live the career* (pp. 105-131). San Francisco, CA: Jossey-Bass.

Fletcher, J. K. (1999). *Disappearing acts: Gender, power and relational practice at work.* Cambridge, MA: MIT Press.

Fletcher, J. K. (2002). *The paradox of post heroic leadership: Gender, power and the "new" organization.* Paper presented at the Academy of Management Annual Meeting, Denver, CO.

Fletcher , J. K. & Jacques, R. (2000). *Relational Practice: an Emerging Stream of Theorizing and its Significance for Organizational Studies.* CGO Working Paper. Center for Gender in Organizations, Simmons Graduate School of Management. Boston, MA.

Fletcher, J. K., Miller, J. B., Jordan, J. V., Parker, V., Harvey, M., & Woodburn, L. (1997). *Contributions of relational theory to models of organizational change.* Symposium presented at the Academy of Management Annual Meeting, Boston.

Follett, M. P. (1924). *Creative Experience.* New York: Longmans, Green.

Fondas, N. (1997). Feminization unveiled: Management qualities in contemporary writings. *Academy of Management Review, 22,* 257-282.

Gary, J. (2001). Beyond business as usual: Managing fear and uncertainty. *Harvard Management Update, 6*(10), 10-11.

Gillespie, G. (2001). *The Mont Fleur Scenario Project, South Africa 1991-1992. The footprints of Mont Fleur.* New York: United Nation Development Program Work Report.

Goleman, D. (1998). *Working with emotional intelligence.* New York: Bantam.

Greenleaf, R. (1977). *Servant leadership.* San Francisco, CA: Jossey-Bass.

Hall, D. T., & Associates (Eds.). (1997). *The career is dead—long live the career.* San Francisco, CA: Jossey-Bass.

Hall, D. T., & Mirvis, P. (1997). The protean worker. In D. T. Hall & Associates. (Eds.), *The career is dead—long live the career.* San Francisco, CA: Jossey-Bass.

Harrington, M. (2000). *Care and equality.* New York: Routledge.

Heenan, D., & Bennis, W. (1999). *Co-leaders: The power of great partnerships.* New York: Wiley.

Heifitz, R. (1994). *Leadership without easy answers.* Cambridge, MA: Harvard University Press.

Heifitz, R., & Laurie, D. (1999). Mobilizing adaptive work: Beyond visionary leadership. In J. Conger, G. Spreitzer, & E. Lawler (Eds.), *The leader's change handbook.* San Francisco, CA: Jossey-Bass.

Held, V. (1990). Mothering vs. contract. In J. Mansbridge (Ed.), *Beyond self interest* (pp. 287-304). Chicago: University of Chicago Press.

Helgeson, S. (1990). *The female advantage.* New York: Doubleday.

Hirschorn, L. (1990). Leaders and followers in a postindustrial age: A psychodynamic view. *The Journal of Applied Behavioral Science, 26*(4), 529-542.

Hosking, D., Dachler, H. P., & Gergen, K. J. (Eds.), (1995). *Management and organization: Relational alternative to individualism.* Aldershot, UK: Ashgate.

Ilgen, D. R. (1999). Teams embedded in organizations. Some implications. *American Psychologist, 54*(2), 129-139.

Isaacs, W. (1999). Dialogue and the art of thinking together. New York: Doubleday.

Jordan, J. (1986). *The meaning of mutuality* (Working Paper 23). Wellesley, MA: Centers for Women, Wellesley College.

Jordan, J., Kaplan, A., Miller, J. B., Stiver, I., & Surrey, J. (1991). *Women's growth in connection.* New York: Guilford.

Jordan, J. V. (1991). *The movement of mutuality and power* (Working Paper No. 53). Wellesley, MA: Wellesley College Centers for Women.

Käufer, K. (2000). *Learning from civic scenario projects: A tool for facilitating social change?* New York: United Nation Development Program Work Report.

Käufer, K., & Fletcher, J. K. (2001). *Distributed leadership.* Paper presented at the Society for Organizational Learning Research Greenhouse, Hartford, CT.

Käufer, K., & Pruyne, E. (in press). *Challenges of change.* Cambridge, MA.

Käufer, K., & Scharmer, C. O. (in press). Dialogue: Moving across four field structures of conversation. Cambridge, MA.

Kahane, A. (2001). How to change the world: Lessons for entrepreneurs from activists. *Reflections, 2*(3), 16-26.

Kegan, R. (1994). *In over our heads.* Cambridge, MA: Harvard University Press.

Kohut, H. (1971). *The analysis of the self.* New York: Interactional Universities Press.

Kouzes, J., & Posner, B. (2002). *The leadership challenge, 3rd ed.* San Francisco, CA: Jossey-Bass.

Kram, K. (1997). Relational aspects of career development. In D. T. Hall & Associates. (Eds.), *The career is dead—long live the career.* San Francisco, CA: Jossey-Bass.

Lave, J., & Wenger, E. (1991). *Situated learning: Legitimate peripheral participation.* New York: Cambridge University Press.

Lipman-Blumen, J. (1996). *The connective edge.* San Francisco, CA: Jossey-Bass.

Lipnack, J., & Stamps, J. (2000). *Virtual teams.* New York: Wiley.

Manz, C. C., & Sims, H. P. (1987). Leading workers to lead themselves: The external leadership of self managing work teams. *Administrative Science Quarterly 32,* 106-128.

Marsick, V., & Watkins, E. (1999). *Facilitating learning organizations: Making learning count.* Aldershot, UK: Gower.

McIntosh, P. (1989). *Feeling like a fraud Part 2* (Working Paper 37). Wellesley, MA: Centers for Women, Wellesley College.

McNamee, S., & Gergen, K. J. (1999). *Relational responsibility: Resources for sustainable dialogue.* Thousand Oaks, CA: Sage.

Meindl, J. R., Ehrlich, S. B., & Dukerich, J. M. (1985). The romance of leadership. *Administrative Science Quarterly, 30,* 78-102.

Meyerson, D. (2000). *Tempered radicals.* Cambridge, MA: Harvard Business School Press.

Meyerson, D., & Fletcher, J. K. (2000, January). A modest manifesto for breaking the glass ceiling. *Harvard Business Review,* 126-136.

Miller, J. B. (1976). *Toward a new psychology of women.* Boston, MA: Beacon

Miller, J. B. (1984). *The development of women's sense of self* (Working Paper No. 12). Wellesley, MA: Wellesley College Centers for Women.

Miller, J. B., & Stiver, I. (1997). *The healing connection.* Boston, MA: Beacon.

Morrison, E., & Milliken, F. (2000). Organizational silence: A barrier to change and development in a pluralistic world. *Academy of Management Review, 25*(4), 706-725.

Northouse, P. G. (2001). *Leadership theory and practice.* (2nd ed.). Thousand Oaks, CA: Sage.

Palmer, P. (1993). *To know as we are known.* San Francisco, CA: HarperCollins.

Pearce, C., & Sims, H. (2000). Shared leadership: Toward a multi-level theory of leadership. In M. Beyerlein, D. Johnson, & S. Beyerlein (Eds.), *Advances in the interdisciplinary studies of work teams, 7,* 115-139. New York: JAI.

Peters, T. (1990, September). The best new managers will listen, motivate, support: Isn't that just like a woman. *Working Woman,* 216-217.

Rapoport, R., Bailyn, L., Fletcher, J. K., & Pruitt, B. (2002). *Beyond work family balance: Advancing gender equity and workplace performance.* San Francisco, CA: Jossey-Bass.

Rosenbaum, J. (1989). Organization career systems and employee misperceptions. In M. Arthur, D. T. Hall, & B. S. Lawrence (Eds.), *Handbook of career theory* (pp. 329-353). Cambridge, MA: Cambridge University Press.

Rosener, J. (1995). *America's Competitive Secret.* New York: Oxford University Press.

Ruddick, S. (1989). *Maternal thinking.* Boston: Beacon.

Ruderman, M., & Ohlott, P. (2002). *Standing at the crossroads.* San Francisco, CA: Jossey-Bass.

Ruderman, M., Ohlott, P., Panzer, K., & King, S. Multiple roles. *Academy of Management Journal, 45*(2), pp. 369-386.

Scharmer, C. O. (2001). Self-transcending knowledge: Organizing around emerging realities. In I. Nonaka & D. Teece (Eds.), *Managing industrial knowledge: creation, transfer and utilization* (pp. 68-90). Thousand Oaks, CA: Sage.

Scully, M., & Donnellon, A. (1994). Teams, performance and rewards: Will the post-bureaucratic organization be a post-meritocratic organization? In C. Heckscher & A. Donnellon (Eds.), *The post-bureaucratic organization* (pp. 63-90). Thousand Oaks, CA: Sage.

Scully, M. & Segal, A. (1997). *Passion with an umbrella: Grassroots activists in the workplace.* MIT Sloan School of Management. Working Paper, Cambridge, MA.

Seely Brown, J., & Duguid, P. (2000). *The social life of information.* Cambridge, MA: Harvard Business School Press.

Senge, P. (1990). *The fifth discipline.* New York: Doubleday.

Senge, P. (1996). Leading learning communities: The bold, the powerful, and the invisible. In F. Hesselbeinet et al. (Eds.), *The leader of the future.* San Francisco, CA: Jossey-Bass.

Senge, P., & Käufer, K. (2001). Communities of leaders or no leadership at all. In S. Chowdhury (Ed.), *Management 21C.* New York: Prentice Hall.

Sharpe, R. (2000). As leaders, women rule. *Business Week, 20,* 78-84.

Smith, K., & Berg, D. (1987). *Paradoxes of Group Life.* San Francisco, CA: Jossey-Bass.

Smith, K., Simmons, V., & Thames, T. (1989). Fix the women: An intervention into an organizational conflict based on parallel process thinking. *Journal of Applied Behavioral Science, 25*(1), 11-29.

Spillane, J. P., Halverson, R. & Diamond, J. B. (1999). *Towards a theory of school leadership practice: Implications of a distributed perspective* (Working paper). Institute for Policy Research, Northwestern University.

Suchman, L. (1987). *Plans and situated actions: The problem of human-machine communication.* New York: Cambridge University Press.

Surrey, J. (1991). Self-in-relation. In J. Jordan, A. Kaplan, J. B. Miller, I. Stiver, & J. Surrey (Eds.), *Women's growth in connection.* New York: Guilford.

Surrey, J. (1985). *The self in relation* (Working Paper No. 13). Centers for Women, Wellesley College, Wellesley, MA.

Thompson, L. L. (2000). *Making the team.* Upper Saddle River, NJ: Prentice Hall.

Tronick, E. (1989). Emotions and emotional communication in the infant. *American Psychologist, 44,* 112-119.

Useem, M. (2001). *Leading up.* New York: Crown.

West, C., & Zimmerman, D. (1991). Doing gender. In J. Lorber & S. Farrell (Eds.), *The social construction of gender* (pp. 13-37). Newbury Park, CA: Sage.

Williams, J. (2000). *Unbending Gender.* Oxford: Oxford University Press.

Winnicott, D. (1958). *The maturational process and the facilitating environment.* New York: International Universities Press.

Yukl, G. A. (1998). *Leadership in organizations* (4th ed.). Englewood Cliffs, NJ: Prentice Hall.

# CHAPTER 3

# Toward a Model of Shared Leadership and Distributed Influence in the Innovation Process

*How Shared Leadership Can Enhance New Product Development Team Dynamics and Effectiveness*

*Jonathan F. Cox*

*Craig L. Pearce*

*Monica L. Perry*

Perhaps reflecting general trends in the leadership literature, commentary on leadership in the new product development (NPD) domain focuses mainly on downward influence by a designated team leader in a position of hierarchical authority (Bass, 1990; Waldman & Bass, 1991). We offer a different perspective on leadership in the NPD domain: shared leadership. Shared leadership relies on a dynamic exchange of lateral influence among peers rather than simply relying on vertical, downward influence by an appointed leader. Given the fact that the NPD context is one composed of knowledge workers with high skill levels, we argue that shared leadership may contribute substantially to the experience of work and to team performance in these type of environments.

Although leadership and empowerment have emerged as critical to understanding the effectiveness of teams (e.g., Yeatts & Hyten, 1998; Yukl, 1998), shared leadership has only recently been explored in the organizational literature (e.g., Avolio, Jung, Murry, & Sivasubramaniam, 1996; Ensley & Pearce, 2000; Pearce, 1997, 1999; Pearce, Perry, & Sims, 2001; Pearce & Sims, 2000, 2002; Pearce, Yoo, & Alavi, in press; Seers, 1996). In applying this alternative conceptualization of leadership to the NPD context, we will discuss the benefits of shared leadership in NPD applications and why NPD contexts may challenge the implementation and maintenance of shared leadership.

We begin by briefly introducing NPD organization and highlighting characteristics of team-based NPD work to set a context for shared leadership. We then define shared leadership as a construct and introduce a limited model describing how shared leadership may influence NPD team outcomes. This model is grounded in the leadership literature as well as in organizational literature on teams and NPD.

## New Product Development Organization and Teams

New product development efforts are primarily organized according to project or program teams. New product development teams are cross-functional work groups organized around interdependent tasks to create or extend a product, process, or service. They provide a forum for members with complementary skills to collaborate in a creative enterprise involving a degree of deliberation, problem solving, mutual adjustment, and coordinated performance. New product development teams share many of these characteristics with a range of enduring, relatively stable, cross-functional, knowledge-intensive work teams. Examples include interdepartmental teams delivering high-value, nonstandard services such as customer support, claims processing, and complex sales (e.g., Perry, Pearce, & Sims, 1999; Wellins, Byham, & Dixon, 1994). However, NPD teams also differ in significant ways. Compared with cross-functional production teams, NPD teams are charged with outcomes that are more fundamentally novel and exploratory. In addition, NPD teams often coalesce temporarily around a pressing project, topical mandate, or time-limited objective. They may also experience changing membership over time through programmed entry and exit of personnel in response to unfolding performance requirements throughout the project life cycle.

These differences in purpose, duration, and stability imply unique performance and leadership challenges. The exploratory nature of their task takes NPD teams into unfamiliar territory, sometimes with significant time pressure and an awareness of high-stakes win/lose potential that can be both exciting and disconcerting. This disorienting novelty—new approaches, solutions, and technologies—broadly complicates teamwork by challenging the skills, and even the comprehension, of leaders and members alike. Programmed turnover compounds these challenges by bringing together members who may be unfamiliar with each other while limiting the time available to build shared understandings and smooth working relationships. Drawing personnel on a temporary basis from existing, often competing, functions may also introduce organizational complications such as turf-protection, competing demands, disputes over resource ownership, and conflicting loyalties among team members (Jassawalla & Sashittal, 1999; Nambisan & Wilemon, 2000;

Thamhain & Wilemon, 1997). Members are likely to bring varying knowledge bases and niche specialties, often highly technical, to the team that may further complicate communication and team integration. It is common for NPD team leaders to find themselves responsible for coordinating smooth execution among matrixed team members with whom they are unfamiliar and over whom they have little formal authority (Thamhain & Wilemon, 1997).

Cross-functional project teams are the preferred method of organizing for developing technology products and processes (Avolio et al., 1996). Reported benefits of cross-functional project teams include faster development and improved product quality (e.g., Brown & Eisenhardt, 1995; Cooper, 1995a, 1995b; Cooper & Kleinschmidt, 1994; Kessler & Chakrabarti, 1996; Kleinschmidt & Cooper, 1995). For example, in a review of more than 100 new product development efforts, Cooper and associates (Cooper, 1995a, 1995b; Cooper & Kleinschmidt, 1994) found the use of cross-functional teams to be a major driver of project timeliness. At their best, development teams pool a base of talent that exceeds the capacity of individual experts while enhancing integrative cross-functional communication, coordination, and information sharing (Donnellon, 1996a, 1996b; Hauptman & Hirji, 1996; Parker, 1994; Sashkin & Sashkin, 1994). On complex projects, NPD teams speed progress by involving the required functional groups early in the development process (Barczack & Wilemon, 1991). The temporary nature of NPD teams and the mobility of team members across projects also makes it possible to more efficiently balance resource demands and retain niche players with highly specialized, expensive-to-acquire skill sets.

The software development community, for example, recognizes team-based system design in many forms, such as chief-programmer teams, joint-application design teams, and walk-through teams (Janz, 1999; Janz & Wetherbe, 1994). Cross-functional NPD teams find ready application in software development, which requires coordinating deep capability across a range of disciplines and technical specialties throughout the project life cycle (e.g., Curtis, Krasner, & Iscoe, 1988). A software project might initially involve specialists in consumer research, market analysis, and competitive benchmarking to assess commercial viability and specify end-user requirements. Follow-on specialists could then be rotated into the team in subsequent phases to assess feasibility, design and pilot the product, test release candidates, confirm usability and end-user acceptance, and ensure appropriate marketing and product maintenance. Software development teams are being implemented against a backdrop of intense pressure to improve the performance of software products and development processes (e.g., Brancheau, Janz, & Wetherbe, 1996). Sobering statistics on the cost performance of NPD efforts are underscored by high-profile failures that have received considerable press attention (e.g., Gibbs, 1994; Glass, 1997; Stengel, 1997). For example, the April 1996 issue of *Computer Economics* estimated that only 18% of software projects are completed within budget, whereas almost a third are abandoned as too expensive.

New product development teams and structured development methods are two common approaches to improving productivity in the NPD process and the quality of NPD output (Sawyer & Guinan, 1998). Research and practice in NPD have tended to adopt a process and technology focus on methods, disciplined project control, and assistive technology and tools (Nambisan & Wilemon, 2000). Formalized approaches such as structured programming, information engineering, and systems development life cycles have been advocated to enhance project control and ensure stable development (e.g., Guinan, Cooprider, & Faraj, 1998; Topper, Ouelette, & Jorgenson, 1994; Yourdon, 1989). Tools and techniques have also been advocated to make NPD more efficient and programmatic (e.g., Card, McGarry, & Page, 1987; Topper et al., 1994). Examples include document preparation tools, modeling software, group decision support systems, requirements engineering, participatory design techniques and joint application development, to name just a few (Guinan et al., 1998).

This process and technology focus has no doubt brought significant advances to the NPD process. However, persistent difficulty delivering NPD outputs that fully meet performance expectations suggests that something more is needed. Nambisan and Wilemon (2000) offer a suggestive alternative by contrasting the NPD focus on "technology to support the development process" with the greater social emphasis of new product development on the "interaction of people and . . . [NPD] processes" (p. 211), and they urge a synthesis of these technology- and socially-oriented approaches around a core emphasis on process, technology, and people.

Sawyer and Guinan (1998) contend that the level of understanding about the human dynamics of NPD—how developers work together effectively—has not kept pace with advances in methodology and tools. Indeed, their research on 40 NPD teams suggests that human interaction has significant effects on NPD effectiveness. They found that social processes such as conflict management, communication, and informal coordination accounted for fully 25 percent of the variance in product quality. In contrast, methodologies and tools explained no variance in quality or team performance. Guinan, Cooprider, and Faraj (1998) similarly found that human interaction variables such as managerial involvement and homogenous team experience contributed more to effective processes in NPD teams than development tools and methods. We focus on one human dimension of NPD: team leadership.

Notwithstanding the dominant process and technology focus of NPD research, our review of the literature found reference to leadership as an important contributor to improving NPD effectiveness. Below, we detail some of the roles that have been proposed for leaders of NPD teams and introduce the construct of shared leadership into this context. We then elaborate a model of shared leadership in NPD teams that links shared leadership, the independent variable, to the dependent variables of team outcomes, including team responses and effectiveness. Our model also includes two groups of antecedent variables, vertical leadership roles and team characteristics, and one group of moderating variables, task characteristics.

# Leading New Product Development Teams

In his review of leadership theory and research, Yukl (1989) offers a catchall definition of leadership as "influence processes involving determination of the group's or organization's objectives, motivating task behavior in pursuit of these objectives, and influencing group maintenance and culture" (p. 5). Downward projection of influence from a focal leader to followers, a familiar pattern that we term vertical leadership, has been found to affect performance through its impact on the attitudes, beliefs, and behaviors of team members (Bass, 1990; Yukl, 1981). Several decades of research have documented the critical importance of leadership for team development, linking leadership to a range of positive outcomes (e.g., Bass, 1990;

Conger, 1999; Manz & Sims, 1989; Yukl, 1989, 1998). This research suggests that leadership interventions have significant potential to enhance the performance of teams, possibly including NPD teams.

## Vertical Leadership

The literature on innovation and new product development often equates effective leadership with efficient project management. For example, Brown and Karagozoglu (1993) describe leadership of NPD teams largely in terms of direct intervention in team communication, integration, and planning. Cooper (1995a, 1995b) portrays effective leaders as monitoring progress and driving task completion. Thamhain and Wilemon (1997) endorse hands-on leadership by "action-oriented" management that provides resources, directs team activity, and resolves problems (p. 131). Rettig and Simons (1993) similarly describe effective NPD team leaders as providing well-defined plans early on, then transitioning to less-structuring facilitation as the team matures. Robert (1977) argues for a supportive, but still largely task-focused, emphasis on reinforcing task accomplishment.

Some researchers also propose expanding the team leader's mandate beyond a task and process focus to stewardship of team attitudes and relational dynamics. For example, Walz, Elam, and Curtis (1993) recommend leader encouragement of team learning, whereas Ward (1997) urges managers to foster the atmosphere of commitment, trust, and openness required by "knowledge workers . . . [who must] think and create in their jobs" (p. 63). Brown and Karagozoglu (1993) invoke the technology and task characteristics of NPD to advocate "participatory leadership . . . to elicit the creativity of team members" (p. 215). Kruglianskas and Thamhain (2000) similarly emphasize the complexity of the NPD process and the need for dynamic problem solving in positioning the leader as a "social architect who understands the interaction of organizational and behavioral variables" (p. 62).

Clearly, opinions vary about what constitutes effective leadership of NPD teams. What stands out in these varied accounts is a consistent emphasis on vertical leadership: Whether coordinating tasks, fostering learning and innovation, or engineering the social architecture of the team, the appointed team leader is positioned as the focus of authority, influence, and control. The NPD team leader's work, it would seem, is never done.

## Shared Leadership

We observe that there are at least two sources of leadership influence in a team (Avolio et al., 1996; Ensley & Pearce, 2000; Ensley, Pearson, & Pearce, in press; Pearce, 1997, 1999; Pearce & Sims, 2000, 2002; Pearce et al., in press; Perry et al., 1999; Seers, 1996). One source, the appointed or emergent team leader, has received considerable treatment in the leadership literature (Bass, 1990; Lawler, 1986; Manz & Sims, 2001; Yukl, 1989, 1998). However, a second powerful source of leadership influence, the team itself, has been the focus of more recent research (e.g., Avolio et al., 1996; Pearce & Sims, 2000, 2002). We use the term shared leadership to describe the condition in which teams collectively exert influence. Under conditions of shared leadership, the relational fabric of the team supplements vertical influence with lateral peer influence. As such, shared leadership is a collaborative, emergent process of group interaction in which members engage in peer leadership while working together. Shared leadership might emerge as a sort of behavioral mechanism through an unfolding series of fluid, situationally appropriate exchanges of lateral influence. In parallel, shared leadership might also emerge as team members negotiate shared understandings about how to navigate decisions and exercise authority.

At a minimum, shared leadership implies that team members have significant authority to chart the team's forward path. As such, shared leadership is consistent with familiar tenets of team empowerment such as power sharing and selective devolution of decision-making authority from management to employees. Team empowerment places authority in the hands of the frontline employees who best understand the work. Frontline empowerment also has the potential to enhance mutual adjustment, communication, coordination, and accountability among peers. Considerable research across industries has explored the benefits of empowering teams with skills, resources, and authority to make decisions and take actions formerly reserved for management (e.g., Hackman, 1986, 1987; Kolodny & Kiggundu, 1980; Lawler, Mohrman, & Ledford, 1992; Mohrman, Cohen, & Mohrman, 1995; Pearce & Ravlin, 1987; Rice, 1955; Trist, Sussman, & Brown, 1977; Walton, 1972). In the NPD arena, Janz (1999) reports that empowered teams can cut development costs, increase customer satisfaction, and improve quality. Kruglianskas and Thamhain (2000) observe a gradual trend away from traditional hierarchy toward empowered teams in technology development contexts. They argue that this trend reflects the increasing complexity of technology and the need for a level of real-time mutual adjustment among collaborative peers that is incompatible with conventional hierarchy. The observations of Kruglianskas and Thamhain (2000) in technology development contexts are consistent with the more general observations a decade earlier by Barry (1991), who argued that relying solely on vertical leadership seems to "ignore leadership dynamics within a group context" (p. 32).

We view shared leadership as a logical extension of the expanded decision-making authority that characterizes truly empowered teams. However, providing an NPD team power and authority to lead itself is not sufficient for shared leadership. Instead, a sequence of conditions must hold for shared leadership to emerge over time (Pearce & Sims, 2000). First, team members must understand that constructive lateral influence is a standing performance expectation. Second, members must accept responsibility for providing and responding appropriately to constructive leadership from their peers. Third, the team members must develop skills as effective leaders and followers. Shared leadership, then, is fully expressed only when team members are prepared to function as savvy agents and targets of lateral influence.

## Benefit of Shared Leadership

Research on empowered teams has found self- and peer-influence in teams, variously termed self-leadership (e.g., Manz & Sims, 1993; Neck, Stewart, & Manz, 1996), distributed leadership (e.g., Barry, 1991), and shared leadership (e.g., Avolio et al., 1996; Ensley & Pearce, 2000; Pearce, 1997, 1999; Pearce & Sims, 2000, 2002; Pearce, Yoo, & Alavi, (in press); Perry et al., 1999; Seers, 1996) to offer significant benefits for team interaction and effectiveness. Empowered teams have been found to experience greater collaboration and coordination, as well as more novel and innovative solutions to problems (e.g., Manz & Sims, 1993; Yeatts & Hyten, 1998). Members of empowered teams may also develop a fuller appreciation of task interdependency and how their behavior affects the enterprise overall (McCafferty & Laight, 1997). Katzenbach and Smith (1993) found that high-performance teams tended to engage in more active peer influence, whereas Pearce (1997, 1999), Avolio et al., (1996), Pearce, Yoo, and Alavi (in press), Pearce and Sims (2002), and Ensley and Pearce (2000) found shared leadership to be an important predictor of team effectiveness.

We believe that shared leadership offers significant benefits for work life and team performance in the complex, knowledge-intensive context of NPD. For example, shared leadership may improve the experience of work by offering an incremental measure of self-determination and opportunity for meaningful impact. This benefit is consistent with the needs of today's workforce, which increasingly expects opportunities for voice and meaningful influence (e.g., Carnevale, 1991). This trend toward higher workforce expectations was evident almost three decades ago to Walton (1972), who identified a mismatch between traditional hierarchy and employees' increasing desire for control over their work lives. Drucker (2000) brings these observations into today's information economy by arguing that retaining knowledge workers requires "turning them from subordinates into fellow executives, and from employees, however well-paid, into partners" (p. 12) Consistent with this assertion, Sonnentag, Brodbeck, Heinbokel, and Stolte (1994) found that a lack of control at work was positively associated with burnout among NPD professionals. By more evenly distributing opportunities for meaningful influence, shared leadership may provide a basis for the full partnership advocated by Drucker.

The benefits of shared leadership may extend even to the essence of NPD work and the core rationale for team-based development. Praeger (1999) observes that technology professionals, for example, gain significant autonomy in organizations because of the relative inaccessibility—the technical mystery—of the work they do. Barriers arising from deep technical expertise may extend even to peers working together on a technology development effort. As mentioned earlier, NPD is often team-based because it requires a range of specialized technical skill sets that exceed the capacity even of skilled individuals (Parker, 1994; Sashkin & Sashkin, 1994). In complex team performance environments, an individual vertical leader is less likely than the team as a whole to have the knowledge and skills required to effectively lead the team (Pearce & Sims, 2000; Perry et al., 1999). Certainly, the knowledge and performance demands of changing technology are a significant challenge for leaders of NPD efforts. Indeed, it is common for technology professionals to work with technology that their formally designated managers know little about (Janz, 1999). King (1998) links NPD team social processes to team effectiveness by observing that the technical orientation of many members and their primary interest in the technology can cause them to resist influence. Shared leadership reaches beyond the limits of individual leader capability through lateral influence among frontline development experts that is potentially better informed and more responsive to momentary task and leadership challenges.

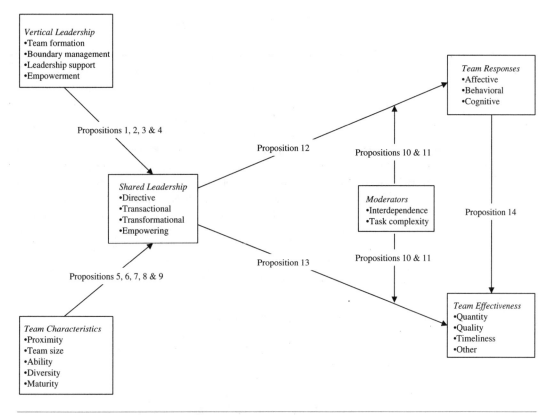

**Figure 3.1**    Conceptual Model of the Role of Shared Leadership in New Product
Development (NPD) Teams

# A Model of Shared Leadership
## in New Product Development Teams

We propose a model of shared leadership in new product development teams that
combines the existing literature on leader behaviors (Bass, 1990; Burns, 1978;
House, 1977; Manz & Sims, 1991; Yukl, 1998) with input-process/throughput-out-
put models from research on teams, particularly empowered teams (e.g.,
Gladstein, 1984; Knight et al., 1999; Tannenbaum, Beard, & Salas, 1992; Yeatts &
Hyten, 1998). We use this model as a foil to describe some of the variables that
might affect the emergence of shared leadership in NPD teams and its impact on
team outcomes. We begin by elaborating our independent variable, shared leadership, and describing two groups of antecedent variables, vertical leadership roles
and team characteristics, that might affect the development and maintenance of
shared leadership. We then introduce potential moderators, task characteristics,
which may affect the relationship between shared leadership and team outcomes.
We conclude with our dependent variables, team outcomes, which are composed
of team responses and team effectiveness. This preliminary model (see Figure 3.1)
is intended to suggest directions for future research on shared leadership in team-
based NPD contexts. As such, our discussion should be considered suggestive.

## Independent Variable: Shared Leadership

Several decades of research on vertical leadership have identified a range of leadership strategies or behaviors that serve as currency in the exchange of influence among leaders and followers (e.g., Bass, 1990; Yukl, 1989, 1998). In shared leadership contexts, these strategies continue to be relevant, with one important caveat: The agents of influence are often peers of the targets of influence. Although vertical leaders continue to play a significant role in developing and maintaining the shared leadership system, lateral influence among peers should typify the experience of leadership under conditions of shared leadership. We position shared leadership as an independent variable, or causal agent, in our model. To describe peer leadership behavior in collectively leading the team, we offer a typology of four leadership strategies, or types, based on an original formulation by Manz and Sims (1991) that was explicated and expanded by Cox (1994), Cox and Sims (1996), Sims and Manz (1996), Pearce (1997), Pearce and Sims (2002), and Pearce, Sims, Cox, et al. (in press). This typology captures much of what has emerged from the established literature on vertical leadership, as well as the emerging literature on shared leadership in teams.

### *Transactional and Transformational Leadership*

We discuss transactional and transformational leadership together because these strategies have been the subject of much academic leadership research in recent years (e.g., Avolio & Bass, 1988; Bass & Avolio, 1993; Brown & Lord, 1999; Conger, 1999). However, a revisionist movement now questions whether scholars are overlooking other appropriate leadership options by coalescing too narrowly on what amounts to a two-factor theory of leadership (Bass & Avolio, 1993; Yukl, 1989). The transactional type of leadership reflects an extensive stream of research encompassing path-goal theory (e.g., House, 1971; House & Mitchell, 1974), expectancy theory (e.g., Vroom, 1964), goal setting theory (e.g., Locke & Latham, 1990), and reinforcement theory (e.g., Luthans & Kreitner, 1985). Transactional leadership entails influencing followers by strategically supplying reinforcement—praise, material rewards, or other valued outcomes—contingent on follower performance. Peer transactional leadership in an NPD team might be expressed through collegial praise for contribution. Colleagues might also negotiate valued assignments or financial distributions based on individual- or team-level attainment of project milestones or quality and functionality targets.

The transformational type of leadership encompasses research on charismatic, transforming, and transformational leadership (e.g., Bass, Waldman, Avolio, & Bebb, 1987; Burns, 1978; Conger, 1989). Whereas transactional leadership emphasizes rewards of immediate value, transformational leadership adopts a more symbolic emphasis on commitment, emotional engagement, or fulfillment of higher-order needs such as meaningful professional impact or desires to engage in breakthrough achievements. NPD teams might engage in shared transformational leadership through peer exhortation or by appealing to collegial desires to design groundbreaking products or launch an exciting new venture.

Transformational influence may be effective in the NPD context because this context depends on significant and necessarily voluntary intellectual investment by skilled professionals. In this context, intellectual stimulation itself can promote effective performance (Waldman & Atwater, 1992; Waldman & Bass, 1991). Hater and Bass (1988) found that internally motivated employees, such as might be expected in the NPD community, respond particularly well to transformational leadership. In a study of 66 industrial research and development teams, Keller (1992, 1995) drew a distinction between research projects involving major or only incremental innovation. He found transformational leadership associated with quality in more innovative research, whereas directive leadership was associated with quality on more routine projects. Brown, McLean, and Straub (1996) advocate a balanced approach by managers that includes a mix of "transactional leadership to produce stability and efficiency, and transformational leadership to produce innovation and effectiveness" (p. 15).

### Directive Leadership

The third leadership type, directive leadership, is inspired by the landmark Ohio State leadership studies (e.g., Fleishman & Hunt, 1973; Halpin & Winer, 1957). Directive leadership involves providing task-focused direction or recommendations (e.g., Manz & Sims, 1991; Schriesheim, House, & Kerr, 1976). Experienced members of an NPD team might well find a receptive audience among less-experienced members for well-meaning direction and prescription. Directive leadership might also be expressed in conversation as peers test each other with prescriptive give-and-take about how to approach tasks, assign accountability, or resolve conflicting points of view. Directive leadership has been advocated in NPD contexts as providing much-needed structure for inherently complex development tasks (Guinan, Cooprider, & Faraj, 1998; Henderson & Lee, 1992). Guinan et al. (1998) found directive leadership to be positively related to NPD team performance as rated by teams themselves and by external stakeholders.

### Empowering Leadership

The last leadership type, empowering leadership, emphasizes employee self-influence rather than top-down control. The empowering leader fosters follower self-influence and, by implication, comprehensive empowerment by modeling self-leadership and by encouraging followers to use self-influence strategies (Manz & Sims, 1987, 1989, 1991, 1993, 2001; Neck, Stewart, & Manz, 1996). Several streams of research relate to empowering leadership, including behavioral self-management (e.g., Mahoney & Arnkoff, 1978), social learning theory (e.g., Bandura, 1977), and cognitive behavior modification (e.g., Meichenbaum, 1977).

In many ways, empowering leadership epitomizes the vertical leadership role under conditions of team-shared leadership. However, like the strategies discussed above, empowering leadership influence can also be projected laterally. Examples of empowering shared leadership in an NPD team might include peer encouragement and support of self-goal setting, self-evaluation, self-reward, and self-development. Empowering leadership largely places default decision-making and control authority in the hands of the followers. Further, it emphasizes building self-influence skills that orchestrate performance while preserving extensive individual autonomy. As such, it may be particularly suited to NPD and technology professionals, who often desire autonomy on the job (e.g., Janz, 1999; Mumford, 1993).

## The Vertical Leadership Role

Shared leadership supplements, but does not replace, vertical leadership in new product development teams (e.g., Pearce & Sims, 2000, 2002). Indeed, the vertical leader, often the formally designated project or program manager, retains a range of important responsibilities even in shared leadership contexts. These responsibilities include forming the team, managing boundaries, providing as-needed leadership support, and maintaining the shared leadership system in the team. We position vertical leadership as an antecedent variable that may affect the extent to which shared leadership emerges in an NPD team.

### Team Formation

Early involvement by the vertical leader in designing the team is critical for long-term success (Yeatts & Hyten, 1998; Perry et al., 1999). The project manager is likely to be the first person assigned to the project and may serve as the nucleus for the growing project team. His or her initial responsibilities may include collaborating with the marketing department to finalize product specifications, scoping the development effort, securing resources, designing the team structure, identifying the core and extended core teams, and launching the project once members have been assembled. Although there is little initial opportunity for shared leadership, the manager's early design decisions and, later, the expectations he or she sets for team interaction and performance, may contribute to the ultimate emergence of shared leadership.

> Proposition 1: Better team formation by the vertical leader is positively associated with the development and display of shared leadership in the team.

### Boundary Management

The vertical leader's ongoing responsibilities include buffering the team from external pressure, facilitating positive relations with the outside organization(s), and securing resources over time (e.g., Ancona & Caldwell, 1992a; Fisher, 1993; Yeatts & Hyten, 1998). Boundary management is critical for the success of NPD efforts (Guinan et al., 1998; Thamhain, 1990). For example, Guinan et al. found positive relationships between leader efforts to manage external relations and external perceptions of team performance. Under the demanding conditions of NPD, such as intense time pressure and lively internal competition for resources and specialized talent, effective boundary management may spell the difference between successful completion and early termination for a development effort. As such, successful boundary managers provide a context in which shared leadership can develop and flourish by providing the necessary resources for the team and simultaneously protecting the team from external interference.

> Proposition 2: Better boundary management by the vertical leader is positively associated with the development and display of shared leadership in the team.

## Leadership Support

Although robust shared leadership can reduce the need for ongoing vertical leadership intervention, periodic leadership support is likely to be required. A key role for the vertical leader—a role that distinguishes shared leadership from the hands-on leadership emphasis of traditional hierarchy—is sparing, judicious intervention on an as-needed basis (Yeatts & Hyten, 1998; Perry et al., 1999). The importance of judicious vertical leadership for maintaining a climate of shared leadership bears particular emphasis: Yeatts and Hyten (1998) found that team member withdrawal, dissatisfaction, and abdication of decision-making responsibility tended to follow when vertical leaders routinely exercised power or stepped into decisions. Moreover, Pearce and Sims (2002) found more vertical leadership than shared leadership in low-performing teams and more shared leadership than vertical leadership in high-performing teams. In shared leadership contexts, the challenge of leadership support involves negotiating a gap-filling balance between abdication at one extreme and disempowering seizure of control at the other.

> Proposition 3: Judicious vertical leader support of the team is positively associated with the development and display of shared leadership in the team.

## Shared Leadership Maintenance

Whereas leadership support should be inherently cautious, maintaining shared leadership requires active encouragement of lateral peer influence. The program manager promotes shared leadership by adopting an empowering leadership emphasis on follower self-leadership and lateral influence. For example, the vertical leader might launch the team by clearly describing shared leadership, illustrating peer leader behaviors, setting clear expectations, and evaluating performance accordingly. He or she might also ensure appropriate training in influence skills or intervene directly with as-needed coaching. An important strategy for the vertical leader is modeling empowering leadership (e.g., Manz & Sims, 1987, 1989, 1991, 2001). Accordingly, the program manager might ask for, rather than propose, solutions (Fisher, 1993; Manz & Sims, 1993); encourage team initiative, goal setting, and problem solving (Manz & Sims, 1993); model productive conflict management (Yeatts & Hyten, 1998); and demonstrate application of situationally appropriate strategies for peer influence.

> Proposition 4: Shared leadership maintenance behaviors by the vertical leader are positively associated with the development and display of shared leadership in the team.

# New Product Development Team Characteristics

Team and task characteristics have been related to process and outcomes in empowered teams (e.g., Hackman & Oldham, 1980; McGrath, 1964; Tannenbaum et al., 1992). The next section will discuss task characteristics in greater detail. In this section we describe five components that collectively constitute our second group of antecedent variables, team characteristics: proximity, size, ability, diversity, and maturity. Like the vertical leadership role, we propose that these team characteristics may affect the extent to which shared leadership emerges in the NPD team.

### Proximity

We cast the term *proximity* broadly to mean conditions that affect vertical and lateral influence by bringing people together or imposing separation. Certainly, proximity refers to physical distance between the vertical leader and the team (e.g., Kerr & Jermier, 1978) or between team members. Although the emergence of shared leadership would seem less likely as distance increases, geographical dispersion may make shared leadership a particularly valuable mechanism for coordination and control that would otherwise be difficult for an individual vertical leader to provide. Beyond geography, a range of other factors may affect the experience of separation, such as technologies that enable location transparency, organizational barriers to cross-functional participation, and legal or contractual barriers among collaborating organizations. For example, participants in large development efforts may represent wholly separate companies, even competitors, in temporary alliance. Under these conditions, shared leadership could provide a welcome measure of real-time lateral influence to knit normally competing organizations together in a coherent development effort. However, nondisclosure agreements may place a legal chokehold on lateral influence by mandating extensive involvement and formal approval by vertical management. As a result, team members may be forced to run a gauntlet while coordinating effort, providing support, and sharing information across organizations.

In a study of NPD teams, Keller (1986) recommended minimizing physical distance to promote team cohesion. However, trends toward increasing multinational collaboration in NPD may make physical proximity harder to achieve in the future (e.g., Carmel, 1997; Gorton & Motwani, 1996). Carmel (1997) cites several reasons for this trend, including a search for top talent, a desire to cut labor costs, the advent of new collaborative technologies, and opportunities to speed development by using time zone differences for around-the-clock development. Networking infrastructure and technologies such as software configuration management have the potential to enable virtual proximity by allowing dispersed team members to collaborate on the same product simultaneously (e.g., Baum, 1995; Boutellier, Gassmann, Macho, & Roux, 1998). Although the implications of proximity factors are as varied as the factors themselves, the impact of proximity on shared leadership should not be underestimated.

> Proposition 5: The proximity of team members is positively associated with the development and display of shared leadership in the team.

### Size

Team size introduces potentially ambiguous effects to our model. Larger teams pool greater collective ability, thus enhancing the value of shared leadership. At the same time, shared leadership may be less likely if size impedes formation of the close working relationships required for credible lateral influence. At some point, sheer size might reasonably amount to a proximity barrier. Research has found team size to have a marginal but negative effect on work integration in cross-functional teams (e.g., Baugh & Graen, 1997; Campion, Medsker, & Higgs, 1993; Guzzo, Salas, & Associates, 1995). Consistent with the team literature generally, Dawson (1992) argues that NPD team effectiveness decreases with increasing size. Moreover, Pearce and Sims (2002) found team size to be negatively related to customer ratings and team self-ratings of team effectiveness. On balance, given the findings on size and team integration, it seems likely that shared leadership will be more difficult to sustain as NPD teams grow larger.

> Proposition 6: Team size is negatively associated with the development and display of shared leadership in the team.

### Ability

Ability refers to the depth and breadth of the collective knowledge, skills, and capabilities of the new product development team. As members of a team grow in capability both individually and collectively, it is likely that vertical leadership will be less necessary (Kerr & Jermier, 1978; Manz & Sims, 1980). Ability encompasses a range of factors including functional and technical knowledge but also interpersonal, leadership, and teamwork skills (Morgan, Salas, & Glickman, 1993). Perry et al. (1999), Morgan et al. (1993), and Barry (1991) suggest that teams may require an evolving mix of functional and leadership/interpersonal skills over time. Fortunately, evidence suggests that the range of team-relevant abilities, though broad, need not involve debilitating trade-offs. For example, highly skilled team members have been found to exhibit more production behavior, but also more relationship-oriented behavior (Sutton & Rousseau, 1979) and boundary-management behavior (Gladstein, 1984) that would seem to enhance the potential for shared leadership. We expect that NPD teams with a robust mix of skills, including interpersonal and leadership skills, are more likely to develop and sustain shared leadership over time.

Twenty years ago, Boehm (1981) advocated an approach to NPD team staffing based on principles of job matching for task and skill congruence, team balance for an appropriate mix of skills, and top talent to keep development teams lean and highly skilled. Staffing to achieve the right blend of skills can be a particular challenge in NPD because personnel with specialized skills are often limited in number (Curtis et al., 1988). As a result, teams often must fill capability gaps through shared learning and integration of knowledge across members (Walz et al., 1993). This learning imperative offers natural opportunities for constructive lateral influence through shared leadership. Shared leadership, in turn, complements knowledge sharing with real-time, issue-relevant peer integration, coordination, and coaching.

Not surprisingly, research has found relationships between group technical ability and team performance (e.g., Curtis et al., 1988; Rash & Tosi, 1992; White & Leifer, 1986). However, NPD researchers and practitioners increasingly recognize the value of balancing technical skills with social or "soft" skills and industry-specific business knowledge to promote teamwork and effective partnering with internal and external customers (e.g., Scott, 1999; Young & Lee, 1997). Walz et al. (1993) view interpersonal skills as critical for team-based NPD, including skills such as team building, negotiation, and teaching. In a survey of recruiting practices among 41 firms, Young and Lee (1997) found that a range of nontechnical skills—verbal skills, ability to perform cross-functional group work, and written communication skills—were key criteria for staffing decisions for high tech workers. Growing acknowledgement of the importance of social competence led Young and Lee (1997) to conclude that technology professionals "can no longer use a technical job function as an excuse for neglecting vital interpersonal skills" (p. 53). Of course, interpersonal skills are just as vital for the extensive mutual adjustment, social give-and-take, and peer influence that characterize shared leadership.

Work styles and nontechnical aspects of the skill mix in NPD contexts may pose certain challenges to shared leadership. For example, conflict resolution skills should be broadly supportive of shared leadership and have been associated with client satisfaction in NPD projects (Sussman & Guinan, 1999). However, technically oriented professionals may not typically have experience openly confronting and resolving conflict (Robey, Farrow, & Franz, 1989; Salaway, 1987). Further, technical contributors may prefer individual contributor roles (e.g., Cheney, 1984; Goldstein & Rockart, 1984; Thamhain & Wilemon, 1997). Thamhain and Wilemon (1997) cite individualism as a specific challenge to collaboration and team building on technology projects, observing that "many of the highly innovative and creative people are . . . individualistically oriented and often admit their aversion to cooperation" (p. 131).

Proposition 7: The greater the abilities of the team members, particularly interpersonal but also technical, the greater the development and display of shared leadership in the team.

## Diversity

Earlier, we described proximity in terms of physical separation, institutional barriers, and other factors largely external to team members. Diversity brings a more personal focus on individual differences among team members that may affect lateral influence through social or relational, rather than physical, separation. Diversity in teams has been operationalized in several ways, including gender and racial composition (e.g., Baugh & Graen, 1997; Nkomo & Cox, 1996); cultural and educational heterogeneity (e.g., Elron, 1997; Kruglianskas & Thamhain, 2000); and functional background, age, and employment tenure diversity (Knight et al., 1999). We view diversity as extending to any number of individual differences, such as incumbent/newcomer effects or barriers to collaboration among members with very different specialties or professional vocabularies (e.g., Ancona & Caldwell, 1992b). Shared leadership depends critically on social interaction and a willingness to respond to peer influence as well as provide it. To the extent that individual differences engender interpersonal barriers, we would expect that shared leadership is less likely under conditions of increasing diversity. However, as research indicates, diversity is a complex phenomenon with effects that are incompletely understood.

Research suggests that diversity may affect a range of team processes in ways that might inhibit shared leadership. For example, diversity has been found to increase conflict, reduce cohesion, hamper communication and coordination, and slow decision making (e.g., Ancona & Caldwell, 1992b; Knight et al., 1999; Pfeffer, 1985; Pfeffer & O'Reilly, 1987). In contrast, team homogeneity, with respect to age and work experience, has been associated with increased communication, social integration, and cohesiveness (e.g., O'Reilly, Caldwell, & Barnett, 1989; Tsui, Xin, & Egan, 1995; Zenger & Lawrence, 1989). With respect to software development,

Carmel (1995) found that highly productive software development teams had diverse formal education but were similar in age, gender, and nationality. Research also finds that NPD teams that mix veteran and novice developers perform at lower levels than more homogeneous teams (Schlosberg, 1996). Schlosberg (1996) and Bozman (1996) offer intriguing anecdotal accounts of skill-based rivalry and resentment between more senior developers with mature knowledge bases and newcomers, sometimes perceived as overconfident, with leading-edge skills. This commentary is suggestive because it implies possible diversity challenges to effective lateral influence that extend beyond familiar characteristics such as race and gender.

Despite these possible challenges, not all research finds negative diversity effects. Further, some findings suggest that diversity may affect team processes mainly in the early stages of team formation. Baugh and Graen (1997) found no difference in the quality of the team working relationships when comparing diverse and homogeneous cross-functional teams. Similarly, Elron (1997) failed to find a relationship between cultural heterogeneity and team cohesion. Watson, Kumar, and Michaelsen (1993) found that early gaps in the effectiveness of team interaction between racially diverse and homogeneous teams tended to disappear over time as diverse teams gained experience working together. Team development interventions may also be helpful in addressing the potential downside of diversity. For example, Knight et al. (1999) concluded that decision-making techniques could be used to address initial difficulties in reaching consensus in diverse teams. The challenge, of course, is appropriate intervention to maximize the benefits of shared leadership in NPD efforts that demand diverse, mission-critical talent—complementary perspectives, experience bases, technical specialties, and skill sets—in an increasingly multinational and multicultural context.

> Proposition 8: Greater diversity among the members of the team is negatively associated with the development and display of shared leadership in the team.

## Maturity

We use the term *maturity* as a summary appraisal of team functioning and interpersonal dynamics. It may include factors such as the level of familiarity among team members, the extent to which responsibilities and relationships have been defined, the extent and effectiveness of consensual performance and relational norms, and the general ease with which members translate team interaction into production and a satisfying experience of work. Team maturity has often been conceptualized as a series of stages, each of which represents an advance in various indicators of performance or interaction (e.g., Gersick, 1988; Jewell & Reitz, 1981; Tuckman, 1965; Tuckman & Jensen, 1977). Maturity models may define stages differently and, to varying degrees, acknowledge periods of retrenchment or recursion in team development. However, models generally assume that time is required for team maturity to progress. We mention maturity last because it stands as a useful cognate for many of the variables already discussed. In more mature teams, for example, effective relationships are likely to have emerged over time as members work together to negotiate the challenges of proximity, ability, diversity, and other factors. As a result, we expect that shared leadership is more likely to emerge among more mature teams.

The NPD literature has described team maturity in process and technology terms, as in the Capability Maturity Model (CMM) (Paulk, Curtis, Chrissis, & Weber, 1993). The CMM defines stages of maturity through increasing technical capability and progressively elaborated control processes that ensure increasing levels of consistency in development. More directly applicable to shared leadership are observations from the literature on interpersonal dynamics in teams. For example, Barry (1991) observed that effective teams spend more time on social familiarization early on and, as a result, are better prepared for shared leadership. As mentioned earlier, Morgan et al. (1993) also found that effective teams differentially emphasize production and team maintenance over the course of team development.

Consistent with stage models generally, Barry (1991) contends that team members are unlikely to appreciate or leverage the leadership skills of their peers unless time is available for team maturation. Unfortunately, given the compressed timeframes and programmed turnover that often characterize cross-functional development efforts, NPD teams may not always have sufficient time to mature. Team maturation might be accelerated if members of a development effort know each other from previous assignments. However, time pressure and temporary membership likely represent a substantial challenge to NPD team maturation and, by implication, to the development of shared leadership.

Proposition 9: Team maturity is positively associated with the development and display of shared leadership in the team.

## Moderating Variables: New Product Development Task Characteristics

Implementing empowered teams may require significant change for many organizations (Manz & Sims, 1993). Further, fully leveraging the potential of empowered teamwork may require significant incremental effort supporting team communication, coordination, and mutual adjustment over and above the effort required to perform the work. The phrase "process loss" has been used to describe this incremental investment in group maintenance (e.g., Steiner, 1972). As a factor that enables empowered teamwork, developing skills in lateral influence may also carry a price tag. Given resource constraints, organizations must ensure that the benefits of teamwork and shared leadership justify the cost of this incremental effort. For example, teams tend to outperform individuals under conditions in which complex tasks and variable production conditions require extensive close coordination and integration of effort (e.g., Cummings & Griggs, 1976/1977; Goodman, Davadas, & Griffeth-Hughson, 1988; Latane, Williams, & Harkins, 1979; Pearce & Ravlin, 1987; Steiner, 1972, 1976).

We include two moderating task characteristics, interdependence and complexity, to capture these conditions. We propose that task characteristics moderate the relationship between shared leadership and team outcomes by affecting the extent to which shared leadership, once developed in the team, is translated into team effectiveness. When task interdependence and complexity hold, as they generally do in NPD contexts (e.g., Kraut & Streeter, 1994), the up-front investment and ongoing process losses of sustaining empowered teamwork and shared leadership are more nearly justified. Further, under these conditions we expect a positive relationship between shared leadership and team outcomes because shared leadership enables the team to better negotiate task demands. In contrast, when tasks are relatively independent or simple—when there is little requirement for coordination or productive collaboration—we would expect to find no relationship, perhaps even a negative relationship, between shared leadership and team outcomes. Under these less challenging conditions, shared leadership would at least be irrelevant. However, shared leadership may have a darker side, expressed in a negative relationship between shared leadership and outcomes, in which more shared leadership behavior actually reduces effectiveness. This negative relationship would reflect the process losses of diverting effort and resources to group maintenance that might be more profitably invested directly in completing relatively discrete, simple tasks.

### Interdependence

Task interdependence is the degree to which goal accomplishment requires completing related or dependent subtasks (e.g., Steiner, 1972). Increasing task interdependence generally requires more effective mechanisms to coordinate and integrate the efforts of team members. However, McIntyre and Salas (1995) note that coordination need not follow from objective task interdependence. Instead, coordination requires active effort among individuals who perceive that they are engaged in interdependent transactions.

As a basis for team collaboration, shared leadership helps meet the need for coordinated effort under conditions of interdependence. Therefore, the investment in developing and sustaining shared leadership should be more justified. Further, the extensive lateral communication implied by shared leadership should enhance shared leadership's durability by promoting an accurate appreciation among team members of their interdependence. As such, task interdependence may facilitate a virtuous cycle in which shared leadership promotes awareness of member interdependence and the need for close collaboration. This awareness, in turn, motivates further shared leadership behavior as a pragmatic solution to the evident challenge of integration, thus spawning a new cycle of lateral communication and advancing awareness. Through rational appeal and modeling, the vertical leader (see vertical leader role, above) could catalyze this cycle by introducing shared leadership as an expected and, over time, self-reinforcing approach to team interaction.

New product development projects involve an extensive series of interdependent development and support activities requiring considerable coordination and commitment by individuals to work as a team (Kraut & Streeter, 1994). NPD projects also require extensive lateral communication (Perry, Staudenmayer, & Votta, 1994), team learning (Walz et al., 1993), and integration of knowledge across multiple disciplines and technical specialties (e.g., Curtis et al., 1988). As mentioned earlier, it is precisely the requirement for coordinated, evolutionary problem solving that motivates development team organization in NPD contexts (e.g., Curtis et al., 1988; Janz, 1999; Kruglianskas & Thamhain, 2000; Nambisan & Wilemon, 2000; Parker, 1994; Sashkin & Sashkin, 1994; Sawyer & Guinan, 1998). Given the demands of task interdependence, we believe that developing and sustaining shared leadership is a particularly productive investment in innovative NPD contexts, but is not as important as, and is potentially harmful in, incremental development contexts that require less interaction and integration across product, task, and system components.

Proposition 10: The level of task interdependence moderates the effect of shared leadership on team responses and team effectiveness.

### Complexity

We follow parallel logic in predicting the likely effect of task complexity on the relationship between shared leadership and new product development team outcomes. Indeed, task interdependence and complexity may be two sides of the same coin. In general, leadership requirements increase with task complexity (Kerr & Jermier, 1978). NPD generally involves a great deal of inherent complexity, both in terms of development tasks and the level of coordination required with outside stakeholders (Kraut & Streeter, 1994). The sheer complexity of translating myriad requirements into workable product specifications can be difficult to comprehend even for skilled developers (e.g., Walz et al., 1993). The complexity of technology projects prompted Kruglianskas and Thamhain (2000) to urge a departure from conventional leadership hierarchy in development settings. They argued that the complex world of evolving technology, in which even basic tasks may require tightly coordinated application of extremely specialized skills, requires "member-generated performance norms and evaluations, rather than hierarchical guidelines, policies, and procedures" (p. 55). Shared leadership enables the relevant, informed evaluation and support recommended by Kruglianskas and Thamhain (2000).

Proposition 11: The level of complexity of the team's task moderates the effect of shared leadership on team responses and team effectiveness.

## Dependent Variables: Team Responses and Effectiveness

In this last section of the model, we turn to our dependent variables, two classes of likely team outcomes that have been discussed in the literature on teams and performance measurement (e.g., Campion et al., 1993; Landy & Farr, 1983; Manz & Sims, 1987, 1993; McGrath, 1964; Yeatts & Hyten, 1998). The first, team responses, pertains to the affective, cognitive, and behavioral impact of shared leadership on the team itself. The second, team effectiveness, pertains to team performance.

### Team Responses

Teams may exhibit affective, cognitive, and behavioral responses to shared leadership. Detailing the full range of responses that might be measured is beyond the scope of this chapter, particularly given the preliminary nature of the present model. However, apart from improving bottom-line team performance, positive responses to shared leadership within the team may have significant value in their own right by enhancing the experience of work, increasing the contribution of development team members in future assignments, and improving the ability of the organization to effectively deploy shared leading teams for future development efforts.

Affective and cognitive responses may include burn out, trust in the team, organizational or team commitment, team potency, satisfaction with the job or team, collective efficacy, and cohesiveness (e.g., Campion et al., 1993; Gladstein, 1984; Guzzo, Yost, Campbell, & Shea, 1993; Janz, 1999; McGrath, 1964; Pearce,

Gallagher, & Ensley, 2002; Pearce & Ravlin, 1987; Sonnentag et al., 1994). Behavioral responses may include effort exerted, motivation, quantity and quality of communication, productivity, specific task performance, absenteeism, task coordination, and citizenship behaviors (e.g., Cox, 1994; Hackman & Oldham, 1980; Janz, 1999; Netemeyer, Boles, McKee, & McMurrian, 1997; Pearce & Giacalone, in press; Pearce & Ravlin, 1987; Tannenbaum et al., 1992). Prior research has found shared leadership to be significantly related to the display of citizenship behavior, networking behavior, and potency in a study of change management teams (Pearce, 1997); to potency, social integration, and problem solving in a study of virtual teams (Pearce, Yoo, & Alavi, (in press)); and to collectively efficacy, potency, extra effort, and satisfaction in a study of teams of undergraduate students working on community improvement projects (Avolio et al., 1996). We would expect this general effect to likewise be important in the context of NPD teams.

Proposition 12: Shared leadership affects team member affective, behavioral, and cognitive responses.

### Team Effectiveness

Evaluating the impact of shared leadership on team effectiveness depends to a great extent on what outcomes are valued, as well as the source of the evaluation. Both qualitative and quantitative indicators of effectiveness might be considered (Pearce & Sims, 2000). Qualitative measures include team self-ratings, external manager ratings, and customer ratings of effectiveness (e.g., Campion et al., 1993; Pearce & Sims, 2000, 2002). Research on NPD teams has evaluated effectiveness from multiple perspectives, including team members, upper management, and customers (e.g., Guinan et al., 1998; Janz, 1999; Sussman & Guinan, 1999). Kemerer (1998) notes that quantifying NPD effectiveness has proven challenging because effectiveness as a criterion is significantly informed by the end product, the processes used in development, and the relative intangibility of many product aspects. Further, effectiveness itself is a moving target: As technologies change and products become more complex and difficult to develop, benchmarks of effectiveness are subject to continual evolution (Kemerer, 1998). The Capability Maturity Model (CMM) (Paulk et al., 1993), discussed earlier, offers benchmarks of team effectiveness from a technical perspective. Additional indices may include quality, cost, and delivery metrics; ease of use; and the maintainability of the deliverables produced by the team (e.g., Kemerer, 1998).

Prior research has found shared leadership to be significantly related to team effectiveness in entrepreneurial top management teams (Ensley & Pearce, 2000), change management teams (Pearce, 1997, 1999; Pearce & Sims, 2002), virtual teams (Pearce, Yoo, & Alavi, (in press)), and teams of undergraduate students (Avolio et al., 1996). We would expect this general effect to likewise be important in the context of NPD teams.

Proposition 13: Shared leadership affects team effectiveness.

### Team Responses and Team Effectiveness

Although we have discussed team responses and team effectiveness separately, team responses are also likely to have a direct impact on the effectiveness of the team. For example, team potency and cohesion, two cognitive responses, have been identified as significant influences on team effectiveness. Team potency, a team's collective belief in its ability to be effective, may well be self-fulfilling through its effect on motivation. Team potency has been found to be related to external ratings of effectiveness (Guzzo, 1986; Guzzo et al., 1993; Pearce et al., 2002; Pearce & Gallagher, 1999, Shea & Guzzo, 1987).

Team cohesion reflects the degree to which team members desire to remain with the team (e.g., Bettenhausen, 1991; Holt, 1990; Seashore, 1954). Cohesiveness has been reported to have a positive relationship with level of effort, work commitment, openness of communication, and adherence to team norms (Bettenhausen, 1991; Holt, 1990; Jewell & Reitz, 1981; Lott & Lott, 1961). Keller (1986), in a study of research and development teams, found cohesiveness to be the strongest predictor of team performance. It is beyond our scope to review all of the potential links between team responses and effectiveness. However, team responses to shared leadership also seem likely to be related to team effectiveness.

Proposition 14: Team responses to shared leadership affect team effectiveness.

## Conclusion

Teams are likely to remain a cornerstone of new product development efforts for the foreseeable future. In many ways, shared leadership seems well-suited to the complexity of team-based NPD, complexity that tests the limits of traditional vertical leadership. Research and theory suggest that lateral peer influence has significant potential under demanding NPD conditions to support the informed and momentary guidance, collaboration, mutual adjustment, and integration required for effectiveness. Although several links have been found between shared leadership and team dynamics (e.g., Avolio et al., 1996; Pearce, 1997; Pearce, Yoo, & Alavi, in press), Avolio et al. (1996) found shared leadership to be predictive of the effectiveness of undergraduate teams, and Pearce (1997, 1999), Pearce and Sims (2002), Pearce, Yoo, and Alavi (in press), and Ensley and Pearce (2000) found shared leadership to be predictive of the effectiveness of work teams—ranging from change management teams to top management teams. As such, shared leadership may positively affect both the experience of work and the effectiveness of NPD teams.

At the same time, the new product development context undeniably presents formidable challenges to implementing and sustaining shared leadership. These challenges include programmed turnover, geographical dispersion, persistent deep specialization, and member characteristics that may not always support ready collaboration. An undercurrent in our discussion is that the very conditions that challenge the development of shared leadership may make it a particularly valuable organizational capability in the NPD context. Given the potential benefits of shared leadership, we recommend future research to address implementation challenges and help the NPD community establish shared leadership as a viable option for team interaction. Implementation challenges notwithstanding, we suggest that sustainable competitive advantage will likely be enjoyed by those who master the difficult aspects of effective organization, not the easy ones.

As a defined construct, shared leadership is too new to have received extensive empirical investigation. Although our model is grounded in established research on empowered teams, leadership, and NPD, it has not yet been field-tested in this context. Field validation of the model among NPD teams is a promising avenue for future research, as is further exploration of the interplay between vertical and shared leadership. Although we have emphasized the continued importance of vertical leadership in shared leadership systems, further definition of supportive vertical leadership roles could offer useful insight into how NPD teams can develop and sustain shared leadership

# References

Ancona, D. G., & Caldwell, D. F. (1992a). Bridging the boundary: External process and performance in organizational teams. *Administrative Science Quarterly, 37,* 527-548.

Ancona, D. G., & Caldwell, D. F. (1992b). Demography and design: Predictors of new product team performance. *Organization Science, 3*(3), 321-341.

Avolio, B. J., & Bass, B. M. (1988). Transformational leadership, charisma, and beyond. In J. G. Hunt, B. R. Baliga, H. P. Dachler, & C. A. Schreisheim (Eds.), *Emerging leadership vistas* (pp. 29-50). Lexington, MA: Lexington.

Avolio, B. J., Jung, D. I., Murry, W., & Sivasubramaniam, N. (1996). Building highly developed teams: Focusing on shared leadership processes, efficacy, trust, and performance. In M. Beyerlein, D. Johnson, & S. Beyerlein (Eds.), *Advances in interdisciplinary studies of work teams: Team leadership* (pp. 173-209). Greenwich, CT: JAI Press.

Bandura, A. (1977). Self-efficacy: Towards a unifying theory of behavioral change. *Psychological Review, 84,* 191-215.

Barczack, G., & Wilemon, D. (1991). Communication patterns of new product development team leaders. *IEEE Transactions on Engineering Management, 38*(2), 101-109.

Barry, D. (1991, Summer). Managing the bossless team: Lessons in distributed leadership. *Organizational Dynamics, 20,* 31-47.

Bass, B. M. (1990). *Bass and Stogdill's handbook of leadership.* New York: Free Press.

Bass, B. M., & Avolio, B. J. (1993). Transformational leadership: A response to critiques. In J. G. Hunt, B. R. Baliga, H. P. Dachler, & C. A. Schriesheim (Eds.), *Emerging leadership vistas* (pp. 29-40). Lexington, MA: Lexington.

Bass, B. M., Waldman, D. A., Avolio, B. J., & Bebb, M. (1987). Transformational leadership and the falling dominoes effect. *Group and Organization Studies, 12,* 73-78.

Baugh, S. G., & Graen, G. B. (1997). Effects of team gender and racial composition on perceptions of team performance in cross-functional teams. *Group and Organization Management, 22,* 366-83.

Baum, D. (1995, August). Unify dispersed development teams. *Datamation, 41*(15), 37-39.

Bettenhausen, K. L. (1991, June). Five years of groups research: What we have learned and what needs to be addressed. *Journal of Management, 17,* 345-381

Boehm, B. R. (1981). *Software engineering economics.* Englewood Cliffs, NJ: Prentice Hall.

Boutellier, R., Gassmann, O., Macho, H., & Roux, M. (1998, January). Management of dispersed product development teams: The role of information technologies. *R & D Management, 28*(1), 13-25.

Bozman, J. S. (1996, January 29). Generating resentment. *Computerworld, 30*(5), 1, 76-77.

Brancheau, J. C., Janz, B. D., & Wetherbe, J. C. (1996). Key issues in information systems management: 1994-1995 SIM Delphi results. *Management Information Systems Quarterly, 20*(2), 225-242.

Brown, C. V., McLean, E. R., & Straub, D. W. (1996, Spring). Partnering roles of the IS executive. *Information Systems Management, 13*(2), 14-18.

Brown, D. J., & Lord, R. G. (1999). The utility of experimental research in the study of transformational/charismatic leadership. *Leadership Quarterly, 10*(4), 531-540.

Brown, S. L., & Eisenhardt, K. M. (1995). Product development: Past research, present findings, and future directions. *Academy of Management Review, 20,* 343-378.

Brown, W. B., & Karagozoglu, N. (1993). Leading the way to faster new product development. *Academy of Management Executive, 7*(1), 36-47.

Burns, J. M. (1978). *Leadership.* New York: Harper & Row.

Campion, M. A., Medsker, G. J., & Higgs, A. C. (1993). Relations between work group characteristics and effectiveness: Implications for designing effective work groups. *Personnel Psychology, 46,* 823-850.

Card, D. N., McGarry, F. E., & Page, G. T. (1987). Evaluating software engineering technologies. *IEEE Transactions in Software Engineering, 7,* 845-851.

Carmel, E. (1995). Cycle time in packaged software firms. *Journal of Product Innovation Management, 12,* 110-123

Carmel, E. (1997, December 8). The explosion of global software teams. *Computerworld, 31*(49), C6.

Carnevale, A. (1991). *America and the new economy.* San Francisco: Jossey-Bass.

Cheney, P. H. (1984). Effects of individual characteristics, organizational factors and task characteristics on computer programmer productivity and job satisfaction. *Information and Management, 7,* 209-214.

Computer Economics. (1996, April). *IS Budget Report.*

Conger, J. A. (1989). *The charismatic leader: Behind the mystique of exceptional leadership.* San Francisco: Jossey-Bass.

Conger, J. A. (1999). Charismatic and transformational leadership in organizations: An insider's perspective on these developing streams of research. *Leadership Quarterly, 10*(2), 145-170.

Conger, J. A., & Kanungo, R.N. (1988). Behavioral dimensions of charismatic leadership. In J. A. Conger & R.N. Kanungo (Eds.), *Charismatic leadership: The elusive factor in organizational effectiveness* (pp. 78-97). San Francisco: Jossey-Bass.

Cooper, R. G. (1995a). Developing new products on time, in time (Part 1). *Research Technology Management, 38*(5), 49-53.

Cooper, R. G. (1995b). Developing new products on time, in time (Part 2). *Research Technology Management, 38*(5), 53-57.

Cooper, R. G., & Kleinschmidt, E. J. (1994). Determinants of timeliness on product development. *Journal of Product Innovation Management, 11,* 381-396.

Cox, J. F. (1994). *The effects of SuperLeadership training on leader behavior, subordinate self-leader behavior, and subordinate citizenship behavior.* Unpublished doctoral dissertation, University of Maryland, College Park.

Cox, J. F., Pearce, C. L., & Sims, H. P., Jr. (in press). Toward a broader agenda for leadership development: Extending the transactional-transformational duality by development directive, empowering and shared leadership skills. In R. E. Riggio & S. Murphy (Eds.), *The Future of Leadership Development.* Mahwah, NJ: Lawrence Erlbaum.

Cox, J. F., & Sims, H. P., Jr. (1996). Leadership and team citizenship behavior: A model and measures. In M. Beyerlein, D. Johnson, & S. Beyerlein (Eds.), *Advances in interdisciplinary studies of work teams: Team leadership* (Vol. 3, pp. 1-41). Greenwich, CT: JAI Press.

Cummings, T. G., & Griggs, W. H. (1976/1977, Winter). Worker reactions to autonomous work groups: Conditions for functioning, differential effects, and individual differences. *Organization and Administrative Sciences, 7*(4), 87-100.

Curtis, B., Krasner, H., & Iscoe, N. (1988). A field study of the software design process for large systems. *Communications of the ACM, 31*(11), 1268-1287.

Dawson, J. (1992). Small teams are essential for success. *Computing Canada, 18*(9), 26.

Donnellon, A. (1996a). Cross-functional teams in product development: Accommodating the structure to the process. *Journal of Product Innovation Management, 10,* 377-392.

Donnellon, A. (1996b). *Team talk: The power of language in team dynamics.* Boston: Harvard Business School Press.

Drucker, P. (2000). Knowledge work. *Executive Excellence, 17*(4), 11-12.

Elron, E. (1997). Top management teams within multinational companies: Effects of cultural heterogeneity. *Leadership Quarterly, 8,* 393-412.

Ensley, M. D., & Pearce, C. L. (2000, June). *Assessing the influence of leadership behaviors on new venture TMT processes and new venture performance.* Paper presented at the 20th annual Entrepreneurship Research Conference, Babson Park, MA.

Ensley, M. D., Pearson, A., & Pearce, C. L. (in press). Top management team process, shared leadership and new venture performance: A theoretical model and research agenda. *Human Resource Management Review.*

Fisher, K. (1993). *Leading self-directed work teams: A guide to developing new team leadership skills.* New York: McGraw-Hill.

Fleishman, E. A. (1973). Twenty years of consideration and structure. In E. A. Fleishman & J. G. Hunt (Eds.), *Current developments in the study of leadership.* Carbondale: Southern Illinois University Press.

Fleishman, E. A., & Hunt, J. G. (1973). *Current developments in the study of leadership.* Carbondale: Southern Illinois University Press.

Gersick, C. J. G. (1988, March). Time and transition in work teams: Towards a new model of group development. *Academy of Management Journal, 31,* 9-41.

Gibbs, W. (1994, September). Software's chronic crisis. *Scientific American, 9,* 86-95.

Gladstein, D. L. (1984, December). Groups in context: A model of task group effectiveness. *Administrative Sciences Quarterly, 29,* 499-517.

Glass, R. (1997). The ups and downs of programmer stress. *Communications of the ACM, 40*(4), 17-19.

Goldstein, J. F., & Rockart, J. F. (1984). An examination of work-related correlates of job satisfaction in programmer/analysts. *MIS Quarterly, 8*(2), 103-115.

Goodman, P. S., Davadas, R., & Griffeth-Hughson, T. L. (1988). Groups and productivity: Analyzing the effectiveness of self-managing teams. In J. P. Campbell & R. J. Campbell (Eds.), *Productivity in organizations: New perspectives from industrial and organizational psychology* (pp. 295-327). San Francisco: Jossey-Bass.

Gorton, I., & Motwani, S. (1996). Issues in co-operative software engineering using globally distributed teams. *Information and Software Technology, 38*(10), 647-655.

Guinan, P. J., Cooprider, J. G., & Faraj, S. (1998). Enabling R&D team performance during requirements definition: A behavioral versus technical approach. *Information Systems Research, 9*(2), 101-125.

Guzzo, R. A. (1986). Group decision making and group effectiveness in organizations. In P. S. Goodman (Ed.), *Designing effective work groups* (pp. 34-71). San Francisco: Jossey-Bass.

Guzzo, R. A., Salas, E., & Associates (1995). *Team effectiveness and decision-making in organizations.* San Francisco: Jossey-Bass.

Guzzo, R. A., Yost, P. R., Campbell, R. J., & Shea, G. P. (1993, November). Potency in groups: Articulating a construct. *British Journal of Social Psychology, 40,* 87-106.

Hackman, J. R. (1986). The psychology of self-management in organizations. In M. S. Pollack & R. O. Perlogg (Eds.), *Psychology and work: Productivity change and employment* (pp. 85-136). Washington, DC: American Psychological Association.

Hackman, J. R. (1987). The design of work teams. In J. W. Lorsch (Ed.), *Handbook of organizational behavior* (pp. 315-342). Englewood Cliffs, NJ: Prentice Hall.

Hackman, J. R., & Oldham, G. R. (1980). *Work redesign.* Reading, MA: Addison-Wesley.

Halpin, A. W., & Winer, B. J. (1957). A factorial study of the leader behavior descriptions. In R. M. Stogdill & E. A. Coons (Eds.), *Leader behavior: Its description and measurement* (pp. 39-51). Columbus: Ohio State University Bureau of Business Research.

Hater, J. J., & Bass, B. M. (1988). Superiors' evaluations and subordinates' perceptions of transformational and transactional leadership. *Journal of Applied Psychology, 73,* 695-702.

Hauptman, O., & Hirji, K. K. (1996). The influence of process concurrency on project outcomes in product development: An empirical study of cross-functional teams. *IEEE Transactions on Engineering Management, 43,* 153-164.

Henderson, J. C., & Lee, S. (1992). Managing I/S design teams: A control theories perspective. *Management Science, 38*(6), 757-777.

Holt, D. H. (1990). *Management: Principles and practices.* Englewood Cliffs, NJ: Prentice Hall.

House, R. J. (1971). A path goal theory of leader effectiveness. *Administrative Science Quarterly, 16,* 321-338.

House, R. J. (1977). A 1976 theory of charismatic leadership. In J. G. Hunt & L. L. Larson (Eds.), *Leadership: The cutting edge* (pp. 16-41). Carbondale: Southern Illinois University Press.

House, R. J., & Mitchell, T. R. (1974). Path-goal theory of leadership. *Journal of Contemporary Business, 3,* 81-97.

Janz, B. D. (1999). Self-directed teams in IS: Correlates for improved systems development and work outcomes. *Information and Management, 35*(3), 171-192.

Janz, B. D., & Wetherbe, J. C. (1994). *Self-directed work teams in IS: Insights gained from a multi-method approach* (Working paper MISRC-WP-91-10). Minneapolis: University of Minnesota, MIS Research Center.

Jassawalla, A. R., & Sashittal, H. C. (1999). Building collaborative cross-functional new product teams. *Academy of Management Executive, 13*(3), 50-63.

Jewell, L. N., & Reitz, H. J. (1981). *Group effectiveness in organizations.* Glenview, IL: Scott, Foresman.

Katzenbach, J. R. & Smith, D. K. (1993). *The wisdom of teams.* Boston: Harvard Business School Press.

Keller, R. (1992). Transformational leadership and the performance of research and development project groups. *Journal of Management, 18*(3), 489-501.

Keller, R. T. (1986). Predictors of the performance of project groups in R&D organizations. *Academy of Management Journal, 29*(4), 715-726.

Keller, R. T. (1995). "Transformational" leaders make a difference. *Research and Technology Management, 38*(3), 41-44.

Kemerer, C. F. (1998). Progress, obstacles, and opportunities in software engineering economics. *Communications of the ACM, 22*(8), 63-66.

Kerr, S., & Jermier, J. M. (1978, December). Substitutes for leadership: Their meaning and measurement. *Organizational Behavior and Human Performance, 22,* 1-14.

Kessler, E. H., & Chakrabarti, A. K. (1996). Innovation speed: A conceptual model of context, antecedents, and outcomes. *Academy of Management Review, 21,* 1143-1191.

King, J. (1998, May 18). Ignoring development guidelines raises costs. *Computerworld, 32*(20), 37-38.

Kleinschmidt, E. J., & Cooper, R. G. (1995). The relative importance of new product success determinants: Perceptions versus reality. *R & D Management, 25,* 281-298.

Knight, D., Pearce, C. L., Smith, K. G., Sims, H. P., Jr., Olian, J. D., Smith, K. A. (1999). Top management team diversity, group dynamics, and strategic consensus: An empirical investigation. *Strategic Management Journal, 20*(5), 445-466.

Kolodny, H., & Kiggundu, M. (1980). Towards the development of a socio-technical systems model in woodland mechanical harvesting. *Human Relations, 33,* 623-645.

Kraut, R., & Streeter, L. (1994). Coordination in R&D. *Communications of the ACM, 38*(3), 69-81.

Kruglianskas, I., & Thamhain, H. J. (2000, February). Managing technology-based projects in multinational environments. *IEEE Transactions on Engineering Management, 47*(1), 55-64.

Landy, F. J., & Farr, J. L. (1983). *The measurement of work performance: Methods, theory and applications.* New York: Free Press.

Latane, B., Williams, K., & Harkins, S. (1979). Many hands make light the work: The causes and consequences of social loafing. *Journal of Personality and Social Psychology, 37,* 822-832.

Lawler, E. E., III (1986). *High-involvement management.* San Francisco: Jossey-Bass.

Lawler, E. E., III, Mohrman, S. A., & Ledford, G. E., Jr. (1992). *Employee involvement and total quality management: Practices and results in Fortune 1000 companies.* San Francisco: Jossey-Bass.

Locke, E. A., & Latham, G. P. (1990). *A theory of goal setting and task performance.* Englewood Cliffs, NJ: Prentice Hall.

Lott, A. J., & Lott, B. E. (1961). Group cohesiveness, communication level and conformity. *Journal of Abnormal and Social Psychology, 62,* 408-412.

Luthans, F., & Kreitner, R. (1985). *Organizational behavior modification and beyond.* Glenview, IL: Scott, Foresman.

Mahoney, M. J., & Arnkoff, D. B. (1978). Cognitive and self-control therapies. In S. L. Garfield & A. E. Borgin (Eds.), *Handbook of psychotherapy and therapy change* (pp. 689-722). New York: Wiley.

Manz, C. C., & Sims, H. P., Jr. (1980). Self-management as a substitute for leadership: A social learning theory perspective. *Academy of Management Review, 5,* 361-367.

Manz, C. C., & Sims, H. P., Jr. (1987). Leading workers to lead themselves: The external leadership of self-managing work teams. *Administrative Science Quarterly, 32,* 106-129.

Manz, C. C., & Sims, H. P., Jr. (1989). *SuperLeadership: Leading others to lead themselves.* New York: Prentice Hall.

Manz, C. C., & Sims, H. P., Jr. (1991). SuperLeadership: Beyond the myth of heroic leadership. *Organizational Dynamics, 19,* 18-35.

Manz, C. C., & Sims, H. P., Jr. (1993). *Business without bosses.* New York: Wiley.

Manz, C. C., & Sims, H. P., Jr. (2001). *The new SuperLeadership: Leading others to lead themselves.* San Francisco: Berrett Koehler.

McCafferty, I., & Laight, D. (1997, June). Empowering the team. *Total Quality Management, 8,* S227-S230.

McGrath, J. E. (1964). *Social psychology: A brief introduction.* New York: Holt, Rinehart & Winston.

McIntyre, R. M., & Salas, E. A. (1995). Measuring and managing for team performance: Emerging principles from complex environments. In R.A. Guzzo & E.A. Salas (Eds.), *Team effectiveness and decision making in organizations* (pp. 9-45). San Francisco, CA: Jossey-Bass.

Meichenbaum, D. (1977). *Cognitive-behavior modification: An integrative approach.* New York: Plenum Press.

Mohrman, S. A., Cohen, S. G., & Mohrman, A. M. (1995). *Designing team-based organizations: New forms for knowledge work.* San Francisco: Jossey-Bass.

Morgan, B. B., Jr., Salas, E. A., & Glickman, A. (1993). An analysis of team evolution and maturation. *Journal of General Psychology, 120,* 277-291.

Mumford, E. (1993). The ETHICS approach. *Communications of the ACM, 36*(4), 82.

Nambisan, S., & Wilemon, D. (2000). R&D and new product development: Potentials for cross-domain knowledge sharing. *IEEE Transactions on Engineering Management, 47*(2), 211-220.

Neck, C. P., Stewart, G. L., & Manz, C. C. (1996). Self-leaders within self-leading teams: Toward an optimal equilibrium. In M. Beyerlein, D. Johnson, & S. Beyerlein (Eds.), *Advances in interdisciplinary studies of work teams: Team leadership Vol. 3* (pp. 43-65). Greenwich, CT: JAI Press.

Netemeyer, R. G., Boles, J. S., McKee, D. O., & McMurrian, R. (1997, July). An investigation into the antecedents of organizational citizenship behaviors in a personal selling context. *Journal of Marketing, 61,* 85-99.

Nkomo, S. M., & Cox, T., Jr. (1996). Diverse identities in organizations. In S. R. Clegg & C. Hardy (Eds.), *Handbook of organization studies* (pp. 338-356). London: Sage.

O'Reilly, C. A., III, Caldwell, D. F., & Barnett, W. P. (1989). Work group demography, social integration, and turnover. *Administrative Sciences Quarterly, 34,* 21-37.

Parker, G. M. (1994). *Cross-functional teams: Working with allies, enemies, and other strangers.* San Francisco: Jossey-Bass.

Paulk, M. C., Curtis, B., Chrissis, M. B., & Weber, C. V. (1993). *Capability maturity model for software version 1.1*. Pittsburgh, PA: Software Engineering Institute. (CMU/SEI-93-TR-24, DTIC Number ADA263403).

Pearce, C. L. (1997). *The determinants of change management team effectiveness: A longitudinal investigation*. Unpublished doctoral dissertation, University of Maryland, College Park.

Pearce, C. L. (1999, August). *The relative influence of vertical vs. shared leadership on the longitudinal effectiveness of change management teams*. Paper presented at the Annual Conference of the Academy of Management, Chicago.

Pearce, C. L. (2002). *Mas allá del liderazco heroico: Como el buen vino, el liderazco es algo para ser compartido*. Revista de empresa.

Pearce, C. L., & Gallagher, C. A. (1999, August). *Potency-effectiveness spirals: A longitudinal investigation of the development and impact of potency in teams*. Paper presented at the Annual Conference of the Academy of Management, Chicago.

Pearce, Craig L., Gallagher, C. A., & Ensley, M. D. (2002). Confidence at the group level of analysis: A longitudinal investigation of the relationship between potency and team effectiveness. *Journal of Occupational and Organizational Psychology, 75,* 115-119.

Pearce, C. L., & Giacalone, R. A. (in press). Teams behaving badly: Counterproductive behavior at the team level of analysis. *Journal of Applied Social Psychology.*

Pearce, C. L., Perry, M. L., & Sims, H. P., Jr. (2001). Shared leadership: Relationship management to improve NPO effectiveness. In T. D. Connors (Ed.), *The nonprofit handbook: Management* (pp. 624-641). New York: Wiley.

Pearce, C. L., & Sims, H. P., Jr. (2000). Shared leadership: Toward a multi-level theory of leadership. In M. Beyerlein, D. Johnson, & S. Beyerlein (Eds.), *Advances in interdisciplinary studies of work teams: Team leadership* (Vol. 7, pp. 115-139). Greenwich, CT: JAI Press.

Pearce, C. L., & Sims, H. P., Jr. (2002). Vertical versus shared leadership as predictors of the effectiveness of change management teams: An examination of aversive, directive, transactional, transformational, and empowering leader behaviors. *Group Dynamics: Theory, Research, and Practice, 6*(2), 172-197.

Pearce, C. L., Sims, H. P., Jr., Cos, J. F., Ball, G., Schnell, E., Smith, K. A., & Trevino, L. (in press). Transactors, transformers and beyond: A multimethod development of a theoretical typology of leadership. *Journal of Management Develoment.*

Pearce, C. L., Yoo, Y., & Alavi, M. (in press). Leadership, social work and virtual teams: The relative influence of vertical vs. shared leadership in the nonprofit section. In R. E. Riggio and S. Smith Orr (Eds.), *Improving leadership in nonprofit organizations.* San Francisco: Jossey-Bass.

Pearce, J. A., & Ravlin, E. C. (1987, November). The design and activation of self-regulating work groups. *Human Relations, 40*(11), 751-782.

Perry, E. E., Staudenmayer, N. A., & Votta, L. G. (1994). People, organizations, and process improvement. *IEEE Transactions on Software Engineering, 11(4),* 36-45.

Perry, M. L., Pearce, C. L., & Sims, H. P., Jr. (1999, Summer). Empowered selling teams: How shared leadership can contribute to selling team outcomes. *Journal of Personal Selling and Sales Management, 3,* 35-51.

Pfeffer, J. (1985, Fall). Organizational demography: Implications for management. *California Management Review, 28,* 67-81.

Pfeffer, J., & O'Reilly, C. (1987). Hospital demography and turnover among nurses. *Industrial Relations, 36,* 158-173.

Praeger, K. P. (1999). Organizational culture and the IT professional: Matching individuals and organizations. *Information Systems Management, 16*(2), 12-17.

Rash, R. H., & Tosi, H. L. (1992). Factors affecting software developers' performance: An integrated approach. *MIS Quarterly,* 395-409.

Rettig, M., & Simons, G. (1993). A project planning and development process for small teams. *Communications of the ACM, 36*(10), 44-56.

Rice, A. K. (1955). Productivity and social organization in an Indian weaving mill; II. A follow-up study of the experimental reorganization of automatic weaving. *Human Relations, 7*(3), 399-428.

Robert, D. W. (1977, Winter). Creating an environment for project success. *Information Systems Management,* 73-77.

Robey, D., Farrow, D. L., & Franz, C. R. (1989). Group process and conflict in system development. *Management Science, 35*(10), 1172-1191.

Salaway, G. (1987). An organizational learning approach to information systems development. *MIS Quarterly, 11,* 245-264.

Sashkin, M., & Sashkin, M. G. (1994). *The new teamwork: Developing and using cross-functional teams.* New York: American Management Association.

Sawyer, S., & Guinan, P. J. (1998). R&D: Processes and performance. *IBM Systems Journal, 37*(4), 552-569.

Schlosberg, J. (1996, June 10). One steamed team. *Computerworld, 30*(24), 76-77.

Schriesheim, C. A., House, R. J., & Kerr, S. (1976). Leader initiating structure: A reconciliation of discrepant research results and some empirical tests. *Organization Behavior and Human Performance, 15,* 297-321.

Scott, G. M. (1999). Top priority management concerns about new product development. *Academy of Management Executive, 13*(3), 77-84.

Seashore, S. (1954). *Group cohesiveness in the industrial work group.* Ann Arbor: Institute for Social Research, University of Michigan.

Seers, A. (1996). Better leadership through chemistry: Toward a model of emergent shared team leadership. *Advances in Interdisciplinary Studies of Work Teams, 3,* 145-172.

Shea, G. P., & Guzzo, R. A. (1987). Group effectiveness: What really matters? *Sloan Management Review, 28,* 25-31.

Sims, H. P., Jr., & Manz, C. C. (1996). *Company of heroes: Unleashing the power of self-leadership.* New York: Wiley.

Sonnentag, S., Brodbeck, F. C., Heinbokel, T., & Stolte, W. (1994). Stressor-burnout relationship in R&D teams. *Journal of Occupational and Organizational Psychology, 67,* 327-341.

Steiner, I. D. (1972). *Group process and productivity.* New York: Academic Press.

Steiner, I. D. (1976). Task-performing groups. In J. W. Thibaut & R. C. Carson (Eds.), *Contemporary topics in social psychology* (pp. 393-422). Morristown, NJ: General Learning Press.

Stengel, R. (1997). An overtaxed IRS. *Time, 67*(20), 58-62.

Sussman, S. W., & Guinan, P. J. (1999). Antidotes for high complexity and ambiguity in software development. *Information & Management, 36*(1), 23-35.

Sutton, R. I., & Rousseau, D. M. (1979). Structure, technology, and dependence on a parent organization: Organizational and environmental correlates of individual responses. *Journal of Applied Psychology, 64,* 675-687.

Tannenbaum, S. I., Beard, R. L., & Salas, E. A. (1992). Team building and its influence on team effectiveness: An examination of conceptual and empirical developments. In K. Kelley (Ed.), *Issues, theory, and research in industrial/organizational psychology* (pp. 117-153). New York: Elsevier Science.

Thamhain, H. J. (1990). Managing technologically innovative team efforts toward new product success. *Journal of Product Innovation Management, 7*(1), 5-18.

Thamhain, H. J., & Wilemon, D. L. (1997). Building high-performing engineering project teams. In R. Katz (Ed.), *The human side of managing technological innovation.* New York: Oxford University Press.

Topper, A., Ouelette, D., & Jorgenson, P. (1994). *Structured methods: Merging models, technologies, and CASE.* New York: McGraw-Hill.

Trist, E. L., Sussman, G. L., & Brown, G. (1977). An experiment in autonomous working in an American underground coalmine. *Human Relations, 30*(3), 201-236.

Tsui, A. S., Xin, K. R., & Egan, T. D. (1995). Relational demography: The missing link in vertical dyad linkage. In S. E. Jackson & M. N. Ruderman (Eds.), *Diversity in work teams:*

*Research paradigms for a changing workplace* (pp. 97-129). Washington, DC: American Psychological Association.

Tuckman, B. W. (1965, December). Developmental sequences in small groups. *Psychological Bulletin, 63,* 384-399.

Tuckman, B. W., & Jensen, M. A. C. (1977). Stages of small group development revisited. *Group and Organization Studies, 2*(4), 419-427.

Vroom, V. H. (1964). *Work and motivation.* New York: Wiley.

Waldman, D., & Atwater, L. (1992). The nature of effective leadership and championing processes at different levels in an R&D hierarchy. *Journal of High Technology Management Research, 5,* 233-245.

Waldman, D., & Bass, B. (1991). Transformational leadership at different phases of the innovation process. *Journal of High Technology Management Research, 2,* 169-180.

Walton, R. E. (1972, November/December). How to counter alienation in the plant. *Harvard Business Review, 50(6),* 70-81.

Walz, D. B., Elam, J. J., & Curtis, B. (1993, October). Inside a software design team: Knowledge acquisition, sharing, and integration. *Communications of the ACM, 36*(10), 62-77.

Ward, J. A. (1997, Winter). Implementing employee empowerment. *Information Systems Management,* 62-65.

Watson, W. E., Kumar, K., & Michaelsen, L. K. (1993, June). Cultural diversity's impact on interaction processes and performance: Comparing homogeneous and diverse task groups. *Academy of Management Journal, 36,* 590-602.

Wellins, R. S., Byham, W. C., & Dixon, G. R. (1994). *Inside teams.* San Francisco: Jossey-Bass.

White, K. B., & Leifer, R. (1986). Information systems development success: Perspectives from project team participants. *MIS Quarterly, 10,* 215-223.

Yeatts, D. E., & Hyten, C. (1998). *High performing self-managed work teams: A comparison of theory to practice.* Thousand Oaks, CA: Sage.

Young, D., & Lee, S. (1997, Winter). Corporate hiring criteria for IS graduates. *Information Systems Management, 14*(1), 47-53.

Yourdon, E. (1989). *Managing the structured technique: Strategies for R&D in the 1990s.* New York: Yourdon Press/Prentice Hall.

Yukl, G. (1981). *Leadership in organizations.* Englewood Cliffs, NJ: Prentice Hall.

Yukl, G. (1989). *Leadership in organizations* (2nd ed.). Englewood Cliffs, NJ: Prentice Hall.

Yukl, G. (1998). *Leadership in organizations* (4th ed.). Englewood Cliffs, NJ: Prentice Hall.

Zenger, T. R., & Lawrence, B. S. (1989). Organizational demography: The differential effects of age and tenure distributions on technical communication. *Academy of Management Journal, 32,* 353-376.

# CHAPTER 4

# Can Team Members Share Leadership?

## Foundations in Research and Theory

*Anson Seers*

*Tiffany Keller*

*James M. Wilkerson*

O rganizations typical of the 20th century built hierarchies of management. These hierarchies established a division of labor that produced differentiated roles. Managers performed mostly cognitive tasks, whereas rank-and-file employees performed manual tasks involving physical resources. Advances in production technology generally reduced the need for workers to be particularly knowledgeable, with automated processes often working systematically to substitute for employee craftsmanship. This rationalization of labor, along with increasing elaboration of organizational structure and related coordination requirements, had the effect of shifting power and influence ever upward in managerial hierarchies of machine bureaucracies (Mintzberg, 1979). Thus, organizational form had a great deal to do with establishing a managerial paradigm characterized by single leaders in formal positions wielding power and influence over multiple followers who had relatively little influence on upper managers' decision making.

AUTHORS' NOTE: The authors wish to acknowledge the suggestions and criticism of Lucy Ford.

# Supervision and the Definition of Leadership

It is possible that our traditional leadership models reflect the particular circumstances of the ubiquity of large, complex hierarchical organizations characteristic of the 20th century. The assumption that leadership arises from the context of formal reporting relationships established within formal bureaucratic authority structures is reflected in traditional definitions of leadership. Indeed, Katz and Kahn's (1978) definition states, "We consider the essence of organizational leadership to be the influential increment over and above mechanical compliance with the routine directives of the organization" (p. 528).

Existing organizational leadership models might be described more precisely as supervisory leadership models. Organizational leadership research over the last 50 years has been guided by a succession of theoretical models that has progressed through three general phases. The earliest studies attempted to identify the basic dimensions of supervisory traits or behavior that were critical to leadership (e.g., Fleishman, 1973; Stogdill, 1948, 1974). In the second phase, attention shifted to attempts to identify situational contingencies that moderated the effects of the leadership behaviors displayed by supervisors (e.g., Fiedler, 1964; Kerr, Schriesheim, Murphy, & Stogdill, 1974). The third stage has been dominated by research pertaining to leader-member exchange theory (e.g., Graen, 1976; Graen & Scandura, 1987) and transformational/charismatic leadership theory (e.g., Bass, 1985; House, 1977). Although these models differ in important ways, they presume that the way in which we can enhance our understanding of leadership is to study patterns of employee supervision. Moreover, much of the research in this stream has relied on the perceptions of employees who are subordinate to organizational managers for the measurement of supervisory behavior. Thus, our literature of organizational leadership assumes, explicitly or implicitly, that leadership reflects a component of supervisory behavior.

## Evolving Organizational Trends

The forces of global economic integration, domestic deregulation, and information technology have reshaped the competitive landscape of the American corporations from which so much of our leadership data are collected (Whitman, 1999). Organizations today feature more emphasis on efficiency and productivity, continuous innovation, decreased stability, more difficulty achieving and maintaining profitability, changed employment relations, and altered internal structures. Many organizations "downsize" and "outsource" functions, rely on contingent employees, and form joint ventures and alliances with other organizations, even former competitors, that might provide useful services complementary to their core business in the most cost-efficient manner.

This pattern of evolution includes the emergence of network forms of organization (Miles & Creed, 1995; Polodny & Page, 1998). As noted by Polodny and Page (1998), so-called network organizations have distinctive attributes that differentiate them from hierarchies. Unlike hierarchical organizations, network organizations do not institutionalize structural authority that can ensure the resolution of conflicting interests. As pointed out by Miles and Creed (1995), the evolution in the popularity of different organizational forms corresponds to the evolution of managerial philosophies. Emerging organizational structures simply cannot rely on the close supervision made possible by tall, hierarchical organizations.

Accordingly, organizations increasingly use self-directing work teams in lieu of hierarchical work supervision. Lawler, Mohrman, and Ledford (1995) reported the escalating use of work teams during the 1990s. Likewise, Joinson (1999) estimated that 80% of the Fortune 500 organizations would have at least 50% of their employees on teams as of the year 2000, and Strozniak (2000) reported that 68% of small company plants used teams to varying extents.

## Away From Positional Leadership Definitions

Some definitions of leadership are compatible with today's organizational landscape and recognize the importance of interpersonal influence rather than position titles or other formal status designations. Stogdill (1974) presented seven different categories for summarizing the various definitions applied in the voluminous research he reviewed. Across all categories, the consistent theme is that leadership involves a social phenomenon in which a person may exert power, persuade, direct a group or individual behavior, facilitate goal achievement, or otherwise influence other people. Despite the variety of definitions, some form of interpersonal influence is consistently included as the central mechanism through which leadership is exercised.

Following Stogdill (1974), we define leadership as a social influence process that must include at least two individuals acting in interdependent roles. At least one individual must act in a follower role, and at least one individual must act in a distinctively influential (leadership) role. Such an influential role relationship may or may not coincide with any formal role designations such as "supervisor" and "subordinate." Under this definition, the question of shared leadership becomes a question of the extent to which more than one individual can effectively operate in a distinctively influential role within the same interdependent role system.

Our approach differs from other concepts of shared leadership. One such idea is implicit in existing leader-member exchange (LMX) research. According to LMX theory (Graen, 1976; Graen & Uhl-Bien, 1995), in-group members should be relatively influential with the boss compared to out-group members. Although this pattern does fit our definition of multiple individuals operating in distinctively influential roles within an interdependent role system, the LMX premise is that the elaboration of roles builds on the foundation of the established hierarchical authority of supervisors. Therefore, existing LMX theory is better suited to addressing relationships across formally designated hierarchical levels than it is for addressing relationships within a self-directing work team.

Our notion of shared leadership also departs from work that addresses self-management as a substitute for supervisory leadership (Gronn, 1999; Manz & Sims, 1991). A fair amount of this work has addressed self-directing work teams (Sims & Manz, 1996; Stewart & Manz, 1995). The focus of such work is on empowering individuals so that they can become "self-leading." These empowered workers share authority and responsibility for work outcomes with formal supervisors. Thus, self-managing workers should achieve a maximal degree of autonomy. The central question in self-management research seems to be how employees might operate with as little interpersonal influence from supervisors as possible. In contrast, our definition of leadership focuses on influence within a context of social interaction. Our central question is how interpersonal influence (e.g., leadership) will operate when individuals do not have formal authority.

Nonetheless, the concept of shared leadership is not new. Hodgson, Levinson, and Zaleznik (1965) analyzed a corporate "executive role constellation" as a manifestation of shared leadership. At that time, the authors noted that their analysis had to draw heavily from small group studies in social psychology because studies of corporate managers provided little insight to shared leadership (Hodgson et al., 1965). The term "shared leadership" has appeared with increasing frequency in the management literature during the 1990s (Barry, 1991; Gerard, 1995; Horner, 1998; Kiernan, 1993; Seers, 1996; Waldersee, Simmons, & Eagleson, 1995; Wheelan & Johnston, 1996). Many of these articles, however, come from the practitioner literature. The concept of shared leadership has drawn little attention in mainstream organizational leadership research and theory.

A notable exception to this is the recent work of Pearce, Sims, and colleagues, who have drawn on Yukl's (1998) view of shared leadership in teams and defined it as leadership that is executed by the members of teams, and not solely by the appointed team leader (Pearce & Sims, 2002; cf. Ensley & Pearce, 2000; Ensley, Pearson, & Pearce, in press; Perry, Pearce, & Sims, 1999). Consistent with influence-based views of leadership (Bass, 1990; Stogdill, 1974), Pearce and Sims (2000) have further detailed that shared leadership "entails the process of shared influence between and among individuals" (p. 116). This new research stream has extended and adapted more traditional, vertical leadership concepts to shared leadership and has contrasted the two kinds of leadership (Ensley & Pearce, 2000; Pearce & Sims, 2002). Pearce and Sims (2000) have also recently discussed some historical research that implicates shared leadership and offered conceptual support for some proposed antecedents (a number of group, task, and environment characteristics).

A close inspection of these antecedents reveals, as Pearce and Sims (2000) note, that some may interact with shared leadership in influencing team outcomes rather than spawn shared leadership in any causal sense. Furthermore, the proposed antecedents are not process mechanisms. Thus, Pearce, Sims, and colleagues have laid some definitional groundwork and begun testing empirical links between shared leadership and outcomes (Pearce & Sims, 2002; cf. Ensley & Pearce, 2000; Ensley, Pearson, & Pearce, in press; Perry, Pearce, & Sims, 1999) The present research stream, however, is largely silent on theoretical reasons for why influence should come to be wielded and reciprocated in any sustained or patterned way across multiple members of work groups. Ironically, more than 35 years after Hodgson et al. (1965) had to rely on small groups research instead of business management literature, our analysis of shared leadership in the context of self-directing work teams also appears to need to draw more heavily on the literature of social psychology than that which is available in business-oriented journals. Research pertaining to power, influence, and leadership that has not been conducted in hierarchically structured organizations appears especially relevant.

Unlike supervisory leadership, shared leadership within self-directing work teams cannot be based on formal hierarchy. Thus, we turn our interest to emergent influence patterns within self-directing work teams. Researchers have long recognized that emergent leaders may be just as important to the facilitation of group task completion as are designated leaders (Bales, 1958; Stogdill, 1974). Goktepe and Schneier (1989) defined emergent leaders as group members who exert significant influence over other members of the group although no formal authority has been vested in them. Some emergent leadership research has focused on the emergence of a single, informal leader, and Pearce and Sims (2002) acknowledge the relevance of emergent leadership research to shared leadership but consider the phenomenon to be focused on informal selection of a single team leader (cf. Pearce & Sims, 2000). Research on emergent leadership processes, however, has not shown that it is always restricted to only one individual at any given time in a team. Given that self-directing work teams generally operate without the constant influence of a formal supervisor, these work groups may provide especially fertile contexts for the study of emergent and shared leadership.

## The Emergence of Leaders

Early studies of emergent leadership literature include those of Bales and his colleagues (Bales, 1958; Bales & Slater, 1955; Borgatta & Bales, 1956; Slater, 1955). These studies focused on the process of role differentiation but predate significant elaborations of role theory by Katz and Kahn (1966) and Sarbin and Allen (1968). Many subsequent studies of emergent leadership, however, shifted attention away from the role-making process. In part, this may be attributable to the complexity of Bales's methodology (Bales, Cohen, & Williamson, 1979). Another factor is continued interest in the effects of individual attributes on leader emergence. These studies often trace their interest back to the reviews by Mann (1959) and Stogdill (1948) on the effect of personality traits on leadership, and less often cite role process studies such as those of Bales.

Gender has perhaps been most frequently investigated as an independent variable predicting leadership emergence. By 1991, a sufficient number of gender studies had accumulated for Eagly and Karau to conduct a meta-analysis, which showed that women emerged as leaders more frequently in socially oriented groups, even though gender bias usually favored males. Kent and Moss (1994) found gender role to be a better predictor of emergence than actual gender. Nonetheless, subsequent studies have continued to investigate the effects of gender on emergence (e.g., Kolb, 1997).

Lord, De Vader, and Alliger (1986) reported a meta-analysis of other predictors of leadership emergence. They found that several personality trait variables, specifically intelligence, dominance, and masculinity, predicted leadership emergence. Several subsequent studies (Foti & Hauenstein, 1996; Morrow & Stern, 1990; Roberts, 1996) also found dominance and intelligence to predict leader emergence. Other subsequent studies explored other individual difference predictors of leadership emergence. For example, Zaccaro, Foti, and Kenny (1991) found that self-monitoring and perception of team requirements predicted emergence. DeSouza and Klein's (1995) study showed that task ability and commitment to team goals predicted leader emergence.

Among the leader emergence studies that focus on patterns of interpersonal behavior rather than on personal characteristics, considerable evidence indicates that individuals who verbalize more most often emerge as leaders (Burke, 1974; Mullen, Salas, & Driskell, 1989; Regula & Julian, 1973; Skvoretz, 1988; Sorrentino &

Boutellier, 1975). Beyond the quantity of talking, Guastello (1995) found that emergent leaders facilitate others' creativity as well as suggesting their own ideas. Johnson and Bechler (1998) found emergent leaders to listen more effectively than individuals not identified as emergent leaders. However consistent, much of the research literature that investigates predictors of emergent leadership is empirically driven, with relatively little elaboration of theoretical models.

Three areas in which theoretical frameworks potentially useful for analyzing the emergence of leaders have been developed are organizational role theory (Katz & Kahn, 1978), social exchange theory (Homans, 1958), and expectation states theory (Berger & Zelditch, 1998). Theory in these three areas is better suited to facilitate an understanding of the process through which leaders may emerge than of the individual attributes that may be brought to the process by likely emergent leaders. We submit that, to understand shared leadership, researchers need theoretical guidance on the structuring (e.g., role configurations as described in role theory), emergence and reciprocation (e.g., social exchange theory's focus), and social endorsement (such as that derived from expectation states) of shared influence. We will review work in each of these areas in turn and suggest ways in which this work might, in combination, help to provide a theoretical foundation on which a model of shared leadership might be developed.

## Revisiting the Theoretical Roots of Role Making

The basic process of role differentiation has been documented over decades of research. With respect to leadership, Bass's (1949) analysis noted that two individual group members often emerged into complementary roles. One of these leaders was generally the member most respected for his or her contributions to the accomplishment of tasks within the group. The other was generally the best-liked member, who was most respected for his or her contribution and support of friendly interaction among members. Similar results were reported by Carter (1954), as well as in the aforementioned studies of Bales and his associates.

It is important to note that not all of these studies consistently showed the emergence of the same pattern of two differentiated, high-status leadership roles and resulting follower roles for the remaining group members. For example, Bales and Slater (1955) found that member roles were also differentiated along a third dimension, which simply reflected the member's activity level. An interesting finding from the Slater (1955) study was that the degree of group consensus in the identification of the status hierarchy was related to the pattern of role differentiation. The strongest consensus was generally achieved when the two most active individuals emerged into distinct roles, one as task specialist and the other as a relationship specialist. The task specialist would then have the highest status, and the relationship specialist would have the second-highest status. Consensus was lowest when the most active member did not score highly on either the task or relational dimensions. This dissension resulted in some members accepting considerable influence from an individual who participated a great deal despite making relatively little contribution to group maintenance or task achievement.

Many studies of role emergence since the 1950s have been conducted as laboratory studies using college students as subjects, without explicit attention to leadership and how it operates in work organizations. Such studies have generally taken pains to avoid the possibility of confounded interpretations due to previous relationships among subjects, as their prior acquaintance could overcome any experimental manipulation of socialization cues. Yet we know that most self-directing work teams in ongoing organizations will actually be composed of members who have prior acquaintance with each other from past work experience and expectations of working together in the foreseeable future. One might then question the usefulness of the findings from the long stream of psychological laboratory studies, not only regarding the emergence of influential leaders of higher status but indeed regarding any of the interpersonal and group dynamics material to the function of work teams. Failing to consider the implications of this massive body of research for the leadership of organizational work teams, however, risks reinvention of the wheel.

Even though most leader emergence studies have investigated leadership as a manifestation of individual personality attributes, findings from these studies appear quite compatible with inferences drawn from studies of role differentiation processes. The effects of the most frequently documented individual difference predictors, including amount of verbalization, intelligence, domination, and gender role, can be readily reconciled with findings from studies in the role-making tradition. To the extent that these individual differences manifest their effects in the form of individual contributions that elicit respect and deference from other members in the group, explanations of leadership emergence coincide between personality predictions and studies that build on the role-making tradition (Berger & Zelditch, 1998).

## Advances of Role Theory

For both social exchange theory and organizational role theory, much of the conceptual development occurred from the 1950s to the 1970s, in light of the extensive stream of research on role differentiation. Katz and Kahn (1966, 1978) offered a particularly useful framework that can address the task functions of groups and their members simultaneously with the psychological and social facets of group behavior. As described by Katz and Kahn (1978), roles constitute patterns of behavior established by the interaction of members of a social unit. These roles allow individuals to know both what others expect of them and what to expect from others. Roles evolve over time as members of a social unit exchange interactions and thus construct meaningful relationships. An important implication of roles for the members of a work team is that when the members of a work group know what they will need to do and how interdependent others will react, less communication is needed for the coordination of their activities (Sarbin & Allen, 1968). Thus, misunderstandings, wasted efforts, and associated psychological tensions are minimized, and time may be used more efficiently. Empirical evidence that role differentiation benefits group performance is available (e.g., Roger & Reid, 1982).

Analyses of the role-making process generally look at the interaction between the occupant of a focal role and those interdependent others who constitute the role set. In team-based organizations, an employee's team may constitute most, or all, of the role set (Seers, 1989). Focal members may generalize across the perceived expectations of the other team members into a summary notion of what their team expects of them. They learn the role over time through a process of socialization (Moreland & Levine, 1982), but it is important to keep in mind that much of the reality they are learning is simultaneously being socially invented by the very group interaction in which they are participating. When role making takes place in a newly formed team, it simultaneously constitutes the group development process (Moreland & Levine, 1984).

Because roles become defined within a specific social context, they are inherently cross-level phenomena that will involve constructs at an individual level of analysis and at one or more social unit analytic levels. The social unit(s) may be dyads; small groups; or large, abstract societal groupings. Thus, the roles people play may distinguish husband versus wife, in-group member versus out-group member, and ethnic minority versus ethnic majority citizen. In self-directing work teams, the roles of interest are defined in relation to the team as a unit, although dynamics of dyadic social exchanges within the team may also be of great interest. Some analyses of the role-making process have focused on interactions between members within dyads (e.g., Graen, 1976; Graen & Scandura, 1987), whereas others have brought into focus role development in a group context (Levine & Moreland, 1990; Moreland & Levine, 1982, 1984).

Our focus is on the emergence of influential group roles in self-directing work teams. Role interactions allow individuals to gain favorable self-validation from role responses within the group, while the systemic character of the group develops through the interaction of its members. As members come to conform to their role expectations, those expectations shared in common among the members become the norms of the group. Acting in concert, they consensually validate (Festinger, 1950; Weick, 1979) their social reality. A group that is generally successful in gaining productive contributions from its members through effective roles and positive norms will best be able to achieve organizational goals. From this perspective, the group owes not only its identity to how it is perceived by its members but also the entirety of its performance. When groups establish norms that are respectful of balanced, reciprocal influence, shared leadership should emerge.

With respect to members within self-directing work teams, Seers (1989) presented a role-making analysis applicable to leadership emergence. He proposed the construct of team member exchange quality (TMX) to assess the reciprocity between a member and the peer group. The reciprocity addressed by TMX involves the member's contribution of ideas, feedback, and assistance to other members in exchange for the member's receipt of information, help, and recognition from other team members. Although Seers's (1989) analysis of TMX relationships focused on the development of cooperation, collaboration, and teamwork, TMX role differentiation within groups can operate vertically as well as horizontally. Analogous to how Graen's (1976) LMX construct indicates the quality of a subordinate's working relationship with the supervisor, the quality of TMX indicates the effectiveness of the member's working relationship to the peer group. Just as high-LMX relationships endow work group members with enhanced status and influence (Cashman, Dansereau, Graen, & Haga, 1976), high TMX should also endow team members with enhanced status and influence among peers.

## Social Exchange Theory

The foremost theoretical works in this area are those of Homans (1961) and Blau (1964); however, other noteworthy early contributions came from Emerson

(1962), Hollander (1964), and Thibaut and Kelley (1959). Common across these approaches is the premise that interactions among group members are characterized by reciprocity, and that this reciprocity engenders the elaboration of the differentiated roles of group members. Extensive reviews of this literature have been published over the years (e.g., Cook, 1987; Ekeh, 1974; Gergen, Greenberg, & Willis, 1980), which facilitate our ability to draw on literature accumulated over several decades. That literature has established that the ability to exert interpersonal influence is given to those who influence by those who are influenced by them.

Homans's (1961) analysis of social exchange as the most elementary form of social behavior advanced the view that all interpersonal dynamics, including influence, grew out of the development of patterns of exchange between individuals. Homans suggested that much influence could be explained by individuals trading their willingness to comply with the preferences of other individuals of higher social status simply for the social acceptance of those higher-status individuals. Even in relationships not involving marked status differences, Homans suggested that greater exchange between individuals would result in a relationship characterized by increased reciprocal influence. In Homans's (1961) terms, "influence over others is purchased at the price of allowing one's self to be influenced by others" (p. 286).

Blau (1964) is generally credited as the first theorist to extend exchange analysis beyond social exchange within dyads. His analysis, however, depicts the group as a single, collective actor conceptually substituted for one of the individual members of a dyad. Hollander (1964) and Jacobs (1970) took comparable approaches in analyses specific to leadership. Although other theorists (e.g., Emerson, 1962; Graen, 1976) argued that only individuals can act meaningfully, within dyads, a group role can be defined only through group members coming to a consensus regarding a set of expectations and the ability and legitimacy of a particular individual for fulfilling those expectations.

Both Hollander (1964) and Jacobs (1970) suggested that subordinate group members collectively reciprocated the leadership contributions from a supervisor by legitimizing that individual's leadership role. In particular, Hollander became well-known for his argument that individuals had to develop "idiosyncrasy credits" for their contributions to a group for their leadership behaviors to be accepted rather than rejected as behavior that violated common member norms. According to Jacobs (1970), member roles become differentiated through a competitive process of elimination through which a status hierarchy is negotiated, and which determines who will influence whom. The major causes for elimination from the influence hierarchy competition include evidencing a lack of information regarding the group's goals, inadequate participation, a lack of flexibility, authoritarianism, and offensive verbalizations, all of which violate member expectations for a leadership role.

Neither Hollander (1964) nor Jacobs (1970) was able to develop arguments well grounded in articulated theoretical formulations of social exchange that recognized *collective* action. Although American research highlighted social exchange in dyads, analysis of social exchange in collective action was proceeding in Europe (Ekeh, 1974; Heath, 1976; Lévi-Strauss, 1969). The work of Lévi-Strauss (1969) in France produced an extension of social exchange theory beyond dyads that did not simply require the reader to imagine the group as an actor parallel to an individual member of a dyad. Ekeh (1974) introduced Lévi-Strauss's construct of generalized social exchange to American readers. Generalized social exchange describes an emergent pattern in which individuals exhibit group-directed behaviors that are reciprocated by other group members. Specifically, Member A may exhibit group-directed behaviors, for which reciprocal behaviors by Member B may be directed to the group in general or to Member C rather than being directed specifically to Member A. By way of example, Ekeh (1974) points out that Neighbor A intervenes by calling the fire department on noticing Neighbor B's house on fire, not simply under the expectation that B will reciprocate if A's house ever burns but also expecting that any other neighbor, C through Z, will reciprocate.

Thus, Ekeh (1974) suggested the coexistence of two forms of social exchange, based on two different principles of reciprocity. He labeled the form of social exchange assumed by most exchange theorists as "restricted" exchange. Restricted exchange is dyadic and adheres closely to direct, mutual reciprocity. In contrast, Ekeh (1974) described "generalized" exchange as multilateral, indirect exchange in which individual contributions are spread over time and across various group members. Generalized exchanges require greater trust from the participants, as they lack the clear accountability of restricted exchanges. Because actors make generalized exchange contributions with expectations that returns will be spread over time and across various group members, generalized exchange builds group solidarity much more effectively than does restricted exchange.

Ekeh's (1974) concept of generalized exchange differs from the use of the term "generalized reciprocity" by Sparrowe and Liden (1997) and Sahlins (1972). The latter authors described generalized reciprocity as a form of exchange within dyads that is relatively altruistic and indefinite in reciprocation obligations. This suggests a continuum in which reciprocity ranges, from generalized reciprocity through balanced reciprocity to negative reciprocity. Sparrowe and Liden (1997) proposed that this continuum helps to explain the differentiation of high-LMX dyads (generalized) from medium- and low-LMX dyads (balanced and negative). Because generalized exchanges involving three or more team members as conceptualized by Ekeh (1974) can coexist with dyadic relationships within a team, they can help explain group-level dynamics that are not inherently dyadic phenomena, such as norms, cohesiveness and, we suggest, shared leadership.

After Ekeh's (1974) elaboration of the generalized exchange construct, relatively few studies involving generalized exchange can be found. Studies by O'Connell (1984), Gillmore (1987), and Uehara (1990), however, found generally positive outcomes associated with generalized exchange, including greater interpersonal trust, social support, group solidarity, and satisfaction with relationships. Yamagishi and Cook (1993) argued that the problem of free riding would be inherent in generalized exchange. They reported a laboratory network study in which individuals, constrained to give resources directly to one other individual and linked in a circular manner, contributed more than when resources were simply pooled and then divided equally. In their design, however, individual subjects remained completely anonymous, all outcomes accrued to specific individuals, and no social structure was or could be established that would involve a group identity, sense of community, or collective action (such as a group sanction against individuals who violated a norm). Bearman (1997) took issue with the premise that generalized exchange would exacerbate the problem of free riding. Instead, his results suggested that individuals who violate the norm of reciprocity in generalized exchange would be subject to greater pressure for conformity from sanction of the entire group rather than that of single dyadic partners.

Lazega and Pattison (1999) presented a network study of exchange within a law firm. They found that work ties organized around both dyadic and generalized exchanges, advice ties clustered locally and hierarchically, and friendship ties organized around local clusters. They interpreted the pattern of relationship ties as indicating that generalized exchange was critical to the evolution of the social structure of the firm. Using the same data, Lazega (2000) showed how this social structure allowed the partners to collectively enforce norms supporting group-oriented efforts, and thus achieve critical outcomes through shared influence.

Yamagishi, Jin, and Kiyonari (1999) summarized a stream of studies based on Tajfel and Turner's (1979) social identity theory and concluded that generalized social exchange provided the most plausible explanation for in-group favoritism. Takahashi (2000) presented a rational choice argument that generalized exchange was unlikely to persist due to rational reactions to free riding individuals. He reported, however, an "evolutionary" computer simulation (e.g., Axelrod, 1986) that showed an incentive structure emerged in which generalized exchange became rational.

Collectively, these studies suggest that generalized exchange contributes to group solidarity. We should then expect that as the overall level of generalized exchange in groups increases, those groups should exhibit greater integration (Hechter, 1987; Lindenberg, 1998) wherein group norms support interlocking, reciprocal influence among the members that allows shared leadership to operate. Still, as members of groups remain unique individuals, individual differences should remain among members with respect to their characteristic level of generalized exchange with the group. Certainly, what is within each individual member's discretion is his or her contributions to exchange relationships (both dyadic and generalized) rather than receipts from exchange relationships. Individuals with characteristically high levels of contributions to generalized exchange should emerge as "model citizens." This role should legitimize their influence with other members.

Seers (2000) suggested that the pattern of generalized social exchange within self-directing work teams should promote emergent leadership as some individuals become more influential than others. For example, Seers, Ford, Wilkerson, and Moorman (2001) examined influence among members of managerial work groups in relation to both generalized TMX with their peers and their dyadic LMX with the supervising manager. The TMX measure was split into symmetric subscales (exchange contributions and exchange receipts) to reflect the reciprocal nature of social exchange. Both LMX and TMX contributions predicted upward influence and lateral influence, but exchange receipts had no significant effect on influence. The results were interpreted as indicating that the contribution side of social exchanges provides the basis for the process of legitimation (Blau, 1964; Ridgeway, 1984) through which leadership roles stabilize.

In sum, a considerable body of evidence has built on the insights of such seminal thinkers as Homans (1961) and Blau (1964). This evidence clearly supports the basic premise of social exchange theory that exchange relationships generate influence. These relationships engage the parties in interdependent patterns of interaction. To maintain the stability of an exchange relationship, both parties must continue to respond to each other. Should the behavior of either party cease to influence the other to reciprocate, the relationship deteriorates. Nonetheless, the extent of influence wielded by each party can differ notably. Our third theoretical pillar, expectation states theory, is perhaps most useful for analyzing variation within a group with respect to the development of influential roles.

## Expectation States Theory

Berger, Cohen, and Zelditch (1972) presented the initial formulation of expectation states theory, and Berger and Zelditch (1998) reported a comprehensive review of subsequent theoretical developments and empirical studies. Expectation states theory suggests that as members begin working together, they intuitively note other members' status characteristics (personal qualities indicative of ability or prestige) and form associated performance expectations. Those possessing superior status characteristics are expected to provide superior contributions, including more numerous and varied actions and greater input and guidance. They also wield influence over others by evaluating their ideas, and can more readily reject others' influence attempts.

According to the theory, individuals' expectations about other members result from both specific status characteristics and diffuse status characteristics. Specific status characteristics are qualities that relate to each individual's ability to perform the task at hand, whereas diffuse status characteristics are general qualities that individuals may perceive to be linked to ability, such as sex, age, or ethnicity. Researchers have largely confirmed that individuals with more specific and diffuse status characteristics usually command relatively great authority in groups (Berger & Zelditch, 1985; Ridgeway & Walker, 1995; Wagner & Berger, 1993; Wilke, 1996).

This relatively cognitive approach has withstood a challenge from advocates of a more behavioralistic "demeanor" explanation for the emergence of dominant members in groups. For example, Lee and Ofshe (1981) found that deference-demanding body language, including a relatively loud, fast, and firm tone of voice with little hesitation, strong eye contact, and traditional business attire, yielded high influence. Deferential body language, including soft, slow, and hesitating speech with disjunctive pauses, poor eye contact, and overly casual attire, yielded low influence, whereas the identification of an individual as holding a high- versus low-status job title had no effect on the resulting influence. A 1984 study by Tuzlak and Moore found effects on influence both for demeanor and for status. The effect of demeanor, however, was found to diminish over time, suggesting the possibility that the behavioral cues of demeanor might serve as a temporary surrogate for the more enduring cues of role expectations in establishing which members lead and which members follow.

Ridgeway (1984) formulated a model that integrated the demeanor and expectation states approaches and found support for it in a subsequent study (Ridgeway, 1987). An important feature of Ridgeway's (1984) model for our purposes is its characterization of demeanor "contests" as dyadic phenomena although the emergence of a status hierarchy requires the establishment of an effective degree of consensus across the entire group membership. Ridgeway (1984) presumes that group members process the same set of status-relevant information about each other, such that they generally arrive at a shared set of role expectations without significant conflict or deliberate efforts toward achieving consensus. The evidence cited by Ridgeway (1984) characterizes the allocation of status across group members as a generally cooperative process based on voluntary deference to status signs and contribution by high-status members of behaviors serving the group's shared interests.

Members of newly formed teams need to sort out their expectations for how members can facilitate various task and relational needs of the group. If they have prior knowledge of each other's group behavior patterns, we should simply expect this knowledge to be incorporated into their sent expectations for these other group members. Nonetheless, the role definition process that resolves what pattern of interpersonal influence will characterize a group can clearly reach an apparently stable resolution within a very short period of time after members of that group begin their interaction, even when the members have no prior acquaintance. Expectation states theory clearly suggests that shared leadership can arise only when multiple members come to the group with impressive status characteristics. It would also appear to suggest, however, that shared leadership *should* arise, and remain stable, when multiple members come to the group with impressive status characteristics. This is consistent with Pearce and Sims's (2000) assertion that shared leadership is more likely when group members are highly skilled in their assigned tasks. Furthermore, we should expect that differing status characteristics may be associated with different goals, objectives, and group needs. The variety of such goals, needs, and objectives should thus promote the development of shared leadership, as well.

# Toward a Theoretical Model of Shared Influence

Thus far, we have outlined three areas of theory that may facilitate our analysis of shared emergent influence. Although there is a fairly long line of leader emergence studies, no succinct theoretical model has emerged from this work. On the other hand, organizational role theory, social exchange theory, and expectation states theory provide complementary conceptual frameworks for the analysis of the development of influence. Each of these three theories has received support from empirical research, but none of the three has found much application to emergent leadership in work organizations. LMX theory has drawn on both role theory and social exchange theory, with considerably more explication of the former (e.g., Graen, 1976) than the latter. There is a comparatively great accumulation of empirical studies bearing on expectation states theory (see Berger & Zelditch, 1998), but virtually none of this work has studied employees working in organizational contexts.

The present authors see the three theoretical frameworks as complementary foundations for a model of shared leadership. Role theory is most capable of supporting structural specification for organizational patterns (e.g., role sets), whereas social exchange theory is most capable of supporting specification of the behavioral incentives that motivate interaction patterns (e.g., interpersonal acceptance), and expectation states theory is most capable of supporting specification of the perceptual and cognitive dynamics of individuals (e.g., specific expectations) in the process of establishing influence patterns. Although future work is needed to carefully integrate these three theoretical bases in the service of explaining shared leadership in work groups, the present analysis should suffice for outlining some of the major factors that may serve as barriers to shared leadership, as well as those that may serve to facilitate it. These factors are identified below and summarized in Table 4.1.

## Barriers to Shared Leadership

Skepticism regarding the prospects for shared leadership seems to have been around as long as the concept itself. Berkowitz (1953) reported an early study of

**Table 4.1**   Shared Leadership: Facilitators Versus Barriers

| Facilitators of Shared Leadership | Barriers to Shared Leadership |
| --- | --- |
| 1. Task requires role differentiation and multiple exchange relationships | 1. People don't like the idea |
| 2. Larger group size, up to the point where coordination requires formalization | 2. Evolutionary evidence of status differentials |
| 3. Higher ratings of each other's abilities to contribute toward goal | 3. One or two leaders usually emerge in leaderless groups |
| 4. High interpersonal attraction | 4. Individual differences in status seeking |
| 5. Generalized exchange norms | 5. Implicit leadership theories |
| | 6. Demographic composition of group |

participant reactions to shared leadership in conference groups. His results indicated that participants reacted quite negatively to shared leadership. The more strongly leader roles were differentiated from participant member roles, the greater were cohesiveness, productivity, and satisfaction with the conference.

The evidence suggests that influence is largely a matter of lower-status individuals deferring to higher-status individuals. This characteristic pattern of social behavior seems quite ubiquitous, even beyond human groups. For example, Mazur (1973) detailed the commonality of the establishment of status hierarchies across species, showing the greatest similarity between humans and similar primates. Although Mazur (1973) acknowledged that human status processes exhibited more differences than similarities compared to lower animals, he did discuss the near linearity of emergent "pecking orders" as perhaps the most visible sign of hierarchical status differentiation with lower animals such as chickens. To the extent that status differentials create monotonic order within groups (i.e., such that leadership ultimately rests with the single individual of highest status), informally emerging status hierarchies might mirror the formal institutionalization of supervisory leadership. Indeed, the literature suggests that status differentials within groups are inevitable. Some of the earliest systematic research on work group leadership showed that "leaderless groups," free from outside influence, usually anoint one or two informal leaders (Bales, 1958; Borgatta & Bales, 1956; Carter, 1954; Slater, 1955). Usually, leadership positions are reserved for those with the highest status within the group. This would suggest that members of self-directing work teams would not share leadership in a manner fundamentally different from groups using traditional supervisory leadership.

Research on the emergence of influential roles within peer groups in social psychology has also long suggested that status differentials within groups are inevitable. First, since status is socially desirable, some individual members may compete for status. Individuals actively seeking status may be more likely to tell others what they should do, interpret others' statements, confirm or dispute others' views, and summarize or reflect on the discussion (Stiles et al., 1997; Stiles, Orth, Scherwitz, Hennrikus, & Vallbona, 1984). In short, individuals seeking status often initiate conversations, shift the topic to their own area of competence, and talk more than individuals who do not seek status (Cappella, 1985; Godfrey, Jones, & Lord, 1986). Individuals who choose not to seek status may effectively defer leadership to others, thereby creating de facto leadership differentials.

Implicit leadership theory also suggests a potential barrier to shared leadership, as cognitive biases may affect leadership perceptions. According to implicit leadership theory, the label "leader" serves as a cognitive category to classify individuals as either "leaders" or "nonleaders." Individuals are classified as leaders based on how well they resemble the leadership schema. If they bear a close resemblance to the leadership prototype, observers categorize them as "leaders." Once activated, the leadership schema may cause individuals to selectively attend to, encode, and retrieve schema-consistent information as well as misremember schema-consistent information when it does not exist (Lord, Foti, & De Vader, 1984; Lord & Maher, 1991; Phillips & Lord, 1982). Thus, group members may expect individuals who fit their mental leader images to act in leadership roles, even if these individuals have neither the ability nor the inclination to do so. Conversely, groups may too readily dismiss individuals who do not fit the type, such as women, from consideration for leadership positions. Accordingly, group members may rely on cognitive prototypes with potentially irrelevant cues to restrict assigned status within groups, effectively narrowing the set of individuals who might be considered leaders.

Perhaps an even more fundamental way in which such cognitive biases might serve as a barrier to shared leadership involves the assumptions implicit in the language used to describe leadership. The term *leader* is used most often in the singular form, as contrasted with the typical use of *followers* or *members* in the plural form. The implicit notion is that a leader is a singular individual "rising above" ordinary members.

Finally, the demographic composition of the group may present a barrier to shared leadership. Organizational demography suggests that being different from others in terms of age, education, sex, and race can affect individuals' attitudes and behavior toward others and the organization (Tsui, Egan, & O'Reilly, 1992; Tsui & Gutek, 1999). Individuals' evaluations of their groups are likely to reflect the values institutionalized by the organization's culture. In particular, members of low-status groups are likely to perceive their own group's attributes as inconsistent with the organizational requirements for success (Tajfel, 1981). Likewise, sex functions as a diffuse status characteristic for women in minority situations, leading them to formulate stereotypical expectations that women are compliant, docile followers and that men are dominant, influential leaders (Lockheed, 1985).

Ridgeway (1988) argues that individuals have a strong cognitive preference for having their expectations about reality supported. Therefore, if women expect men to hold higher-status positions—an expectation that she argues is supported by a disproportionate number of men in positions of organizational authority—they will prefer to engage in a level and range of task behavior that are commensurate with low performance and status. Women will lack task confidence and task motivation, engage in fewer directive behaviors, and concentrate instead on socioemotional concerns (Ridgeway, 1988). In short, women are inclined to emulate the characteristics stereotypically associated with women as a group and to evaluate themselves unfavorably in relation to requirements for success.

Organizational demography has direct implications for shared leadership in teams. If the group is composed primarily of white men, women and minorities may not perceive themselves as leaders. Consequently, they may refrain from engaging in directive behaviors that are typically associated with leadership. Accordingly, group members may be less inclined to view them as leaders, thus creating a self-fulfilling prophecy.

In summary, although the philosophy of the self-directing team is one that embraces shared leadership, such a reality may be difficult to achieve. Some individuals may actively seek status, whereas others do not. Some individuals may possess certain traits or characteristics relevant for the task, whereas others do not. Finally, some individuals may better fit the prototype of leader, whereas others do not. Shared leadership might be particularly difficult if members believe that status hierarchies are inexorably part of human nature.

## Facilitators of Shared Leadership

Although there are practical as well as theoretical reasons to question how effectively shared leadership can operate in self-directing work teams, our review of research and theory produces neither theoretical reason to see it as impossible nor evidence that it does not occur. We have proposed that it should occur, subject to known processes of leader emergence. Our review indicates that the differentiation of roles with respect to influence is likely ubiquitous, such that informal leaders likely emerge even in a system that includes formally designated leaders (Wheelan & Johnston, 1996). Yet we have little clear evidence regarding the likely distribution of influential roles within groups. Thus, one very basic question involves how appropriate different possible mathematical models may be to represent this distribution. Given the grounding of the research we have reviewed within the realm of extant research on human behavior, we surmise that the distribution of influence across group members will likely fit the normal curve, as does the variance of most individual attributes. There is little basis here for expecting to find many groups in which a rectangular distribution would provide a good fit (i.e., we would not suggest that shared leadership would be manifested in cases in which all members truly share influence equally). There is also little basis, however, for expecting many groups in which a negative exponential distribution would provide a good fit (i.e., a monopoly of influence in which only one person ever exercises any leadership).

The few existing empirical studies that provide evidence regarding the dispersion of power and influence in groups suggest that the extent of this dispersion is important at the group level of analysis. Feldman (1973) analyzed the distribution of power in children's camp groups in relation to member characteristics, group size, and group process variables. Dispersion of power was related to three factors, in decreasing order of variance accounted. First, it was greatest in groups in which the members reported greater interpersonal attraction (liking); second, dispersion was higher in larger groups; and third, dispersion was also higher when members reported higher ratings of each others' abilities to contribute toward achieving group goals. Notably, dispersion of power was unrelated to the extent of sharing of group norms.

Dispersion of power and influence within self-directing work teams must involve the group dynamics through which group members achieve differentiated roles. Although it may be premature to expect resolution of the question of if, and how, shared leadership naturally occurs through the dispersion of power and influence, a clear implication of the role differentiation process is that various members of a group can and do simultaneously contribute influence to activities within the work group.

The notion of distributed influence within a team seems quite consistent with the considerable body of role research cited above that has found multiple group members simultaneously fulfilling influential task, consideration, and activity roles. Thus, evolution toward differentiated roles in a group that are mutually complementary should facilitate shared leadership. For shared leadership to develop, this differentiation must involve different bases, as well as different degrees, of status and influence. Factors leading to the existence of differing bases of status and influence may be found among the nature of a group's task, the attributes brought to the group by its members, and the process dynamics of the group as a social system.

For groups having a complex task, or multiple tasks, there is a broader base for individuals to make the kind of unique contributions to group goals that social exchange theory suggests are reciprocated by following behaviors. Accordingly, we concur with Pearce and Sims's (2000) recent suggestion that task complexity is positively associated with shared leadership. Indeed, a complex task, or multiple tasks, may require *multiple* exchange relationships among members. This should be the case especially when task interdependencies require complementary skills and abilities among group members. Self-directing work teams, which presumably may rely on shared leadership, are used for such tasks with increasing frequency.

As the use of work teams has become more popular, teamwork and leadership abilities have become increasingly valued employee characteristics. Beyond the complementarity of skills and abilities brought to teamwork by group members, the perceptions and reactions of individuals may also facilitate shared team leadership. The work of Feldman (1973), described above, suggests that group members may facilitate shared leadership to the extent that they perceive each other as likable and rate each others' abilities favorably. Thus, any given team member's salutary personal characteristics can be the basis for teammates' expectations of, and ready deference to, the member's influence.

Social exchange research presents perhaps the clearest implications for how group dynamics can facilitate shared influence. First, the parties to any exchange relationship may develop a great deal of reciprocal influence, such as appears to be the ideal of leadership in the LMX model (Graen & Uhl-Bien, 1995). This can produce an in-group of employees whose influence exceeds that of out-group members. Little research or theory, however, has addressed the implications of vertical dyad differentiation for peer group dynamics. Unlike restricted exchange within dyads, generalized peer group exchange relationships allow every group member to develop reciprocity that engages the group in general, which allows each member at least some opportunity to influence the group as a whole. When we watch influence flowing in this reciprocal relationship from the group to the individual, we see the conformity of members to group norms. When we watch the flow from individual to group, we see leadership, so generalized exchange should provide a mechanism enabling multiple members to share leadership. We should expect generalized exchange contributions to persist only if group norms arise that reinforce it. Under these conditions, shared leadership should become an implicit, common expectation of group members.

A final group characteristic that may be important for facilitating shared leadership may be an appropriate group size. Pearce and Sims (2000) held that group size should influence shared leadership, and we concur in light of role and task coordination concerns. In Feldman's (1973) study, dispersion of power and influence increased with group size. Very small groups may provide little opportunity for shared leadership, and may also have fewer members who are relatively willing and able to take on particularly influential roles. It is important to note that the range of group size in Feldman's study was only between 6 and 13 members, but there are additional reasons to expect that larger group size may not always facilitate shared leadership. The formalization of hierarchy has long been the typical result occasioned by the coordination problems of especially large groups. We would not expect shared leadership to occur for groups large enough to develop internal hierarchy, nor in any situation where needs for efficient coordination become paramount.

## Research Issues

The amount of evidence documenting the existence, let alone benefits, of dispersed or shared leadership is modest. Neubert (1999) found that dispersion (measured by the proportion of members nominated as a group's emergent leader) correlated with manufacturing team cohesion, but the correlation with performance fell short of significance. Pearce and Sims (2002) operationalized shared leadership in terms of participants' perceptions of teammates' leadership behaviors, and found that shared leadership positively predicted multisource ratings of team effectiveness. Also, shared leadership was a more useful predictor of team effectiveness than was vertical leadership. Ensley and Pearce (2000) observed significant associations between top management team-shared leadership measures and firm sales growth and volume. Taggar, Hackett, and Saha (1999) found evidence for shared leadership in student work teams, even as their results showed that team members reached a high level of agreement about which single individual member scored highest on peer-rated leadership. In a multiple regression analysis, the average leadership rating of participants other than the single highest-rated individual significantly predicted team performance, whereas the regression weight for the single highest-rated individual was not significant. The interaction between the average participant leadership score and the single highest-rated individual's score, however, was significant. The pattern of this interaction reflected a conjunctive model, such that high performance resulted only from the combination of relatively high leadership from the single highest individual with a high average level of leadership from the other participants.

Even if shared leadership does prove beneficial to performance, future research is needed to establish the reliability over time of emergent team leadership. The type of leadership that we have been considering in this chapter has many parallels to the dyadic leadership studied by Graen and his associates (e.g., Graen & Uhl-Bien, 1995). The most fundamental parallel may be the underlying concept of leadership. Here, both TMX and LMX owe a clear conceptual heritage to the definition of Katz and Kahn (1978) of leadership as an influence increment that goes beyond routine role compliance linked to formal organizational sanctions and rewards. Evidence from LMX research indicates that dyadic leadership is quite stable over time. Yet the foundation of LMX clearly rests on how a supervisor can build on her or his positional resources and formal authority as the personal representative of the organization (Graen, 1976). Emergent team leadership is clearly influence without authority. Its stability may turn out to depend on the stability of task and goal requirements. Self-directing work teams are often used when much flexibility is required due to changing task requirements, and the ability of individuals to maintain a role based on their special abilities to contribute to group task effectiveness might change almost as suddenly as goals may change.

Our analysis also suggests that future research should address the question of the conditions under which shared leadership may occur. If we grant that shared leadership is possible, when is it *likely*? Would there be conditions under which it would be *required*? These questions may prove particularly important for self-directing work teams. Organizations that have adopted self-directing work teams have not always subsequently benefited from improved performance (Cohen & Bailey, 1997). Although it is clear that self-directing work teams should substitute, or at least supplement, employee authority and responsibility for supervisory authority and responsibility (Manz & Sims, 1987), the effectiveness of this substitution might be constrained if a single emergent leader simply assumes much the same influence role as the former formal supervisor.

Another issue involves the extent to which shared or distributed leadership may be specifically applicable in self-directing work teams. Seers, Petty, and Cashman (1995) argued that autonomous work teams "experience more peer-directed role-making interaction" (p. 21). As differentiated team roles reflect the various initiatives of different group members, those taking respected initiatives in different areas important to the group may all serve as leaders to some extent. Seers (1996) suggested that long recognized patterns of differentiation between and among various group task and relationship roles provided one possible scenario for self-directing work teams to employ simultaneous leadership contributions from multiple members.

The preceding two issues combine to suggest additional issues: How stable and effective is distributed or shared team leadership? Do groups revert to operating with a single leader atop a social hierarchy? Why might a structure of shared leadership endure? Why not? Shared leadership might be unstable if the implication of a long line of research on status hierarchy competition in small groups supports Ludwig's (2002) argument that the nature of leadership is that humans automatically compete so as to produce a pyramidal status hierarchy. Alternatively, shared leadership might conceivably exhibit greater stability than unitary leadership if it produces a leadership cadre whose collective skills and abilities provide a better match for evolving tasks and goals than do the skills and abilities of a single individual. This stability may develop as a function of group learning over time, such that shared leadership supplants group tendencies toward unitary leadership with repeated successful applications of distributed influence.

Future research should also investigate the relationship between task factors and influence patterns in self-directing work teams. Much of the research on the differentiation of influential roles and emergent leadership has been done in laboratory studies with simplified tasks in which a single shared goal is salient for all group members. Such tasks greatly oversimplify the often complex interdependencies within employee work teams. Organizational work groups rarely have only a single shared goal for which contributions can be rewarded with greater influence. It is possible that self-directing work teams may have complex tasks, such that different dimensions of specific status characteristics become relevant as the group's attention turns to different goals. Perhaps diffuse status characteristics can also have multiple bases within groups, such that different individuals are respected, and deferred to, for different reasons. Similarly, with respect to generalized exchange, individuals who contribute to different group needs, such as task performance versus the maintenance of harmonious relationships, may jointly derive complementary influence.

Because different tasks and goals may fluctuate over time in their importance, this suggests additional temporal dynamics of shared leadership that should be of interest. Perhaps shared leadership might be found to operate in its most stable manifestation in the group's division of labor as attention turns from one task or function to another. This suggests, however, that leadership might be shared only in the sense of a rotation in which only one individual will act as a leader at any one point in time. Such rotation appears to be assumed in Pearce and Sims's (2002) suggestion that "the concept of shared leadership might be thought of as 'serial emergence' of multiple leaders over the life of a team" (p.176).

Finally, the extent to which dyadic versus generalized exchange may underlie emergent leadership is certainly an issue that requires resolution through further research. Much of what is familiar to students of social exchange processes in leadership has been framed by the dyadic conceptualization underlying theory and research addressing the leader-member exchange model (Graen & Uhl-Bien, 1995). Indeed, a study by Gerstner and Tesluk (2000) constructed a peer group leadership measure as a composite of peer dyadic relationship measures. The only existing study in which dyadic assessments of peer working relationships have been competitively examined in comparison to the TMX approach may be that of Keup (2000). In Keup's study, a composite measure of dyadic peer exchange relationships across work teams, at the individual level of analysis, was used in conjunction with the Seers (1989) TMX measure. Both the dyadic measure and the original measure significantly predicted organizational commitment, job satisfaction, and perceived group performance, but the predictions were stronger for TMX than for the dyadic measure for each outcome.

# Conclusion

Our heritage of research from industrial-organizational psychologists, social psychologists, and sociologists may serve us well as the machine bureaucracies of the 20th century give way to more flexible organizations. The clear trend is toward the design of organizations that must change much too quickly to have the bulk of their human resource investment tied up in elaborate structures of formal authority. Research and theory on emergent and shared leadership should indeed prove even more useful in the future than it has been in the past.

What little evidence exists appears to suggest that shared leadership is possible and even beneficial. We have many more questions than answers, however. Nonetheless, we see this as befitting the current state of transition in which new organizational forms are emerging, which differ from previous bureaucratic hierarchical forms that gave birth to our leadership theories. Self-managed teams constitute one of the most prominent features of post–industrial era organizations. Whether shared leadership is possible within those teams, and through what processes such influence is gained, may be key questions on the frontier of leadership research for 21st-century organizations.

# References

Axelrod, R. (1986). An evolutionary approach to norms. *American Political Science Review, 80,* 1095-1111.

Bales, R. F. (1958). Task roles and social roles in problem-solving groups. In E. E. Maccoby, T. M. Newcomb, & E. L. Hartley (Eds.), *Readings in social psychology* (pp. 437-447). New York: Henry Holt.

Bales, R. F., Cohen, S. P., & Williamson, S. A. (1979). *SYMLOG: A system for the multiple level observation of groups.* New York: Free Press.

Bales, R. F., & Slater, P. E. (1955). Role differentiation in small decision-making groups. In T. Parsons & R. F. Bales (Eds.), *Family, socialization, and interaction processes* (pp. 259-306). New York: Free Press.

Barry, D. (1991). Managing the bossless team: Lessons in distributed leadership. *Organizational Dynamics, 21*(1), 31-47.

Bass, B. M. (1949). An analysis of the leaderless group discussion. *Journal of Applied Psychology, 33,* 627-633.

Bass, B. M. (1985). Leadership and performance beyond expectations. New York: Free Press.

Bass, B. M. (1990). *Bass and Stogdill's handbook of leadership: Theory, research, and managerial applications* (3rd ed.). New York: Free Press.

Bearman, P. (1997). Generalized exchange. *American Journal of Sociology, 102,* 1383-1415.

Berger, J., Cohen, B. P., & Zelditch, M. (1972). Status characteristics and social interaction. *American Sociological Review, 37,* 241-255.

Berger, J., & Zelditch, M. (1985). *Status, rewards, and influence: How expectations organize behavior.* San Francisco: Jossey-Bass.

Berger, J., & Zelditch, M. (1998). *Status, power, and legitimacy: Strategies and theories.* New Brunswick, NJ: Transaction.

Berkowitz, L. (1953). Sharing leadership in small decision-making groups. *Journal of Abnormal and Social Psychology, 48,* 231-238.

Blau, P. M. (1964). *Exchange and power in social life.* New York: Wiley.

Borgatta, E. F., & Bales, R. F. (1956). Sociometric status patterns and characteristics of interaction. *Journal of Social Psychology, 43,* 289-297.

Burke, P. J. (1974). Participation and leadership in small groups. *American Sociological Review, 35,* 832-843.

Cappella, J. N. (1985). Controlling the floor in conversation. In A. W. Siegman & S. Feldstein (Eds.), *Multichannel integrations of nonverbal behavior* (pp. 69-103). Hillsdale, NJ: Erlbaum.

Carter, L. F. (1954). Recording and evaluating the performance of individuals as members of small groups. *Personnel Psychology, 7,* 477-484.

Cashman, J., Dansereau, F., Graen, G., & Haga, W. J. (1976). Organizational understructure and leadership: A longitudinal investigation of the managerial role-making process. *Organizational Behavior and Human Performance, 15,* 278-296.

Cohen, S. G., & Bailey, D. E. (1997). What makes teams work: Group effectiveness research from the shop floor to the executive suite. *Journal of Management, 23,* 239-290.

Cook, K. S. (1987). *Social exchange theory.* Newbury Park, CA: Sage.

DeSouza, G., & Klein, H. J. (1995). Emergent leadership in the group goal-setting process. *Small Group Research, 26,* 475-496.

Eagly, A. H., & Karau, S. J. (1991). Gender and the emergence of leaders: A meta-analysis. *Journal of Personality and Social Psychology, 60,* 685-710.

Ekeh, P. P. (1974). *Social exchange theory: The two traditions.* Cambridge, MA: Harvard University Press.

Emerson, R. M. (1962). Power-dependence relations. *American Sociological Review, 27,* 31-41.

Ensley, M. D., & Pearce, C. L. (2000, June). *Vertical and shared leadership in new venture top management teams: Implications for new venture performance.* Paper presented at the 20th Annual Entrepreneurship Research Conference, Babson College, Babson Park, MA.

Ensley, M. D., Pearson, A., & Pearce, C. L. (in press). Top management team process, shared leadership, and new venture performance: A theoretical model and research agenda. *Human Resource Management Review.*

Feldman, R. A. (1973). Power distribution, integration, and conformity in small groups. *American Journal of Sociology, 79,* 639-665.

Festinger, L. (1950). Informal social communication. *Psychological Review, 57,* 271-282.

Fiedler, F. E. (1964). A contingency model of leadership effectiveness. In L. Berkowitz (Ed.), *Advances in experimental social psychology* (pp. 149-190). New York: Academic Press.

Fleishman, E. A. (1973). Twenty years of consideration and structure. In E. A. Fleishman & J. G. Hunt (Eds.), *Current developments in the study of leadership* (pp. 1-40). Carbondale: Southern Illinois University Press.

Foti, R. J., & Hauenstein, N. M. A. (1996, April). Linking leadership emergence to leadership effectiveness and team performance in a military population. In R. Foti (Chair), *Linking leadership emergence to assessment centers, leadership effectiveness, and development.* Symposium presented at the Society for Industrial and Organizational Psychology, San Diego, CA.

Gerard, R. J. (1995). Teaming up: Making the transition to a self-directed, team-based organization. *Academy of Management Executive, 9*(3), 91-93.

Gergen, K. J., Greenberg, M. S., & Willis, R. H. (1980). *Social exchange: Advances in theory and research.* New York: Plenum Press.

Gerstner, C., & Tesluk, P. E. (2000, April). Peer leadership in self-managing teams: Examining team leadership through a social network analytic approach. In J. L. Cordery (Chair), *Leadership and team effectiveness.* Symposium presented at the Society for Industrial and Organizational Psychology, New Orleans, LA.

Gillmore, M. R. (1987). Implications of general versus restricted exchange. In K. S. Cook (Ed.), *Social exchange theory* (pp. 170-189). Newbury Park, CA: Sage.

Godfrey, D. K., Jones, E. E., & Lord, C. G. (1986). Self-promotion is not ingratiating. *Journal of Personality and Social Psychology, 50,* 106-115.

Goktepe, J. R., & Schneier, C. E. (1989). Role of sex, gender roles, and attraction in predicting emergent leaders. *Journal of Applied Psychology, 74,* 165-167.

Graen, G. (1976). Role making processes within complex organizations. In M. D. Dunnette (Eds.), *Handbook of industrial and organizational psychology* (pp. 1201-1245). Chicago: Rand McNally.

Graen, G. B., & Scandura, T. A. (1987). Toward a psychology of dyadic organizing. In L. L. Cummings & B. M. Staw (Eds.), *Research in organizational behavior* (pp. 175-208). Greenwich, CT: JAI Press.

Graen, G. B., & Uhl-Bien, M. (1995). Relationship-based approach to leadership: Development of leader-member exchange (LMX) theory of leadership over 25 years: Applying a multi-level multi-domain perspective. *Leadership Quarterly, 6,* 219-247.

Gronn, P. (1999). Substituting for leadership: The neglected role of the leadership couple. *Leadership Quarterly, 10,* 41-62.

Guastello, S. J. (1995). Facilitative style, individual innovation, and emergent leadership in problem solving groups. *Journal of Creative Behavior, 29,* 225-239.

Heath, A. (1976). *Rational choice and social exchange: A critique of exchange theory.* Cambridge, UK: Cambridge University Press.

Hechter, M. (1987). *Principles of group solidarity.* Berkeley, CA: University of California Press.

Hodgson, R. C., Levinson, D. J., & Zaleznik, A. (1965). *The executive role constellation: An analysis of personality and role relations in management.* Boston: Harvard University Division of Research.

Hollander, E. P. (1964). *Leaders, groups, and influence.* New York: Oxford University Press.

Homans, G. C. (1958). Social behavior as exchange. *American Journal of Sociology, 63,* 597-606.

Homans, G. C. (1961). *Social behavior: Its elementary forms.* New York: Harcourt Brace & World.

Horner, M. A. (1998). The process of shared team leadership: A study of key leadership behaviors and who exhibits them. *Dissertation Abstracts International, 58* (11B), 6265 (AAG9816141).

House, R. J. (1977). A 1976 theory of charismatic leadership. In J. G. Hunt & L. L. Larson (Eds.), *Leadership: The cutting edge* (pp. 189-207). Carbondale: Southern Illinois University Press.

Jacobs, T. O. (1970). *Leadership and exchange in formal organizations.* Alexandria, VA: Human Resources Research Organization.

Johnson, S. D., & Bechler, C. (1998). Examining the relationship between listening effectiveness and leadership emergence: Perceptions, behaviors, and recall. *Small Group Research, 29,* 452-471.

Joinson, C. (1999). Teams at work. *HRMagazine, 44*(5), 30-36.

Katz, D., & Kahn, R. L. (1966). *The social psychology of organizations.* New York: Wiley.

Katz, D., & Kahn, R. L. (1978). *The social psychology of organizations* (2nd ed.). New York: Wiley.

Kent, R. L., & Moss, S. E. (1994). Effects of sex and gender role on leader emergence. *Academy of Management Journal, 37,* 1335-1346.

Kerr, S., Schriesheim, C. A., Murphy, C. J., & Stogdill, R. M. (1974). Toward a contingency theory of leadership based upon the consideration and initiating structure literature. *Organizational Behavior and Human Performance, 12,* 62-82.

Keup, L. C. (2000). *A network of working relationships and its influence on individual job outcomes.* Unpublished doctoral dissertation, University of Manitoba, Winnipeg.

Kiernan, M. J. (1993). The new strategic architecture: Learning to compete in the twenty-first century. *Academy of Management Executive, 7*(1), 7-21.

Kolb, J. A. (1997). Are we still stereotyping leadership? A look at gender and other predictors of leader emergence. *Small Group Research, 28,* 370-393.

Lawler, E. E., Mohrman, S. A., & Ledford, G. E. (1995). *Creating high performance organizations: Practices and results of employee involvement and total quality management in Fortune 1000 companies.* San Francisco: Jossey-Bass.

Lazega, E. (2000). Rule enforcement among peers: A lateral control regime. *Organization Studies, 21,* 193-214.

Lazega, E., & Pattison, P. (1999). Multiplexity, generalized exchange and cooperation in organizations: A case study. *Social Networks, 21,* 67-90.

Lee, M. T., & Ofshe, R. (1981). The impact of behavioral style and status characteristics on social influence: A test of two competing theories. *Social Psychology Quarterly, 44,* 73-82.

Levine, J. M., & Moreland, R. L. (1990). Progress in small group research. *Annual Review of Psychology, 41,* 585-634.

Lévi-Strauss, C. (1969). *The elementary structures of kinship* (2nd ed.). Boston: Beacon.

Lindenberg, S. (1998). Solidarity: Its microfoundations and macro dependence. In P. Doreian & T. J. Fararo (Eds.), *The problem of solidarity: Theories and models* (pp. 61-112). London: Gordon & Breach.

Lockheed, M. E. (1985). Sex and social influence: A meta-analysis guided by theory. In J. Berger & M. Zelditch, Jr. (Eds.), *Status, rewards and influence: How expectations organize behavior* (pp. 406-429). San Francisco: Jossey-Bass.

Lord, R. G., De Vader, C. L., & Alliger, G. M. (1986). A meta-analysis of the relationships between personality traits and leadership perceptions. *Journal of Applied Psychology, 71,* 402-410.

Lord, R. G., Foti, R. J., & De Vader, C. L. (1984). A test of leadership categorization theory: Internal structure, information processing, and leadership perceptions. *Organizational Behavior and Human Performance, 34,* 343-378.

Lord, R. G., & Maher, K. J. (1991). *Leadership and information processing: Linking perceptions and performance.* Boston, MA: Rutledge.

Ludwig, A. M. (2002). *King of the mountain: The nature of political leadership.* Lexington, KY: University Press of Kentucky .

Mann, R. D. (1959). A review of the relationships between personality and performance in small groups. *Psychological Bulletin, 56,* 241-270.

Manz, C. C., & Sims, H. P. (1987). Leading workers to lead themselves: The external leadership of self-managing work teams. *Administrative Science Quarterly, 32,* 106-128.

Manz, C. C., & Sims, H. P. (1991). Super leadership: Beyond the myth of heroic leadership. *Organizational Dynamics, 19,* 18-35.

Mazur, A. (1973). Cross species comparison of status in established small groups. *American Sociological Review, 38,* 513-530.

Miles, R. E., & Creed, W. E. D. (1995). Organizational forms and managerial philosophies: A descriptive and analytical review. *Research in Organizational Behavior, 17,* 333-372.

Mintzberg, H. (1979). *The structuring of organizations.* Englewood Cliffs, NJ: Prentice Hall.

Moreland, R. L., & Levine, J. M. (1982). Socialization in small groups: Temporal changes in individual-group relations. *Advances in Experimental Social Psychology, 15,* 137-192.

Moreland, R. L., & Levine, J. M. (1984). Role transitions in small groups. In V. L. Allen & E. van de Vliert (Eds.), *Role transitions: Explorations and explanation* (pp. 181-195). New York: Plenum.

Morrow, I. J., & Stern, M. (1990). Stars, adversaries, producers, and phantoms at work: A new leadership typology. In K. Clark & M. Clark (Eds.), *Measures of leadership* (pp. 419-440). West Orange, NJ: Leadership Library of America.

Mullen, B., Salas, E., & Driskell, J. E. (1989). Salience motivation and artifact as contributions to the relation between participation rate and leadership. *Journal of Experimental Social Psychology, 25,* 545-559.

Neubert, M. J. (1999). Too much of a good thing or the more the merrier? Exploring the dispersion and gender composition of informal leadership in manufacturing teams. *Small Group Research, 30,* 635-646.

O'Connell, L. (1984). An exploration of exchange in three social relationships: Kinship, friendship, and the marketplace. *Journal of Social and Personal Relationships, 1,* 333-345.

Pearce, C. L., & Sims, H. P., Jr. (2000). Shared leadership: Toward a multi-level theory of leadership. *Advances in Interdisciplinary Studies of Work Teams, 7,* 115-139. Greenwich, CT: JAI Press.

Pearce, C. L, & Sims, H. P., Jr. (2002). Vertical versus shared leadership as predictors of the effectiveness of change management teams: An examination of aversive, directive, transactional, transformational, and empowering leader behaviors. *Group Dynamics, 6,* 172-197.

Perry, M. L., Pearce, C. L., & Sims, H. P., Jr. (1999). Empowered selling teams: How shared leadership can contribute to selling team outcomes. *Journal of Personal Selling & Sales Management, 19*(3), 35-51.

Phillips, J. S., & Lord, R.G. (1982). Schematic information processing and perception of leadership in problem solving groups. *Journal of Applied Psychology, 67,* 486-492.

Polodny, J. M., & Page, K. L. (1998). Network forms of organization. *Annual Review of Sociology, 24,* 57-76.

Regula, R. C., & Julian, J. W. (1973). The impact of quality and frequency of task contributions on perceived ability. *Journal of Social Psychology, 89,* 115-122.

Ridgeway, C. L. (1984). Dominance, performance, and status in groups: A theoretical analysis. In E. J. Lawler (Ed.), *Advances in group processes* (Vol. 1, pp. 59-93). Greenwich, CT: JAI Press.

Ridgeway, C. L. (1987). Nonverbal behavior, dominance, and the basis of status in task groups. *American Sociological Review, 52,* 683-694.

Ridgeway, C. L. (1988). Gender differences in task groups: A status and legitimacy account. In M. Webster & M. Foschi (Eds.), *Status generalization: New theory and research* (pp. 188-206). Stanford, CA: Stanford University Press.

Ridgeway, C. L., & Walker, H. A. (1995). Status structures. In K. S. Cook, G. A. Fine, & J. S. House (Eds.), *Sociological perspectives on social psychology* (pp. 281-310). Boston: Allyn & Bacon.

Roberts, H. E. (1996, April). *Investigating the role of personal attributes in leadership emergence.* Paper presented at the 11th annual meeting of the Society for Industrial and Organizational Psychology, San Diego, CA.

Roger, D. B., & Reid, R. L. (1982). Role differentiation and seating arrangements: A further study. *British Journal of Social Psychology, 21,* 23-29.

Sahlins, M. (1972). *Stone age economics.* New York: Aldine De Gruyter.

Sarbin, T. R., & Allen, V. L. (1968). Role theory. In G. Lindzey & E. Aronson (Eds.), *Handbook of social psychology: Vol. 1* (pp. 488-567). Reading, MA: Addison-Wesley.

Seers, A. (1989). Team-member exchange quality: A new construct for role making research. *Organizational Behavior and Human Decision Processes, 43,* 118-135.

Seers, A. (1996). Better leadership through chemistry: Toward a model of shared team leadership. In M. Beyerlein (Ed.), *Advances in interdisciplinary studies of work teams* (pp. 145-172). Greenwich, CT: JAI Press.

Seers, A. (2000, April). Leadership in self-directed work teams: Toward a role-making analysis of leadership emergence. In J. L. Cordery (Chair), *Leadership and team effectiveness.* Symposium presented at the Society for Industrial and Organizational Psychology, New Orleans, LA.

Seers, A., Ford, L. R., Wilkerson, J. M., & Moorman, T. E. (2001, September). *The generation of influence: Effects of leader-member exchange and team-member exchange.* Paper presented at annual meeting of the Southern Management Association, New Orleans, LA.

Seers, A., Petty, M. M., & Cashman, J. F. (1995). Team-member exchange under team and traditional management: A naturally occurring quasi-experiment. *Group and Organization Management, 20,* 18-38.

Sims, H. P., Jr., & Manz, C. C. (1996). *Company of heroes: Unleashing the power of self-leadership.* New York: Wiley.

Skvoretz, J. (1988). Models of participation in status-differentiated groups. *Social Psychology Quarterly, 51,* 43-57.

Slater, P. E. (1955). Role differentiation in small groups. *American Sociology Journal, 20,* 300-310.

Sorrentino, R. M., & Boutellier, R. G. (1975). The effect of quantity and quality of verbal interaction on ratings of leadership ability. *Journal of Experimental Social Psychology, 28,* 199-205.

Sparrowe, R. T., & Liden, R. C. (1997). Process and structure in leader-member exchange. *Academy of Management Review, 22,* 522-552.

Stewart, G. L., & Manz, C. C. (1995). Leadership for self-managing work teams: A typology and integrative model. *Human Relations, 48,* 347-370.

Stiles, W. B., Orth, J. E., Scherwitz, L., Hennrikus, D., & Vallbona, C. (1984). Role behaviors in routine medical interviews with hypersensitive patients: A repertoire of verbal exchanges. *Social Psychology Quarterly, 47,* 224-254.

Stiles, W. B., Lyall, L. M., Knight, D. P., Ickes, W., Waung, M., Hall, C. L., & Primeau, B. E. (1997). Gender differences in verbal presumptuousness and attentiveness. *Personality and Social Psychology Bulletin, 23,* 759-772.

Stogdill, R. M. (1948). Personal factors associated with leadership: A survey of the literature. *Journal of Psychology, 25,* 35-71.

Stogdill, R. M. (1974). *Handbook of leadership: A survey of the literature.* New York: Free Press.

Strozniak, P. (2000, September 18). Teams at work. *Industry Week, 47-50.*

Taggar, S., Hackett, R., & Saha, S. (1999). Leadership emergence in autonomous work teams: Antecedents and outcomes. *Personnel Psychology, 52,* 899-926.

Tajfel, H. (1981). *Human groups and social categories.* Cambridge, UK: Cambridge University Press.

Tajfel, H., & Turner, J. C. (1979). An integrative theory of intergroup conflict. In W. G. Austin, & S. Worchel (Eds.), *The psychology of intergroup relations* (pp. 33-48). Monterey, CA: Nelson-Hall.

Takahashi, N. (2000). The emergence of generalized exchange. *The American Journal of Sociology, 105,* 1105-1134.

Thibaut, J., & Kelley, H. H. (1959). *The social psychology of groups.* New York: Wiley.

Tsui, A. S., Egan, T. D., & O'Reilly, C. A. (1992). Being different: Relational demography and organizational attachment. *Administrative Science Quarterly, 37,* 549-579.

Tsui, A. S., & Gutek, B. A. (1999). *Demographic differences in organizations: Current research and future directions.* New York: Lexington Books/Macmillan, Inc.

Tuzlak, A., & Moore, J. C. (1984). Status, demeanor, and influence: An empirical reassessment. *Social Psychological Quarterly, 47,* 178-183.

Uehara, E. (1990). Dual exchange theory, social networks, and informal social support. *American Journal of Sociology, 96,* 521-557.

Wagner, D. G., & Berger, J. (1993). Status characteristics theory: The growth of a program. In J. Berger & M. Zelditch, Jr. (Eds.), *Theoretical research programs: Studies in the growth of theory* (pp. 24-63). Stanford, CA: Stanford University Press.

Waldersee, R., Simmons, R., & Eagleson, G. (1995). Pluralistic leadership in service change programs: Some preliminary findings. *Academy of Management Annual Meeting Best Paper Proceedings* (pp. 296-300). Vancouver, Canada: Madison Omnipress.

Weick, K. E. (1979). *The social psychology of organizing* (2nd ed.). Reading, MA: Addison Wesley.

Wheelan, S. A., & Johnston, F. (1996). The role of informal member leaders in a system containing formal leaders. *Small Group Research, 27,* 33-55.

Whitman, M. N. (1999). *New world, new rules: The changing role of the American corporation.* Boston: Harvard Business School Press.

Wilke, H. A. M. (1996). Status congruence in small groups. In E. Witte & J. H. Davis (Eds.), *Understanding group behavior: Small group processes and interpersonal relations* (pp. 67-91). Mahwah, NJ: Erlbaum.

Yamagishi, T., & Cook, K. S. (1993). Generalized exchange and social dilemmas. *Social Psychology Quarterly, 56,* 235-248.

Yamagishi, T., Jin, N., & Kiyonari, T. (1999). Bounded generalized reciprocity: Ingroup boasting and ingroup favoritism. *Advances in Group Processes, 16,* 161-197.

Yukl, G. A. (1998). *Leadership in organizations* (4th ed.). Englewood Cliffs, NJ: Prentice Hall.

Zaccaro, S. J., Foti, R. J., & Kenny, D. A. (1991). Self-monitoring and trait-based variance in leadership: An investigation of leader flexibility across multiple group rotations. *Journal of Applied Psychology, 76,* 308-315.

# CHAPTER 5

# The Role of Shared Cognition in Enabling Shared Leadership and Team Adaptability

*C. Shawn Burke*

*Stephen M. Fiore*

*Eduardo Salas*

O rganizations are increasingly using teams as a predominant strategy when faced with environments characterized by complexity and ambiguity. These teams are typically composed of two or more members who work interdependently and adaptively to accomplish a common goal or mission. Such teams typically have specific role assignments and they often disband once the goal is reached or mission is completed (Salas, Dickinson, Converse, & Tannenbaum, 1992). Moreover, due to the complicated nature of the tasks facing those in industry and the military, these teams are increasingly becoming cross-functional (see Northcraft, Polzer, Neale, & Kramer, 1995; Knight et al., 1999). Despite the proposed benefits of work teams (see Swezey & Salas, 1992), many real world examples have illustrated that they are not always effective (Hackman, 1990). Key among the reasons for the failure of teams to live up to their potential are (a) the failure to smoothly coordinate member action and (b) a lack of effective leadership to guide the coordination process. In fact, some have argued that the team leader's failure to guide and structure team experiences that facilitate the development and maintenance of coordinative, adaptive action can be a key factor in ineffective performance (Stewart & Manz, 1995). Clearly, coordinative, adaptive action is vital to successful team performance.

Although coordinative action has been studied extensively, team adaptability, or coordinative adaptive action, has received less attention. Nonetheless, there has recently been an increased focus on how to create team adaptability. With this increased attention comes several varied definitions of team adaptability, including (a) the ability of the team to continually improve team process by reconfiguring the network to meet the immediate contingencies within the environment (Kozlowski, Gully, Nason, & Smith, 1997), (b) learning new ways to perform a job (Noe & Ford, 1992), (c) the ability to make the necessary modifications in order to meet new challenges (Klein & Pierce, 2001), and (d) a shift in attention or focus in response to unpredictable and uncertain work conditions (Pulakos, Arad, Donovan, & Plamondon, 2000). Along with the various definitions, there has also been a distinction made between two major forms of adaptability, internal and external (Klein & Pierce, 2001). Internal adaptability refers to instances in which a team needs to make changes within its own structure, whereas external adaptability is the dynamic replanning that takes place during the execution of a plan or strategy. Moreover, both types of adaptability are often necessary (Klein & Pierce, 2001), especially in complex and ambiguous situations.

Within the leadership literature, it has been widely acknowledged that leadership functions can have a substantial impact on subordinate outcomes (Bass, 1990; House, 1977; Yukl, 1998). Similarly, team researchers have begun to argue that leadership can greatly affect the effectiveness and quality of team processes and outcomes (Burke, 1999; Kozlowski, Gully, Salas, & Cannon-Bowers, 1996; Marks & Zaccaro, 1997). One method by which team leadership can affect team effectiveness is by promoting both internal and external team adaptability. Although it is possible for the team leader to help in promoting both forms of team adaptability, the primary focus of this chapter will be on a form of *shared* team leadership (see Pearce, Perry, & Sims, 2001) that we argue will promote internal adaptability, albeit as a dynamic response to changing needs. Specifically, shared leadership refers to a leadership process in which the leadership function is dynamically transferred within the team. The transference of leadership functions is an adaptive response to either internal or external demands currently being imposed on the team. Given the above, the purpose of this chapter is twofold. First, we present a framework that serves to guide our thinking on the role that shared cognition has in shared leadership. This framework forms the theoretical basis for our approach to melding shared cognition with shared leadership. Second, we suggest a set of research propositions derived from this framework in order to form the foundation for a principled approach to research in this neglected but important area of team effectiveness.

# Team Leadership

Although there has been a wealth of research on the leadership of individuals, and on teams in general, until recently here has been a relatively small amount of research aimed at team leadership. For example, leadership researchers (see Komaki, Desselles, & Bowman, 1989) note that, despite the extensive leadership literature base, "neglected are the crucial differences between supervising individuals within teams and supervising individuals as individuals" (p. 522). Team researchers (see Marks & Zaccaro, 1997) similarly argue that, "the team literature either ignores leadership altogether or treats it as one of many performance functions, without recognizing the vital role it may play in driving other functions" (p. 3).

# Shared Team Leadership

Most of the work on leadership has been conducted on vertical leadership in which one individual projects downward influence on individuals (Pearce & Sims, 2000). As organizations become increasingly complex, however, vertical leadership may not be the most effective way to lead organizational teams. For example, Pearce and Sims (2002) found that another form of team leadership, shared leadership, was more effective than was the traditional process of vertical leadership. Others have similarly discussed the effect that shared team leadership can have on team effectiveness (see Avolio, Jung, Murry, & Sivasubramaniam, 1996; Barry, 1991; Klenke, 1997; Yukl, 1998).

Shared leadership is seen as a group process by which leadership is distributed among, and stems from, team members (Pearce & Sims, 2000). Others have defined it as: (a) leadership distributed among organizational units (Rawlings, 2000); and (b) a management model based on a philosophy of shared governance, in which those performing the work are the ones who best know how to improve the process (Jackson, 2000; Spooner, Keenan, & Card, 1997). Although a variety of definitions of shared leadership have recently been offered, there are underlying similarities among the differing approaches. Invariant among these is the notion that, as teams are increasingly composed of members who are multifunctional and highly skilled, coordination within the team may be improved if the team takes advantage of individual member strengths in terms of leadership.

For the purposes of this chapter, we define shared leadership as the transference of the leadership function among team members in order to take advantage of member strengths (e.g., knowledge, skills, attitudes, perspectives, contacts, and time available) as dictated by either environmental demands or the developmental stage of the team. Within environments using shared leadership, the leadership functions are transferred among team members dependent on the type of skills needed at each juncture of the team's development or driven by the demands of the situation. This transference of leadership functions may happen many times during the progression toward goal attainment or mission completion. As leadership functions are dynamically transferred among team members, effectiveness is heavily dependent on the smooth transference among team members (i.e., coordinated leadership transfer).

## Theoretical Basis

Although a relatively new concept, the notion of shared leadership fits either explicitly or implicitly within several theories of team leadership. For example, one of the most popular approaches to team leadership is the functional approach (see Lord, 1977). This approach builds on the open systems perspective that states that organizations are not static entities, but affect and are affected by the environment (Katz & Kahn, 1978). The functional approach (see McGrath, quoted in Hackman & Walton, 1986) argues that "the leader's main job is to do, or get done, whatever is not being adequately handled for group needs. If the leader manages by whatever means to ensure that critical team functions are being met, then the leader is considered effective" (p. 75). This approach relates to shared leadership in several ways. First, it recognizes that leadership is not defined by a specific set of behaviors, but by a generic set of responses that must be tailored to the individual situation. Task characteristics, interdependency level, and stage of team development are a few of the factors that may interact to cause the need to tailor generic leadership competencies. Second, although the leader must ensure that key functions are handled, these functions do not physically have to be accomplished by one person. As such, this approach may be argued to imply that key leadership functions can be shared or distributed throughout the team.

Another team leadership theory that supports the notion of sharing or distributing leadership within the team is that proposed by Kozlowski and colleagues. These researchers implicitly suggest that the leadership process can be shared due to the team needing different leadership functions as they progress developmentally. Within this framework, the sharing of leadership would be due to internal demands of the team that prepare them to face external challenges from the environment. Specifically, Kozlowski and colleagues argue that teams progress through approximately four developmental stages during which the leadership requirements change (Kozlowski, Gully, Nason, & Smith, 1997; Kozlowski, Gully, Salas, & Cannon-Bowers, 1997). Team leader functions range from that of a mentor, to instructor, to coach, and finally to facilitator, dependent on the stage of team development. As each leadership function requires different leadership competencies, it could be argued that team members may vary in their ability to carry out each of the leadership functions—forming the groundwork for shared leadership. An example of how shared leadership might unfold within this framework follows. While mentoring, the leader (a) melds members to the team, (b) clarifies the mission and team goals, (c) builds and clarifies norms for interaction, and (d) builds shared affect and attitudes. Conversely, while instructing, the leader (a) builds individual skill and proficiency and (b) develops member self-efficacy, knowledge, and cognitive structures. As these two functions may require different knowledge, skills, and abilities (KSAs), as well as different methods by which to achieve the goal of each function, team members may be differentially suited to assume each particular function.

Another approach to leadership that implicitly argues for shared team leadership is the work that has been done on empowered or self-managed teams (see Manz & Sims, 1987, 1989, 1993). This work has acknowledged that team members can and do take on leadership roles and functions that have been traditionally held by authority figures outside the team (i.e., vertical leadership). Moreover, within this framework Manz and Sims (1989) argue that the primary objective of the leader is to develop self-leadership abilities in followers (e.g., team members). The view taken within this approach is that shared leadership would occur in response to demands within the overall work environment, as opposed to internal team demands.

Although the above leadership approaches implicitly suggest the notion of shared or distributed leadership, other approaches explicitly argue for the sharing of leadership. For example, Klenke (1997) developed a model of *distributed leadership* in high-performance information systems teams. These teams perform work that is highly cognitive, involves continuous learning, and requires intensive interactive communications. As such, the distributed leadership model would be expected to generalize best to teams who have similar characteristics (e.g., cross-functional teams operating in complex environments). Thus, although this model was developed for application in a particular industry, many of its tenets transfer to other interdependent teams. The basis of this model is the contention that leadership styles and outcomes for effective teams will vary as a function of the work unit and the stage of team development. For example, within the teams studied, leaders function as coordinators, facilitators, coaches, and communicators, but not as authoritarians. Effective teams were also found to have a structure in which the leadership functions were distributed among members (i.e., different members performing the leadership functions at different times) with the knowledge and norm that the team as a whole is ultimately responsible for its performance. The distributed leadership model also suggests that each member must take initiative for his or her own development of leadership abilities and facilitate the leadership of other team members by cultivating leadership processes, functions, and roles in order to maximize performance at each stage of team development (Klenke, 1997).

In sum, there are several theories as well as limited research (see Avolio et al., 1996; Pearce & Sims, 2000; Perry, Pearce, & Sims, 1999) within the area of leadership that either implicitly or explicitly notes the value of shared leadership. From a practical standpoint, shared leadership makes good "business" sense in that, as complexity increases, a sole team leader may have a difficult time completing the necessary and varied leadership functions now required to keep the team successful. For example, the cognitive demands may be such that one individual is no longer able to perform all the leadership functions (e.g., multitasking). In addition, as complexity increases it becomes probable that no one individual will have all the requisite knowledge, skills, abilities, and network contacts that would enable him or her to accomplish all of the leadership functions without distributing them among the team. Finally, the transference of the leadership function from one member to another helps the team remain adaptive to internal and external team demands. Nonetheless, what is lacking is a characterization of the antecedent conditions necessary for the effective implementation of shared leadership. Toward that end, we next discuss the theoretical framework developed to articulate the factors that drive shared leadership. More specifically, although we have articulated two distinct forms of shared leadership, we focus our framework on the more dynamic form of leadership transfer occurring within particular situations and driven by environmental demands.

# Framework

The framework that is presented in Figure 5.1 illustrates the four cognitive drivers that we suggest are foundational to the effective enactment of shared team leadership: mental models, situation assessment, metacognition, and attitudes (see Table 5.1 for definitions of key model constructs). Two of these cognitive drivers are dynamic because they are enacted within the context of a particular need, whereas two are static because they represent cognitive products used by team members.

**Table 5.1**  Definition of Key Cognitive Constructs Pertaining to the Enablement of Shared Leadership.

| Construct | Definition |
|---|---|
| Situation assessment | Interpretation of stimuli from the environment, primarily the external environment. Interpretation of cues and cue relevance used to recognize that a problem exists and some action is required (Orasanu, 1990). |
| Metacognition | Awareness of one's own cognitive processes and the ability to understand, control, and manipulate these processes (Davidson et al., 1994). |
| Mental models | Cognitive structures containing knowledge of the equipment, task, team, and situation (Rouse et al., 1992). |
| Shared mental models | Possession of compatible mental models among team members. These structures have been purported to enable coordination (Orasanu, 1990). |
| • Team mental models | Model containing knowledge pertaining to the individual's role in the team, the role of fellow team members, their characteristics, and the collective requirements needed for effective team interaction (Cannon-Bowers, Salas, & Converse, 1993). |
| • Situation mental model | Developed while the team is actively engaged in the task, context-specific, and changing as the situation changes. Represents the team's collective understanding of the situation at any given point in time and makes use of preexisting mental models (Cooke et al., 2000). |
| Member attitudes | Beliefs and dispositional attributes held by team members. |
| • Collective efficacy | Shared belief that a group can execute a specific task (Guzzo et al., 1993); an individual's belief in his or her team's ability to achieve a desired level of performance (Zaccaro et al., 1995). |
| • Collective orientation | The tendency to coordinate, evaluate, and use task inputs from other group members in an interdependent manner when performing a group task (Driskell & Salas, 1992). |

Within this model, the dynamic cognitive processes are composed of (a) situation assessment (i.e., the interpretation of stimuli from the external environment) and (b) metacognition (i.e., the dynamic monitoring of one's interpretation of the external environment in conjunction with internal factors). The static cognitive drivers consist of: (a) mental models (i.e., cognitive structures containing knowledge of the equipment, task, team, and situation) and (b) member attitudes (i.e., beliefs and dispositional attributes held by team members, in this case related to shared leadership). The confluence of these factors can be considered a *situation mental model*, which is a dynamic model arising in the context of specific events.

Effective use of these drivers can best be understood through the use of the shared cognition construct. In order for a team to make use of these factors, there

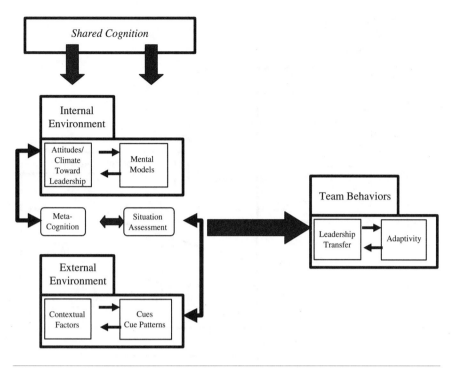

**Figure 5.1**     Schematic of Shared Cognition As It Relates to Shared Team Leadership and Team Adaptivity

has to be a degree of overlap in the team's understanding of each driver (i.e., the knowledge and procedures associated with the team need to be in congruence). We suggest that the cognitive drivers depicted in Figure 5.1 work together to enable shared team leadership in the following manner. Shared mental models describe the degree to which long-term memory structures held by team members are aligned such that substantial agreement exists. This shared knowledge serves to guide coordinated action and affects the development of shared situational assessment among team members. Shared situation assessment involves the scanning of the environment and the perceiving of cues and patterns in a dynamic context. Information gained during this assessment process is then integrated into existing knowledge structures serving to update members' shared mental models (Salas, Cannon-Bowers, Fiore, & Stout, 2001). Simultaneous to this dynamic assessment process is the requirement to regulate one's own monitoring and interpretation of input, that is, to engage in metacognitive processes that allow one to modify active mental models to provide a context-sensitive assessment of the current situation. Within the team, this assessment needs to be shared to promote a common awareness of the situation, which serves to guide action. Nonetheless, it is not enough that team members have a common understanding of the situation; there also needs to be a shared recognition among members that, due to something in the environment, the leadership function needs to, or is about to, change.

The final enabling factor within the model is an attitudinal factor: There needs to be a "climate" created such that members feel it is acceptable to have fluid

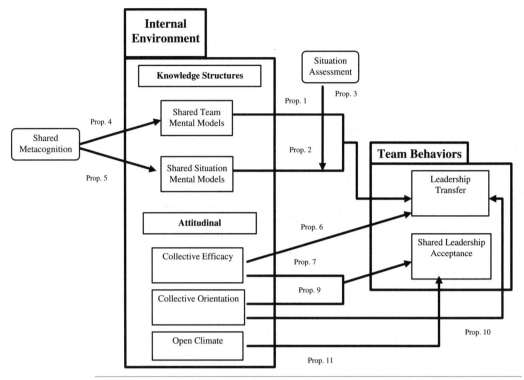

**Figure 5.2**  Graphical Representation of Propositions Set Forth Within the Chapter

leadership roles. This not only involves the realization that some ambiguity is to be expected but also that members are comfortable with taking guidance and cues from different people, dependent on who is currently assuming the leadership function. The confluence of these factors is a smooth transference of leadership from one member to another and the facilitation of adaptive team behaviors. We next describe the cognitive drivers presented in our framework along with a set of propositions concerning their relation to shared team leadership. See Figure 5.2 for a graphical depiction of all propositions.

## Shared Mental Models

Within the team literature, many argue that teams are able to collectively coordinate their actions and adapt to a changing performance environment through the use of shared or compatible mental models (e.g., Cannon-Bowers & Salas, 2001; Cannon-Bowers, Salas, & Converse, 1990; Mathieu, Heffner, Goodwin, Salas, & Cannon-Bowers, 2000; Minionis, 1994; Rouse & Morris, 1986). Dependent on the domain within which the term is used, definitions of mental models vary somewhat. For example, within cognitive science, mental models are described as structured knowledge involved in the comprehension of a given phenomena, and they are used to assist in drawing inferences (e.g., Johnson-Laird, 1983). Human factors researchers analogously suggest that mental models allow one to both generate descriptions of systems, as well as make predictions about future system states (e.g., Rouse, Cannon-Bowers, & Salas, 1992). Organizational psychologists argue that mental models are representations of knowledge elements in an employee's environment along with the elements' interrelations (Klimoski & Mohammed, 1994).

In terms of teams and shared leadership, it is not enough that members possess mental models; they must also be shared or hold compatible knowledge (Cannon-Bowers & Salas, 1990; Orasanu, 1990). The possession of compatible mental models have an impact on shared team leadership because they allow members to operate under a common set of assumptions. These assumptions or expectations serve to guide how both individuals and the team as a whole respond to environmental cues as well as what aspects of the situation or task elicit their attention. More specifically, shared mental models serve to guide the coordinated action needed for the smooth transference of leadership functions among team members. In order for shared mental models to be functional in terms of promoting shared leadership, at least two prerequisites need to be met. First, team members must be aware that the expectations arising from mental models are shared or else they may not act on these expectations (Klimoski & Mohammed, 1994; Rentsch & Hall, 1994). For example, fellow team members must have the expectation that in situations having characteristics "X," team Member A will assume the leadership function, enabling smooth transference without explicit communication. Second, *flexible* shared mental models need to be possessed by the team so that members do not fall into the trap of conformity norms in which they feel there is only one right way to do things, possibly blocking using new strategies or the updating of existing mental models. For example, in time-pressure situations, team Member B may normally assume the leadership function. It may be, however, that in the current situation there is time pressure, but team Member B is already overloaded. The individual knowledge structures of the team need to be flexible enough to account for this, which means that team members must be aware of standard procedures yet also be aware of which member could act as a substitute if the team is to appropriately adapt.

Although there are many mental models that, when shared, serve to guide team performance (e.g., equipment, task, team, and situation; see Cannon-Bowers, Salas, & Converse, 1993), we focus on two that are most relevant to enabling shared leadership—team and situation models. The team mental model is a mental model that contains declarative, procedural, and strategic knowledge (Converse & Kahler, 1992). It contains knowledge pertaining to (a) the individual's role in the task, (b) the role(s) of fellow team members (i.e., team member characteristics—their task knowledge, skills, abilities, and preferences), and (c) the individual and collective requirements needed for effective team interaction. This includes how each member's role and responsibilities intersect with those of other members on the team, allowing members to anticipate and sequence their collective actions. Given that this mental model contains knowledge related to team member characteristics, it serves as a key resource for team members to determine to whom the leadership function needs to transfer. For example, the situation may demand the need for immediate boundary spanning—based on team mental models, the team should know which member is best suited to handle this function. Shared team mental models are also important to the implementation of shared leadership in that they contain the basis for determining the value of member contributions (via knowledge of team member characteristics). We offer the following proposition with respect to shared mental models:

Proposition 1: Team mental models play a key role in the smooth transference of the leadership function as they guide the action of to whom the leadership should be transferred, based on members' knowledge of their fellow teammates.

The situation model is perhaps the most dynamic of the mental models. Cooke, Salas, Cannon-Bowers, and Stout (2000) argue that this model is developed while the team is actively engaged in the task, is context-specific, and changes as the situation changes. The situation model represents the team's collective understanding of the situation at any given point in time and makes use of preexisting team models. As this model represents the team's collective understanding of the specific situation at a given point in time, its role in the implementation of effective shared leadership is that it guides the determination of when the leadership function should transfer. Given these factors, we offer the following proposition:

Proposition 2: Shared situation models guide the determination of when the leadership function needs to be transferred.

## Shared Situation Assessment

Related to shared mental models is the second component within our framework, situation assessment. Situation assessment refers to (a) the interpretation of cues and cue relevance used to recognize that a problem or opportunity exists and that some action or decision is required (Orasanu, 1990); and (b) the process whereby knowledge contained in members' mental models is integrated with information within the environment in order to understand, explain, and predict behavior in the context at hand (Cooke, Stout, & Salas, 1997; Stout, Cannon-Bowers, & Salas, 1996). Through this process, the importance of the environmental cues and cue patterns is determined with the resultant product being a state of situation awareness (e.g., see Endsley, 1997; Endsley & Garland, 2000) leading to the decision of whether action is required at the current time. This suggests an almost iterative process whereby multiple exposures to environmental stimuli (e.g., differing experiences in differing contexts) and the resultant situation assessment taking place serve to aid in both the construction and the modification of mental models.

Although this process is typically thought of as one whereby individuals are assessing the environment outside the team, an alternative viewpoint is that members may also be assessing the environment within the team to determine, from a developmental view, when leadership function(s) need to change. With either function, the processes involved in situation assessment are (a) dynamic, (b) iterative, and (c) have been found to be one of the most critical facets of successful knowledge acquisition and application (see Bransford, Franks, Vye, & Sherwood, 1989; Bruner, Goodnow, & Austin, 1956; Cannon-Bowers & Bell, 1997; Chi, Glaser, & Farr, 1988; Endsley, 1989a, 1989b; Gibson, 1969; Kaempf & Klein, 1994; Klayman, 1988; Klein, 1989; Perfetto, Bransford, & Franks, 1983; Rumelhart, 1980; Salas et al., 2001). As such, shared situation assessment should aid in the determination of when the leadership function should transfer. Within the context of shared team leadership, the *process* of situation assessment requires the *product* of shared mental models.

Specifically, although situation assessment is an inherently individual process to the degree that the team members overlap in their knowledge (i.e., possess shared mental models), the appropriate interpretation of, and reactions to, the environment can make this a shared process. As discussed previously, these shared mental models include the cognitive structures involved in coordinating routines as well as the task knowledge within the team (Artman, 2000). Thus, existing mental models will guide the determination of cue information that is critical and what information within the situation assessment process needs to be shared with whom (Salas et al., 2001). For shared leadership to occur within teams, shared situation assessment needs to occur so that members know when the transference of the leadership function needs to happen. Team members need to establish a norm for periodically communicating relevant aspects of individual situation assessments to ensure that members are operating from similar perceptions regarding the current state of the team and its environment.

Within highly complex and dynamic environments, the process of sharing information to create shared situation assessment is critical for it is likely that members may each perceive different aspects of the environment. Furthermore, dependent on the distribution of members and the complexity of the situation, it is possible that one member may assess a certain situation and subsequently engage in leadership behavior toward the team, whereas in another situation a different member plays a similar role. What is critical is that this assessment is communicated so that members are able to have the common ground needed to effectively transfer the leadership function.

As such, the following proposition is offered in terms of how shared situation assessment drives effective shared team leadership.

> Proposition 3: Shared situation assessment moderates the relationship between shared situation models and the determination of when the leadership function should transfer.

## Shared Metacognition

Another enabling mechanism to shared leadership is the requirement to regulate one's monitoring and interpretation of input, which means to engage in meta-cognitive processes that allow one to modify active mental models—providing a context sensitive assessment of the current situation. Metacognition has been investigated in many domains and can be described as an awareness of one's own cognitive processes and the ability to understand, control, and manipulate these processes (Davidson, Deuser, & Sternberg, 1994; Flavell, 1976; Lord & Emrich, 2001; Osman & Hannafin, 1992). Similarly, Garner (1994) suggests that metacognition involves knowledge of oneself, of the tasks we engage in, and of the strategies used while engaged in tasks.

Metacognition has been shown to have a substantial impact on (a) learning and the development of expertise (Osman & Hannafin, 1992; Sternberg, 1998), (b) performing when training for complex team tasks (Ford, Smith, Weissbein, Gully, & Salas, 1998), and (c) social intelligence (i.e., the ability to perceive sensitive social requirements) allowing one to adjust behavior accordingly (Zaccaro, Gilbert, Thor, & Mumford, 1991). In terms of its relation to shared leadership, we argue that although teams are progressing through the dynamic assessment process involved in shared situation assessment, the requirement also exists for team members to be dynamically regulating one's monitoring and interpretation of input. Metacognition describes this process whereby effective teams evaluate themselves during the interaction context (Lord & Emrich, 2001). The monitoring of actions in this manner allows members to more effectively select the appropriate behavioral scripts and modify active mental models.

Within the context of shared leadership, we argue that metacognition is the process that allows members to guide action and, more specifically, guide the choice of when the leadership function should change. This is important for it allows a context-sensitive assessment of the current situation. When combined with team shared mental models, metacognition allows the shared diagnosis of to whom the leadership role must transfer enabling the seamless coordination of leadership transfer.

> Proposition 4: Shared metacognition enables the development (i.e., updating) of appropriate shared team mental models, which, in turn, guide members in determining to whom the leadership function needs to transfer.

> Proposition 5: Shared metacognition enables the development (i.e., updating) of appropriate shared situation models, which, in turn, guide members in determining when the leadership function needs to change.

We suggest that shared leadership in dynamic environments is made up of the convergence of (a) the appropriate team knowledge that results in shared mental models, (b) the interaction experience that leads to the ability to engage in shared situation assessment, and (c) the activation and application of the metacognitive processes that lead members to recognize when something in the environment requires that the leadership function needs to, or is about to, change. We next discuss the final contributing factor that enables shared leadership, the set of attitudes conducive to a flexible, dynamic leadership process.

## Shared Attitudes

For leadership transfer to be effectively implemented, team members must possess a core set of shared attitudes that promote this form of leadership. Attitudes have commonly been defined (Cannon-Bowers, Tannenbaum, Salas, & Volpe, 1995) as "an internal state that influences an individual's choices or decisions to act in a certain way under particular circumstances" (p. 354). Others have theorized that shared attitudes are a necessary, but not sufficient, component in the development of shared mental models in newly forming teams (Fiore, Salas, & Cannon-Bowers, 2001). Here we argue that team members must possess attitudes that allow them to feel comfortable with (a) fluidity, (b) ambiguity, and (c) taking guidance from different people, dependent on who is leading the team. As such, we suggest that three specific attitudes will have a direct effect on the successful implementation of shared team leadership: (a) collective efficacy, (b) collective orientation, and (c) perception of an open climate.

## Collective Efficacy

Original conceptualizations of collective efficacy referred to a team or group's ability to perform effectively as a unit, given some set of specific task demands (Bandura, 1986). Others have defined it as (a) assessment of the team's collective ability to perform that task at hand (Riggs, 1989), (b) shared conviction that a group can execute a specific task (Guzzo, Yost, Campbell, & Shea, 1993), and (c) an individual's belief in their team's ability to achieve a desired level of performance (Zaccaro, Blair, Peterson, & Zazanis, 1995).

Although a number of empirical studies have documented its positive relationship with team performance (Bandura, 1986; Zaccaro et al., 1995; Pearce, Gallagher, & Ensley, in press; Spink, 1990), we would also argue for its importance in the process of shared team leadership. Specifically, within the context of shared leadership, collective efficacy is relevant because it reflects an attitude or feeling of confidence regarding the abilities of fellow teammates. When more than one individual will occupy the leadership role, as with shared leadership, it is necessary that fellow team members have confidence in the ability of each member assuming the leadership role at any given time. Without a belief in that person's ability, members may be reluctant to follow guidance or direction given by that member. Similarly, Jackson (2000) has argued that a lack of respect for fellow members' contributions can be a key barrier to the implementation of effective leadership. As such, we propose the following relationship between collective efficacy and shared team leadership:

> Proposition 6: Collective efficacy will be positively related to effective transference of the leadership function among team members.

> Proposition 7: Collective efficacy will be positively related to team members feeling comfortable taking guidance from fellow team members, as they occupy the leadership role.

## Collective Orientation

Collective orientation has been defined (Driskell & Salas, 1992) as "the tendency to coordinate, evaluate, and use task inputs from other group members in an interdependent manner in performing a group task" (p. 278). This includes the capacity to take others' behavior into account and the belief that the team's goals should have higher priority than the goals of individual members.

Collective orientation represents a necessary environmental component for enabling the implementation of shared team leadership for the following reasons. First, some suggest that individual career goals may be a barrier to the effective implementation of shared leadership (Porter-O'Grady, Hawkins, & Parker, 1997). Individuals high in collective orientation may put the team's goals above individual goals and should be less susceptible to this barrier. Second, individuals scoring high on collective orientation scales typically enjoy working and coordinating with others (Driskell & Salas, 1992). Given that shared team leadership involves a high level of this type of coordination and integration of other member inputs, this suggests a positive relationship. Third, as collective orientation involves the capacity to take others' behavior into account (Driskell & Salas, 1992), members who are high on this attitude may be more likely to respect other member contributions and be open to fellow members' input (Fiore et al., 2001).

Although high levels of collective orientation may promote the effective implementation of shared team leadership, it could also be argued that this attitude may inhibit members from assuming the leadership role. For example, individuals high on this dimension may not seek a leadership role as it could be construed as counter to their values (e.g., putting their needs above that of the team). It would, however, seem that the potentially detrimental effect of high levels of collective orientation could be mitigated dependent on the framing of the situation. Nonetheless, future research needs to investigate this possibility. Overall we argue that collective orientation will enable shared team leadership, and we put forth the following propositions:

> Proposition 8: High levels of collective orientation will be positively related to the acceptance of shared team leadership.

> Proposition 9: High levels of collective orientation will enable the transference of leadership.

### Organizational Climate

The climate that exists in an organization will be a key determinant of the effectiveness with which shared team leadership is implemented. At its most basic, shared team leadership involves a partnership among team members. In order for this partnership to be successful, members need to perceive that they are part of an open climate in which ideas and opinions are freely exchanged and respected. When organizational norms are perceived to favor collective efforts, people are more likely to seek assistance and thus improve overall performance. Following this, it may be that such organizational cultures will similarly favor the open transference of leadership. Specifically, individuals occupying the leadership role need to understand not only their own strengths and weaknesses (enabled by metacognition) but also need to be comfortable learning from fellow teammates (when the leadership role is transferred). The only way in which this will happen is if members feel connected and that they are operating in an open climate.

The creation of an organizational climate that is not only perceived as being open, but also is one in which the norm is created that this type of leadership structure is not only possible and acceptable but also highly valued, is a necessity in order for shared leadership to be effective. Because American work culture has traditionally promoted individualism as opposed to a collective orientation, such a shift in leadership norms has been problematic for many organizations. Shared leadership is perhaps the truest form of collectivism, even more so than team-based work structures.

> Proposition 10: An open organizational climate will be positively related to the effective implementation of shared team leadership.

> Proposition 11: The creation of a shared attitude, at both the team and organizational level, regarding the advantages of a fluid leadership structure will have a positive relationship with the implementation of effective shared team leadership.

## Summary

It may be that the promotion of shared attitudes among members and the organization as a whole is one of the most difficult, yet important, barriers to overcome in the implementation of shared team leadership. Because attitudes are, in general, difficult to modify, encouraging the adoption of the attitudes necessary to enable shared leadership is expected to be a challenge. Furthermore, the type of shared attitudes needed to enable effective shared leadership is contrary to the status quo within much of corporate America. Specifically, in order to enable shared leadership, members must share the power and authority. In addition, members need to have certain competencies, such as behavioral flexibility and adaptability. This, in turn, is what will allow members to not only feel comfortable with some level of ambiguity, but also provide them with the behavioral repertoire to function within this type of adaptive, dynamic environment.

# Conclusion

As environments continue to become increasingly complex and ill defined, organizations are increasingly turning to teams as a key strategy. These teams are being required to dynamically adapt to both changing internal and external demands as well as rapidly changing situations. Work has begun to show that the team leader can play a key role in team adaptivity (Burke, 1999; Kozlowski et al., 1996; Marks, Zaccaro, & Mathieu, 2000). As teams are increasingly becoming cross-functional and environmental complexity increases, however, it becomes more likely that a sole team leader may not be the most efficient use of team resources. Many are beginning to speak of a system in which leadership is dynamically shared among team members dependent on the specific competencies required by the current situation or context. Although this type of leadership fits within the context of some organizational needs and may even become a necessity as management structure continues to change, the initial implementation of such a system produces many challenges. Therefore, it becomes important to begin to understand and investigate the factors that may contribute to effective shared team leadership.

Our goal with the presented framework, along with the propositions enumerated, was to stimulate thinking along this critical but neglected area of team effectiveness. Within this chapter, we have argued for a set of four cognitive drivers that together enable the smooth transference of leadership and facilitate adaptive team behavior. These drivers include more static (shared mental models, shared attitudes) as well as more dynamic processes (shared metacognition, shared situation assessment). These processes interact with one another such that team members are able to recognize when the leadership function needs to change and to whom it needs to change, as well as create the shared attitude that the ambiguity contained within this process is acceptable both at a team and organizational level. We argued that shared mental models drive shared situational assessment, an iterative process, the results of which are integrated back into members' mental models. Simultaneous to this, metacognitive processes allow members to update situation mental models and contribute to an assessment of member strengths and weaknesses. Finally, members must also share the team attitudes that enable the acceptance of leadership transfer.

As the process of shared team leadership is a relatively new area, there is much work that remains to be done. First, future work should be more consistent in its use of terminology and better operationalize what is meant by the term "shared leadership." It would seem that the two factors that distinguish shared leadership from other forms of leadership are (a) the dynamic transference of the leadership function and (b) that team members themselves are assuming the leadership functions, a factor requiring a certain level of empowerment within teams. These two factors are not always readily apparent in many of the definitions that were found. Second, the propositions set forth in the current chapter need to be empirically evaluated and others factors should also be investigated. For example, the process of shared leadership raises several questions concerning advancement and reward allocation. Questions such as the following become important at the management level: "How should rewards be parsed?" "How do people advance within such a system?" And as the leadership process is fluid, "How do people receive credit?" In terms of the actual implementation of shared leadership, research needs to investigate the environmental situations in which it may be the most appropriate. Other questions involve the team itself and how it may affect the effectiveness of shared leadership. For example, is this form of leadership only appropriate for expert teams or can novices be taught the requisite KSAs needed to enact this process? Similarly, Pearce and Sims (2000) argue that the stage of group maturity may affect the display and form of shared leadership displayed within the group. Furthermore, with respect to training shared leadership, is it feasible for the real-time training to be used, or will selection to such teams be necessary a priori? If these KSAs are taught to novices, what is the best way to proceed in order to not to overload them? Finally, organizational change issues surrounding how to create the appropriate culture for shared leadership need to be examined.

In addition to many questions concerning what will serve to expand the nomological framework of shared team leadership are questions concerning measurement. Currently, most of the measures of shared leadership are based on self-reports. Behavioral observations along with knowledge elicitation techniques may be other methods by which to examine this phenomenon. Future research should continue to evaluate measurement instruments. In sum, the more rigorous the research and the more systematic the thinking on the relationship between shared cognition and shared leadership, the more principles and guidelines the field can offer to benefit organizational practice.

# References

Artman, H. (2000). Team situation assessment and information distribution. *Ergonomics, 43*(8), 1111-1128.

Avolio, B. J., Jung, D. I., Murry, W., & Sivasubramaniam, N. (1996). Building highly developed teams: Focusing on shared leadership processes, efficacy, trust, and performance. *Advances in Interdisciplinary Studies of Work Teams, 3,* 173-209. Greenwich, CT: JAI Press.

Bandura, A. (1986). *Social foundations of action and thought: A social cognitive view.* Englewood Cliffs, NJ: Prentice Hall.

Barry, D. (1991). Managing the bossless team: Lessons in distributed leadership. *Organizational Dynamics, 20*(1), 31-47.

Bass, B. M. (1990). *Bass and Stogdill's handbook of leadership: Theory, research, and managerial applications* (3rd ed.). New York: Free Press.

Bransford, J. D., Franks, J. J., Vye, N. J., & Sherwood, R. D. (1989). New approaches to instruction: Because wisdom can't be told. In S. Vosniadou & A. Ortony (Eds.), *Similarity and analytical reasoning* (pp. 470-497). New York: Cambridge University Press.

Bruner, J. S., Goodnow, J. J., & Austin, G. A. (1956). *A study of thinking.* New York: Wiley.

Burke, C. S. (1999). Examination of the cognitive mechanisms through which team leaders promote effective team processes and adaptive team performance. Unpublished doctoral dissertation, George Mason University, Virginia.

Cannon-Bowers, J. A., & Bell, H. R. (1997). Training decision makers for complex environments: Implications of the naturalistic decision making perspective. In C. Zsambok & G. Klein (Eds.), *Naturalistic decision making* (pp. 99-110). Hillsdale, NJ: Lawrence Erlbaum.

Cannon-Bowers, J. A., & Salas, E. (1990, April). *Cognitive psychology and team training: Training shared mental models of complex systems.* Paper presented at the Annual Meeting of the Society for Industrial and Organizational Psychology, Miami, FL.

Cannon-Bowers, J. A., & Salas, E. (2001). Reflections on shared cognition. *Journal of Organizational Behavior, 22,* 195-202.

Cannon-Bowers, J. A., Salas, E., & Converse, S. A. (1990). Cognitive psychology and team training: Training of shared mental models of complex systems. *Human Factors Society Bulletin, 33*(12), 1-4.

Cannon-Bowers, J. A., Tannenbaum, S. I., Salas, E., & Volpe, C. E. (1995). Defining competencies and establishing team training requirements. In R. Guzzo & E. Salas (Eds.), *Team effectiveness and decision making in organizations* (pp. 333-380). San Francisco: Jossey-Bass.

Chi, M., Glaser, R., & Farr, M. (1988). *The nature of expertise.* Hillsdale, NJ: Lawrence Erlbaum.

Cooke, N. J., Salas, E., Cannon-Bowers, J. A., & Stout, R. J. (2000). Measuring team knowledge. *Human Factors, 42*(1), 151-175.

Cooke, N. J., Stout, R. J., & Salas, E. (1997). Broadening the measurement of situation awareness through cognitive engineering methods. *Proceedings of the 41st annual meeting of the Human Factors and Ergonomics Society,* Santa Monica, CA, 215-219.

Converse, S. A., & Kahler, S. E. (1992, August). *Shared mental models, team performance, and knowledge acquisition.* Paper presented at the annual meeting of the American Psychology Association, Washington, DC.

Davidson, J. E., Deuser, & R., Sternberg, R. J. (1994). The role of metacognition in problem solving. In J. Metcalfe & A. P. Shimamura (Eds.), *Metacognition: Knowing about knowing* (pp. 207-226). Cambridge, MA: MIT Press.

Driskell, J. E., & Salas, E. (1992). Collective behavior and team performance. *Human Factors, 34*(3), 277-288

Endsley, M. R. (1997). The role of situation awareness in naturalistic decision making. In C. E. Zsambok & G. Klein (Eds.), *Naturalistic decision making. Expertise: Research and applications* (pp. 269-283). Hillsdale, NJ: Lawrence Erlbaum.

Endsley, M. R. (1989a). *Final report: Situation awareness in an advanced strategic mission* (NOR DOC 89-32). Hawthorne, CA: Northrop.

Endsley, M. R. (1989b). *Pilot situation awareness: The challenge for the training community.* Paper presented at the Interservice/Industry Training Systems Conference, Fort Worth, TX.

Endsley, M. R., & Garland, D. J. (Eds.). (2000). *Situation awareness analysis and measurement.* Mahwah, NJ: Lawrence Erlbaum.

Fiore, S. M., Salas, E., & Cannon-Bowers, J. A. (2001). Group dynamics and shared mental model development. In M. London (Ed.), *How people evaluate others in organizations* (pp. 309-336). Mahwah, NJ: Lawrence Erlbaum.

Flavell, J. H. (1976). Metacognitive aspects of problem solving. In L. B. Resnick (Ed.), *The nature of intelligence* (pp. 231-235). Hillsdale, NJ: Lawrence Erlbaum.

Ford, J. K., Smith, E. M., Weissbein, D. A., Gully, S. M., & Salas, E. (1998). Relationships of goal-orientation, metacognitive activity, and practice strategies with learning outcomes and transfer. *Journal of Applied Psychology, 83,* 218-233.

Garner, R. (1994). Metacognition and executive control. In H. R. B. Rudell, M. R. Rudell, & Singer (Eds.), *Theoretical models and processes of reading* (4th ed., pp. 715-732). Newark, DE: International Reading Association.

Gibson, E. J. (1969). *Principles of perceptual; earning and development.* New York: Appleton Century-Crofts.

Guzzo, R., Yost, P., Campbell, R., & Shea, G. (1993). Potency in groups: Articulating a construct. *British Journal of Social Psychology, 32,* 87-106.

Hackman, J. R. (1990). *Groups that work and those that don't: Creating conditions for effective teamwork.* San Francisco, CA: Jossey-Bass.

Hackman, J. R., & Walton, R. E. (1986). Leading groups in organizations. In P. S. Goodman & Associates (Eds.), *Designing effective work groups* (pp. 72-119). San Francisco: Jossey-Bass.

House, R. J. (1977). A 1976 theory of charismatic leadership. In J. G. Hunt & L. L. Larson (Eds.), *Leadership: The cutting edge* (pp. 189-207). Carbondale: Southern Illinois University Press.

Jackson, S. (2000). A qualitative evaluation of shared leadership barriers, drivers, and recommendations. *Journal of Management in Medicine, 14*(3/4), 166-178.

Johnson-Laird, P. (1983). *Mental models.* Cambridge, MA: Harvard University Press.

Kaempf, G. L., & Klein, G. (1994). Aeronautical decision making: The next generation. In N. Johnston, N. McDonald, & R. Fuller (Eds.), *Aviation psychology in practice* (pp. 223-254). Brooksfield, VT: Ashgate.

Katz, D., & Kahn, R. L. (1978). *The social psychology of organizations* (2nd ed.). New York: Wiley.

Klayman, J. (1988). Cue discovery in probabilistic environments: Uncertainty and experimentation. *Journal of Experimental Psychology: Learning, Memory, and Cognition, 14,* 317-330.

Klein, G. (1989). Recognition-primed decisions. In W. Rouse (Ed.), *Advances in Man-Machine Systems Research, 5,* 47-92.

Klein, G., & Pierce, L. (2001). *Adaptive teams.* (Draft Report, Purchase Order H438556(A) for Link Simulation and Training Division/Army Prime Contract No. DAAD17-00-A-5002). Fairborn, OH: Klein Associates.

Klenke, K. (1997). Leadership dispersion as a function of performance in information systems teams. *Journal of High Technology Management Research, 8(1),* 149-169.

Klimoski, R., & Mohammed, S. (1994). Team mental model: Construct or metaphor? *Journal of Management, 20,* 403-437.

Knight, D., Pearce, C., L., Smith, K. G., Olian, J. D., Sims, H. P., Smith, K. A., et al. (1999). Top management team diversity, group process, and strategic consensus. *Strategic Management Journal, 20,* 445-465.

Komaki, J .L., Desselles, M. L., & Bowman, E. D. (1989). Definitely not a breeze: Extending an operant model of effective supervision to teams. *Journal of Applied Psychology, 74,* 522-529.

Kozlowski, S. W. J., Gully, S. M., Nason, E. R., & Smith, E. M. (1997). Developing adaptive teams: A theory of compilation and performance across levels and time. In D. R. Ilgen & D. Pulakos (Eds.), *The changing nature of work and performance: Implications for staffing, personnel actions, and development* (Vol. 15, pp. 253-305). Greenwich, CT: JAI Press.

Kozlowski, S. W. J., Gully, S. M., Salas, E., & Cannon-Bowers, J. A. (1996). Team leadership and development: Theory, principles, and guidelines for training leaders and teams. *Advances in Interdisciplinary Studies of Work Teams* (Vol. 3, pp. 253-291). Greenwich, CT: JAI Press.

Lord, R. G. (1977). Functional leadership behavior: Measurement and relation to social power and leadership perceptions. *Administrative Science Quarterly, 22,* 114-133.

Lord, R. G., & Emrich, C. G. (2001). Thinking outside the box by looking inside the box: Extending the cognitive revolution in leadership research. *Leadership Quarterly, 11(4)*, 551-579.

Manz, C. C., & Sims, H. P., Jr. (1987). Leading workers to lead themselves: The external leadership of self-managing work teams. *Administrative Science Quarterly, 32*, 106-129.

Manz, C. C., & Sims, H. P., Jr. (1989). Self-management as a substitute for leadership: A social learning theory perspective. *Academy of Management Review, 5*, 361-367.

Manz, C. C., & Sims, H. P., Jr. (1993). *Business without bosses: How self-managing teams are building high-performing companies.* New York: Wiley.

Marks, M. A., & Zaccaro, S. J. (1997). *Leader-team dynamics in hierarchical decision making teams.* Presentation at the 1997 meetings of the Academy of Management, Boston, MA.

Marks, M. A., Zaccaro, S. J., & Mathieu, J. E. (2000). Performance implications of leader briefings and team interaction training for team adaptation to novel environments. *Journal of Applied Psychology, 85*(6), 971-986.

Mathieu, J. E., Heffner, T. S., Goodwin, G. F., Salas, E., & Cannon-Bowers, J. A. (2000). The influence of shared mental models on team process and performance. *Journal of Applied Psychology, 85*(2), 273-283.

Minionis, D. P. (1994). *Enhancing team performance in adverse conditions: The role of shared mental models and team training on an interdependent task.* Unpublished doctoral dissertation, George Mason University, Fairfax, VA.

Noe, R., & Ford, K. J. (1992). Emerging issues and new directions for training research. *Research in Personnel and Human Resource Management, 10*, 345-384.

Northcraft, G. B., Polzer, J. T., Neale, M. A., & Kramer, R. M. (1995). Diversity, social identity, and performance: Emergent social dynamics in cross-functional teams. In S. E. Jackson & M. N. Ruderman (Eds.), *Diversity in work teams: Research paradigms for a changing workplace* (pp. 69-96). Washington, DC: American Psychological Association.

Orasanu, J. M. (1990, October). *Shared mental models and crew performance.* Paper presented at the 34th Annual Meeting of the Human Factors Society, Orlando, FL.

Osman, M. E., & Hannafin, M. J. (1992). Metacognition research and theory: Analysis and implications for instructional design. *Educational Technology Research & Development, 40*, 83-99.

Pearce, C. L., Gallagher, C. A., & Ensley, M. D. (2002). Confidence at the group level of analysis: A longitudinal investigation of the relationship between potency and team effectiveness. *Journal of Occupational and Organizational Psychology, 75*, 115-119.

Pearce, C. L., Perry, M. L., & Sims, H. P., Jr. (2001). Shared leadership: Relationship management to improve nonprofit organization effectiveness. In T. D. Conners (Ed.), *The nonprofit handbook: Management* (3rd ed., pp. 624-641). New York: Wiley.

Pearce, C. L., & Sims, H. P. (2000). Shared leadership: Toward a multi-level theory of leadership. *Advances in interdisciplinary studies of work teams* Vol.7, pp. 115-139. Greenwich, CT: JAI Press.

Pearce, C. L., & Sims, H. P. (2002). Vertical *versus* shared leadership as predictors of the effectiveness of change management teams: An examination of aversive, directive, transactional, transformational, and empowering leader behaviors. *Group Dynamics: Theory, Research, and Practice, 6* (2), 172-197.

Perfetto, G. A., Bransford, J. D., & Franks, J. J. (1983). Constraints on access in a problem solving context. *Memory and Cognition, 11*, 24-31.

Perry, M. L., Pearce, C. L., & Sims, H. P., Jr. (1999). Empowered selling teams: How shared leadership can contribute to selling team outcomes. *Journal of Personal Selling and Sales Management, 19*(3), 35-51.

Porter-O'Grady, T., Hawkins, M., & Parker, M. (Eds.). (1997). *Whole systems shared governance: Architecture for integration.* Gaithersburg, MD: Aspen.

Pulakos, E. D., Arad, S., Donovan, M. A., & Plamondon, K. E. (2000). Adaptability in the workplace: Development of a taxonomy of adaptive performance. *Journal of Applied Psychology, 85*(4), 612-624.

Rawlings, D. (2000). Collaborative leadership teams: Oxymoron or new paradigm? *Consulting Psychology Journal: Practice and Research, 52*(1), 36-48.

Rentsch, J. R., & Hall, R. J. (1994). Members of great teams think alike: A model of team effectiveness and schema similarity among team members. *Advances in Interdisciplinary Studies of Work Teams, 1,* 223-261. Greenwich, CT: JAI Press.

Riggs, M. L. (1989, April). *The development of self-efficacy and outcome scales for general applications.* Paper presented at the annual meeting of the Society of Industrial and Organizational Psychology, Boston.

Rouse, W. B., Cannon-Bowers, J. A., & Salas, E. (1992). The role of mental models in team performance in complex systems. *IEEE Transactions on Systems, Man, and Cybernetics, 22,* 1296-1308.

Rouse, W. B., & Morris, N. M. (1986). On looking into the black box: Prospects and limits in the search for mental models. *Psychological Bulletin, 100,* 349-363.

Rumelhart, D. E. (1980). Schemata: The building blocks of cognition. In R. Spiro, B. Bruce, & W. Brewer (Eds.), *Theoretical issues in reading comprehension* (pp. 33-58). Hillsdale, NJ: Lawrence Erlbaum.

Salas, E., Cannon-Bowers, J. A., Fiore, S. M., & Stout, R. J. (2001). Cue-recognition training to enhance team situational awareness. In M. McNeese, E. Salas, & M. Endsley (Eds.), *New trends in cooperative activities: Understanding system dynamics in complex environments.* Santa Monica, CA: Human Factors and Ergonomics Society.

Salas, E., Dickinson, T. L., Converse, S. A., & Tannenbaum, S. I. (1992). Toward an understanding of team performance and training. In R. J. Swezey & E. Salas (Eds.), *Teams: Their training and performance* (pp. 3-29). Norwood, NJ: Ablex.

Spink, K. S. (1990). Collective efficacy in the sport setting. *International Journal of Sport Psychology, 21,* 380-395.

Spooner, S., Keenan, R., & Card, M. (1997). Determining if shared leadership is being practiced: Evaluation methodology. *Nursing Administrative Quarterly, 22*(1), 48.

Sternberg, R. J. (1998). Metacognition, abilities, and developing expertise: What makes an expert student? *Instructional Science, 26,* 127-140.

Stewart, G. L., & Manz, C. C. (1995). Leadership for self-managing work teams: A typology and integrative model. *Human Relations, 48*(7), 747-770.

Stout, R. J., Cannon-Bowers, J. A., & Salas, E. (1996). The role of shared mental models in developing team situational awareness: Implications for training. *Training Research Journal, 2,* 85-116.

Swezey, R. J., & Salas, E. (Eds.). (1992). *Teams: Their training and performance.* Norwood, NJ: Ablex.

Yukl, G. A. (1998). *Leadership in organizations* (4th ed.). Upper Saddle River, NJ: Prentice Hall.

Zaccaro, S. J., Blair, V., Peterson, C., & Zazanis, M. (1995). Collective efficacy. In J. E. Maddux (Ed.), *Self-efficacy, adaptation, and adjustment: Theory, research, and application* (pp. 305-328). New York: Plenum.

Zaccaro, S. J., Gilbert, J. A., Thor, K. K., & Mumford, M. M. (1991). Leadership and social intelligence: Linking social perceptiveness and behavioral flexibility to leader effectiveness. *Leadership Quarterly, 2,* 317-342.

# CHAPTER 6

# Self-Leadership and SuperLeadership

## The Heart and Art of Creating Shared Leadership in Teams

*Jeffery D. Houghton*

*Christopher P. Neck*

*Charles C. Manz*

> *"If you give a man a fish, he will have a single meal. If you teach him how to fish, he will eat all his life."*
>
> — Kwan-Tzu

The competitive environment facing many organizations is rapidly changing in the face of today's fast moving, information-based world. Driven by technology and global competition, many companies are moving toward more organic and decentralized organizational forms. Through the decentralization of power, authority, and decision-making responsibilities, organizations are finding the flexibility and rapid response capabilities necessary to remain competitive in high-tech or service-oriented marketplaces. This decentralization of organizational power is creating unprecedented opportunities for organizational members at all levels to take greater responsibility for their own job tasks and work behaviors (Shipper & Manz, 1992). In addition, this trend has placed an emphasis on participatory management concepts such as employee empowerment (e.g., Conger & Kanungo, 1988; Thomas & Velthouse, 1990) and self-managing work teams (e.g., Cohen & Ledford, 1994; Hackman, 1986). Because this trend is likely to continue well into the 21st century, organizational leaders will find an increasing need to depend on individual employees to share the responsibility for leading themselves rather than relying on traditional, hierarchical forms of leadership.

It is hardly surprising that the concept of shared leadership is gaining in popularity, particularly in the context of self-managing work teams. Shared leadership is a process through which individual team members share in performing the behaviors and roles of a traditional, hierarchical team leader (e.g., Bradford & Cohen, 1998; Perry, Pearce, & Sims, 1999; Spooner, Keenan, & Card, 1997). Shared leadership concepts have been successfully applied in a variety of organizational settings including healthcare (e.g., Spooner et al., 1997), human services (e.g., Sweeney, 1996), and telecommunications (e.g., Reshef, Kizilos, Ledford, & Cohen, 1999). Like shared leadership, the concept of self-leadership (the process of influencing oneself) also appears to have impressive potential for application in today's dynamic organizational environments characterized by empowerment and self-managing teams. Indeed, self-leadership has often been presented as a primary mechanism in both empowerment (e.g., Anderson & Prussia, 1997; Manz, 1992; Prussia, Anderson, & Manz, 1998; Shipper & Manz, 1992) and the successful implementation of self-managing work teams (e.g., Manz, 1990; Manz & Sims, 1986; Manz & Sims, 1987; Neck, Stewart, & Manz, 1996). Self-leadership is a systematic set of strategies through which individuals can lead themselves to higher levels of performance and effectiveness (Manz, 1986; Manz & Neck, 1999; Manz & Sims, 2001). As the organizational empowerment movement continues to grow, both self-leadership and shared leadership are likely to remain popular organizational interventions.

Although self-leadership and shared leadership are two examples of popular empowerment interventions, it is important to note that they are two distinct, yet complementary, concepts. Indeed, in this chapter we will contend that self-leadership can and should play an important role in the facilitation of shared leadership. We will suggest that team members who are effective self-leaders will willingly, confidently, and enthusiastically accept shared leadership roles and responsibilities. We will further develop the idea that self-leadership skills, strategies, and behaviors are integral components in the successful implementation and maintenance of shared leadership processes. We will also propose that the primary role for the vertical team leader is to become a SuperLeader, that is, a leader who leads followers to lead themselves though empowerment and the development of self-leadership skills (Manz & Sims, 1987, 1989, 1991, 2001). Finally, we will present a model that shows the facilitative relationships between SuperLeadership, self-leadership, and shared leadership. As our model and discussion will demonstrate, the primary message of our chapter is that self-leadership is central to effective empowerment and shared leadership.

## Shared Leadership

Leadership is often described as a process of influence toward the accomplishment of objectives (e.g., Bass, 1960; Katz & Kahn, 1966; Nahavandi, 2000; Yukl, 1998). In a team setting, this process of influence can originate from a traditional vertical leader or from the team members themselves (Pearce, 1997; Perry et al., 1999). Vertical leadership, that is, leadership originating from a higher level in the organizational hierarchy, can play a significant part in shaping team processes and outcomes. In this traditional approach to team leadership, power and authority are invested in a single appointed leader who serves as the primary source of influence, wisdom, and guidance for team members. In contrast, shared leadership is a collaborative team process in which team members share key leadership roles (Perry et al, 1999.). Within this approach to team leadership, team members share the responsibility of providing influence and guidance to one another, engaging in various leadership behaviors within the team as needed. Shared leadership is hypothesized to influence team affective responses such as commitment, satisfaction, potency, and cohesiveness, as well as team behavioral responses such as effort, communication, and citizenship behaviors (Perry et al., 1999). Team affective and behavioral responses, in turn, may positively affect overall team effectiveness (Perry et al., 1999).

Although many of the vertical leader's traditional roles such as directing and monitoring team member activities are undertaken and shared by the team members themselves, there are, nevertheless, several important roles for the vertical leader in the shared leadership process (Perry et al., 1999). First, the vertical leader must carefully identify and select team members with the appropriate mix of both leadership and technical skills necessary to successfully share leadership roles and responsibilities. Second, the vertical leader should strive to develop essential but lacking leadership skills in team members. Third, the vertical leader should fill in skill areas in which team member skills are lacking or still developing. Fourth, the vertical leader should dedicate a significant amount of time to managing boundaries between the team and the rest of the organization. Finally, the vertical leader should empower team members by providing the team with the full authority to make decisions, solve problems, set objectives, and develop and pursue appropriate courses of action. In short, the vertical leader's primary responsibility in the shared leadership process is to facilitate and encourage the sharing of leadership roles and behaviors among team members.

Based on established and emerging leadership literature, there are at least five primary categories of leadership behaviors that can and should be shared by team members. These include transactional behaviors, transformational behaviors, directive behaviors, empowering behaviors, and social supportive behaviors (Perry et al., 1999). Transactional leadership behaviors involve creating and maintaining reward contingencies (Bass, 1985; Burns, 1978). In other words, the leader offers certain material rewards in exchange for compliance and performance. In contrast, transformational leadership behaviors entail being charismatic, intellectually stimulating, and inspirational (Bass, 1985). A key aspect of the transformational leadership style is the development and communication of an appealing higher-level vision that is capable of eliciting an emotional response from followers. Directive leadership behaviors include assigning tasks and roles, issuing commands, and closely monitoring follower compliance (Katz, Maccoby, Gurin, & Floor, 1951; Stogdill & Coons, 1951). Empowering leadership behaviors encourage the development of followers who can make independent decisions, think and act autonomously without direct supervision, and generally take responsibility for their own work behaviors (Conger & Kanungo, 1988). In short, the empowerment process strives to create followers who are effective self-leaders (Manz & Sims, 2001). Finally, social supportive leadership behaviors are especially important within the team leadership context. Social supportive behaviors facilitate the social development of the team and include efforts to deal with social and emotional issues such as personality conflicts and individual power struggles (Barry, 1991). Because each of these categories of behaviors are well-represented in the leadership literature, it seems likely that each type of behavior would need to be present in order for a team to operate in a self-sufficient manner, independent of significant hierarchical leadership influences.

The sharing of leadership roles among several people has certain advantages over a single multirole leader. For instance, research has indicated that leadership roles are often split in small groups between directive and social supportive leaders in the face of difficult or trying situations (Bales, 1951). This may be because the directive or task-oriented leader often creates tension within the group through the assignment of tasks. This person, then, may not be in the best position to fill the social supportive role of solving or soothing the problems created by the task-related tension (Burke, 1967). Thus, it may be most effective to have a second peson provide social supportive behaviors to help the group deal with the socioemotional issues created by task assignments (Waldersee, Simmons, & Eagleson, 1995).

To effectively undertake this wide array of leadership responsibility, team members must be both able and willing to engage in the shared leadership process (Perry et al., 1999). In other words, team members must have both the requisite skills and the necessary desire in order to effectively share leadership roles and engage in key leadership behaviors. Even if appropriate levels of leadership skills are present in the composition of the team, team member confidence in their own abilities to exercise these skills may be lacking. In particular, team members may be low in self-efficacy for sharing leadership roles and behaviors. Self-efficacy has been described as a person's belief in his or her ability to perform a certain task or behavior (Bandura, 1986, 1991; Gist, 1987). If team members are low in self-efficacy for sharing leadership responsibilities, then they will likely be unwilling and perhaps even unable to undertake important leadership activities within the team. The reluctance or inability of team members to embrace the shared leadership concept can be a major hindrance to its effective implementation.

Fortunately, leadership skills can be developed along with the confidence, desire, and self-efficacy necessary to apply these skills in a shared leadership environment. Although leadership skills may be developed in a number of ways, we suggest that self-leadership strategies are ideally suited for developing the skills, confidence, desire, and self-efficacy needed for team members to successfully share leadership. *Self-leadership* is a term used to describe a comprehensive theory of self-influence that has great potential for application in the context of shared leadership. Indeed, we will argue that self-leadership is an integral part of the overall shared leadership process.

## Self-Leadership: The Heart of Shared Leadership

Self-leadership is defined as a process through which people influence themselves to achieve the self-direction and self-motivation needed to perform (Manz, 1986; Manz & Neck, 1999). Self-leadership uses specific sets of behavioral and cognitive strategies designed to shape individual performance outcomes. In recent years, self-leadership concepts have drawn considerable attention from organizational executives and academics alike as evidenced by the large number of practitioner-oriented books and articles on the subject (e.g., Blanchard, 1995; Cashman, 1995; Manz, 1991; Manz & Neck, 1991, 1999; Manz & Sims, 1989, 1994, 2001; Sims & Manz, 1996; Waitley, 1995) and by coverage in an increasing number of management and leadership textbooks (e.g., Ivancevich & Matteson, 1999; Kreitner & Kinicki, 2001; McShane & Von Glinow, 2000; Nahavandi, 2000). Corporate leaders have also embraced self-leadership concepts through training programs designed to increase self-leadership skills and behaviors (e.g., Cox, 1993; Neck & Manz, 1996; Stewart, Carson, & Cardy, 1996).

Self-leadership strategies are deeply rooted in related theories of self-regulation (Kanfer, 1970; Carver & Scheier, 1981), self-control (Cautela, 1969; Mahoney & Arnkoff, 1978, 1979; Mahoney & Thoresen, 1974; Thoresen & Mahoney, 1974), and self-management (Andrasik & Heimberg, 1982; Luthans & Davis, 1979; Manz & Sims, 1980). Self-regulation (e.g., Kanfer, 1970) can be viewed as a process of reducing variation from a set standard. The self-regulation process is often compared to the operation of a mechanical thermostat. A thermostat senses temperature variations relative to a given standard and signals the heating or cooling system to take appropriate action to reduce the discrepancy. In self-regulation theory, standards are simply assumed to exist and little attention is paid to how standards are determined. In an organizational setting, self-regulatory standards are based primarily on existing organizational standards and objectives. As long as organizational policies, rules, and procedures are followed, deviation reduction will occur. Thus, in the short run, the process of deviation reduction becomes relatively automatic and self-perpetuating. In other words, due to its largely automatic and unconscious responses to external demands, self-regulation can be viewed as a weaker form of self-influence than either self-management or self-leadership.

In contrast to self-regulation theory, which provides no prescriptions concerning *how* discrepancy should be reduced, self-management theory (e.g., Andrasik & Heimberg, 1982; Luthans & Davis, 1979; Manz & Sims, 1980) provides specific strategies for managing behaviors in order to regulate discrepancy from set standards (Manz, 1986). Self-management is defined as a process through which an individual chooses an unattractive or low probability behavior from among a variety of short-run behavioral alternatives (Manz, 1986; Manz & Sims, 1980; Mills, 1983; Thoresen & Mahoney, 1974). In other words, the individual chooses behaviors that are undesirable in the short-term in order to gain valued long-term outcomes. Self-management is founded on concepts of self-control originally developed in clinical psychology (e.g., Cautela, 1969; Mahoney & Arnkoff, 1978, 1979; Mahoney & Thoresen, 1974; Thoresen & Mahoney, 1974). Specific self-control strategies include self-observation, self–goal setting, cueing strategies, self-reinforcement, self-punishment, and rehearsal (Mahoney & Arnkoff, 1978, 1979). These strategies, when adapted to organizational settings, are often relabeled "self-management" (Andrasik & Heimberg, 1982; Luthans & Davis, 1979; Manz & Sims, 1980). These same strategies form the basis for the behavior-focused strategies of self-leadership (Manz, 1986; Manz & Neck, 1999).

Self-leadership is generally portrayed as a broader concept of self-influence than either self-regulation or self-management (Manz, 1986). Self-leadership subsumes the behavior-focused strategies of self-regulation, self-control, and self-management, and then specifies additional sets of cognitive-oriented strategies derived from intrinsic motivation theories (e.g., Deci, 1975; Deci and Ryan, 1985), social cognitive theory (Bandura, 1986, 1991), and clinical cognitive psychology (Beck, Rush, Shaw, & Emery, 1979; Burns, 1980, Ellis, 1977; Seligman, 1991). Taken together, self-leadership represents a diversified portfolio of self-influence strategies that are hypothesized to positively influence individual behavior, thought processes, and related outcomes.

Self-leadership strategies are often divided into three broad categories: behavior-focused strategies, natural reward strategies, and constructive thought pattern strategies (Anderson & Prussia, 1997; Manz & Neck, 1999; Prussia et al., & 1998). Behavior-focused strategies are intended to increase self-awareness leading to the management of behaviors involving necessary but perhaps unpleasant tasks (Manz & Neck, 1999). Originating in self-control and self-management theory, self-leadership's behavior-focused strategies include self-observation, self–goal setting, self-reward, self-correcting feedback, and practice. Self-observation is a process of closely examining one's own behavior in order to increase awareness of when and why one engages in certain behaviors. Through self-observation, an individual can identify behaviors that should be changed, enhanced, or eliminated (Mahoney & Arnkoff, 1978, 1979; Manz & Sims, 1980; Manz & Neck, 1999). For example, a person who is unhappy with his or her level of job performance could make informal notes documenting the occurrence of unproductive office behaviors such as phone conversations, lingering near the water cooler, or daydreaming. This heightening of awareness of negative behaviors is an important first step toward changing such behaviors. Given this increased awareness of current behaviors, an individual can now more effectively set personal goals that may lead to improved performance levels (Manz, 1986; Manz & Neck, 1999; Manz & Sims, 1980). A multitude of research has suggested that goals should be both challenging and specific in order to be optimally effective (Locke & Latham, 1990). For instance, a person might set a goal of developing five new accounts over the next quarter or of completing an important project one week ahead of schedule.

When used in conjunction with self-set goals such as these, self-rewards can be quite effective in energizing and directing behaviors toward goal attainment (Mahoney & Arnkoff, 1978, 1979; Manz & Sims, 1980; Manz & Neck, 1999). Self-rewards can be tangible, like a nice restaurant meal or a weekend vacation following the completion of a difficult project at work, or self-rewards can be as simple as the mental visualization of a favorite place or experience. Like self-rewards, self-correcting feedback can also be used to effectively shape desired behaviors. An introspective yet positively framed examination of negative behaviors and failures can be much more effective in correcting such behaviors than excessive self-punishment based on habitual guilt and self-criticism (Manz & Sims, 2001). Finally, the rehearsal or practice of desired behaviors before actual performance can allow for the correction of problems and the avoidance of costly miscues (Manz, 1992; Manz & Neck, 1999; Manz & Sims, 1980; Thoresen & Mahoney, 1974). In short, behavior-focused self-leadership strategies are designed to encourage positive, desirable behaviors that lead to successful outcomes, while suppressing negative, undesirable behaviors that lead to unsuccessful outcomes.

Natural reward strategies focus attention on the positive aspects of a given task or activity. Natural or intrinsic rewards result when a person engages in a task or activity primarily for its own sake and is motivated or rewarded by the task itself

(Manz & Neck, 1999; Manz & Sims, 2001). Steven Jobs of Apple Computer seems to serve as an example of the power of natural rewards. On returning to Apple as CEO in 1997 after an extended leave of over ten years, Jobs refused to accept any pay or stock for his efforts. Instead, he received a token $1 annual salary. Jobs (2000) commented, "I didn't return to Apple to make a fortune. . . . I just wanted to see if we could work together to turn this thing around when the company was literally on the verge of bankruptcy. The decision to go without pay has served me well" (p. 76). For Jobs, it would seem that the work itself is naturally rewarding. Natural reward strategies encompass two primary approaches. The first involves building more pleasant and enjoyable features into a given task or activity so that value is obtained from the task itself and the job becomes naturally rewarding (Manz & Neck, 1999; Manz & Sims, 2001). The second involves changing one's perceptions of an activity by focusing on the task's inherently rewarding aspects (Manz & Neck, 1999; Manz & Sims, 2001). To illustrate, a person might try to create a work environment that is more enjoyable by playing soft music, hanging pictures, or adding other personal touches. Alternatively, a person could mentally shift attention to the aspects of the job that they most enjoy such as working outdoors or engaging customers in conversation. By employing natural reward strategies such as these, a person may increase performance levels simply by focusing on the pleasant aspects of work.

Constructive thought pattern strategies deal with the creation or alteration of cognitive thought processes. Essentially, this set of strategies includes three primary ways through which thought patterns may be altered: self-analysis and improvement of belief systems, mental imagery of successful performance outcomes, and positive self-talk (Manz & Neck, 1999). Taken together, constructive thought pattern strategies are often referred to as *thought self-leadership* (e.g., Manz & Neck, 1991; Neck & Manz, 1992, 1996). Thought self-leadership suggests that individuals can influence and control their own thoughts through the use of specific cognitive strategies designed to facilitate the formation of constructive thought patterns or habitual ways of thinking that can positively affect performance (Manz & Neck, 1999; Neck & Manz, 1992).

Dysfunctional thought processes, a common and serious hindrance to individual performance, generally result from underlying dysfunctional beliefs and assumptions that are often triggered by stressful or troubling situations (Burns, 1980; Ellis, 1977). Through a process of self-analysis, thought self-leadership strives to identify, confront, and replace dysfunctional beliefs and assumptions with more rational ones (Beck, 1979; Burns, 1980; Ellis, 1977; Manz & Neck, 1999; Neck & Manz, 1992). In a similar manner, thought self-leadership suggests that negative and destructive self-talk should be replaced more positive and constructive self-dialogues. Self-talk is defined as what we covertly tell ourselves (Ellis, 1962; Neck & Manz, 1992, 1996). Self-dialogues usually take place at unobservable levels as individuals evaluate, instruct, and mentally react to themselves (Ellis, 1962, 1977; Manz & Neck, 1991; Neck & Manz, 1992). Through an analysis and evaluation of self-talk patterns, an individual can learn to suppress and discourage negative and pessimistic self-talk while fostering and encouraging optimistic self-dialogues (Seligman, 1991). By replacing negative and dysfunctional self-talk patterns with more constructive internal dialogues, performance may be enhanced (Manz & Neck, 1999).

Finally, the thought self-leadership strategy of mental imagery is generally defined as the symbolic, covert, mental invention or rehearsal of an experience or task in the absence of actual, overt physical muscular movement (cf. Driskell, Copper, & Moran, 1994; Finke, 1989). Through the use of mental imagery, it may be possible to create and symbolically experience behavioral outcomes prior to actual performance (Manz & Neck, 1991; Neck & Manz, 1992, 1996). This technique has also been variously referred to as imaginary practice (Perry, 1939), covert rehearsal (Corbin, 1967), symbolic rehearsal (Sackett, 1934), and mental practice (Corbin, 1972). Those individuals who envision the successful performance of a task or activity beforehand are much more likely to perform successfully when faced with the actual situation (Manz & Neck, 1999). Research evidence supports this assertion. For example, a recent meta-analysis of 35 empirical studies (Driskell et al., 1994) suggests that mental practice generally has both a positive and significant effect on performance outcomes.

Thought self-leadership proposes that an individual's beliefs, self-talk, and mental imagery combine to affect the individual's thought patterns. An individual's thought pattern is basically a person's habitual way of thinking (Manz & Neck, 1999; Neck & Manz, 1992). Individuals tend to fall into one of two opposing patterns of habitual thought: opportunity thinking or obstacle thinking (Manz & Neck, 1999; Neck & Manz, 1992). Opportunity thinking involves habitually thinking in terms of worthwhile challenges, opportunities, and constructive approaches to difficult or unpleasant situations. Obstacle thinking, in contrast, focuses on reasons to give up and retreat from problems and difficulties. Opportunity thinkers tend to exert greater effort and persistence in dealing with challenges and difficulties, whereas obstacle thinkers tend to focus on the negative and discouraging aspects of a challenging situation (Manz, 1986; Seligman, 1991).

Generally, the effectiveness of thought self-leadership strategies has been supported by a wide variety of disciplines. Specifically, the effects of self-talk and mental imagery on performance have been empirically supported in sports psychology (e.g., Andre & Means, 1986; Clark, 1960; Feltz & Landers, 1983; Kendall, Hrycaiko, Martin, & Kendall, 1990; Lee, 1990; Mahoney & Avener, 1977; Meyers, Cooke, Cullen, & Liles, 1979; Ryan & Simons, 1981; Wrisberg & Anshel, 1989; Zecker, 1982; Ziegler, 1987), clinical psychology (Bonadies & Bass, 1984; Crowder, 1989; Harrell, Chambless, & Calhoun, 1981; Meichenbaum & Goodman, 1971; Rosin & Nelson, 1983; Schill, Monroes, Evans, & Ramanaiah, 1978; Steffy, Meichenbaum, & Best, 1970; Turner, Kohl, & Morris, 1982; Velten, 1968), counseling psychology (Baker, Johnson, Kopala, & Strout, 1985), and communication (Boice, 1985). In addition, clinical psychologists have described processes through which an individual's beliefs and assumptions can result in a variety of cognitive distortions often leading to depression (Beck et al., 1979; Burns, 1980; Ellis, 1977). Finally, in the organizational literature, employees who participated in a thought self-leadership training intervention experienced significant increases in mental performance, positive affect, and job satisfaction relative to those not receiving the training (Neck & Manz, 1996).

A primary objective of all three categories of self-leadership strategies is the enhancement of self-efficacy perceptions, which should in turn lead to higher levels of performance (e.g., Manz, 1986; Manz & Neck, 1999; Neck & Manz, 1992, 1996; Prussia et al., 1998). As mentioned earlier, self-efficacy refers to a person's beliefs regarding his or her capabilities to perform a specific task (Bandura, 1986, 1991; Gist, 1987). High levels of self-efficacy for engaging in a specific task lead to higher performance standards (Bandura, 1991), greater effort, and greater persistence in the pursuit of goals and objectives (e.g., Bandura & Cervone, 1983, 1986).

Substantial empirical evidence supports the effectiveness of self-leadership strategies in increasing self-efficacy perceptions. For instance, Frayne and Latham (1987) and Latham and Frayne (1989) showed a positive relationship between self-management training and self-efficacy for reducing absenteeism. In addition, Neck and Manz (1996) demonstrated a significant difference in self-efficacy levels between a group that had received thought self-leadership training and a nontraining control group. More recently, Prussia and his colleagues (Prussia et al., 1998) examined the hypothesized role of self-efficacy as a mediator of the relationship between self-leadership strategies and performance. Their analysis indicated significant relationships between self-leadership strategies, self-efficacy perceptions, and task performance. These findings suggest that self-efficacy may serve as the primary mechanism through which self-leadership strategies affect performance. Taken together, these results suggest significant positive effects for self-leadership strategies on both self-efficacy and related performance outcomes.

Given self-leadership's positive relationship to both self-efficacy and performance outcomes, self-leadership has considerable potential for acting as a primary mechanism in the development of team members who are both willing and able to engage in the sharing of leadership roles. Through the use of the various self-leadership strategies, team members can effectively increase their self-efficacy beliefs for undertaking various leadership roles and responsibilities within the team. Constructive thought strategies may be particularly useful in increasing team members' self-efficacy beliefs for sharing leadership roles. For instance, a team member may be suffering from dysfunctional beliefs and assumptions and from negative self-talk relative to his ability to engage in leadership behaviors. This person may be thinking, "I feel like no one on the team ever pays any attention to me. I have absolutely no influence with my team. How could I possibly share the responsibility of leading the team?" This is an example of irrational thinking and mental distortion. It is unlikely that any single team member has absolutely no influence within the team. Irrational thought processes such as these should be openly challenged and replaced with more reasonable and constructive thought processes and internal dialogues. In this example, the team member could tell himself, "I know a lot about some of the most important aspects of our team's work process. I know I can share this knowledge with my team members in helping to direct their behaviors in positive ways. I'm also a good counselor. People often come to me for social and emotional support. Maybe I can share in the leadership process after all." In addition, this person could engage in mental imagery and visualize himself successfully performing various leadership roles within the team. By challenging irrational beliefs and assumptions, by replacing negative self-dialogues with more positive ones, and by visualizing successful performance of leadership behaviors, this team member may increase his belief in his ability to share in various leadership processes, thus bolstering his confidence and desire to undertake such roles.

The process through which increased self-efficacy beliefs for sharing leadership roles are translated into shared leadership behaviors can be further explained using Fishbein and Ajzen's (1975) general model of behavioral intentions as a theoretical framework. According to this model, beliefs help shape attitudes, which are defined as an evaluative response to an object, person, or event. Attitudes in turn lead to behavioral intentions for engaging in specific behaviors. Behavioral intentions are viewed as the single best predictor of actual behaviors. In the case of shared leadership, higher self-efficacy beliefs for sharing leadership roles are likely to lead to more positive

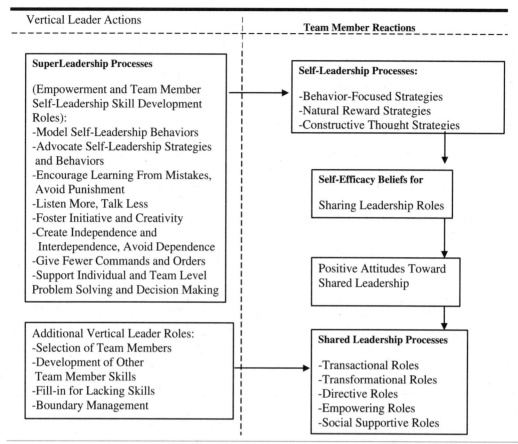

**Figure 6.1** The Role of SuperLeadership and Self-Leadership Strategies in Facilitating Shared Leadership

attitudes toward shared leadership behaviors. Indeed, empirical evidence lends support to this theoretical linkage. For instance, Thoms, Moore, and Scott (1996) demonstrated a positive relationship between self-efficacy for participating in self-managed work groups and general attitudes toward self-managing work groups. More positive attitudes toward shared leadership processes are likely to result in behavioral intentions to engage in shared leadership behaviors, and ultimately in shared leadership behaviors themselves. The suggested relationships between self-leadership strategies, self-efficacy beliefs for shared leadership, attitudes toward shared leadership, and shared leadership behaviors, as outlined above, are shown in Figure 6.1.

In summary, we believe that self-leadership is a prime ingredient in the facilitation of shared leadership. Our belief is based on the concept that team members must first learn to lead themselves before they can effectively influence and lead their fellow team members. In addition, we suggest that self-leadership, operating through self-efficacy beliefs and attitudes toward shared leadership, can serve as a principal mechanism for developing team members who have the motivation, the confidence, and the desire necessary to share leadership roles. In short, we view self-leadership as lying at the very heart of shared leadership.

# SuperLeadership:
# The Art of Facilitating Shared Leadership

If self-leadership is the heart of shared leadership, then SuperLeadership may be viewed as the art of creating and facilitating self-leadership and shared leadership in team members. SuperLeadership is a term used to describe the process of leading others to lead themselves (Manz & Sims, 1987, 1989, 1991, 2001). In other words, SuperLeadership is an approach that strives to develop followers who are effective self-leaders. The SuperLeader is often contrasted with three other common leadership types: the Strongman, the Transactor, and the Visionary Hero (Manz & Sims, 1991, 2001). The Strongman focuses primarily on the directive leadership roles of giving commands, assigning goals, and threatening or intimidating followers into a fear-based compliance. The Transactor focuses on transactional roles such as creating reward contingencies and exchange relationships with followers that result in a calculated compliance. The Visionary Hero focuses on the transformational roles of creating and communicating a higher-level vision in a charismatic way that elicits an emotional response and commitment from the followers. In contrast, the SuperLeader focuses primarily on the empowering roles of helping, encouraging, and supporting followers in the development of personal responsibility, individual initiative, self-confidence, self–goal setting, self–problem solving, opportunity thinking, self-leadership, and psychological ownership of their work tasks and duties (Manz & Sims, 2001).

Shared leadership suggests that the directive, transactional, and transformational roles traditionally filled by the Strongman, the Transactor, and the Visionary Hero types of leaders respectively are best shared by the team members themselves (Perry et al., 1999). As these traditional leadership roles are redistributed among the team members, the vertical leader's main function is to serve as a facilitator of the shared leadership process. Specifically, the vertical leader should engage in the facilitating roles of selecting team members, developing team member skills, filling in for lacking skills, managing boundaries, and empowering team members. Although each of these roles is important, perhaps no two facilitating roles are as critical to the ultimate success of the shared leadership process as the empowerment and development of team members. If team members are not provided necessary skills and the power to apply them, they will lack the confidence and the desire to engage in the sharing of leadership roles. In addition, due to the key role of self-leadership strategies in shaping shared leadership self-efficacy beliefs, attitudes, and behaviors, self-leadership skills appear to be among the more important skills that should be developed in team members. Thus, the vertical leader should be largely concerned with developing self-leadership skills in followers and empowering them to use them.

The principal goals of SuperLeadership are to develop self-leadership skills in followers and to empower them to effectively use these skills to lead themselves and others. Hence, we suggest that the primary responsibility of the vertical leader in facilitating shared leadership is to act as a SuperLeader. A SuperLeader can develop empowered, self-leading followers by engaging in a variety of specific actions and behaviors (Manz & Sims, 2001). Specifically, the SuperLeader should model self-leadership behaviors and advocate the use of self-leadership strategies. The SuperLeader also avoids the use of punishment, viewing mistakes as learning opportunities. The SuperLeader listens more and talks less, while asking more questions and providing fewer answers. Rather than providing answers, the SuperLeader encourages individual and team problem solving and decision making. A SuperLeader strives to replace conformity and dependence among followers with initiative, creativity, independence, and interdependence. As shown in Figure 6.1, SuperLeadership processes such as these facilitate shared leadership processes indirectly by developing self-leading capabilities in team members, which in turn affect self-efficacy beliefs and attitudes relating to shared leadership.

Figure 6.1 also reflects the more direct influence of the remaining vertical leadership roles in facilitating shared leadership. These additional vertical leader roles, though important, are more supportive in nature. If team members have low self-efficacy for sharing leadership roles and negative attitudes toward the shared leadership process, then team members will likely be unwilling or unable to share leadership roles regardless of how effectively boundaries are managed or how carefully team members are selected. Engaging in these roles alone would likely accomplish very little in the way of facilitating shared leadership behaviors. Thus, we submit that the SuperLeadership process of empowering team members and developing their self-leadership skills is the central way in which the vertical leader facilitates shared leadership.

Although we advocate SuperLeadership as a primary means for creating shared leadership in teams, this leadership approach is not without certain limitations and disadvantages, and it may not be the most appropriate leadership style for every situation. For instance, leaders who choose a SuperLeadership approach may appear weak to some (i.e., not directive or decisive enough), and the perception might arise that they are shirking their leadership responsibilities. Indeed, choosing a SuperLeadership approach could threaten future promotions or opportunities for increased leadership responsibilities if superiors prefer a more directive leadership style. In addition, SuperLeadership will often produce poorer results at first as followers are learning how to handle increased responsibilities. SuperLeadership can also be more time consuming than simply giving orders or doing the task oneself. In urgent situations, time is often at a serious premium. Finally, without realizing it, leaders may sometimes "talk the talk" of SuperLeadership (i.e., employee empowerment) while behaving much more autocratically. For example, a would-be SuperLeader might say something like this: "Of course I trust you and empower you to handle this situation on your own. So go ahead and work on it. . . . And by the way, I would like you to check in with me every couple of hours so that I can monitor your progress." Clearly, this person is not acting as a genuine SuperLeader.

In addition to difficulties such as these, SuperLeadership may not always be the most appropriate choice given the constraints of the situation. Consistent with Hersey and Blanchard's well-known Situational Leadership Model (e.g., Hersey & Blanchard, 1969; Hersey, Blanchard, & Johnson, 2001), newer or less experienced employees will likely need significant guidance initially before being allowed and encouraged to engage in much more self-leadership later on. The SuperLeadership approach differs, however, from the Situational Leadership Model in that facilitating self-leadership is seen as an important investment in the future and not just as a contingency option to be used when conditions are suitable. In addition, SuperLeadership is generally characterized as most effective when the leader wants commitment from the follower, the situation is not urgent, and there is adequate time for developing self-leadership in followers (Manz & Sims, 2001). If, in contrast, the leader is interested *only* in follower compliance (an interest seemingly at odds with the concept of shared leadership), then either the Strongman or Transactor approach would be acceptable. If the leader wants commitment and the situation is urgent, then a more visionary or inspirational style is probably needed, at least in the short run. For the long run, however, when followers need to develop independence and when knowledge is to be drawn from all involved, SuperLeadership tends to be the more effective leadership approach. Thus, we maintain that a SuperLeadership style can serve an important role in facilitating shared leadership though the long-term development of capable self-leading team members who are eager to assume leadership responsibilities.

# Conclusion

The high-tech, information-oriented reality of today's business environments will most likely continue to demand flexible, responsive organizations populated with highly independent, well-educated knowledge workers. In response, organizational structures will continue the evolution toward more decentralized organizational forms founded on concepts like empowerment and self-managing teams. As we have discussed, the sharing of leadership roles among team members can be a key factor in maximizing the effectiveness of team-based structures. In this chapter, we have argued that self-leadership is an integral component in the facilitation of shared leadership within self-managing teams. More precisely, we have suggested that self-leadership strategies could be quite effective in developing high self-efficacy beliefs among team members for sharing leadership roles and responsibilities. Higher self-efficacy beliefs for sharing leadership in turn are apt to foster positive attitudes toward the shared leadership process in general. High self-efficacy and positive attitudes will tend to result in confident and enthusiastic team members who are willing and able to share leadership roles.

We have also proposed that the primary responsibility of the vertical leader in facilitating shared leadership is to become a SuperLeader, that is, a leader who seeks to empower and develop self-leadership skills in team members. Indeed, we believe that SuperLeadership represents an ideal leadership style through which the vertical leader can facilitate effective self-leadership and ultimately effective shared leadership among team members. Overall, we view self-leadership as the central component in the process of developing empowered organizational members who are willing to share the responsibilities of leadership. In ordinary terms, we see self-leadership as the means by which team members can "learn how to fish" rather than having someone else "fish for them." Indeed, we are convinced that, in the years to come, organizations operating on the basis of empowerment and shared leadership will not only survive in the midst of turbulent global competition; they will flourish.

# References

Anderson, J. S., & Prussia, G. E. (1997). The self-leadership questionnaire: Preliminary assessment of construct validity. *Journal of Leadership Studies, 4,* 119-143.

Andrasik, F., & Heimberg, J. S. (1982). Self-management procedures. In L. W. Frederikson (Ed.), *Handbook of organizational behavior management* (pp. 219-247). New York: Wiley.

Andre, J. C., & Means, J. R. (1986). Rate of imagery in mental practice: An experimental investigation. *Journal of Sports Psychology, 8,* 123-128.

Baker, S. B., Johnson, E., Kopala, M., & Strout, N. J. (1985). Test interpretation competence: A comparison of microskills and mental practice training. *Counselor Education and Supervision, 25,* 31-43.

Bales, R. F. (1951). *Interaction process analysis.* Cambridge, MA: Addison-Wesley.

Bandura, A. (1986). *Social foundations of thought and action: A social cognitive theory.* Englewood Cliffs, NJ: Prentice Hall.

Bandura, A. (1991). Social cognitive theory of self-regulation. *Organizational Behavior and Human Decision Processes, 50,* 248-287.

Bandura, A., & Cervone, D. (1983). Self-evaluative and self-efficacy mechanisms governing the motivational effects of goal systems. *Journal of Personality and Social Psychology, 45,* 1017-1028.

Bandura, A., & Cervone, D. (1986). Differential engagement of self-reactive influences in cognitive motivation. *Organizational Behavior and Human Decision Processes, 38,* 92-113.

Barry, D. (1991). Managing the bossless team: Lessons in distributed leadership. *Organizational Dynamics, 20,* 31-47.

Bass, B. M. (1960). *Leadership, psychology, and organizational behavior.* New York: Harper & Row.

Bass, B. M. (1985). *Leadership and performance beyond expectations.* New York: Free Press.

Beck, A. T., Rush, A. J., Shaw, B. F., & Emery, G. (1979). *Cognitive theory of depression.* New York: Guilford Press.

Blanchard, K. (1995). Points of power can help self-leadership. *Manage, 46* (3), 12.

Boice, R. (1985). Cognitive components of blocking. *Written Communication, 2,* 91-104.

Bonadies, G. A., & Bass, B. A. (1984). Effects of self-verbalizations upon emotional arousal and performance: A test of rational-emotive theory. *Perceptual and Motor Skills, 59,* 939-948.

Bradford, D. L., & Cohen, A. R. (1998). *Power up: Transforming organizations through shared leadership.* New York: Wiley.

Burke, P. J. (1967). The development of task and socio-emotional role differentiation. *Sociometry, 30,* 379-392.

Burns, D. D. (1980). *Feeling good: The new mood therapy.* New York: William Morrow.

Burns, J. M. (1978). *Leadership.* New York: Harper & Row.

Carver, C. S., & Scheier, M. F. (1981). Attention and self-regulation: A control theory approach to human behavior. New York: Springer-Verlag.

Cashman, K. (1995). Mastery from the inside out. *Executive Excellence, 12* (12), 17.

Cautela, J. R. (1969). Behavior therapy and self-control: Techniques and applications. In C. M. Franks (Ed.), *Behavioral therapy: Appraisal and status* (pp. 323-340). New York: McGraw-Hill.

Clark, L. V. (1960). Effect of mental practice on the development of a complex motor skill. *Research Quarterly, 31,* 560-569.

Cohen, S. G., & Ledford, G. E., Jr. (1994). The effectiveness of self-managing teams: A quasi-experiment. *Human Relations, 47,* 13-43.

Conger, J., & Kanungo, R. (1988). The empowerment process: Integrating theory and practice. *Academy of Management Review, 13,* 639-652.

Corbin, C. B. (1967). Effects of mental practice on skill development after controlled practice. *Research Quarterly, 38,* 534-538.

Corbin, C. B. (1972). Mental practice. In W. P. Morgan (Ed.), *Ergogenic aids and muscular performance* (pp. 93-118). San Diego, CA: Academic Press.

Cox, J. F. (1993). *The effects of superleadership training on leader behavior, subordinate self-leadership behavior, and subordinate citizenship.* Unpublished doctoral dissertation, University of Maryland, College Park, MD.

Crowder, R. G. (1989). Imagery for musical timbre. *Journal of Experimental Psychology: Human Perception and Performance, 15,* 477-478.

Deci, E. L. (1975). *Intrinsic motivation.* New York: Plenum.

Deci, E. L., & Ryan, R. M. (1985). *Intrinsic motivation and self-determination in human behavior.* New York: Plenum.

Driskell, J. E., Copper, C., & Moran, A. (1994). Does mental practice enhance performance? *Journal of Applied Psychology, 79,* 481-492.

Ellis, A. (1962). *Reason and emotion in psychotherapy.* New York: Lyle Stuart.

Ellis, A. (1977). *The basic clinical theory of rational-emotive therapy.* New York: Springer.

Feltz, D. L., & Landers, D. M. (1983). The effects of mental practice on motor skill learning and performance: A meta-analysis. *Journal of Sport Psychology, 5,* 25-57.

Finke, R. A. (1989). *Principles of mental imagery.* Cambridge, MA: MIT Press.

Fishbein, M., & Ajzen, I. (1975). *Belief, attitude, intention and behavior: An introduction to theory and research.* Reading, MA: Addison-Wesley.

Frayne, C. A., & Latham, G. P. (1987). Application of social learning theory to employee self-management of attendance. *Journal of Applied Psychology, 72,* 387-392.

Gist, M. E. (1987). Self-efficacy: Implications for organizational behavior and human resource management. *Academy of Management Review, 12,* 472-485.

Hackman, J. R. (1986). The psychology of self-management in organizations. In M. S. Pollack & R. O. Perlogg (Eds.), *Psychology and work: Productivity change and employment* (pp. 85-136). Washington, DC: American Psychological Association.

Harrell, T. H., Chambless, D. L., & Calhoun, J. F. (1981). Correlational relationships between self-statements and affective states. *Cognitive Therapy and Research, 5,* 159-173.

Hersey, P., & Blanchard, K. H. (1969). *Management of organizational behavior: Utilizing human resources.* Englewood Cliffs, NJ: Prentice Hall.

Hersey, P., Blanchard, K. H., & Johnson, D. E. (2001). *Management of organizational behavior: Leading human resources* (8th ed.). Upper Saddle River, NJ: Prentice Hall.

Ivancevich, J. M., & Matteson, M. T. (1999). *Organizational behavior and management* (5th ed.). Boston: Irwin/McGraw-Hill.

Jobs, S. (2000, January 24). Apple's One-Dollar-A-Year Man. *Fortune,* 76.

Kanfer, F. H. (1970). Self-regulation: Research, issues, and speculations. In C. Neuringer & J. L. Michael (Eds.), *Behavioral modification in clinical psychology* (pp. 178-220). New York: Appleton-Century-Crofts.

Katz, D., & Kahn, R. L. (1966). *The social psychology of organizations.* New York: Wiley.

Katz, D., Maccoby, N., Gurin, G., & Floor, L. (1951). *Productivity, supervision, and morale among railroad workers.* Ann Arbor: Survey Research Center, University of Michigan.

Kendall, G., Hrycaiko, D., Martin, G. L., & Kendall, T. (1990). The effects of an imagery rehearsal, relaxation, and self-talk package on basketball game performance. *Journal of Counseling Psychology, 32,* 263-271.

Kreitner, R., & Kinicki, A. (2001). *Organizational behavior* (5th ed.). Boston: Irwin/McGraw-Hill.

Latham, G. P., & Frayne, C. A. (1989). Self-management training for increasing job attendance: A follow-up and replication. *Journal of Applied Psychology, 74,* 411-416.

Lee, C. (1990). Psyching up for a muscular endurance task: Effects of image content on performance and mood state. *Journal of Sport and Exercise Psychology, 12,* 66-73.

Locke, E. A., & Latham, G. P. (1990). *A theory of goal setting and task performance.* Englewood Cliffs, NJ: Prentice Hall.

Luthans, F., & Davis, T. (1979). Behavioral self-management (BSM): The missing link in managerial effectiveness. *Organizational Dynamics, 8,* 42-60.

Mahoney, M. J., & Arnkoff, D. B. (1978). Cognitive and self-control therapies. In S. L. Garfield & A. E. Borgin (Eds.), *Handbook of psychotherapy and therapy change* (pp. 689-722). New York: Wiley.

Mahoney, M. J., & Arnkoff, D. B. (1979). Self-management: Theory, research, and application. In J. P. Brady & D. Pomerleau (Eds.), *Behavioral medicine: Theory and practice* (pp. 75-96). Baltimore: Williams & Williams.

Mahoney, M. J., & Avener, M. (1977). Psychology of the elite athlete: An exploratory study. *Cognitive Therapy and Research, 1,* 135-141.

Mahoney, M. J., & Thoresen, C. E. (Eds.). (1974). *Self-control: Power to the person.* Monterey, CA: Brooks/Cole.

Manz, C. C. (1986). Self-leadership: Toward an expanded theory of self-influence processes in organizations. *Academy of Management Review, 11,* 585-600.

Manz, C. C. (1990). Beyond self-managing work teams: Toward self-leading teams in the workplace. In R. Woodman & W. Pasmore (Eds.), *Research in organizational change and development* (pp. 273-299). Greenwich, CT: JAI Press.

Manz, C. C. (1991). Developing self-leaders through SuperLeadership. *Supervisory Management, 36* (9), 3.

Manz, C. C. (1992). Self-leadership . . . The heart of empowerment. *The Journal for Quality and Participation, 15* (4), 80-89.

Manz, C. C., & Neck, C. P. (1991). Inner leadership: Creating productive thought patterns. *The Executive, 5,* 87-95.

Manz, C. C., & Neck, C. P. (1999). *Mastering self-leadership: Empowering yourself for personal excellence* (2nd ed.). Upper Saddle River, NJ: Prentice Hall.

Manz, C. C., & Sims, H. P., Jr. (1980). Self-management as a substitute for leadership: A social learning perspective. *Academy of Management Review, 5,* 361-367.

Manz, C. C., & Sims, H. P., Jr. (1986). Leading self-managed groups: A conceptual analysis of a paradox. *Economic and Industrial Democracy, 7,* 141-165.

Manz, C. C., & Sims, H. P., Jr. (1987). Leading workers to lead themselves: The external leadership of self-managing work teams. *Administrative Science Quarterly, 32,* 106-128.

Manz, C. C., & Sims, H. P., Jr. (1989). *Superleadership: Leading others to lead themselves.* Englewood Cliffs, NJ: Prentice Hall.

Manz, C. C., & Sims, H. P., Jr. (1991). Superleadership: Beyond the myth of heroic leadership. *Organizational Dynamics, 19,* 18-35.

Manz, C. C., & Sims, H. P., Jr. (1994). *Business without bosses: How self-managing work teams are building high performing companies.* New York: Wiley.

Manz, C. C., & Sims, H. P., Jr. (2001). *The new Superleadership: Leading others to lead themselves.* San Francisco, CA: Berrett-Koehler.

McShane, S. L., & Von Glinow, M. A. (2000). *Organizational behavior.* Boston: Irwin/McGraw-Hill.

Meichenbaum, D., & Goodman, J. (1971). Training impulsive children to talk to themselves: A means of developing self-control. *Journal of Abnormal Psychology, 77,* 115-126.

Meyers, A. W., Cooke, C. J., Cullen, J., & Liles, L. (1979). Psychological aspects of athletic competitors: A replication across sports. *Cognitive Therapy and Research, 3,* 361-366.

Mills, P. K. (1983). Self-management: Its control and relationship to other organizational properties. *Academy of Management Review, 8,* 445-453.

Nahavandi, A. (2000). *The art and science of leadership* (2nd ed.). Upper Saddle River, NJ: Prentice Hall.

Neck, C. P., & Manz, C. C. (1992). Thought self-leadership: The impact of self-talk and mental imagery on performance. *Journal of Organizational Behavior, 12,* 681-699.

Neck, C. P., & Manz, C. C. (1996). Thought self-leadership: The impact of mental strategies training on employee behavior, cognition, and emotion. *Journal of Organizational Behavior, 17,* 445-467.

Neck, C. P., Stewart, G. L., & Manz, C. C. (1996). Self-leaders within self-leading teams: Toward an optimal equilibrium. In M. Beyerlein (Ed.), *Advances in Interdisciplinary Studies of Work Teams: Vol. 3* (pp. 43-65). Greenwich, CT: JAI Press.

Pearce, C. L. (1997). *The determinants of change management and team effectiveness: A longitudinal investigation.* Unpublished doctoral dissertation, University of Maryland.

Perry, H. M. (1939). The relative efficiency of actual and imaginary practice in 5 selected tasks. *Archives of Psychology, 4,* 5-75.

Perry, M. L., Pearce, C. L., & Sims, H. P., Jr. (1999). Empowered selling teams: How shared leadership can contribute to selling team outcomes. *Journal of Personal Selling & Sales Management, 14,* 35-51.

Prussia, G. E., Anderson, J. S., & Manz, C. C. (1998). Self-leadership and performance outcomes: The mediating influence of self-efficacy. *Journal of Organizational Behavior, 19,* 523-538.

Reshef, Y., Kizilos, M., Ledford, G. E., Jr., & Cohen, S. G. (1999). Employee involvement programs: Should unions get involved? *Journal of Labor Research, 20,* 557-569.

Rosin, L., & Nelson, W. M. (1983). The effects of rational and irrational self-verbalizations on performance efficiency and levels of anxiety. *Journal of Clinical Psychology, 39,* 208-213.

Ryan, E. D., & Simons, J. (1981). Cognitive demand, imagery, and frequency of mental rehearsal as factors influencing acquisition of motor skills. *Journal of Sport Psychology, 3,* 35-45.

Sackett, R. S. (1934). The influence of symbolic rehearsal upon the retention of a maze habit. *Journal of General Psychology, 10,* 376-395.

Schill, T., Monroe, S., Evans, R., & Ramanaiah, N. (1978). The effects of self-verbalizations on performance: Test of the rational-emotive position. *Psychotherapy: Theory, Research, and Practice, 15,* 2-7.

Seligman, M. E. P. (1991). *Learned optimism.* New York: Alfred Knopf.

Shipper, F., & Manz, C. C. (1992). Employee self-management without formally designated teams: An alternative road to empowerment. *Organizational Dynamics, 20* (3), 48-61.

Sims, H. P., Jr., & Manz, C. C. (1996). *Company of heroes: Unleashing the power of self-leadership.* New York: Wiley.

Spooner, S. H., Keenan, R., & Card, M. (1997). Determining if shared leadership is being practiced: Evaluation methodology. *Nursing Administration Quarterly, 22,* 47-57.

Steffy, R. A., Meichenbaum, D., & Best, J. A. (1970). Aversive and cognitive factors in the modification of smoking behavior. *Behavioral Research and Therapy, 8,* 115-125.

Stewart, G. L., Carson, K. P., & Cardy, R. L. (1996). The joint effects of conscientiousness and self-leadership training on self-directed behavior in a service setting. *Personnel Psychology, 49,* 143-164.

Stogdill, R. M., & Coons, A. E. (Eds.). (1951). *Leader behavior: Its description and measurement* (Research Monograph No. 88). Columbus: Ohio State University, Bureau of Business Research.

Sweeney, K. (1996). A shared leadership model for human services program management. *International Journal of Public Administration, 19,* 1105-1121.

Thomas, K. W., & Velthouse, B. A. (1990). Cognitive elements of empowerment: An interpretive model of intrinsic task motivation. *The Academy of Management Review, 15,* 666-681.

Thoms, P., Moore, K. S., & Scott, K. S. (1996). The relationship between self-efficacy for participating in self-managed work groups and the big five personality dimensions. *Journal of Organizational Behavior, 17,* 349-362.

Thoresen, C. E., & Mahoney, M. J. (1974). *Behavioral self-control.* New York: Holt, Rinehart, and Winston.

Turner, P. E ., Kohl, R. M., & Morris, L. W. (1982). Individual differences in skilled performance following imagery of bilateral skill. *Perceptual and Motor Skills, 55,* 771-780.

Velten, E. (1968). A laboratory task for induction of mood states. *Behavioral Research and Therapy, 6,* 473-482.

Waitley, D. (1995). *Empires of the mind: Lessons to lead and succeed in a knowledge-based world.* New York: William Morrow.

Waldersee, R., Simmons, R., & Eagleson, G. (1995). Pluralistic leadership in service change programs: Some preliminary findings. *Academy of Management Best Papers Proceedings 1995,* 296-302.

Wrisberg, C. A., & Anshel, M. H. (1989). The effect of cognitive strategies on the free throw shooting performance of young athletes. *The Sport Psychologist, 3,* 95-104.

Yukl, G. (1998). *Leadership in organizations* (4th ed.). Upper Saddle River, NJ: Prentice Hall.

Zecker, S. G. (1982). Mental practice and knowledge of results in the learning of a perceptual motor skill. *Journal of Sport Psychology, 4,* 52-63.

Ziegler, S. G. (1987). Comparison of imagery styles and past experience in skills performance. *Perceptual and Motor Skills, 64,* 579-586.

Part II

# METHODOLOGICAL ISSUES IN THE STUDY OF SHARED LEADERSHIP

# CHAPTER 7

# Assessing Shared Leadership

*Development and Preliminary Validation of a Team Multifactor Leadership Questionnaire*

*Bruce J. Avolio*

*Nagaraj Sivasubramaniam*

*William D. Murry*

*Don Jung*

*John W. Garger*

n recent years, a great deal of interest has been generated in the United States and abroad regarding the use of teams to build and rebuild organizations (Amason, Thompson, Hochwater, & Harrison, 1995; Cascio, 1995; Hackman, 1992; Kirkman & Rosen, 2001). Pressures to downsize and restructure organizations have led to a reduction in levels of management, with more emphasis now being placed on creating flexible forms of work, greater degrees of worker empowerment, and more interdependence among workers to accomplish their tasks (Smith, Peterson, & Misumi, 1994). These changes have led to repeated calls for implementing the work team concept in organizations. As more organizations turn to the use of teams, the need to examine the leadership processes that make teams successful has become more imperative (Pearce, Yoo, & Alavi, in press).

There has been considerable evidence accumulated to support the organization-wide benefits of implementing work teams (Cohen & Bailey, 1997; Avolio, Jung, Murry, & Sivasubramaniam, 2002), especially in the context of high-performance work systems (Huselid, 1995; MacDuffie, 1995). There is, however, some research evidence that indicates not all experiences with the implementation and use of teams have been successful (Hackman, 1992). One of the common causes of failures to implement work teams successfully has been ineffective leadership (Katzenbach, 1997; Sinclair, 1992; Stewart & Manz, 1994). Ironically, only a few authors have even included leadership in their models of team effectiveness (see Kozlowski, Gully, Salas, & Cannon-Bowers, 1996). Moreover, when focusing on leadership in teams, most authors have examined the behavior of an individual appointed leader as opposed to the leadership exhibited by all members of the team (Ireland & Hitt, 1999; Perry, Pearce, & Sims, 1999).

The omission of leadership in team models may be due, in part, to the construct of leadership being traditionally associated with an individual as opposed to a team. As we intend to demonstrate in this chapter, however, many of the constructs typically associated with individual leadership may also apply to the shared leadership displayed by a team.

Our main premise is that leadership exhibited by individuals and the team can each predict team performance (Ireland & Hitt, 1999; Perry et al., 1999; Yukl, 1998). Indeed, Pearce et al. (in press) have already provided evidence showing that shared leadership was a more powerful predictor of team performance than vertical or individual leadership. They also reported that shared leadership accounted for a greater occurrence of unique variance in potency, social integration, and problem-solving quality than leadership exhibited by a single appointed leader.

## Leadership "of" Versus "by" the Team

Most prior research focusing on leadership in teams has assessed the leadership exhibited by a single individual appointed to lead a team (Cohen, Chang, & Ledford, 1997; Ilgen, Major, Hollenbeck, & Sego, 1993). Although several authors have introduced the concept of "collective" or "distributed" leadership exhibited by teams (Katzenbach, 1997; Kozlowski et al., 1996; Manz & Sims, 1993; Zaccaro, Blair, Peterson, & Zazanos, 1995), there have been few attempts to measure leadership as a group-level construct. Dunphy and Bryant (1996) reviewed the literature on teams and concluded that future research must include leadership *by* the team, as well as *of* the team, when modeling team effectiveness. Similarly, Ilgen et al. (1993) recommended, "As we consider work teams and research on them in the 1990s, we cannot overlook the role of leaders and leadership" (p. 248). Moreover, Yukl (1998) stated, "The extent to which leadership can be shared, . . . the success of shared leadership, and the implications for design of organizations are important and interesting questions that deserve more research" (p. 504).

# Building the Team Leadership Construct

## Defining Team Leadership

Of the thirteen articles published in a two-part special issue of the *Leadership Quarterly* on multiple-level approaches to studying leadership, only two considered the possibility of leadership being observed and evaluated at the group level. Both articles introduced the idea of examining leadership "by" the group (Avolio & Bass, 1995; Markham & Markham, 1995), rather than "of" the group by a single individual. For example, Avolio and Bass (1995) argued that individualized consideration, a component of transformational leadership, could be examined at either an individual or group level. Specifically, team members can collectively exhibit concern for each member's needs and development. In this example, the concern for individuals can be shared by all members of the team versus any single individual within the team.

Other articles in this special issue that focused on group level leadership examined the grouping of multiple raters of a single leader (Hall & Lord, 1995), versus examining multiple raters evaluating the shared leadership within a team. The position taken here is that if one accepts the idea that leadership can be defined as a social influence process, then it can be operationally defined at either an individual or group level of analysis. By moving the assessment of leadership to the group level, the target of ratings becomes the shared leadership of the team.

We are not by any means the first to describe leadership as representing a shared social influence process, as noted above (Astin & Astin, 1996; Bales, 1954; Bowers & Seashore, 1966; House & Aditya, 1997; Waldersee & Eagleson, 1996). For example, while summarizing the Harvard Laboratory Studies on leadership, Bales (1954) referred to the term "co-leadership," suggesting that it might be beneficial for groups to allocate the task and relational leadership roles to multiple individuals. Waldersee and Eagleson (1996) provided support for Bales's position, demonstrating that the implementation of major change programs in hotels was more effective when the task and relational roles were shared between two individuals on the change management team.

House and Aditya (1997) refer to collective leadership in their review of the leadership literature, borrowing the term "peer leadership" from work published by Bowers and Seashore (1966). House and Aditya state, "It is also possible that some of the specific leader behaviors required to enact generic functions can be distributed throughout the entire work group or work unit being managed. Thus several individuals would enact the same specific leadership behaviors contemporaneously" (p. 458). House and Aditya go on to conclude, "The research by Bowers and Seashore (1966) clearly demonstrates that the exercise of leaders' behaviors can be shared by members of work units, as well as conducted by formal work unit managers" (p. 459).

Hughes, Ginnett, and Curphy (1998) define leadership as, "the process of influencing an organized group toward accomplishing its goals" (p. 9). Our only modification to their general process definition of leadership is that we focus specifically on *how all members of the team collectively influence each other toward accomplishing its goals*. An extension of this definition could involve examining how a team's shared leadership influences others, such as with top management teams in organizations. This extension, however, goes beyond the scope of the present study.

## Teams as Our Target of Analysis

Teams create a particular identity that guides the behavior of individual members. The identity stems from shared expectations and beliefs held by members of the team (Martin, 1993), or what Neck and Manz (1994) referred to as "group self leadership." As the team's identity becomes more central to its members, the mental model in each member's head of what the collective or team accepts, supports, and criticizes can influence individual and collective actions of all team members. For example, the very act of being a part of the team might inspire and stimulate individual members to reach performance levels beyond expectations in very much the same way as an individual leader influences his or her followers to perform when they are inspired (Bass, 1985). This may explain why Gully, Joshi, and Incalcaterra (2001) reported that team efficacy added incrementally to the self-efficacy ratings of team members in predicting team performance, and why Feltz and Lirgg (1998) were able to show that the team efficacy levels of hockey teams predicted their performance beyond aggregated individual self-efficacy perceptions.

We define team leadership in terms of how members of the group evaluate the influence of the group on members, as opposed to one individual within or external to the group. The theoretical meaning and operational definition of team leadership integrates the perspective taken by the team member in assessing leadership, as well as the level at which the phenomenon of leadership is examined, which we define here as the group or team. Our strategy for measuring team leadership is consistent with recommendations by Tesluk, Zaccaro, Marks, and Mathieu (1997), who suggested that group level phenomena can be assessed by having each individual rate the group on attributes defined at that level. Using this strategy, ratings are then averaged to reflect the group (also see Campion, Papper, & Medsker, 1996; Chan, 1998; Hyatt & Ruddy, 1997; Zaccaro & Marks, 1996, for a discussion on methods to evaluate team constructs).

### Parallel Team Concepts Viewed at the Group Level

There are a number of concepts that have been defined at an individual level that have subsequently been raised to a group level of analysis. Many of these concepts are related directly and indirectly to the shared leadership exhibited by teams. Kirkman and Rosen (1999) discuss five such concepts generally associated with individuals that were escalated to the team level in their discussion of a model of team effectiveness. The concepts included *meaningfulness, autonomy, empowerment, proactivity,* and *commitment.* Team meaningfulness was defined as what members of the team collectively considered important in their work. For autonomy they examined whether the team determined on its own, and how and what things were to be done. For empowerment they examined the extent to which the team felt it had the appropriate degrees of freedom to take action. Kirkman and Rosen adapted Bateman and Crant's (1993) measure of individual proactivity to assess how proactive the team was as a unit. Finally, commitment was measured using a scale adapted from Shapiro and Kirkman (1999), which assessed how committed individuals were collectively to the team.

In each instance, Kirkman and Rosen (1999) have taken constructs that were described at an individual level of analysis and escalated those constructs to describe a team. Taking this approach, Kirkman and Rosen concluded that oftentimes what is needed to examine team effectiveness is to have measures that simultaneously examine constructs at both individual and group levels.

Similar attempts to escalate concepts that are relevant to leadership processes in teams have appeared in the literature (Bandura, 1986; Bettenhausen & Murninghan, 1985; George, 1990; George & Bettenhausen, 1991; Moreland & Levine, 1992; Orasanu, 1990; Pearce & Sims, 2001). George (1990) discussed the affect of groups versus the affect of individuals. Bandura (1986, 1997) suggested that efficacy could be linked to a group's shared expectations of what it is capable of accomplishing. Bandura (1997) defines team efficacy as a team's "shared beliefs in its conjoint capabilities to organize and execute the course of actions required to produce given levels of attainment" (p. 477). George and Bettenhausen (1991) discussed how groups collectively exhibited "prosocial behavior." Klimoski and Mohammed (1994) discussed "cognition" as a group-level process in which members of the group retain information by sharing with their group in a way that transcends the cognitive facilities of any one individual. Similarly, both Orasanu (1990) and Moreland and Levine (1992) discuss how teams develop a common or shared understanding for problem identification.

Kozlowski et al. (1996) discussed team effectiveness in terms of team abilities, team decision making, team coherence, and team cohesion. They refer to each of these constructs as group-level constructs similar to the examples cited above. Underlying the "collective" base for each construct is a "shared system" of expectations and perceptions. For example, when discussing team coherence, they described it as a shared system of meaning among members. Kozlowski et al. concluded that effective teams possess common mental models that provide a basis for establishing mutual roles and expectations.

To conclude, across a very wide spectrum, constructs that have been tied to the individual level have now been escalated to a group level of analysis in models of team effectiveness. In all of the cases described above, there was reference to shared mental frameworks/models that result in the formation of constructs such as *collective* or *shared* thinking, esteem, coherence, problem-solving capability, efficacy, prosocial behavior, and, in our view, the leadership that characterizes high performing teams.

## Four Ways to Assess Leadership

Figure 7.1 offers a framework to summarize how leadership is conceptualized and measured in the literature reviewed above. The four different conceptualizations are classified using a two-dimensional framework whereby we include both the level of analysis and frame-of-reference, which can be associated with the rater's perspective of leadership.

### Level of Analysis

For many years, researchers (House, Rousseau, & Thomas-Hunt, 1995; Rousseau, 1985; Tosi, 1992; Yammarino, 1998) have been calling for more studies on leadership that examine mesolevel effects. In Hunt's (1991) multilevel model of leadership, he specifically calls for researchers to think of "team leadership" rather than just focus on a single leader (p. 298).

The theoretical framework should be the primary determinant of one's choice of an appropriate level of analysis for a specific construct. If leadership were not expected to be shared by all team members, then it should be assessed at the *individual level,* or what Klein, Dansereau, and Hall (1994) described as a *parts* view. In contrast, if there is reason to believe that group members are consistent in their perceptions of leadership, then there is justification to escalate leadership to a higher level of analysis, which we generally refer to here as the *group-level.*

### Rater Referent of Leadership

The frame of reference used by a respondent to evaluate leadership also determines one's measurement scheme. Most research on leadership has examined the leadership behaviors exhibited by an individual—the supervisor, the assigned team leader, or the distant leader such as the division head, vice president, or CEO. Yet, leadership can also be represented by members' perceptions of the work unit of which they are members by shifting the referent from an *individual* to the *group.* This strategy has been repeatedly used by researchers who have examined group-level constructs such as organizational citizenship behavior (Podsakoff, Ahearne, & MacKenzie, 1997), team climate (Kivimaki et al., 1997), team efficacy (Bandura, 1997), as well as other work group characteristics (Campion, Medsker, & Higgs, 1993).

### Classification of Measurement Approaches

By combining the rater's leadership perspective and levels of analysis, we created a four-cell typology of leadership measurement. We have provided a description of key facets in each quadrant as well as a pictorial metaphor to capture the essence of different measurement schemes. In Figure 7.1, *smaller circles* represent individuals, whereas a *larger circle* represents the group. Lines represent the direction of influence among the elements. Quadrant 1 in Figure 7.1 represents the most common strategy in which a rater is asked to evaluate a leader, and the analysis is at the *individual level.* Dansereau et al. (1995) found strong support for this individualized leadership in their multilevel study of leadership.

Chan (1998) offered a typology of composition models to specify the functional relationships among constructs at different levels of analysis. According to Chan, Quadrant 1's measurement scheme represents an additive model in which individual perceptions of the leader are averaged or aggregated to develop an index of leadership.

Quadrant 2 represents the approach commonly used to study leadership *of* teams. Researchers examine leadership at a focal leader's level, after statistically establishing that the followers have common perceptions of that individual's leadership *of* the team. Chan (1998) refers to this approach as the direct consensus model, meaning that individual leadership is derived from consensus among followers. Within-group agreement is considered adequate evidence to aggregate individual ratings of the leader. An ellipse that loosely envelops the individual members represents the within-group agreement on ratings of a focal leader pictorially.

Quadrants 3 and 4 are uncommon in leadership research. There are few empirical studies of leadership in which leadership was defined as shared, except for research on co-leadership and recent work by Pearce and Sims (2001). As noted earlier, however, examples abound in related literature in which researchers have examined constructs such as efficacy (Bandura, 1986), affect (George, 1990), and climate

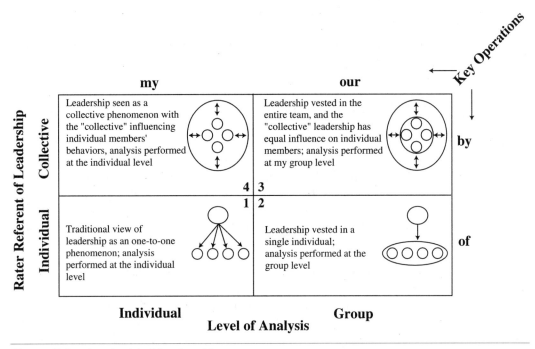

**Figure 7.1**    Leadership Membership

(Anderson & West, 1998) at the group level. Group members are seen as being able to provide assessments of their group while being part of the collective (e.g., members of my group encourage each other when someone is down; we monitor each other to maintain a higher standard of work performance). Quadrant 3 represents a referent-shift consensus model (Chan, 1998) in which respondents are asked to shift the referent from an individual to a group, and evidence for escalation to a higher level is provided by within-group agreement concerning the construct. The picture in Quadrant 3 depicts the collective influence of the group on individual members.

Anderson and West (1998) escalated the construct of team climate to the group level of analysis (Quadrant 4) by establishing that team members held shared perceptions of team climate. Measurement of shared perceptions at the group level is a core characteristic of Quadrant 4, where there is relatively equal influence on individual members; thus the analysis should be performed at the group level. We represent this form of shared leadership by indicating that individuals still have their own identity, as represented by the smaller circles, inside of the larger circle, which represents the team they are embedded within.

Kivimaki et al. (1997) examined team climate as a collective phenomenon with a large Finnish sample of government employees, using the measurement perspective described in Quadrant 3. Here each rater individually rated the climate of the team at the group level using the Team Climate Inventory (Anderson & West, 1994). Podsakoff et al. (1997) assessed team members' perceptions of the work unit's organizational citizenship behaviors (OCB) and aggregated individual members' assessment to the group level. They then used group-level OCB to predict both quantity and quality of workgroup output, a core illustration of Quadrant 4.

Operative words are provided in Figure 7.1 to illustrate how each quadrant can be distinguished from one another. For example, Quadrant 1 is described using the operative words, *my* assessment of the leadership *of* individuals. In Quadrant 3 we refer to the raters as a group, providing *our* assessment of leadership developed by a shared understanding or consensus, a procedure recommended by Kirkman and Rosen (1999).

## Extending Transformational Leadership Theory to Groups and Teams

Recently, Burns (1996) extended his original thinking on individual transformational leadership to include a focus on collective or shared leadership. Burns (1996) wrote in a paper titled "Empowerment for Change," that there was "the existence of webs of potential collective leadership" (p. 1). Substituting the term "initiators" for "leadership" due to the fact that leadership is typically assigned to an individual, Burns went on to suggest, "The initiator may continue as a single dominating 'leader' à la Castro, but more typically he or she will merge with others in a series of participant interactions that will constitute collective leadership. . . . I see crucial leadership acts in the collective process" (pp. 2-3).

In his extension of transformational leadership theory to teams, Bass (1998) notes that, "transformational leadership could be shared among the team members" (p. 157). He suggests that in such teams, substitutes for leadership may evolve that help support the team's higher levels of achievement. For example, Bass (1998) states,

> We might see a small military team whose esprit had been built by a previous history of success, gallantry, and mutual support of members for each other. Its formally appointed officer might find the membership on the team provided sufficient member self-esteem without any effort on the part of the officer. . . . Instead of motivation being supplied by identification of members with an idealized, charismatic leader, similar motivation would be supplied by identification with the team. . . . Inspiration would come from a sharing of mutually articulated goals. . . . Empowered, self-managed work teams ideally epitomize substitution for much of what was done before by the formal hierarchical leader (p. 157).

Bass refers to substitution in terms of team leadership development, in much the same way as Kerr and Jermier (1978) and Meindl, Ehrlich, and Dukerich (1985) do in referring to substitutes for leadership. Taking a temporal view of the development of team leadership, Bass points to the role an individual leader may play in initiating a "social contagion" process in a group over time, which may manifest by potentially substituting for individual leadership in the team (see Gully, 2000, for a discussion of a temporal view of team development). For example, the leader may repeatedly emphasize the need to control mistakes to avoid life-threatening events, and over time the need to control mistakes becomes part of its shared behavior.

Avolio and Bass (1995) have argued that transformational and transactional leadership can be considered multilevel constructs, as their theoretical meaning holds even when generalized across levels. Specifically, the type of "individualized" relationship that a leader builds with each follower can also emerge at a group level of analysis as demonstrated by the various relationships among team members (Avolio, Jung, Murry, & Sivasubramaniam, 1996; Kozlowski et al., 1996).

In the present study, we extended Burns's (1978) operational definition of transforming leadership, suggesting that teams can collectively display a transformational style. Our extension escalates the individual transformational and transactional styles of leadership involving a leader and his or her followers to the team level, whereby members of the team share in influencing each other to perform for the "good of the team," as Burns originally described transforming leadership. Team members also develop shared expectations of each other as typically defined by transactional leadership.

In this chapter, we decided to focus only on examining transformational, transactional, and avoidant (laissez-faire) leadership behaviors, as described by Bass and Avolio (1994). These leadership constructs represent a significant subset of potential leadership styles that we would expect to observe within teams. Thus we assume there are other factors that may also be relevant to measuring team leadership that have not yet been explored.

### Components of a MultiFactor Leadership Model

Recent evidence provided by Avolio, Bass, and Jung (1999) indicated support for at least six factors or components comprising what Bass and Avolio (1994) have referred to as a multifactor model of leadership. Three of these components represented transformational leadership, two represented transactional leadership, and one was associated with a passive/avoidant leadership style. These components or factors were validated in two separate confirmatory factor analyses with large samples of leaders, all of whom were rated by their respective followers at an individual level of analysis (Avolio et al., 1999).

Bass and Avolio (1994) labeled the three component transformational scales as Inspiring Leadership (IL), Intellectual Stimulation (IS), and Individualized Consideration (IC). Two component scales represented transactional leadership. One scale measured transactional contingent reward leadership (CR). The other scale measured Managing-by-Exception–Active (MA). The sixth scale represented Passive/Avoidant Leadership (PA).

In sum, we make the case here for extending the multifactor leadership model to the group or team level, by using the measurement perspectives defined in Quadrants 3 and 4 of Figure 7.1. Using this framework we can assess how members of the group evaluate their group's collective leadership in terms of the components of the multi theory of leadership.

# Phase 1: Exploratory Study

## Method

### Sample

Data were gathered from 189 undergraduates majoring in business at a large public university in the Northeastern U.S. Students were enrolled in two different sections of an introductory organizational behavior course during the fall term. All participants were randomly assigned to 37 groups of mixed gender and ethnicity and were required to complete a series of group projects by meeting on weekly basis. There were approximately an even number of males and females in the sample.

## Instrument

Items included in the team multifactor leadership questionnaire (TMLQ) were developed based on four sources. The first source included the definitions of constructs comprising Bass and Avolio's multifactor leadership model. The second source was the team literature and references made to leadership *of* and *by* teams. The third source was the Multi-factor Leadership Questionnaire (Form 5X) (Avolio et al., 1999). The MLQ measures the individual transformational, transactional, and avoidant leadership styles that were used as a basis for developing the team leadership constructs. The fourth source was from individuals who were interviewed and had worked in teams for at least one year. Approximately 30 teams participated in interviews lasting two hours each. These teams were employed by four different organizations including a large financial services firm, a performing arts organization, and two global manufacturing organizations. Open-ended questions were used asking members, for example, to describe stages of team development, how members lead teams, how teams reinforced high potential, and how leadership differed in team systems versus more traditional organizational settings.

All the team interviews were videotaped. The videotaped interviews were then reviewed for leadership content and sample items were developed for inclusion in the TMLQ. Four experts in the field of leadership independently classified the items into component scales based on the multifactor leadership model, while also evaluating each item for clarity and understanding. Items were retained if they were successfully classified into the original scales comprising the MLQ (Form 5X) at least 80% of the time. The initial version of the TMLQ used in the exploratory study contained 43 leadership items.

## Data Collection Process

Students' perceptions of group-level leadership were gathered using the TMLQ questionnaire after all group projects were submitted, but before any form of evaluation was made on projects. On average, these teams had worked together for nearly three months, meeting approximately two hours a week. Questionnaire items were rated using a five-point response scale: (1) not at all, (2) once in a while, (3) sometimes, (4) fairly often, and (5) frequently, if not always. Participants were asked to judge how frequently, on average, did their *group* display the behavior described in each statement.

## Analysis

Because the dimensionality of the TMLQ was not yet established, we assessed the factor structure using exploratory factor analysis (Gorsuch, 1983). We used the eigenvalues and scree test to help guide us in determining the factor structure underlying the measurement of shared leadership. Previous research (e.g., Tucker, Koopman, & Linn, 1969) has shown the scree test to be an effective preliminary method for determining the factor structure of a survey instrument.

Results of the extracted eigenvalues indicated breaks at five or six factors. We used the principal axis method for factor extraction and the Harris-Kaiser oblique rotation method to transform the final factor solution to a simple solution for interpretation (Harris & Kaiser, 1964). Previous research (Hakstian, 1971) has shown the Harris-Kaiser rotation to be superior to other methods for recovery of a known structure. We then analyzed a range of factor solutions from three factors to six factors based on prior transformational and transactional leadership literature.

## Results

We started with 43 items, representing the leadership factors originally conceptualized and identified, to construct the questionnaire. Our principal axis method of exploratory analysis initially revealed a six-factor solution (see Table 7.1). We used two criteria for considering an item as representing the factor: a factor loading of greater than .45 (Gorsuch, 1983) and item cross loading on other factors that were no greater than .3. The first five factors exhibited clear loading patterns, whereas the sixth factor was not interpretable. The first factor was mostly comprised of items representing Intellectual Stimulation (IS) with one item from the original Individualized Consideration scale (IC) significantly loading on this factor. We chose the first four items that met the two selection criteria described above. The second factor represented items from the Passive/Avoidant Leadership (PA) scale. The first five items loading onto this factor met the dual criteria and were retained for the validation study. The third factor was mostly composed of items representing Inspiring Leadership (IL), and five items met the criteria for retention. The fourth factor was made up of items representing Contingent Reward (CR) and Individualized Consideration (IC). Three items from the CR scale and two items from the IC scale met the selection criteria. Management-by-Exception–Active (MA) items, along with one item representing passive/avoidant leadership, loaded on to the fifth factor. Three MA items and one active avoidant leadership item were selected to represent this factor based on our selection criteria.

In all, we retained 23 items representing five different factors that exhibited clear loading patterns. Our goal here was to develop a short survey instrument for research purposes. The five team leadership factors extracted at this stage were Inspiring leadership (5 items), Intellectual Stimulation (4 items), Individualized Consideration (5 items), Management-by-Exception–Active (4 items), and Passive/Avoidant Leadership (5 items).

Consistent with prior research on individual leadership, the pattern of intercorrelations among the transformational, transactional, and passive/avoidant scales were similar to those intercorrelations reported at an individual level of analysis (Bass, 1997; Lowe, Kroeck, & Sivasubramaniam, 1995). Specifically, the three transformational scales were all positively intercorrelated, and negatively correlated with the other two scales. Active management-by-exception and passive/avoidant scales were modestly and positively correlated.

Results of this exploratory factor analysis were quite similar to the factor structure reported by Avolio et al., (1999) for individual leadership ratings, except that they found evidence for considering IC and CR as two separate factors rather than as a single factor. They also, however, reported that each of these lower-order factors loaded on a single higher-order factor.

**Table 7.1**   Exploratory Factor Analysis—Student Sample

| Brief Item Descriptions | Item | Factor 1 | Factor 2 | Factor 3 | Factor 4 | Factor 5 | Factor 6 |
|---|---|---|---|---|---|---|---|
| IS–look at problems differently | I42 | **80** | 7 | −3 | 14 | −10 | 2 |
| IC–provide advice | I43 | **61** | 0 | 12 | 21 | 2 | 6 |
| IS–seek broad perspectives | I34 | **59** | −22 | 6 | −1 | −4 | 1 |
| IS–question others strategy | I7 | **48** | 1 | −1 | 3 | 30 | 9 |
| IC–teach and coach each other | I27 | 46 | −7 | 34 | −9 | 4 | 25 |
| CR–recognize accomplishments | I40 | 42 | −5 | 25 | 36 | −8 | −8 |
| IM–set high standards | I5 | 42 | −15 | 9 | 6 | 31 | 6 |
| IC–develop others' strengths | I18 | 38 | −2 | 33 | 5 | 5 | 22 |
| IS–encourage rethinking of ideas | I16 | 32 | −12 | 31 | 15 | 12 | 20 |
| MP–delay actions until serious | I10 | 17 | **81** | −13 | 2 | 3 | −19 |
| MP–act when things go wrong | I28 | −10 | **75** | −2 | −1 | 14 | −8 |
| MP–allow performance to fall | I2 | −30 | **58** | 7 | −5 | 2 | 8 |
| LF–delay responding | I35 | −26 | **57** | −10 | −2 | 9 | 22 |
| LF–avoid problems | I8 | 19 | **57** | 3 | −31 | −19 | 6 |
| LF–no follow-up on requests | I17 | −33 | 48 | 30 | −19 | −1 | 1 |
| MBEP–not broke, don't fix it | I37 | −15 | 22 | −2 | −16 | 15 | 5 |
| II–talk up trust | I30 | −5 | 12 | **80** | −8 | 13 | 3 |
| IM–optimistic about future | I23 | −10 | −16 | **65** | 29 | −9 | −4 |
| IM–articulate vision | I41 | 12 | −9 | **61** | 15 | −3 | 17 |
| M–envision possibilities | I14 | 31 | −2 | **52** | 17 | 5 | 5 |
| II–collective sense of mission | I39 | 40 | −13 | 50 | 2 | −6 | −7 |
| IM–talk about importance of work | I32 | 28 | −30 | 47 | −4 | 15 | −2 |
| CR–agree on expectations | I13 | 4 | −6 | −3 | **70** | −6 | 29 |
| CR–clear communication | I6 | 17 | 8 | 1 | **69** | 5 | −2 |
| IC-listen attentively to each other | I9 | 10 | −27 | 4 | **55** | 18 | −25 |
| CR–provide assistance for effort | I22 | −2 | −7 | 30 | **53** | −11 | 23 |
| IC–treat others as individuals | I36 | 17 | −7 | 19 | **49** | 0 | −23 |
| II–clarify purpose | I21 | 11 | −20 | 29 | 31 | 7 | 9 |
| MA–track mistakes | I29 | −2 | 12 | 4 | 9 | **65** | 11 |
| MA–focus on mistakes | I4 | 8 | −3 | 6 | 8 | **65** | −10 |
| MA–attention on failure | I38 | −6 | −5 | 1 | −10 | **65** | −18 |
| MP–tell others of mistakes | I19 | −23 | 24 | 4 | −6 | **54** | 18 |
| MA–always put out fires | I20 | −6 | 32 | 6 | −16 | 43 | 27 |

NOTE: Shaded rows represent variables that were excluded from the validation study. Items were selected if their loading on the target factor was greater than .45 and loadings on other factors did not exceed .30. Bolded items in table indicate the specific factor loadings per scale.

In the following section, we describe the next set of studies that were conducted to validate the dimensionality of TMLQ.

# Phase 2: Validation Studies

## Method

### Validation Study 1

Participants were 165 business majors enrolled in the same introductory organizational behavior course that was offered in the spring term of the following year. Participants were randomly assigned to 42 groups to ensure an even mix of gender and ethnicity. Forty-four percent of the sample was women. Ratings on the TMLQ were collected in classroom settings after teams had interacted on average for three months, but prior to receiving any formal feedback on their team project.

### Validation Study 2

Data were gathered from 359 soldiers in the U.S. Army, who came from 18 light infantry platoons. Each soldier was asked to complete the TMLQ survey rating the shared leadership of his platoon. We included those who had been with their platoon for at least three months to ensure equivalence with the student sample as well as to reduce the effects of possible bias in the responses of newcomers to the platoon. Complete data were available for 309 soldiers, who were all male.

### Validation Study 3

Participants were 118 business majors enrolled in two sections of an introductory organizational behavior course. Participants were randomly assigned to 34 groups to ensure an even mix of gender and ethnicity. Ratings on the TMLQ were collected in classroom settings after teams had interacted on average for three months, but prior to receiving any feedback on their group project.

### Instrument and Data Collection

The same questionnaire used in the exploratory study was used in validation Studies 1 and 3, except the items were reordered. None of the students had been exposed to the questionnaire in any other class, and hence had no awareness of the properties of the instrument prior to survey administration. The questionnaire used with the Army sample was similar to the student version of TMLQ. Several items, however, were reworded to reflect the unique context in which teamwork is performed in the U.S. Army. Three content experts from the U.S. military made suggestions for rewording these items, which were checked by the first author to assure the meaning of items were not altered by using military jargon. The TMLQ data for the student groups and Army platoons were collected in large groups in a classroom setting, under the direct supervision of the researchers involved with this study. Participation in the Army sample was voluntary and produced a participation rate of 90%. The loss of data was due to soldiers being off base at the time of data collection.

### Analysis

We used confirmatory factor analysis (CFA) to validate the factor structure described above in the Phase 1 exploratory study, using each sample separately. The CFA was implemented using LISREL and AMOS. In addition to testing the factor structure derived at the exploratory stage, we also tested eight other competing models that were theoretically feasible, in line with recommendations made by James, Mulaik, and Brett (1982) and Anderson and Gerbing (1988). The "target" model was the five-factor model determined by exploratory factor analysis, whereas all other models were treated as competing models. The competing models examined here represent alternative factor structures of the multifactor model proposed by other researchers at an individual level of analysis (Avolio et al., 1999; Wofford, Goodwin, & Whittington, 1998; Yammarino, Dubinsky, & Spangler, 1998). We present the details of the target model and the eight competing models in Table 7.2.

We examined different methods of assessing whether the hypothesized factor structure adequately described the observed data. Given that traditional model fit indices of structural equation models such as $\chi^2$, root-mean-squared residual (RMSR), and goodness-of-fit index (GFI) are inadequate and considerably influenced by sample size and departures from multivariate normality, many researchers have proposed alternative fit indices (Medsker, Williams, & Holohan, 1994). We chose three fit indices that have been strongly recommended when assessing nested models—Normed Fit Index (NFI2) proposed by Mulaik et al. (1989), Comparative Fit Index (CFI) proposed by Bentler (1990), and root-mean-squared error of approximation (RMSEA) suggested by Browne and Cudeck (1993). We also used the $\chi^2$/df ratio as recommended by Marsh and Hocevar (1985) and La Du and Tanaka (1989). Values of this ratio between 2 and 5 are considered acceptable, whereas values closer to 1 indicate superior fit. We also used the $\chi^2$ difference test to examine whether any of the competing models was a more parsimonious representation of the observed data than the target 5-factor model. Our strategy of reporting and using multiple fit indices is in line with Gerbing and Anderson's (1992) suggestion that a single index of model assessment should not be used to the exclusion of other possible fit indices.

## Results

Descriptive statistics and intercorrelations for the three validation samples are presented in Table 7.3. Scale reliabilities were computed using the method proposed by Fornell and Larcker (1981) for LISREL models. Means for the Army sample were significantly lower than for the first student sample for all three transformational team leadership scales and significantly higher than both student samples for the other two-team leadership scales, with Individualized Consideration (IC), Management-by-Exception—Active (MA), and Passive/Avoidant (PA) scales showing the largest differences. The scale reliabilities for all scales excepting MA were at

**Table 7.2**    Description of the Competing Models Tested in the Validation Stage

| Model | Description |
|---|---|
| Model 1: One-Factor Model | All items were hypothesized to load on to a single factor representing team leadership. |
| Model 2: Two-Factor Model | All items representing different facets of transformational team leadership were hypothesized to load on to one factor and all items representing the passive leadership dimensions were constrained to load on to the second factor. |
| Model 3: Three-Factor Model | All transformational leadership items were represented by one factor. Items representing Management-by-Exception—Active (MA) were hypothesized to load on to the second factor, whereas items representing the Passive/Avoidant (PA) dimension loaded on to the third factor. |
| Model 4: Four-Factor Model | Items representing Inspiring Leadership (IL) were differentiated from the other transformational leadership items and constrained to load on to a separate factor. Third and fourth factors were same as Model 3. |
| Model 5: Four-Factor Model | Items representing Individualized Consideration (IC) were differentiated from the other transformational leadership items and constrained to load on to a separate factor. Third and fourth factors were same as Model 3. |
| Model 6: Five-Factor Model (Target Model) | Two other transformational leadership dimensions were identified – Intellectual Stimulation (IS) and Individualized Consideration (IC). This model is the theoretical model to be validated and included all five leadership dimensions identified in the exploratory stage |
| Model 7: Second-order Factor Model I | The two transformational leadership factors—IS and IC—were conceptualized to be represented by a second-order factor, whereas the other leadership dimensions remain as first-order factors. |
| Model 8: Second-order Factor Model II | The two transformational leadership factors—IL and IS—were conceptualized to be represented by a second-order factor, whereas the other leadership dimensions remain as first-order factors. |
| Model 9: Second-order Factor Model III | All three transformational leadership factors—IL, IS, and IC-CR—were hypothesized to be represented by a second-order factor labeled Transformational Team Leadership, whereas the two passive dimensions—MA and PA—remain as first-order factors. |

**Table 7.3** Descriptive Statistics and Inter-Correlations for Validation Samples

| Dimensions | Study 1[a] | | Correlations & Scale Reliabilities[d] | | | | |
|---|---|---|---|---|---|---|---|
| | Mean | SD | 1 | 2 | 3 | 4 | 5 |
| 1. Inspiring (IL) | 3.15 | .88 | .84 | | | | |
| 2. Intellectual Stimulation (IS) | 3.57 | .74 | .60 | .79 | | | |
| 3. Individualized Cons (IC) | 3.85 | .70 | .55 | .72 | .80 | | |
| 4. Mgmt-by-exception–Active (MA) | 2.56 | .71 | −.06 | .06 | −.22 | .61 | |
| 5. Passive/Avoidant (PA) | 1.95 | .82 | −.20 | −.49 | −.55 | .39 | .87 |

| Dimensions | Study 2[b] | | Correlations & Scale Reliabilities[d] | | | | |
|---|---|---|---|---|---|---|---|
| | Mean | SD | 1 | 2 | 3 | 4 | 5 |
| 1. Inspiring (IL) | 3.03 | .89 | .82 | | | | |
| 2. Intellectual Stimulation (IS) | 3.17 | .89 | .77 | .81 | | | |
| 3. Individualized Cons (IC) | 3.21 | .86 | .69 | .73 | .80 | | |
| 4. Mgmt-by-exception–Active (MA) | 3.22 | .95 | −.24 | −.21 | −.24 | .66 | |
| 5. Passive/Avoidant (PA) | 2.48 | .85 | −.50 | −.53 | −.53 | .46 | .80 |

| Dimensions | Study 3[c] | | Correlations & Scale Reliabilities[d] | | | | |
|---|---|---|---|---|---|---|---|
| | Mean | SD | 1 | 2 | 3 | 4 | 5 |
| 1. Inspiring (IL) | 3.00 | .96 | .84 | | | | |
| 2. Intellectual Stimulation (IS) | 3.22 | .89 | .86 | .86 | | | |
| 3. Individualized Cons (IC) | 3.42 | .84 | .80 | .88 | .90 | | |
| 4. Mgmt-by-exception–Active (MA) | 2.83 | .68 | .29 | .32 | .18 | .60 | |
| 5. Passive/Avoidant (PA) | 2.39 | .81 | −.31 | −.41 | −.50 | .26 | .80 |

a. Student Sample 1: N = 165.
b. Army Sample: N = 309.
c. Student Sample 2: N = 118.
d. Diagonals show scale reliability. Intercorrelations are presented on off-diagonals. Absolute values of correlation above .2 significant at $p < .01$.

or above minimum standards recommended in the literature and reported in Table 7.3. The MA scale was marginally acceptable in terms of reliability. Scale reliabilities for the three studies were quite similar, except for the Individualized Consideration (IC) and Passive/Avoidant (PA) scales. It is interesting to note that the MA scale was not correlated with the transformational scales in student sample 1, but negatively and significantly correlated with all three transformational scales in the Army sample, which may be due in part to the high-risk environment in this context, and the need to anticipate and avoid mistakes.

## Study 1: Student Sample 1

The covariance matrix was used as input into LISREL. The parameters of the measurement model were estimated using the maximum-likelihood estimation method. Results of the CFA are reported in Table 7.4. Compared to the first five models, the target model (Model 6) fit the data best as indicated by acceptable values for NFI2 and CFI. RMSEA was below .08, indicating that the target model yielded a reasonable approximation of the model. The $\chi^2/df$ ratio was also below 2, indicating an acceptable model fit. The competing models, although more parsimonious than the target model in terms of the number of parameters estimated, did not fit the observed data as well as the target model did. Simpler conceptualizations of the factor structure compared to the five-factor model resulted in poorer fit, indicating that a five-factor structure best described the observed data. The $\chi^2$ difference test between the target model and each of the competing models were all significant, indicating deterioration in fit for the alternative models when compared with the five-factor model.

We also examined the magnitude and significance of the factor loadings. All factor loadings were significant with $t$-values ranging between 3.5 and 13.5. Excepting for two items, factor loadings were well above .5 demonstrating adequate item reliabilities. The pattern of correlations among the five latent factors was similar to the exploratory study in that the three transformational factors were not correlated with MA and negatively correlated with PA.

## Study 2: Army Platoons

As noted above, item wording for this sample reflected the work context of the platoons. All but one of the final 23 items used in Study 1 were identical to those used in Study 2. The lone exception was an item representing the MA scale. The item "members of my team track each other's mistakes" was omitted from the questionnaire used for the Army sample. We conducted the CFA with the remaining three items in the MA scale, which are the minimum recommended items per scale for CFA. The covariance matrix was used as input into LISREL. The parameters of the measurement model were estimated using the maximum-likelihood estimation method.

The CFA results are presented in Table 7.5. The target model (Model 6) fit the data very well as indicated by high values for NFI2 and CFI. RMSEA was also below .05, indicating that the data fit the model very well. Also, the $\chi^2/df$ ratio was well below the recommended value of 2 for the target model. Again, alternate conceptualizations of the factor structure were not empirically supported. Even though the two-, three-, and four-factor models produced adequate fit indices, the difference in $\chi^2$ between these alternate models and the five-factor model were highly significant, indicating that the five-factor model had the best fit as compared to other first-order factor models. The lone exception was Model 5, the four-factor model in which we treated IC, MA, and LF as separate factors and combined IL and IS into a single factor. The difference in $\chi^2$ between this model and the target model was marginally significant ($\Delta\chi^2 = 8.7$, $p < .08$), indicating that the four-factor model fit the data as well as the five-factor model did. The RMSEA value was also below .05 and insignificant ($p < .84$). We examined the four- versus five-factor model using a

**Table 7.4**   LISREL Results: Student Sample 1

| Model Description | $\chi^2$ | df | $\chi^2$/df | RMSEA[a] | CFI[b] | NFI2[c] | $\Delta \chi^2$ (df)[d] |
|---|---|---|---|---|---|---|---|
| Null Model | 1919.08 | 253 | | | | | |
| Model 1: One-Factor Model | 928.10 | 230 | 4.04 | .136 | .581 | .587 | 511.63 (10) |
| Model 2: Two-Factor Model | 669.72 | 229 | 2.92 | .108 | .735 | .739 | 253.25 (9) |
| Model 3: Three-Factor Model | 614.87 | 227 | 2.71 | .102 | .767 | .771 | 198.40 (7) |
| Model 4: Four-Factor Model (IL separate) | 453.66 | 224 | 2.03 | .079 | .862 | .865 | 37.19 (4) |
| Model 5: Four-Factor Model (IS separate) | 575.38 | 224 | 2.57 | .098 | .789 | .793 | 158.91 (4) |
| **Model 6: Five First-order factors** | 416.47 | 220 | 1.89 | .073 | .882 | .884 | — |
| Model 7: Five first-order factors—one second-order factor only for IS & IC | 439.44 | 222 | 1.98 | .077 | .869 | .872 | 22.97 (2) |
| Model 8: Five first-order factors—one second order factor only for IL and IS | 430.73 | 222 | 1.94 | .075 | .875 | .877 | 14.26 (2) |
| Model 9: One second-order factor for the three transformational factors | 450.96 | 224 | 2.01 | .078 | .864 | .866 | 34.49 (4) |

a. The RMSEA (root-mean squared error of approximation) was suggested by Browne and Cudeck (1993) as a way to compare nested models by compensating for the effects of model complexity; values below .05 indicate a close fit of the model, whereas values less than .08 indicate a reasonable error of approximation. We also tested the null hypothesis that RMSEA $\leq$ .05; all RMSEA values reported above were significantly greater than .05.

b. The CFI (comparative fit index) proposed by Bentler (1990) is identical to McDonald and Marsh's (1990) relative noncentrality index (RNI) and is strongly recommended by Bagozzi, Yi, and Phillips (1991) and Medsker, Williams, and Holohan (1994).

c. NFI2, proposed by Mulaik et al. (1989), is conceptually similar to the Normed Fit Index proposed by Bentler and Bonnett (1980), excepting that the degrees of freedom of the target model is subtracted from the Null model chi-square in the denominator.

d. $\Delta \chi^2$ calculated by subtracting the $\chi^2$ value associated with the five-factor model (Model 5) from the value associated with the competing model. The differences in the degrees of freedom (the degrees of freedom gained by setting more constraints) are reported in parentheses along side. All values were significant at $p < .001$.

**Table 7.5**    LISREL Results: Army Platoons[a]

| Model Description | $\chi^2$ | df[b] | $\chi^2$/df | RMSEA[c] | CFI | NFI[2] | $\Delta \chi^2$ (df) |
|---|---|---|---|---|---|---|---|
| Null Model | 3004.71 | 231 | | | | | |
| Model 1: One-Factor Model | 696.08 | 209 | 3.33 | .087 | .824 | .826 | 376.96 (10) |
| Model 2: Two-Factor Model | 417.60 | 208 | 2.01 | .057 | .924 | .925 | 98.48 (9) |
| Model 3: Three-Factor Model | 344.13 | 206 | 1.67 | .047 | .950 | .951 | 25.01 (7) |
| Model 4: Four-Factor Model (IL separate) | 331.21 | 203 | 1.63 | .045 | .954 | .954 | 12.09 (4) |
| Model 5: Four-Factor Model (IC separate) | 327.82 | 203 | 1.62 | .045 | .955 | .955 | 8.7ns (4) |
| **Model 6: Five First-order factors** | 319.12 | 199 | 1.60 | .044 | .957 | .957 | — |
| Model 7: Five first-order factors—one second-order factor only for IS & IC | 323.14 | 201 | 1.61 | .044 | .956 | .956 | 4.02ns (2) |
| Model 8: Five first-order factors—one second-order factor only for IL & IS | 319.93 | 201 | 1.59 | .044 | .957 | .958 | 0.81ns (2) |
| Model 9: One second-order factor for the three transformational factors | 326.58 | 203 | 1.61 | .044 | .955 | .956 | 7.46ns (4) |

a. The questionnaire distributed among student teams had an additional MA item, "Members of my team track each other's mistakes." This item was dropped from the questionnaire used for the Army platoons, as it was considered not appropriate for this sample by our content experts.

b. The number of raters completing TMLQ.

c. RMSEA values below .057 not significantly different than .05 in the above sample.

higher-order factor conceptualization below. The factor loadings for the 22 items were all well above .5 and the t values ranged between 6 and 16. Unlike the student sample 1, the three transformational scales were significantly and negatively correlated with the MA scale.

**Table 7.6**   AMOS Results: Student Sample 2

| Model Description | $\chi$ | $df^a$ | $\chi^2/df$ | RMSEA | CFI | NFI2 | $\Delta \chi^2$ (df) |
|---|---|---|---|---|---|---|---|
| Null Model | 1917.26 | 253 | | | | | |
| Model 1: One-Factor Model | 610.55 | 230 | 2.66 | .119 | .771 | .774 | 172.77 (10) |
| Model 2: Two-Factor Model | 491.70 | 229 | 2.15 | .099 | .842 | .844 | 53.92 (9) |
| Model 3: Three-Factor Model | 463.52 | 227 | 2.04 | .094 | .858 | .860 | 25.74 (7) |
| Model 4: Four-Factor Model (IL separate) | 453.47 | 224 | 2.02 | .094 | .862 | .864 | 15.69 (4) |
| Model 5: Four-Factor Model (IC separate) | 457.43 | 224 | 2.04 | .094 | .860 | .862 | 19.65 (4) |
| **Model 6: Five First-order factors** | 437.78 | 220 | 1.99 | .092 | .879 | .872 | — |
| Model 7: Five first-order factors—one second-order factor only for IS & IC | 442.68 | 222 | 1.94 | .092 | .867 | .870 | 4.90ns (2) |
| Model 8: Five first-order factors—one second-order factor only for IL & IS | 439.85 | 222 | 1.98 | .092 | .869 | .871 | 2.07ns (2) |
| Model 9: One second-order factor for the three transformational factors | 445.58 | 224 | 1.99 | .092 | .867 | .869 | 7.80ns (4) |

a. The number of raters completing TMLQ.

## Study 3: Student Sample 2

Results of the CFA are reported in Table 7.6. Compared to the first five models, the target model (Model 6) fit the data best as indicated by acceptable values for NFI2. For CFI, models 6 and 8 tied for the best fit with an index of .88. RMSEA was .09 indicating that target model yielded a reasonable approximation of the model. The $\chi^2/df$ ratio was also below 2, indicating an acceptable model fit. The competing models, although more parsimonious than the target model in terms of the number of parameters estimated, tended not to fit the observed data as well as the target model did. Simpler conceptualizations of the factor structure compared to the five-factor model resulted in poorer fit, indicating that a five-factor structure best described the observed data. The $\chi^2$ difference test between the target model and each of the competing models was significant.

We also examined the magnitude and significance of the factor loadings. All factor loadings excepting one were significant with t-values ranging between 3.275 and 11.617. Only one of the indicators had a nonsignificant critical ratio of 1.282. All factor loadings excepting three were well above .5, ranging from .60 to .86 and demonstrating adequate item reliabilities.

## Higher-Order Constructs

We tested three additional alternative conceptualizations of the factor structure of the Team Multifactor Leadership Questionnaire (TMLQ). Consistent with the theoretical descriptions of transformational leadership as being a higher-order construct (Bass, 1985; Bass & Avolio, 1994) and the empirical demonstration at the individual level of analysis, we tested three models that examined whether the three components of transformational leadership could be represented by a higher-order construct. We conducted a second-order CFA examining Models 7, 8, and 9 (refer to Table 7.2). Our underlying assumption for testing these models was that a higher-order transformational leadership factor could represent the first-order transformational team leadership factors. The three competing models depicted the conceptualization of the higher-order factor differently. In Model 7, two transformational factors—intellectual stimulation and individualized consideration—were linked to a higher-order factor based on results reported by Avolio et al. (1999), while retaining Inspiring Leadership (IL) as a separate or unique first-order factor. In Model 8, consistent with the notion of a higher-level of transformational leadership suggested by Avolio and Bass (1995), we linked inspiring leadership and intellectual stimulation to a higher-order factor while retaining individualized consideration as a separate factor. In Model 9, we included all three first-order transformational factors in a higher-order factor, in line with arguments that have described transformational leadership as a higher-order construct at an individual leadership level (Bass & Avolio, 1994).

In student sample 1 (Table 7.4), the higher-order factors did not fit the data as well as the target model did, and produced a significant deterioration in overall fit as indicated by the $\chi^2$ difference test. For instance, Model 8, although estimating two fewer parameters than Model 6, produced significantly worse fit ($\Delta\chi^2 = 14.26$, $p < .001$). In the Army sample (Table 7.5), however, the second-order factor models had as good a fit as the target model did, and the $\chi^2$ difference test was insignificant for all three competing models (Model 7: 2 $\Delta\chi^2 = 4.02$, $p > .15$; Model 8: 2 $\Delta\chi^2 = .81$, $p > .80$; Model 7: 2 $\Delta\chi^2 = 7.46$, $p > .10$). Model 8 provided the most parsimonious representation of the data in that two fewer parameters were estimated without significant deterioration in overall model fit over the target model. Model 8 also produced superior fit in comparison to the other competing models. Hence, in the Army sample, there is stronger evidence to support a higher-order conceptualization of IL and IS while retaining IC, MA, and LF as first-order, correlated factors. Similar to the Army sample, the second-order factor models of student sample 2 (table 7.6) had as good fit as the target model, and the $\chi^2$ difference test was insignificant for all three competing models (Model 7: 2 $\Delta\chi^2$ = 4.90, $p$ > .1; Model 8: 2 $\Delta\chi^2$ = .2.07, $p$ > .5; Model 7: 2 $\Delta\chi^2$ = 7.80, $p$ > .1).

## Within-Group Convergence

In post hoc analyses, we used James's (1982) procedure for estimating within group inter-rater agreement to determine whether there was convergence in the perceptions of team members about the leadership phenomena. Using this aggregation procedure, we examined how much agreement there was among members within various groups in terms of ratings of their team's leadership behavior. In student sample 1 with a sample of 42 undergraduate student groups working together for 3 months, over 83% of those groups exhibited a sufficient degree of consistency to support our conceptualization of the team leadership construct. Specifically, the within-group agreement in these groups exceeded the cutoffs recommended by James (1982) of .7 for all the leadership scales. James indicates that .7 cutoff is a sufficient level for determining aggregation to a higher level of interest. Schriesheim, Cogliser, and Neider (1998) agree that .7 is the acceptable level for indicating group level convergence. The convergence of team leadership ratings indicated that members of a team had agreement about the phenomena they were asked to evaluate.

In general, within-group agreement in the 18 Army platoons was lower than for student teams in student sample 1. At least 12 of the 18 platoons (67%) exceeded the .7 value for all leadership scales excepting Management-by-Exception–Active, in which only three platoons exceeded the .7 cut-off. The mean within-group agreement exceeded .7 for four of the five scales with MA being the exception. These results provided some additional support for conceptualizing the leadership construct at the team level.

Within-group agreement analysis for the 34 teams in student sample 2 yielded 28 teams exceeding the .7 value for all leadership scales with 100% of the groups exceeding the .7 value for Passive/Avoidant, Individualized Consideration, and Active Management-by-Exception. Intellectual Stimulation had 90% of the groups exceed .7 and Inspiring Leadership had 81%. Like the Army sample, these results provided additional support for conceptualizing the leadership construct at the team level.

In addition, we tested all of the samples for between-groups variance using one-way ANOVAs. The results of these analyses indicated significant between-group variance on each factor with "$F$" values ranging from 1.08 to 2.29 for the student samples across the respective scales, and 1.71 to 2.77 for the Army sample. All analyses were significant at the .05 level or higher except for the Management-by-Exception–Active factor for student validation samples 1 and 2 and the Inspiring Leadership factor for student sample 2.

## Summary

Results of the CFA generally provided support for the five-factor model, as indicated by superior fit indices and significant differences in model fit with other first-order competing models. In all three samples, the incremental fit indices were at least marginally acceptable, and the $\chi^2/df$ ratio was less than 2 for the target model, providing support for the five-factor model. The RMSEA values were also in the acceptable range for the three samples. In the Army sample, we found evidence in support of a hierarchical structure for the transformational leadership components of the team multifactor leadership questionnaire. This hierarchical structure now needs to be tested in other independent samples, before any firm conclusions about the factor structure underlying these leadership dimensions can be drawn.

# Discussion

A basic premise for conducting the current series of studies was that shared leadership processes are critical ingredients to team success (Kozlowski et al., 1996; Pearce & Sims, 2002). In this study, team leadership was defined as the shared leadership within a group.

A primary assumption underlying this study was that leadership constructs defined at an individual level of analysis could be elevated to the group level (Avolio & Bass, 1995). With respect to the multifactor leadership model discussed by Bass and Avolio (1994), constructs such as "individualized consideration" can be examined in terms of the relationship between a leader and follower, or in terms of how team members collectively treat each other, whereby recognizing team members' needs, abilities, and motivation. Although some behaviors may differ across levels of analysis, we assumed here that many leadership indicators and constructs were applicable at *both* an individual and team level of analysis.

Avolio et al. (1996) reported evidence demonstrating that early in a team's formation, leadership styles such as individualized consideration operated at an individual level of analysis, in which some raters indicated the team was considerate of each other's needs, whereas others saw the team as exhibiting very little consideration. In other words, there were individual differences in how members perceived this team leadership construct. Yet, after several months of interaction, team members described the team's leadership styles with a high degree of consistency, indicating, for example, that the team generally displayed individually considerate behaviors. Results provided by Avolio et al. (1996) indicated that the passage of time and the nature of team members' interactions might be significant factors in evaluating when individual perceptions of team leadership emerge to a group level of analysis. In addition, the type of team and the context it operates within could also affect the way leadership is perceived by members of the team. For example, the leadership in a temporary student team, as opposed to an Army platoon or top management team, may be viewed differently due to the context in which each of those teams are embedded. Specifically, the Army context represents a hierarchical leadership system, whereas the student team is more like a flattened or horizontally structured organization.

As team members interact over time, their level of agreement regarding their ratings on specific leadership factors are expected to become more congruent within the team, for example, everyone comes to agree that the group manages itself by focusing too much on mistakes. We expect all members will share a mental model of what is and is not appropriate behavior in the team as the team develops over time. Such mental models and shared expectations may actually substitute for individual leadership. As time passes and the team becomes more cohesive, we speculate that the 5 factors found for the TMLQ, or a more differentiated factor model of team leadership, presented here could receive stronger support as a measure of shared leadership. We take this position, in part, because items included in the survey were rated based on frequency of occurrence. Thus, we expect team members to agree more with each other's evaluation of collective leadership as the team accumulates a longer history of interactions. This is consistent with the model of team effectiveness described by Kozlowski et al. (1996) and work by Seers (1989) on team leadership. It also builds on the work of Weick (1979), who indicated that over time teams evolve to "creating interlocking role expectations" (p. 368).

In sum, our set of studies provides preliminary support for a five-factor model of team leadership style, with some evidence for a hierarchical factor structure representing transformational leadership. What this series of studies does not examine is a comprehensive list of team leadership constructs or all items relevant to measuring team leadership. Certainly, there are other styles of leadership that may be relevant to team leadership not included here. Our purpose was to use a model of leadership tested at the individual level that had justification for escalation to measuring team leadership. Thus there are styles of leadership that were omitted that now must be considered in further assessments of team leadership.

## Recommendations for Future Research, Limitations, and Implications

There are several directions future research can take with respect to improving the TMLQ survey, and to further test a multifactor model of leadership at the team level. First, preliminary evidence now indicates that team members may need a sufficient amount of time to interact with each other before ratings on the TMLQ should be collected. For example, Avolio et al. (1996) reported the reliability for the active management-by-exception scale was unacceptably low, when examined one month after a team was formed. When team members evaluated their leadership after three months of interaction, however, the reliability for this scale improved and was nearly identical to all other TMLQ scales. Since mistakes by definition may follow a more unpredictable pattern, it may be necessary to expand the time period before such ratings are collected to obtain a stable, reliable estimate of this scale. In the present study, this scale generated the lowest reliability (.60, .61, and .66, respectively), but was within Nunnally's (1978) level of acceptability for new scale development.

Second, a more parsimonious team leadership model may be represented by a three-factor model, for example, transformational/transactional, active management-by-exception, and passive/avoidant leadership. Given the preliminary nature of this study, however, we strongly recommend the retention of all items included in at least the five factors for subsequent research. Since leadership is by definition contextually based, there is a need to include a broader sampling of teams from a wide range of contexts to maximize the construct validity of measures of team leadership. Avolio and Sivasubramaniam (2001) argue that the sample characteristics alone, regardless of size, can constrain our ability to test more complex models of leadership.

Obviously, these results should be viewed cautiously, since the samples used in validating this new instrument came from only two unique populations. Indeed, there may be some potential biases associated with the student samples that may have affected the pattern of results obtained in the present study. These biases might include an expectation that the teams had a limited lifespan, that members had little discretion over rewards for each other, that participants had relatively little full-time work experience, and that leadership ratings had no impact on how individuals or teams were evaluated in these courses.

With regard to the platoon sample, the hierarchical command structure of the military may have made it difficult for soldiers to view their unit as a team, which on average was comprised of 32 members. Moreover, in filling out the TMLQ, soldiers had to take into consideration all members including their platoon leader and sergeant. Thus, the soldiers' ratings of shared leadership may have been affected by their evaluations of their individual or formally designated leaders' ability to display self-management leadership behaviors (Cohen et al., 1997). This problem may account for the broader range of within-group agreement with platoons' TMLQ ratings reported above. Finally, there was a great deal of turnover in these platoons that may have affected the development of a collective identity and subsequently perceptions of shared leadership.

We now recommend that the TMLQ survey be used with teams who have a longer history of interacting with each other, and that have accumulated more work experience and perhaps a wider range of challenges, than is associated with teams involved in the current research. Another recommendation is to examine teams that have been independently identified as *high* versus *low* performing, to determine whether their team leadership styles differ from those teams, who produce average or below average performance. Based on the leadership characteristics that Katzenbach and Smith (1993) attributed to "high performing" teams, we would expect them to be rated as exhibiting more transformational and active transactional leadership.

As is true of all survey measures of leadership, we are not sure what the target of reference was in each rater's mind when they completed the TMLQ. It would be helpful to have raters orally describe how they conceptualized their team, while evaluating its leadership to see whether raters are thinking *team* or about specific individuals in the team or some combination.

All teams are clearly not the same. As noted above, future research must examine how the context in which teams operate affects the patterns of relationships observed in survey measures like the TMLQ. For example, how management-by-exception is perceived in a military culture may be quite different than in a high-tech organizational culture. Finally, even though we believe replication of studies such as this advances our understanding about construct development and generalizability, we strongly urge researchers to avoid the temptation of merely picking up the TMLQ and doing "quick and dirty" studies of team leadership. We now must develop a deeper understanding of what constitutes "shared" leadership, and how it can be developed in teams using multiple methods to assess shared leadership.

Overall, our goal here was to address an area in team assessment that has been largely neglected in research and training efforts. Most discussions of team leadership have focused on identifying a particular leader of a team, and how that person leads that team. Although clearly relevant to many teams, we have argued the more highly developed teams share their leadership responsibilities when taking on challenges and opportunities. This does not negate in any way the importance of how a project supervisor leads a team. Rather, we have attempted to add another dimension to the discussion of team leadership by examining how it manifests itself at the group level of analysis, while also developing a survey to measure team leadership behavior.

# References

Amason, A. C., Thompson, K. R., Hochwater, W. A., & Harrison, A. W. (1995). Conflict: An important dimension in successful management teams. *Organizational Dynamics, 24,* 20-35.

Anderson, J., & Gerbing, D. W. (1988). Structural equation modeling in practice: A review and recommended two-step approach. *Psychological Bulletin, 103,* 411-423.

Anderson, N. R., & West, M. A. (1994). Measuring climate for work group innovation: Development and validation of the team climate inventory. *Journal of Organizational Behavior, 19,* 235-258.

Astin, H. S., & Astin, A. W. (1996). *A social change model of leadership development guidebook, version 3.* Los Angeles.: Higher Education Research Institute, University of California.

Avolio, B. J., & Bass, B. M. (1995). Individual consideration viewed at multiple levels of analysis: A multi-level framework for examining the diffusion of transformational leadership. *Leadership Quarterly, 6,* 199-218.

Avolio, B. J., Bass, B. M., & Jung, D. (1999). Re-examining the components of transformational and transactional leadership using the Multifactor Leadership Questionnaire. *Journal of Organizational and Occupational Psychology, 72,* 441-462.

Avolio, B. J., Jung, D., Murry, W., & Sivasubramaniam, N. (1996). Building highly developed teams: Focusing on shared leadership process, efficacy, trust, and performance. In M. M. Beyerlein, D. A. Johnson, & S. T. Beyerlein (Eds.), *Advances in interdisciplinary studies of work teams* (pp. 173-209). Greenwich, CT: JAI Press.

Avolio, B. J., & Sivasubramaniam, N. (2001). *Re-examining the components of the multi-factor leadership theory: When too few is probably not enough.* Unpublished manuscript, State University of New York at Binghamton.

Bagozzi, R. P., Yi, Y., & Phillips, L. W. (1991). Assessing construct validity in organizational research. *Administrative Science Quarterly, 36,* 421-458.

Bales, R. F. (1954). In conference. *Harvard Business Review, 32,* 44-50.

Bandura, A. (1986). *Social foundations of thought and action: A social cognitive theory.* Englewood Cliffs, NJ: Prentice Hall.

Bandura, A. (1997). *Self-efficacy: The exercise of control.* New York: Freeman.

Bass, B. M. (1985). *Leadership and performance beyond expectations.* New York: Free Press.

Bass, B. M. (1997). Does the transactional-transformational leadership paradigm transcend organizational and national boundaries? *American Psychologist, 52,* 130-139.

Bass, B. M. (1998). *Transformational leadership: Industrial, military and educational impact.* Hillsdale, NJ: Erlbaum.

Bass, B. M., & Avolio, B. J. (1994). *Improving organizational effectiveness through transformational leadership.* Thousand Oaks, CA: Sage.

Bateman, T. S., & Crant, J. M. (1993). The proactive component of organizational behavior: A measure and correlates. *Journal of Organizational Behavior, 14,* 105-118.

Bentler, P. M. (1990). Comparative fit indexes in structural models. *Psychological Bulletin, 107,* 238.

Bentler, P. M., & Bonnett, D. G. (1980). Significance tests and goodness of fit in the analysis of covariance structures. *Psychological Bulletin, 88,* 588-606.

Bettenhausen, K., & Murninghan, J. K. (1985). The emergence of norms in competitive decision-making groups. *Administrative Science Quarterly, 30,* 350-372.

Bowers, D. G., & Seashore, S. E. (1966). Predicting organizational effectiveness with a four factor theory of leadership. *Administrative Science Quarterly, 11,* 238-263.

Browne, M. W., & Cudeck, R. (1993). Alternative ways of assessing model fit. In K. A. Long & K. A. Bollen (Eds.), *Testing structural equation models* (pp. 136-161). Newbury Park, CA: Sage.

Burns, J. M. (1978). *Leadership.* New York: Free Press.

Burns, J. M. (1996). *Empowerment for change.* Unpublished manuscript, Kellogg Leadership Studies Project, University of Maryland.

Campion, M. A., Medsker, G. J., & Higgs, A. C. (1993). Relations between work group characteristics and effectiveness: Implications for designing effective work groups. *Personnel Psychology, 46,* 823-850.

Campion, M. A., Papper, E. M., & Medsker, G. J. (1996). Relations between work group characteristics and effectiveness: A replication and extension. *Personnel Psychology, 49,* 429-452.

Cascio, W. F. (1995). Whither industrial and organizational psychology in a changing world of work? *American Psychologist, 50,* 928-939.

Chan, D. (1998). Functional relations among constructs in the same content domain at different levels of analysis: A typology of composition models. *Journal of Applied Psychology, 83,* 234-246.

Cohen, S. G., & Bailey, D. E. (1997). What makes teams work: Group effectiveness research from the shop floor to the executive suite. *Journal of Management, 23,* 239-290.

Cohen, S. G., Chang, L., & Ledford, G. E. (1997). A hierarchical construct of self-management leadership and its relationship to quality of work life and perceived work group effectiveness. *Personnel Psychology, 50,* 275-308.

Dansereau, F., Yammarino, F. J., Markham, S. E., Alutto, J. A., Newman, J., Dumas, M., et al. (1995). Individualized leadership: A new multi-level approach. *Leadership Quarterly, 6,* 413-450.

Dunphy, D., & Bryant, B. (1996). Teams: Panaceas or prescriptions for improved performance? *Human Relations, 49,* 677-699.

Feltz, D. L., & Lirgg, C. D. (1998). Perceived team and player efficacy in hockey. *Journal of Applied Psychology, 83,* 557-564.

Fornell, C., & Larcker, D. F. (1981). Evaluating structural equation models with unobservable variables and measurement error. *Journal of Marketing Research, 18,* 39-50.

George, J. (1990). Personality, affect, and behavior in groups. *Journal of Applied Psychology, 75,* 107-116.

George, J., & Bettenhausen, K. (1991). Understanding prosocial behavior, sales performance, and turnover: A group-level analysis in a service context. *Journal of Applied Psychology, 75,* 698-709.

Gerbing, D. W., & Anderson, J. C. (1992). Monte Carlo evaluations of goodness of fit indices for structural equation models. *Sociological Methods and Research, 21,* 132-160.

Gorsuch, R. L. (1983). *Factor analysis.* Hillsdale, NJ: Erlbaum.

Gully, S. M. (2000). Work teams research. In M. M. Beyerlein (Ed.), *Work teams: Past, present, and future* (pp. 25-44). Netherlands: Kluwer Academic Publishers.

Gully, S. M., Joshi, A., & Incalcaterra, K. A. (2001, April). *A meta-analytic investigation of the relationships among team efficacy, self-efficacy and performance.* Paper presented at the Society for Industrial and Organizational Psychology Conference, San Diego, CA.

Hackman, J. R. (1992). *Groups that work (and those that don't).* San Francisco, CA: Jossey-Bass.

Hakstian, A. R. (1971). A comparative evaluation of several prominent methods of oblique rotation. *Psychometrika, 38,* 175-193.

Hall, R. J., & Lord, R. G. (1995). Multi-level information processing explanations of followers' leadership perceptions. *Leadership Quarterly, 6,* 265-287.

Harris, C. W., & Kaiser, H. F. (1964). Oblique factor rotation analytic solutions by orthogonal transformations. *Psychometrika, 29,* 347-362.

House, R. J., & Aditya, R. N. (1997). The social scientific study of leadership: Quo vadis? *Journal of Management, 23,* 409-473.

House, R. J., Rousseau, D. M., & Thomas-Hunt, M. (1995). The meso paradigm: A framework for the integration of micro and macro organizational behavior. In L. L. Cummings & B. Shaw (Eds.), *Research in Organizational Behavior* (Vol. 17, pp. 71-114), Greenwich, CT: JAI Press.

Hughes, R. L., Ginnett, R. C., & Curphy, G. J. (1998). *Leadership: Enhancing the lessons of experience.* Chicago: Irwin.

Hunt, J. G. (1991). *Leadership: A new synthesis.* Newbury Park, CA: Sage.

Huselid, M. A. (1995). The impact of human resource management practices on turnover, productivity, and corporate financial performance. *Academy of Management Journal, 38,* 635-672.

Hyatt, D. E., & Ruddy, T. M. (1997). An examination of the relationship between work group characteristics and performance: Once more into the breech. *Personnel Psychology, 50,* 553-585.

Ilgen, D., Major, D., Hollenbeck, J., & Sego, D. (1993). Team research in the 1990s. In M. Chemers & R. Ayman (Eds.), *Leadership theory and research: Perspectives and directions* (pp. 245-270). New York: Academic Press.

Ireland, R. D., & Hitt, M. A. (1999). Achieving and maintaining strategic competitiveness in the 21st century: The role of strategic leadership. *Academy of Management Executive, 13,* 43-57.

James, L. R. (1982). Aggregation bias in estimates of perceptual agreement. *Journal of Applied Psychology, 67,* 219-229.

James, L. R., Mulaik, S. A., & Brett, J. M. (1982). *Causal analysis: Assumptions, models, and data.* Beverly Hills, CA: Sage.

Katzenbach, J. R. (1997). *Teams at the top: Unleashing the potential of both teams and individual leaders.* Boston, MA: Harvard Business School Press.

Katzenbach, J. R., & Smith, D. K. (1993). *The wisdom of teams.* Boston, MA: Harvard Business School Press.

Kerr, S., & Jermier, J. M. (1978). Substitutes for leadership: Their meaning and measurement. *Organizational Behavior and Human Performance, 22,* 375-403.

Kirkman, B. L., & Rosen, B. (1999). Beyond self-management: Antecedents and consequences of team empowerment. *Academy of Management Journal, 42,* 58-74.

Kirkman, B .L., & Rosen, B. (2001, winter). Powering up teams. *Organizational Dynamics,* 48-66.

Kivimaki, M., Kuk, G., Elovainio, M., Thomson, L., Kalliomaki-Levanto, T., & Heikkila, A. (1997). The Team Climate Inventory (TCI)-four or five factors? Testing the structure of the TCI in samples of low and high complexity jobs. *Journal of Occupational and Organizational Psychology, 70,* 375-389.

Klein, K. J., Dansereau, F., & Hall, R. J. (1994). Levels issues in theory development, data collection, and analysis. *Academy of Management Review, 19,* 195-229.

Klimoski, R., & Mohammed, S. (1994). Team mental model: Construct or metaphor? *Journal of Management, 20,* 403-437.

Kozlowski, S., Gully, S., Salas, E., & Cannon-Bowers, J. (1996). Team leadership and development: Theories, principles, and guidelines for training leaders and teams. In M. M. Beyerlein, D. A. Johnson, & S. T. Beyerlein (Eds.), *Advances in interdisciplinary studies of work teams* (pp. 253-291). Greenwich, CT: JAI Press.

La Du, T. J., & Tanaka, J. S. (1989). Influence of sample size, estimation method, and model specification on goodness-of-fit assessments in structural equation models. *Journal of Applied Psychology, 74,* 625-635.

Lowe, K. B., Kroeck, K. G., & Sivasubramaniam, N. (1995). Effectiveness correlates of transformational and transactional leadership: A meta-analytic review of MLQ literature. *Leadership Quarterly, 7,* 385-425.

MacDuffie, J. P. (1995). Human resource bundles and manufacturing performance: Organizational logic and flexible production systems in the world auto industry. *Industrial and Labor Relations Review, 48,* 197-221.

Manz, C. C., & Sims, H. P., Jr. (1993). *Businesses without bosses: How self-managing teams are building high performance companies.* New York: Wiley.

Markham, S. E., & Markham, I. S. (1995). Self-management and self-leadership reexamined: A levels-of-analysis perspective. *Leadership Quarterly, 6,* 343-359.

Marsh, H. W., & Hocevar, D. (1985). Applications of confirmatory factor analysis to the study of self-concept: First- and higher-order factor models and their invariance across groups. *Psychological Bulletin, 97,* 562-582.

Martin, D. (1993). *Team think.* New York: Dutton.

McDonald, R. P., & Marsh, H. W. (1990). Choosing a multivariate model: Noncentrality and goodness-of-fit. *Psychological Bulletin, 107,* 247-255.

Medsker, G. J., Williams, L. J., & Holohan, P. J. (1994). A review of current practices for evaluating causal models in organizational behavior and human resource management research. *Journal of Management, 20,* 439-464.

Meindl, J. R., Ehrlich, S. B., & Durkerich, J. M. (1985). The romance of leadership. *Administrative Science Quarterly, 30,* 78-102.

Moreland, R. L., & Levine, J. M. (1992). Problem identification in groups. In S. Worchal, W. Wood, & J. A. Simpson (Eds.), *Group process and productivity* (pp. 17-47). Newbury Park, CA: Sage.

Mulaik, S. A., James, L. R., Alstine, J. V., Bennett, N., Lind, S., & Stillwell, C. D. (1989). An evaluation of goodness-of-fit indices for structural equation models. *Psychological Bulletin, 105,* 430-445.

Neck, C. P., & Manz, C. C. (1994). From groupthink to teamthink: Toward the creation of constructive thought patterns in self-managing work teams. *Human Relations, 47,* 929-952.

Nunnally, J. C. (1978). *Psychometric theory.* New York: McGraw-Hill.

Orasanu, J. (1990). *Shared mental models and crew performance.* Paper presented at the 34th Annual meeting of the Human Factors Society, Orlando, FL.

Pearce, C. L., & Sims, H. P., Jr. (2002). Vertical versus shared leadership as predictors of the effectiveness of change management teams: An examination of aversive, directive, transactional, transformational, and empowering leader behaviors. *Group Dynamics: Theory, Research, and Practice, 6*(2), 179-197.

Pearce, C. L., Yoo, Y., & Alavi, M. (in press). Leadership, social work and virtual teams: The relative influence of vertical vs. shared leadership in the nonprofit section. In R. E. Riggio and S. Smith Orr (Eds.), *Improving leadership in nonprofit organizations.* San Francisco: Jossey-Bass.

Perry, M. L., Pearce, C. L., & Sims, H. P., Jr. (1999). Empowered selling teams: How shared leadership can contribute to selling team outcomes. *Journal of Personal Selling and Sales Management, 19,* 33-52.

Podsakoff, P. M., Ahearne, M., & MacKenzie, S. B. (1997). Organizational citizenship behavior and the quantity and quality of work group performance. *Journal of Applied Psychology, 82,* 262-270.

Rousseau, D. M. (1985). Issues of level in organizational research: Multi-level and cross-level perspectives. In L. L. Cummings & B. M. Staw (Eds.), *Research in organizational behavior* (Vol. 7, pp. 1-37), Greenwich, CT: JAI Press.

Schriesheim, C. A., Cogliser, C. C., and Neider, L. L. (1998). Ohio State model: Is it "trustworthy"? A multiple-levels-of-analysis reexamination of an Ohio State leadership study, with implications for future research. In F. Dansereau & F. J. Yammarino (Eds.), *Leadership: The multiple-level approaches* (Vol. 24, pp. 3-64). Greenwich, CT: JAI Press.

Seers, A. (1989). Team-member exchange quality: A new construct for role-making research. *Organizational Behavior and Human Decision Processes, 43,* 118-135.

Shapiro, D. L., & Kirkman, B. L. (1999). Employees' reaction to the change to work teams: The influence of "anticipatory" injustice. *Journal of Organizational Change Management, 12,* 51-75.

Sinclair, A. (1992). The tyranny of a team ideology. *Organization Studies, 13,* 611-626.

Smith, P. B., Peterson, M. F., & Misumi, J. (1994). Event management and work team effectiveness in Japan, Britain, and USA. *Journal of Occupational and Organizational Psychology, 67*, 33-43.

Stewart, G., & Manz, C. (1994, April). *Leadership for self-managing work teams: A theoretical integration.* Paper presented at the Society for Industrial and Organizational Psychologists Conference, Nashville, TN.

Tesluk, P. E., Zaccaro, S. J., Marks, M., & Mathieu, J. (1997). Task and aggregation issues in the analysis and assessment of team performance. In M. Brannick & E. Salas (Eds.), *Assessment and measurement of team performance: Theory, research and applications* (pp. 197-224). Greenwich, CT: JAI Press.

Tosi, H. L. (Ed.). (1992). The environment/organization/person (EOP) contingency model: A meso approach to the study of organization. *Monographs in organizational behavior and industrial relations* (Vol. 14). Greenwich, CT: JAI Press.

Tucker, L. P., Koopman, R. F., & Linn, R. L. (1969). Evaluation of factor analytic research procedures by means of simulated correlation matrices. *Psychometrika, 34*, 421-459.

Waldersee, R., & Eagleson, G. (1996). *The efficacy of distributed leadership in implementing change.* Unpublished manuscript, Australian Graduate School of Management, University of New South Wales, Sydney, Australia.

Weick, K. E. (1979). *The social psychology of organizing.* Reading, MA: Addison-Wesley.

Wofford, J. C., Goodwin, V. L., & Whittington, J. L. (1998). A field study of a cognitive approach to understanding transformational and transactional leadership. *Leadership Quarterly, 9*, 55-84.

Yammarino, F. J. (1998). Multivariate aspects of the varient/WABA approach: A discussion and leadership illustration. *Leadership Quarterly, 9*, 203-227.

Yammarino, F. J., Dubinsky, A. J., & Spangler, W. D. (1998). Transformational and contingent reward leadership: Individual, dyad, and group level of analysis. *Leadership Quarterly, 9*, 27-54.

Yukl, G. A. (1998). *Leadership in organizations.* (4th ed.). Englewood Cliffs, NJ: Prentice Hall.

Zaccaro, S. J., Blair, V., Peterson, C., & Zazanos, M. (1995). Collective efficacy. In J. E. Maddux (Ed.), *Self-efficacy, adaptation, and adjustment: Theory, research and application* (pp. 305-328). New York: Plenum.

Zaccaro, S. J., & Marks, M. (1996). Collecting data from groups. In F. T. L. Leong & J. T. Austin (Eds.), *The psychology research handbook: A guide for graduate and research assistants* (pp. 155-164). Thousand Oaks, CA: Sage.

# CHAPTER 8

# A Group Exchange Structure Approach to Leadership in Groups

*Scott E. Seibert*

*Raymond T. Sparrowe*

*Robert C. Liden*

**M**uch has been written about the "romance" of leadership (Meindl & Ehrlich, 1987; Pfeffer, 1977). It is undeniably true that much leadership theory has focused on the leader, whether the leader's personality, behavior, or charisma (Yukl, 2002). Since the 1970s, much romance has also been associated with teams and the notion that employees can manage themselves and businesses can operate "without bosses" (Manz & Sims, 1993; Yukl, 2002). The danger of an overly romantic view of either the leader or the team is that too great an attachment to the object of devotion can lead to a failure to focus on important behaviors and processes that bring about effective performance. Shared leadership theory represents an attempt to overcome this shortcoming by focusing on the behavior of group members. As developed by Pearce and Sims (2000), shared leadership theory describes how influence is not solely the prerogative of formal leaders, but may be shared by members of groups or teams. Complementing research that focuses on the effects of the formal leader on group outcomes, proponents of shared leadership suggest that it explains variance in group outcomes, such as potency and problem solving (Pearce, Yoo, & Alavi, in press), effectiveness ratings

(Pearce, 1999), and new venture revenue and growth rates (Ensley & Pearce, 2000). Pearce and Sims (2000) describe the influence of comembers by likening it to a substitute for leadership because it has the potential of suppressing the necessity for formal leadership. Shared leadership thus bridges the distance between theories that focus on the effects of formal leaders on group performance and those that focus on wholly self-managing teams. Moreover, because the emphasis is on members participating in influence processes, traditional groups with formal leaders and self-managed teams can manifest shared leadership.

We find that the general approach to shared leadership offered by Pearce and Sims (2000) is a promising initiative. Indeed, initial empirical evidence (Pearce & Sims, 2002) suggests that shared leadership is an important predictor of group effectiveness. Our goal in this chapter is to add to the conversation about shared leadership by offering a somewhat different theoretical account of its origins, key processes, and salient outcomes. The work to date (Pearce & Sims, 2000, 2002) treats shared leadership empirically as a group-level construct in which the level of influence among individual members is *relatively equal among individuals*. We are interested in describing the emergence of shared leadership in groups and its effects on outcomes from a theoretical perspective that focuses on *differing levels of individual influence* among group members. Furthermore, we develop the idea that equal sharing of influence among members is but one among several potentially interesting configurations of influence structures in groups. Equal sharing of influence among members would constitute the "ideal" type of shared leadership; nothing in the Pearce and Sims (2000) formulation, however, excludes the possibility of influence being arrayed among members in different structural configurations. Pursuit of this perspective leads us to a methodologically unique approach to the study of shared leadership.

Our argument proceeds in three steps. We begin by grounding the theory of shared leadership within the literature on influence processes in small groups. We then reframe the shared leadership concept within an approach based on social exchange structures in groups. Finally, we conclude by addressing the role of vertical or hierarchical leadership in managing group network structures in order to improve group process and effectiveness.

# Shared Leadership, Individuals, and Group Influence

To be clear about our topic, it is necessary to distinguish the concept of shared leadership from other concepts applied to work in teams such as task rotation, task sharing, empowerment, or participative management. These practices involve the assignment of specific group tasks, such as ordering parts or scheduling the work, to one or more members on either a temporary or an ongoing basis. Ideas regarding the assignment of such tasks fit comfortably within established notions of job design and the delegation of authority and responsibility. The notion of group leadership as used here does not refer to such specific group tasks but rather refers to the management of the group itself. Such leadership functions may include internal and external information processing, planning regarding task performance strategies, decision making and problem solving, coordinating and monitoring performance, and developing and enforcing appropriate group norms (Hackman, 1987).

Leadership implies the use of influence over these functions and shared leadership implies a role for the multiple group members in this influence process.

Pearce and Sims (2000) define shared leadership as a group-level construct that entails the process of shared influence between and among individuals. Although the specific approach taken by Pearce and Sims is new, it calls to mind an extensive program of research on social influence processes in groups begun in the late 1940s at the University of Michigan by Leon Festinger and his colleagues (see McGrath, 1984). These researchers posited a group-level construct, group cohesion, and defined it as the sum total of forces attracting members to a group (Cartwright, 1968). Group cohesion reflects the upper limit of a group's ability to influence its members. The more attractive a group is to a particular member, the more the threat of ostracism from that group is likely to bring about compliance to the group's norms and expectations.

It was tempting for researchers to assume that group cohesion would be related to group task performance but, alas, 50 years of research have painted a more complex picture. Recent meta-analyses (Evans & Dion, 1991; Mullen & Copper, 1994; Podsakoff, MacKenzie, & Ahearne, 1997) show that although there is a small positive effect of group cohesion on group performance, the stronger effect flows from performance success to group cohesion. The most powerful determinant of the group cohesion leading to group performance relationship is the type of performance norms developed within the group. Performance norms are important because groups may be highly cohesive but not share organizational performance goals (Hackman, 1976; Roethlisberger & Dickson, 1939). Cohesive groups with high performance norms (e.g., high output, quality work, and cooperation with other groups) are more productive than less cohesive groups with high performance norms. This is because cohesive groups are better able to enforce group member conformity to norms than are less cohesive groups. Thus, cohesion functions just as it was originally intended to—as an indicator of group influence on individual members—and is only indirectly related to group performance.

The intriguing implication of these observations regarding group cohesion is that we should expect shared leadership to benefit group performance only under certain conditions. That is, we should expect groups that have a high overall level of shared leadership to have more influence over group members, especially with regard to the enforcement of conformity to group production norms. Only when such norms are supportive of task accomplishment should we expect higher group performance.

We thus are led to suggest that the definition of shared leadership as "shared influence" needs to be sharpened to account for the fact that influence among group members may cover a broader domain of attitudes and behaviors than what most scholars would consider leadership. Equating influence with leadership makes sense when group members exert influence to achieve broader organizational goals and performance objectives. Neither group members, however—nor, for that matter, formal leaders—can always be assumed to share organizational goals and objectives. This distinction becomes important in addressing how shared leadership relates to group performance.

We now turn to the question of how influence is shared among group members. Treating influence as being shared relatively equally among members (e.g., Pearce & Sims, 2000) certainly is plausible; moreover, it effectively represents the ideal of self-managed teams in which all members are on an equal footing. There are reasons, however, to expect that the distribution of influence among members might not be equal in all groups, thus opening the possibility of other informal structures of shared leadership. Early research on groups strongly suggests exactly this dynamic in leaderless groups (see Hollander, 1978; McGrath, 1984). Although the actual interaction processes varied from one experimental protocol to the next, the research showed that the emergence of differentiated leadership roles in task groups generally followed a common trajectory. Group members initially share ideas that are potentially relevant to the group's task, and those ideas are informally (either explicitly or implicitly) evaluated by other members of the group. Ideas that win acceptance bring provisional legitimacy to the task-relevant knowledge of the individual who offers them and, with legitimacy, that individual is able to initiate structure, such as organizing the work, assigning tasks, or rejecting the ideas of others. These interactions generated socioemotional tensions, as when an individual's ideas are ignored, ridiculed, or rejected, or when he or she loses in the competition for legitimacy and influence. In task groups, expressive leadership emerges when a group member behaves in ways that reduce tensions by suggesting compromises, affirming the value of an individual who has offered a rejected idea, or injecting humor into the discussion. Bales (1953) traced this interplay between instrumental and expressive leadership through the actual actions and responses of group members and suggested that effective groups achieve dynamic equilibrium.

Early research in emergent leadership also indicated that these differentiated roles arrange themselves vertically in status hierarchies such that, in task groups, the individual who emerges as the instrumental leader (the "idea man" [*sic*]) enjoys greater influence than do other members (Bales & Slater, 1955). Slater (1965) observed that as the time groups spend in interaction increases, so also does role differentiation. In order for a group to act cooperatively, some level of consensus among members regarding which individual legitimately fills which role is necessary. When groups fail to achieve consensus, research (see Slater, 1965) found that differentiated roles are "sharp and divisive" (p. 626).

Our assumption regarding differentiated roles is that the capabilities possessed by group members vary, thus potential contributions to group outcomes also vary. Informal leaders emerge by virtue of differentiated roles and status hierarchies that reflect varying degrees of influence. So although we agree with Pearce and Sims' (2000) perspective that distributed influence is indicative of shared leadership, existing research and theory suggests that significant differences in influence among group members should be expected. From our perspective, those cases in which influence is shared equally among members are especially interesting insofar as they manifest equality and mutuality, rather than differentiated influence and emergent status hierarchies.

The shared leadership construct as developed by Pearce and Sims reflects more than just the overall level of influence among group members in that it specifies five distinct behavioral influence strategies (Pearce & Sims, 2000): aversive, directive, transactional, transformational, and empowering. These behavioral influence strategies have some obvious parallels to existing taxonomies of influence tactics (e.g., Yukl & Tracey, 1992). For example, the aversive, transactional, and transformational dimensions of shared leadership would appear to parallel the influence tactics of pressure, exchange, and inspirational appeals, respectively. Directive behavioral influence appears to overlap with assertiveness or a simple request based on legitimate power, and empowering influence may be conceptually related to the consultation influence tactic (Yukl & Falbe, 1990).

Here again, grounding the theory of shared leadership in what we already know about the social influence process seems to be the most promising approach for advancing knowledge. It has been demonstrated that some tactics (consultation, inspirational appeals, and rational persuasion) are most likely to produce commitment in the target of influence, whereas others (pressure, exchange, coalition, and legitimating tactics) are more likely to produce only overt compliance or even resistance (Yukl, Kim, & Falbe, 1996; Yukl & Tracey, 1992). Indeed, these findings nicely parallel Pearce's (1997) results from a second-order confirmatory factor analysis of the behavioral influence strategies that discriminated between catalyzing and controlling factors. Yet the most fundamental lesson learned from research on influence tactics is that both the individual's choice of influence tactics and the likely effectiveness of a tactic is highly contingent on such factors as the nature of the influence agent's power, the objective of the influence attempt, prevailing social (or group) norms regarding the use of a specific tactic, and the difficulty faced by the target in complying with the request. The specific combination of different influence tactics and the sequential timing of their use are also related to the effectiveness of an influence attempt (Falbe & Yukl, 1992; Yukl & Tracey, 1992).

The implication of these findings for a theory of shared leadership is that the relationship between the behavioral influence strategies used in the group and aspects of group effectiveness may be mediated by member's task commitment. In general, the influence strategies associated with "catalyzing leadership" should be associated with more commitment among group members to carry out the requested task or activity. This may be especially true for groups without a formal leader because other group members are unlikely to have the kind of formal power derived from a hierarchical position necessary to allow pressure and exchange tactics to be effective.

Finally, what appears to be most central to the shared influence point of view is the idea that group members exert influence on each other. Just as we have argued that there are likely to be groups in which members do not share influence equally, we also expect that individuals would employ differing behavioral influence strategies. Although it is conceivable that a particular style of influence is both widely used and effective in engendering commitment in some groups, it would seem important to entertain the possibility that members use different strategies and do so at different levels of intensity. That is, we would need to distinguish between "Group A" in which all members use a moderate level of aversive behavioral influence and "Group B" in which half of the members are high and half are low in the use of aversive behavioral influence. Notice that this issue is not addressed by measures of perceptual agreement. Asked to report the level of aversive behavioral influence used by the group as a whole, members of Group B may indeed all agree that, on average, there is a moderate reliance on aversive influence in the group. Yet we should expect these two groups to function quite differently. We might expect Group A to be quite unified, perhaps to the point of developing group norms regarding appropriate influence strategies, whereas Group B may tend toward severe polarization.

Furthermore, it is likely that group members themselves differentiate among influence agents and demonstrate a more subtle and nuanced reaction to influence attempts from different individual group members. Due to the important role that contingency factors play in determining the effectiveness of influence attempts, the attributes of the influence agent—for example, the informal status of the influence agent—may be quite important. An extensive literature on minority influence (Moscovici, 1985) and coalition dynamics in groups (Murnighan, 1985) also suggests that the position of other group members on a particular issue will have an important role in determining the success of a particular influence attempt.

Finally, we expect that member influence is differentiated in the strategies used by one individual to influence another. This issue has, of course, been addressed in the leadership literature before. Leader-member exchange theory (e.g., Dansereau, Graen, & Haga, 1975) argues that leaders develop differentiated relationships with each of their followers. These theorists argue that meaningful variance in leader behavior is lost if researchers aggregate followers' ratings to derive an indication of average leader behavior. Although perceptual agreement regarding group influence strategies among group members does indicate consistency in behavior among subordinates, it does not rule out the possibility that meaningful variance also exists among subordinates.

# A Group Exchange Approach to Shared Leadership

A core idea of the shared leadership point of view is that a request or influence attempt by one person, whether he or she is the formal leader or a peer, will be reinforced by the influence of the other group members. Blau (1964), in his examination of social exchange processes and leadership, commented on the important role subordinates play in legitimating the authority of the leader. According to Blau (1964), "A man [*sic*] in authority does not have to enforce compliance with his orders, because the structural constraints that exist among subordinates do so for him" (p. 209). In arguing for differentiated influence patterns among group members, we seek to recognize (a) that the group might not be unified in its attitude toward a specific goal or objective, (b) that individual members might employ different influence tactics, and (c) that group members distinguish among individuals in choosing the type of influence tactic employed or their reaction to a specific influence attempt. What we attempt to develop in this section is a more fine-grained analysis of the pattern of influence among group members in order to develop an operational approach to understanding shared leadership and the effects of the "structural constraints" to which Blau (1964) refers.

The first step in our approach is to move from a focus on influence tactics to a broader focus on relationships among group members. Although a focus on influence tactics provides some information on group functioning, we believe that a more encompassing approach is to focus on the nature of the exchange relationships among group members. That is, a focus on the nature of social relationships among group members reveals information about a number of important social processes in the group, including, but not limited to, influence tactics. We use social exchange theory to develop a theory-based view of shared leadership in groups. Social exchange theory has already been extensively employed to enhance our understanding of leadership and social interaction in groups and organizations (e.g., Blau, 1964; Hollander, 1978; Liden & Graen, 1980; Thibaut & Kelley, 1959). We expect social exchange theory to be useful in developing our understanding of shared leadership processes as well. Seers (1989) has proposed a construct he identified as team-member exchange that is also an application of social exchange theory to teams, but team-member exchange, like the shared leadership construct of Pearce and Sims (2000), is conceptualized and measured at the group level. Consistent with our argument regarding shared leadership, we would suggest that team-member exchange quality is likely to be differentiated among members—and that differences among team member exchange quality are relevant for explaining team outcomes. What we are suggesting is unique because it is a structural approach focusing on the overall pattern of exchange relationships among group members.

A basic distinction growing out of social exchange theory is that between economic and social exchange. According to Blau (1964), economic exchange involves specific and quantifiable goods or services. Social exchange, on the other hand, involves unspecified obligations that the other party trusts will be discharged in only rough equivalence over time. Social, but not economic, exchange tends to engender feelings of personal obligation, gratitude, and trust (Blau, 1964). The distinction between social and economic exchange is fundamental to the leader-member exchange model of leadership (Settoon, Bennett, & Liden, 1996; Sparrowe & Liden, 1997). According to Sparrowe and Liden (1997),

> Low-quality leader-member relations have been characterized in terms of economic (contractual) exchanges that do not progress beyond what is specified in the employment agreement, whereas high-quality leader-member relations have been characterized in terms of social exchanges that extend beyond what is required of the employment contract. (p. 523)

Sparrowe and Liden (1997) extend this conceptualization of leader-member exchange (LMX). Drawing from the work of Sahlins (1972), they discuss three types of exchange relationships: generalized, balanced, and negative. Balanced exchange relationships correspond with low LMX relationships in that they are characterized by equivalent and immediate exchanges, as in a quid pro quo arrangement. Generalized exchange corresponds to high LMX relationships in that strict equivalence in exchange is not required and balance is presumed to work itself out over the long run. The relationship is also characterized by trust, respect, and a concern for the welfare of the partner. Negative exchange extends current conceptualizations of LMX in that exchange partners pursue only self-interest and may even seek to harm the other. This extension is useful to our theory of group exchange structures developed below.

An extensive literature documents the benefits that subordinates enjoy in terms of performance appraisals, raises, promotions, and career success, as a result of maintaining a high-quality relationship with their immediate superior (Liden, Sparrowe, & Wayne, 1997). But the benefits of a high-quality social exchange relationship are not limited to leader-subordinate relationships. Similar to Granovetter's (1973) concept of a strong tie, social exchange relationships are likely to involve frequent and extensive information sharing, multiple types of resources flows, trust and mutual obligations, and social support and approval. These interpersonal processes should benefit each of the interacting partners in a number of ways. For example, information sharing between bargaining partners is an important factor related to the level of mutual outcomes in negotiation situations

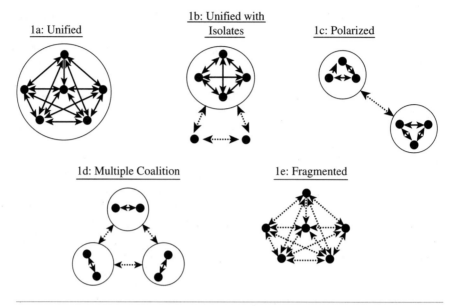

**Figure 8.1**   Group Exchange Structures

NOTE: Solid lines represent Generalized Exchange Relationships. Dashed lines represent Negative
    Exchange Relationships.

(Kimmel, Pruitt, Magenau, Konar-Goldband, & Carnevale, 1980). People who are
central in trust and advice networks (i.e., they possess a relatively large number of
such relationships) are seen as more powerful and exhibit higher job performance
(Brass & Burkhardt, 1992; Sparrowe, Liden, Wayne, & Kraimer, 2001).

In terms of the influence processes that are the focus of shared leadership
theory, we would expect members of high-quality social exchange relationships to
have high levels of mutual influence over each other. Since the choice of influence
tactic is highly context sensitive, we expect the nature of the exchange relationship
to play a determining role. For example, use of coercive pressure or quid pro quo
exchange tactics is likely to be seen as inappropriate in the context of a high-quality
social exchange relationship. We would therefore expect greater reliance on the soft
influence tactics within generalized social exchange relationships, greater reliance
on explicit exchange tactics within balanced relationships, and reliance on aversive
and coalition tactics within negative exchange relationships.

The second step necessary to develop our approach to shared leadership is to
move our focus from the dyad to the group. In order to illustrate the general outlines of such an approach, we present and discuss five prototypical group exchange
structures in Figure 8.1. For simplicity of presentation, we portray only generalized
and negative social exchange relationships. Lines between circles represent all
relationships of the corresponding dyads. Although we do not pursue it here, additional complexity can be introduced by adding balanced social exchange relationships, and by distinguishing reciprocal (those in which both dyad report the same
type of relationships) from nonreciprocal relationships (those in which members
of the dyad report different types of relationship with each other).

The examples in Figure 8.1 encourage one to view the group as a social network. A great deal of research within the social network tradition has focused on the implications of group (or network) structure for interpersonal influence processes and outcome (Friedkin, 1998; Marsden & Friedkin, 1994). Based in social comparison theory (Festinger, 1954), the simplest influence model predicts a focal individual's attitude as a function of the attitudes of the other individuals with which the actor has contact. Such direct effects models predict that groups with extensive positive relationships will move toward consensus (Harary, 1959). More general models of group influence, however, allow for probabilistic influence ties, effects of prior attitudes, random disturbance terms, and differential weighting of influence based on individual attributes or social distance. Under these more general models, groups may move toward consensus, toward greater polarization, or may settle at some equilibrium point in which disagreement continues to exist (Marsden & Friedkin, 1994). Exactly which model best characterizes the group influence process is an empirical question that continues to receive considerable research attention.

The implication of this research is that the pattern of relationships among group members can have a major impact on the ability of a group to function effectively. We should expect the pattern of exchange relations to affect information sharing, cooperation, conflict resolution, group decision-making style, and member satisfaction within the group. This approach should be regarded as "structural" in the sense that the pattern of relations is as important as the number or content of relations. Notice, for example, that a group-level measure might indicate a moderate level of transformational influence tactics for all of the groups depicted in Figures 8.1a through 8.1d. For the group depicted in Figure 8.1a, reliance on this influence tactic may be distributed evenly among group members. Within the group depicted in Figure 8.1c, however, dyads within the circle may each rely on high levels of transformational influence even though all relationships across circles may use very little transformational influence—still resulting in a moderate overall level of transformational influence. We should, however, expect very different group processes and outcomes in each of these groups. These structural exchange relationships are likely to be especially relevant and important as a determinant of group process and performance when a differentiated leadership role is not present, as in the self-managed team.

# Speculations on Group Exchange Structure and Group Process

The multiple ways in which group social exchange structure affects group process and performance is, we believe, an area ripe for empirical exploration. This task is beyond the limits of the current chapter, but in this section we encourage research work by developing a number of ideas detailing the types of processes and outcomes we expect to be associated with each of the example structures of Figure 8.1.

Figure 8.1a depicts what we have labeled as a unified group. All relationships among group members are generalized exchange relationships. Based on our description of generalized exchange in dyads, the group should be typified by extensive information sharing, good coordination, high mutual trust, cooperation, effective conflict resolution, and a strong tendency toward consensus. Indeed, this structure appears to be the one assumed by the group-as-a-whole approach to shared leadership, in which a single group-level measure represents influence processes in the group and no differences are expected in terms of influence strategies or influence effectiveness as a result of an individual's position within the group.

We should expect the unified group exchange structure to have a number of positive effects on group process consistent with the positive outcomes associated with generalized social exchange in dyads. Because of the high levels of mutual influence among group members, we should expect the group to readily move toward consensus on attitudes, decisions, and even group norms. Initial tendencies toward disagreement should generally be low, and when healthy disagreements arise we should expect conflict resolution styles to be accommodating or compromising. The completely connected structure in Figure 8.1a does not engender power differences among members because all members are equally central. We therefore expect the use of soft influence strategies to predominate and internalized commitment to group norms and tasks to result. Studies of communication networks and group problem solving (Shaw, 1964) show that a decentralized group structure such as this one is best for solving problems with complex information processing requirements. Furthermore, individual group members are more satisfied with their level of participation and influence in the group in such decentralized structures (Shaw, 1964).

Transactive memory theory (Moreland, 1999; Wegner, 1987) also leads us to expect high group performance from the unified group exchange structure. Transactive memory theory focuses on the mechanisms by which group members discover "who knows who" and "who knows what" within the group and its effects on group performance. Due to extensive interaction among members in the unified group exchange structure, all members should possess a good understanding of the skills, abilities, and expertise of the other group members. Because group members are better able to make use of the knowledge and expertise possessed by the group, group process losses associated with the inaccurate weighting of member inputs (Steiner, 1972) should be minimized and performance enhanced.

Yet this same structure is perhaps the most susceptible to a number of the process losses associated with conformity in cohesive groups (Steiner, 1972). High mutual influence will lead the group to become homogeneous with respect to attitudes and opinions over time (Harary, 1959). The negative effects of homogeneity on group creativity and problem-solving performance have been well documented (Shaw, 1981). Group polarization, the tendency for groups to make decisions that are more extreme than the average decisions of individual group members, is also a product of conformity processes in groups (Burnstein & Vinokur, 1977; Isenberg, 1986). Group polarization may in fact be the simple result of differentiated influence among members in which consensus decisions gravitate toward the view of the most influential individual (Friedkin, 1999). Seibert and Goltz (2001) demonstrated that interacting groups were more susceptible to the escalation of commitment decision trap than noninteracting groups due to polarization processes. Groupthink (Janis, 1972) is an extreme example of dysfunctional consequences of conformity in group decision making. Thus, there are also a number of negative group process effects one might expect from such a structure.

We have labeled the group depicted in Figure 8.1b as unified with isolates. Although the majority of group members share generalized exchange structures, some members have only negative exchange relationships with the other group members, including each other. Actors with few or no positive relationships with other actors are often referred to as isolates within the social network literature. We would expect the group within the circle to function much as the unified group of Figure 8.1a only with the level of performance somewhere between that predicted by the abilities and resources of (in this example) a four-member group and a six-member group. That is, the knowledge, information, coordination, and workload of a six-member group will be realized only through higher transaction costs because the group will be relatively inefficient at influencing the behavior of the isolates. When task demands do not exceed the resources of a four-person team, we expect group performance to be similar to that of the unified group. But when task demands require interdependence among group members and exceed the resources of a four-person team, we expect the group in Figure 8.1b to experience some loss of information sharing, coordination, and subsequent performance.

Vertical dyad linkage theory (Dansereau et al., 1975) might identify group members within the circle in Figure 8.1b as the in-group, whereas those outside the circle might be described as the out-group. The difference in our approach is that the in-group is determined by the structure of relationships among group members rather than the relationship of the group members with the formal leader. Although there may be considerable overlap between the leader's in-group and out-group and the subgroups that form based on relationships among group members, it is conceivable that the formal leader might be one of the isolates or a member of the out-group. This would certainly have implications for the effectiveness of the formal leader, as explored briefly below.

Figure 8.1c differs from Figure 8.1b chiefly in that the out-group members have formed generalized social exchange relationships with each other, although all of the relationships between members of different subgroups remain negative exchange relationships. In fact, given the distribution of members in the example of Figure 8.1c, there is no structural basis for labeling either group as an in-group or out-group. Rather, the group is characterized as polarized. Here we might expect a level of group performance even below that predicted for a three-person group because of the potential for competition, conflict, and active blocking of goal accomplishment by the other subgroup. Although presumably designed as a single group, the dynamics of intergroup relations may be more predictive of the inter-personal processes likely to take place (Alderfer, 1987). Among these processes are group identity formation, out-group stereotyping, and the escalation of conflict and competition. In a group that is highly polarized, the net effect of shared influence among group members may be zero.

Figure 8.1d presents a group in which several generalized exchange relationships exist among subgroups but only negative exchange relationships exist between members of different subgroups. Each subgroup represents a coalition in itself, with restricted information sharing, coordination, and cooperation occurring between subgroups. But perhaps the more important processes in the group depicted in Figure 8.1d relate to the dynamics of coalitions taking place among the multiple subgroups (see McGrath, 1984; Murnighan, 1991). Theories of coalition behavior attempt to predict which partners will form coalitions and the distribution of resources among coalition partners (Gamson, 1961; Komorita, 1974). Research has shown that group members strive to form coalitions (or subgroups) containing the fewest members necessary to obtain a majority of the total resources or decision-making influence within the whole group. This is because the rewards of being part of the winning coalition will be larger when shared with fewer coalition members. Because coalitions tend to be unstable and open to exploitation, we would not expect the kind of entrenched conflict processes likely to occur in a polarized group and would predict group performance to reach a level somewhat above that of the winning "minimum coalition" predicted by the theories. Specifically, although the winning coalition, due to its monopoly on resources, influence, and rewards, will contribute most to group performance, the remaining group members will make small additions to group performance as well, perhaps through tasks delegated from winning coalition members.

Finally, Figure 8.1e depicts what we have labeled as a fragmented group exchange structure. In this pure type, all relationships are characterized as negative exchanges. Members pursue their own self-interest without regard for the welfare of others, and there is a low level of trust and reciprocity. Information sharing is likely to be minimal and strategic; knowledge and expertise will be subject to hoarding and use for political purposes. Consensus will not be easily obtained and the ability of peers to influence or sanction each other will be minimal. Influence agents are likely to rely on coercion, balanced exchange, or negative exchange. Commitment and satisfaction among individual group members is likely to be low. Here again, a group-level influence construct may adequately represent the group but does not convey many of the other dynamics captured by the focus on the nature of negative exchange relationships.

# Differentiation of Exchange Relationships and the Formation of Group Structures

In a previous section, we reviewed many positive outcomes that we expect to be the product of generalized social exchange relationships at the dyadic level. In our review of group exchange structures, the most promising structure to emerge with respect to expected benefits and the fewest drawbacks was the unified structure. One might therefore readily draw the conclusion that all of the members of a group should form generalized social exchange relationships with each other, as depicted in Figure 8.1a. This question parallels a debate in the LMX literature concerning whether leaders should form all high-quality LMX relationships with subordinates or should differentiate among group members in the type of relationships they form (Graen & Uhl-Bien, 1995; Liden, Erdogan, Wayne, & Sparrowe, 2000). In this section, we explore a number of reasons why an individual, whether the leader or group member, may not want or be able to develop generalized social exchange relationships with all of the other group members. Building from the dyadic level, this discussion helps us to understand why group exchange structures other than the one depicted in Figure 8.1a might be expected to exist.

A primary reason an individual might limit the number of generalized exchange relationships involving other group members is that such relationships take considerable time, energy, and resources to develop (Brass, 1995; Sparrowe & Liden, 1997). They also involve mutual unspecified obligations that must be met if the relationship is to be maintained (Blau, 1964). Any given individual will be able to develop only a limited number of such relationships and he or she may not want all of them to be limited to only immediate work group members. A good deal of research indicates that individuals who are strategic in the relationships they choose to form enjoy benefits in terms of influence, job performance, and career success (Brass & Burkhardt, 1992; Burt, 1997, 1994; Seibert, Kraimer, & Liden, 2001; Sparrowe et al., 2001).

Thibaut and Kelley (1959) spend considerable time explicating the cost/benefit logic governing the choice of interaction partners in their analysis of social exchange relationships. A number of characteristics lead one to be perceived as a valuable interaction partner, including similarity to the chooser and individual characteristics such as ability (Berger & Zelditch, 1985; Thibaut & Kelley, 1959). Given that the number of relationships one forms is limited, one may choose to avoid forming generalized social exchange relationships with partners who yield few social or economic rewards (Thibaut & Kelley, 1959). To the extent that group members display a range of values as social interaction partners, one should be selective in choosing the partners with whom he or she invests the time and energy required to develop rich, multidimensional relationships.

A second reason an actor may wish to limit the number of generalized social exchange relationships he or she forms with fellow group members is that such relationships act as a constraint on the range of permissible behavior within a dyad (Blau, 1964). Just as relationship norms prescribe certain behaviors, for example the norm of reciprocity, they may proscribe certain other behaviors, such as the use of exchange or coercive influence tactics. The management of poor performance is a pervasive problem in groups (Liden et al., 1999). If actors form generalized social exchange relationship with low performing group members, they will feel limited in the extent to which they may rely on directive, coercive, or explicit exchange tactics to alter those group members' behavior. Yet under some circumstances, these may be the very influence tactics required (Fiedler & Chemers, 1974).

To put this same point another way, it may be useful to have a few members in the out-group because it is easier to justify treating them less well. Cognitive dissonance theory (Festinger, 1957) can help us to understand the cognitive process team members go through in providing discipline or assign an unpleasant task to another team member. Disciplining a team member involves choices regarding what behaviors are worthy of discipline and the nature and extent of the discipline. Choice leads to cognitive dissonance and produces pressure to bolster the choice already made. In this case, such bolstering would involve deprecating the knowledge, expertise, abilities, or overall value of the disciplined team member. Thus, discipline or the assignment of unpleasant tasks or consequences becomes easier and out-group members are likely to become increasingly devalued over time through a process of self-fulfillment. In layman's terms, it may be comforting for in-group members to have a scapegoat.

A third reason to limit the number of generalized exchange relationships one forms is the effect it has on the perception others might form of one's value as an interaction partner. That is, the greater the number of generalized exchange relationships one forms, the less uniquely valuable one becomes as an interaction partner. In terms of simple extrinsic rewards, the more generalized relationships one maintains, the fewer are the rewards available to be distributed across each relationship. The dynamics involving social rewards are similar if a bit more complex. According to social exchange theory (Blau, 1964), social approval is one of the most important social rewards on which relationships are based. Approval from respected others serves to confirm one's own judgments, to justify one's own conduct, and to validate one's own values and beliefs. But, according to Blau, the significance that a person's approval has for others depends on the others' respect for that person's judgment and "the discrimination he exhibits in furnishing approval" (p. 64). Those who issue approval indiscriminately lose the respect of their peers and lose value as the provider of social rewards. This will be especially true to the extent that one forms generalized social exchange relationships with others who are considered of low value as interaction partners.

Fourth, it may also be unwise to form a generalized social exchange relationship with an actor who consistently views the relationship in terms of negative exchange. That is, it would be unwise to trust someone who seeks only to exploit your good will in order to maximize only his or her own self-interest. In the social network diagrams in Figure 8.1, this could be represented by a nonreciprocal generalized social exchange relationship. A great deal of the research growing out of the interaction matrix developed by Thibaut and Kelley (Thibaut & Kelley 1959; Kelley & Thibaut, 1978) is devoted to the dynamics of behavior in interdependent situations. The evolution of cooperation in dyads is the main issue driving this research (Axelrod, 1984). According to social exchange theory, one's own propensity to form open, trusting, generalized exchange relationships will be moderated by the behavior of one's partner. Someone who forms a generalized social exchange relationship with a partner who seeks only to maximize their own interests [a behavior pattern sometimes termed "the sucker" (Murnighan, 1991)] is likely to experience low returns from the relationship and be evaluated poorly in the eyes of his or her peers.

The pattern of relationships within the group is a fifth constraint on one's ability to form generalized exchange relationships with other group members. There is a strong tendency for social relationships to exhibit balance (Heider, 1958; Krackhardt, 1999), such that the friend of a friend is my friend and the enemy of a friend is my enemy. It is difficult to maintain a generalized social exchange relationship with both members of a dyad who have a negative social exchange relationship with each other (Heider, 1958). One who offers social approval to both members of a dyad who disagree with each other is likely to be seen as lacking in sincerity, and the social value of this person as an interaction partner will decrease (Blau, 1964).

# Vertical Leadership and Shared Leadership

At this point, we are in a position to suggest perhaps a fuller understanding of the role of vertical leadership and its interaction with group exchange processes. The leader's role may be minimal in the unified group structure and, in the case of the unified with isolates structure, necessary only to discourage the isolates from forming a coalition. When a leader may become necessary, however, is in dealing with the shortcomings of suboptimal group processes induced by the other group structures. Ultimately, the responsibilities of the leader include initiating a change in the existing exchange structure of the group in order to create a more effective group network structure. Although group members may understand what needs to be done, it may require a unique position of power and authority to effectuate a change. In what follows, we do not distinguish here between a leader who is formally assigned and enjoys hierarchical power and one who gains informal status within the group.

From the perspective of group exchange structures, the role of the leader is to evolve the group toward the structure depicted in Figure 8.1a or 1b. Which group structure is chosen depends on (a) the distribution of ability and motivation to attain group goals among group members and (b) the leader's ability to remove and recruit new group members. If each group member makes an important contribution to the attainment of group goals and the group task requires the contribution of all group members, then the leader might seek to establish a unified group structure. If one or more members are low in ability or have not responded to positive attempts to increase their motivation, and the leader has the authority to remove members and recruit new members, then the leader might seek to establish the structure depicted in Figure 8.1b as an intermediary form, with the low performing members as the isolates. When the opportunity arises, the leader can remove the low performing members and replace them with members he or she expects to be high performing. Finally, in the situation in which the leader does not have the authority to remove low performing group members, the unified with isolates structure might be sought as a stable group structure. Exchange tactics can be used to induce contributions from the isolated group members when necessary for task performance. Although equality norms might predominate within the in-group, equity norms would predominate in interactions with out-group members.

This evolution is to be accomplished by the leader through the strategic formation of generalized exchange relationships and the development of a cohesive in-group. It is necessary that the leader be seen as a valuable interaction partner with whom it is worthwhile to develop a generalized social exchange relationship. The leader would, of course, seek to establish generalized social exchange relationships with the most valuable interaction partners in the group. Once these dyads are established, the group is a modified version of Figure 8.1b—unified with isolates. From this point, the leader should seek to increase the number of group members sharing generalized social exchange relations within the in-group. The danger at this point is that members of the out-group may form their own coalitions, producing the group structures depicted in Figures 8.1c or 8.1d. In these group structures, the leader's strategy is to establish a generalized social exchange relationship with one out-group member in each coalition. Such relationships would span distinct social circles, thereby constituting what Burt (1992) has termed a structural hole. The leader would then enjoy the benefits of being *tertius gaudens* (Simmel, 1950), controlling the flow of resources exchanged between them and pitting one against the other as necessary to achieve organizational goals.

One final observation on the role of vertical leadership is appropriate. This involves the differentiated role of leaders in the group exchange structure. It may not be necessary for leaders to become involved in generalized exchange relationships with all group members as long as generalized exchange relations are maintained between the other group members. At the extreme, this would involve maintaining one generalized exchange relationship between the leader and one group member. Leaders' influence can be transmitted and reinforced by the multiple and redundant linkages among group members. Such a pattern would be efficient in terms of the leaders' investments in relationships and the need to maintain strong relationships with individuals outside of the immediate work group (Sparrowe & Liden, 1997). It would also impose minimal constraint on the range of behaviors and actions normatively expected of the leader. Finally, it would minimize the opportunity for other group members to exploit their relationship with the leader.

# Future Research Directions

We encourage empirical testing of the ideas presented in our chapter as well as continued theory development on shared leadership. Great potential for advancing knowledge lies in the integration of research on leadership and small groups. The impressive program of experimental research on the leadership of groups during the 1950s (Bass, 1990; Shaw, 1971) that lost its momentum in following decades should be resurrected. Specifically, field research implementing state of the art social network analysis procedures show much potential for informing the literature on leadership sharing in groups. Assessing the dyadic social exchange relationships among all members of groups provides richness not possible with aggregated treatment of group variables. For example, social network analyses could be used to investigate the formation, nature, and consequences of coalitions within intact work groups. Research could explore the extent to which in-groups and out-groups based on social exchange relationships between the formal leader and each group member overlap with subgroups or coalitions that are based on social exchange relationships among group members. Such research would shed light on the extent to which leadership behaviors are shared differentially among group members, as well as provide evidence on the effects of such differentiation on group effectiveness.

Related to the issue of differentiation in work groups is the need to investigate different structures for sharing leadership. For example, studies are needed that examine the implications of shared leadership in which each group member is responsible for a specific leadership behavior or set of behaviors versus shared leadership in which all group members reach consensus in executing leadership behaviors. Degree of task interdependence could be examined for its moderating role in determining the implications of these two forms of shared leadership on group effectiveness. For example, Liden, Wayne, and Bradway (1997) found that the relation between group-level empowerment and influence in decision making and group performance were moderated by task interdependence, such that for low task interdependence groups, group performance suffered as the group was empowered at the group level. It appeared that in low task interdependent groups, individuals who previously held responsibility for a particular task or decision were forced under group empowerment to relinquish that task or decision to the group (see Manz & Angle, 1986). Thus, we feel that it is imperative for investigations to explore the structure of shared leadership and how elements of the context may moderate the relations between the form of shared leadership and group effectiveness.

In this chapter, we have endeavored to expand the shared leadership concept, especially as developed by Pearce and Sims (2000), by developing the implications of differentiated influence structures within groups. By examining shared leadership theory in the context of previous research and theory on groups, we have attempted to highlight areas where leadership theory needs to be developed in greater detail and depth. We have also attempted to develop some possible directions for future theory and research based on our analysis.

# References

Alderfer, C. P. (1987). An intergroup perspective on group dynamics. In J. W. Lorsch (Ed.), *Handbook of organizational behavior* (pp. 190-222). Englewood Cliffs, NJ: Prentice Hall.

Axelrod, R. M. (1984). *The evolution of cooperation.* New York: Basic Books.

Bales, R. F. (1953). The equilibrium problem in small groups. In T. Parsons, R. F. Bales, & E. A. Shils (Eds.), *Working papers in the theory of action* (pp. 111-116). Glencoe, IL: Free Press.

Bales, R. F., & Slater, P. E. (1955). Role differentiation. In T. Parsons & R. F. Bales (Eds.), *The family, socialization, and interaction process* (pp. 259-306). Glencoe, IL: Free Press.

Bass, B. M. (1990). *Bass and Stogdill's handbook of leadership: Theory, research, and managerial applications* (3rd ed.). New York: Free Press.

Berger, J., & Zelditch, M. (Eds.). (1985). *Status, rewards, and influence.* San Francisco: Jossey-Bass.

Blau, P. M. (1964). *Exchange and power in social life.* New Brunswick, NJ: Wiley.

Brass, D. J. (1995). A social network perspective on human resources management. *Research in Personnel and Human Resources Management, 13*, 39-79.

Brass, D. J., & Burkhardt, M. E. (1992). Centrality and power in organizations. In R. G. Eccles & N. Nohria (Eds.), *Networks and organizations: Structure, form and action* (pp. 191-215). Cambridge, MA: Harvard Business School Press.

Burnstein, E., & Vinokur, A. (1977). Persuasive arguments and social comparison as determinants of attitude polarization. *Journal of Experimental Social Psychology, 13*, 315-332.

Burt, R. S. (1992). *Structural holes: The social structure of competition.* Cambridge, MA: Harvard University Press.

Burt, R. S. (1997). The contingent value of social capital. *Administrative Science Quarterly, 42*, 339-365.

Cartwright, D. (1968). The nature of group cohesiveness. In D. Cartwright & A. Zander (Eds.), *Group dynamics* (3rd ed.). New York: Harper & Row.

Dansereau, F., Graen, G., & Haga, W. J. (1975). A vertical dyad linkage approach to leadership within formal organizations. *Organizational Behavior and Human Performance, 13*, 46-78.

Deutsch, M. (1949). A theory of cooperation and competition. *Human Relations, 2*, 129-152.

Ensley, M. D., & Pearce, C. L. (2000, June). *Assessing the influence of leadership behaviors on new venture TMT processes and new venture performance.* Presented to the 20th annual Entrepreneurship Research Conference, Babson Park, MA.

Evans, C. R., & Dion, K. L. (1991). Group cohesion and performance: A meta-analysis. *Small Group Research, 22*, 175-186.

Falbe, C. M., & Yukl, G. A. (1992). Consequences for managers of using single influence tactics and combinations of tactics. *Academy of Management Journal, 35*, 638-653.

Fiedler, F. E., & Chemers, M. M. (1974). *Leadership and effective management.* Glenview, IL: Scott, Foresman.

Festinger, L. (1954). A theory of social comparison processes. *Human Relations, 7*, 117-140.

Festinger, L. (1957). *A theory of cognitive dissonance.* New York: Harper & Row.

Friedkin, N. E. (1998). *A structural theory of social influence.* Cambridge, UK: Cambridge University Press.

Friedkin, N. E. (1999). Choice shift and group polarization. *American Sociological Review, 64*, 856-875.

Gamson, W. A. (1961). A theory of coalition formation. *American Sociological Review, 26*, 373-382.

Graen, G. B., & Uhl-Bien, M. (1995). Development of leader-member exchange (LMX) theory of leadership over 25 years: Applying a multi-level multi-domain perspective. *Leadership Quarterly, 6*, 219-247.

Granovetter, M. (1973). The strength of weak ties. *American Journal of Sociology, 78*, 1360-1380.

Hackman, J. R. (1976). Group influences on individuals. In M. D. Dunnette (Ed.), *Handbook of industrial and organizational psychology, Vol. 3* (pp. 199-267). Chicago: Rand McNally.

Hackman, J. R. (1987). The design of work teams. In J. W. Lorsch (Ed.), *Handbook of organizational behavior* (pp. 315-342). Englewood Cliffs, NJ: Prentice Hall.

Harary, F. (1959). A criterion for unanimity in French's theory of social power. In D. Cartwright (Ed.), *Studies of social power* (pp. 168-182). Ann Arbor, MI: Institute for Social Research.

Heider, F. (1958). *The psychology of interpersonal relations.* New York: Wiley.

Hollander, E. P. (1978). *Leadership dynamics.* New York: The Free Press.

Isenberg, D. J. (1986). Group polarization: A critical review and meta-analysis. *Journal of Personality and Social Psychology, 50,* 1141-1151.

Janis, I. L. (1972). *Victims of groupthink.* Boston: Houghton Mifflin.

Kelley, H. H., & Thibaut, J.W. (1978). *Interpersonal relations: A theory of interdependence.* New York: Wiley.

Kimmel, M. J., Pruitt, D. G., Magenau, J. M., Konar-Goldband, E., & Carnevale, P. J. D. (1980). Effects of trust aspiration and gender on negotiation tactics. *Journal of Personality and Social Psychology, 38,* 9-23.

Komorita, S. S. (1974). A weighted probability model of coalition formation. *Psychological Review, 81,* 242-256.

Krackhardt, D., & Kilduff, M. (1999). Whether close or far: Social distance effects on perceived balance in friendship networks. *Journal of Personality and Social Psychology, 76*(5), 770-782.

Liden, R. C., Erdogan, B., Wayne, S. J., & Sparrowe, R. T. (2000, August). *Leader-member exchange differentiation: Implications for group effectiveness.* Paper presented at Academy of Management Meeting, Toronto, Canada.

Liden, R. C., & Graen, G. (1980). Generalizability of the vertical dyad linkage model of leadership. *Academy of Management Journal, 23,* 451-465.

Liden, R. C., Sparrowe, R. T., & Wayne, S. J. (1997). Leader-member exchange theory: The past and potential for the future. *Research in Personnel and Human Resources Management, 15,* 47-119.

Liden, R. C., Wayne, S. J., & Bradway, L. M. (1997). Task interdependence as a moderator of the relation between group control and performance. *Human Relations, 50,* 169-181.

Liden, R. C., Wayne, S. J., Judge, T. A., Sparrowe, R. T., Kraimer, M. L., & Franz, T. M. (1999). Management of poor performance: A comparison of manger, group member, and group disciplinary decisions. *Journal of Applied Psychology, 84,* 835-850.

Manz, C. C., & Angle, H. (1986). Can group self-management mean a loss of personal control: Triangulating a paradox. *Group and Organization Studies, 11,* 309-334.

Manz, C. C., & Sims, H. P., Jr. (1993). *Business without bosses.* New York: Wiley.

Marsden, P. V., & Friedkin, N. E. (1994). Network studies of social influence. In S. Wasserman & J. Galaskiewicz (Eds.), *Advances in social network analysis* (pp. 3-25). Thousand Oaks, CA: Sage.

McGrath, J. E. (1984). *Groups: Interaction and performance.* Englewood Cliffs, NJ: Prentice Hall.

Meindl, J. R., & Ehrlich, S. B. (1987). The romance of leadership and the evaluation of organizational performance. *Academy of Management Journal, 30,* 90-109.

Moreland, R. L. (1999). Transactive memory: Learning who knows what in work groups and organizations. In L. Thompson, D. Messick, & J. Levine (Eds.), *Sharing knowledge in organizations.* (pp. 3-31). Hillsdale, NJ: Lawrence Erlbaum.

Moscovici, S. (1985). Social influence and conformity. In G. Lindzey & E. Aronson (Eds.), *Handbook of social psychology vol. 2* (3rd ed., pp. 347-412). New York: Random House.

Mullen, B., & Copper, C. (1994, March). The relationship between group cohesiveness and performance: An integration. *Psychological Bulletin, 115,* 224.

Murnighan, J. K. (1985). Coalitions in decision-making groups: Organizational analogs. *Organizational Behavior and Human Decision Processes, 35,* 1-26.

Murnighan, J. K. (1991). *The dynamics of bargaining games.* Englewood Cliffs, NJ: Prentice Hall.

Pearce, C. L. (1997). *The determinants of change management team (CMT) effectiveness: A longitudinal investigation.* Unpublished doctoral dissertation, University of Maryland College Park.

Pearce, C. L. (1999, August). *The relative influence of vertical vs. shared leadership on the longitudinal effectiveness of change management teams.* Presented to the annual conference of the Academy of Management, Chicago, IL.

Pearce, C. L., & Sims, H. P., Jr. (2000). Shared leadership: Toward a multi-level theory of leadership. *Advances in Interdisciplinary Studies of Work Teams, 7,* 115-139. Greenwich, CT: JAI Press.

Pearce, C. L., & Sims, H. P., Jr. (in press). Vertical vs. shared leadership as predictors of the effectiveness of change management teams: An examination of aversive, directive, transactional, transformational and empowering leader behaviors. *Group Dynamics: Theory, research, and practice.*

Pearce, C. L., Yoo, Y., & Alavi, M. (in press). Leadership, social work and virtual teams: The relative influence of vertical vs. shared leadership in the nonprofit section. In R. E. Riggio and S. Smith Orr (Eds.), *Improving leadership in nonprofit organizations.* San Francisco: Jossey-Bass.

Pfeffer, J. (1977). The ambiguity of leadership. *Academy of Management Review, 2*(1), 104-112.

Podsakoff, P. M., MacKenzie, S. B., & Ahearne, M. (1977). Moderating effects of goal acceptance on the relationship between group cohesiveness and productivity. *Journal of Applied Psychology, 82,* 974-983.

Roethlisberger, F. J., & Dickson, W. J. (1939). *Management and the worker.* Cambridge, MA: Harvard University Press.

Sahlins, M. (1972). *Stone age economics.* New York: Aldine De Gruyter.

Scott, J. (2000). *Social network analysis* (2nd ed.). Thousand Oaks, CA: Sage.

Seers, A. (1989). Team-member exchange quality: A new construct for role-making research. *Organizational Behavior & Human Decision Processes, 43,* 118-135.

Seibert, S. E., & Goltz, S. M. (2001). Comparison of allocations by individuals and interacting groups in an escalation of commitment situation. *Journal of Applied Social Psychology, 31,* 134-156.

Seibert, S. E., Kraimer, M. L., & Liden, R. C. (2001). A social capital theory of career success. *Academy of Management Journal, 44,* 219-237.

Settoon, R. P., Bennett, N., & Liden, R. C. (1996). Social exchange in organizations: Perceived organizational support, leader-member exchange, and employee reciprocity. *Journal of Applied Psychology, 81,* 219-227.

Shaw, M. E. (1964). Communication networks. In L. Berkowitz (Ed.), *Advances in experimental social psychology* (2nd ed.). New York: McGraw-Hill.

Shaw, M. E. (1971). *Group dynamics: The psychology of small group behavior.* New York: McGraw-Hill.

Shaw, M. E. (1981). *Group dynamics: The psychology of small group behavior.* 3d ed. New York: McGraw-Hill.

Simmel, G. (1950). *The sociology of George Simmel.* New York: Free Press.

Slater, P. E. (1965). Role differentiation in small groups. In A. P. Hare, E. F. Borgatta, & R. F. Bales (Eds.), *Small groups: Studies in social interaction* (pp. 610-627). New York: Knopf.

Sparrowe, R. T., & Liden, R. C. (1997). Process and structure in leader-member exchange. *Academy of Management Review, 22,* 522-552.

Sparrowe, R. T., Liden, R. C., Wayne, S. J., & Kraimer, M. L. (2001). Social networks and the performance of individuals and groups. *Academy of Management Journal, 44,* 316-325.

Steiner, I. D. (1972). *Group process and productivity.* New York: Academic Press.

Thibaut, J. W., & Kelley, H. H. (1959). *The social psychology of groups.* New York: Wiley.

Wegner, D. M. (1987). Transactive memory: A contemporary analysis of the group mind. In B. Mullen & G. R. Goethals (Eds.), *Theories of group behavior* (pp. 185-208). New York: Springer-Verlag.

Yukl, G. (2002). *Leadership in organizations* (5th ed.). Upper Saddle River, NJ: Prentice Hall.

Yukl, G., & Falbe, C. M. (1990). Influence tactics and objectives in upward, downward, and lateral influence attempts. *Journal of Applied Psychology, 75,* 132-140.

Yukl, G. A., Kim, H., & Falbe, C. M. (1996). Antecedents of influence outcomes. *Journal of Applied Psychology, 81,* 309-317.

Yukl, G. A., & Tracey, B. (1992). Consequences of influence tactics used with subordinates, peers, and the boss. *Journal of Applied Psychology, 77,* 525-535.

# CHAPTER 9

# Shared Leadership in Work Teams

## A Social Network Approach

*Margarita Mayo*

*James R. Meindl*

*Juan-Carlos Pastor*

The dominant paradigm for describing team leadership has been a leader-centered perspective, which emphasizes the behaviors and personal characteristics of individual leaders (see Bass, 1990). In the past few years, however, new follower-centered models of leadership are emerging that challenge this view (e.g., Meindl, 1990; Pastor, Meindl, & Mayo, 2002). The shared leadership perspective adds to this new trend by offering an alternative to the traditional vertical leadership perspective. Whereas vertical leadership models consider leadership as emanating solely from the leader, the shared leadership approach considers the role of mutual influence among team members as another source of leadership for the group (e.g., Pearce & Sims 2002; Perry, Pearce, & Sims, 1999).

The increased interest in shared leadership has resulted in theoretical models and a handful of empirical studies (Pearce, 1997; Pearce & Sims, 2002). These first studies of shared leadership in teams have used measures of aggregation in which, typically, each team member is asked how much influence the team has over aspects of the leadership process and then responses are aggregated at the team level (e.g., Pearce & Sims, 2002). This approach has been useful in showing that traditional dimensions of vertical leadership also apply to shared leadership models.

This is only a first step, however, toward capturing the complexities of shared leadership. An aggregation measure leaves unexplored many issues related to the overall properties of the team, such as: How are leadership functions distributed in the team? Are they evenly distributed among all members of the team? Can we identify subgroups within the team that specialize in specific leadership functions?

This shift in the conceptualization of leadership from a single person to a team model requires new concepts and methods to capture the nature and structure of shared leadership at the level of teams as wholes. Yukl (1998) states that

> viewing leadership in terms of reciprocal, recursive influence processes among multiple parties in a systems context is very different from studying unidirectional effects of a single leader on subordinates, and new research methods may be needed to describe and analyze the complex nature of leadership processes in social systems. (p. 459)

One perspective that may help provide the conceptual framework and methodological tools to study a shared leadership perspective is the social network approach. There are several reasons why a social network perspective can be useful to understand the dynamics of shared leadership in work teams. First, shared leadership is a relational construct that would benefit from a social network approach, which is relational by definition. The social network perspective begins with the assumption that social actors are embedded in a complex web of relationships. As such, the relation is the basic unit of analysis. Second, building on the relation as the basic unit of analysis, the social network perspective has developed concepts and methodological tools to describe and analyze social structures, including small groups. Finally, the essence of shared leadership relies on influence processes, and the social network perspective has widely examined the nature and structure of influence networks.

The purpose of this chapter is to describe a social network approach to shared leadership that extends and complements the emerging research in this area. We provide a model of shared leadership that takes into consideration the nature and distribution of influence among team members as they take leadership responsibilities. To articulate this network approach of shared leadership, we first outline some of the basic principles of social network analysis. We then discuss the nature of leadership networks based on the traditional distinction between transactional and transformational leadership. Finally, we discuss the distributional properties of these leadership networks by describing and applying the concept of network centralization.

# Basic Concepts in Intraorganizational Social Network Analysis

The use of social networks concepts and methods, the traditional domain of sociologists, has been steadily increasing in the organizational behavior (OB) literature in the past few years. Until the early 1990s, only a handful of network scholars were developing research agendas for micro-OB research or intraorganizational networks (e.g., Astley & Sachdeva, 1984; Brass, 1984, 1985; Danowski, 1980;

Krackhardt & Kilduff, 1990; Krackhardt & Porter, 1985, 1986; Rice & Aydin, 1991). Since then, interest in the topic has grown steadily, as reflected in the increased number of social network studies examining organizational issues that have appeared recently in top organizational behavior journals.

The most distinguishing feature of a social network perspective is its emphasis on relationships among social actors and the patterns and implications of these relationships (Wasserman & Faust, 1994). The main difference between network and non-network perspectives is that a network perspective uses theoretical concepts and data on relationships among social actors to test theories. To examine social systems under this paradigm, network analysts have developed a new set of concepts and research methods. We review here some of the key social network concepts as they relate to our model of shared leadership.

## Social Network

In the intraorganizational literature, a *social network* is commonly defined as a set of individuals with a routine and established pattern of interpersonal contacts who can be identified as members of a network exchanging information, resources, influence, affect, or power. Cartwright and Harary (1977) outlined the basic idea of representing groups as a collection of points connected by lines. The resulting "sociogram" represents the network of relations among group members that can be analyzed by using the methods and techniques of social network analysis.

Social networks have more or less defined boundaries. The whole world's population can be thought of as a big social network in which people are connected by fewer than six degrees of separation (it takes fewer than six steps to connect any given pair of individuals on Earth). In the intraorganizational networks literature, the boundaries of the network, by definition, are usually established within the organization. Researchers have typically examined groups ranging from large social systems, representing work units and functional departments from 30 to more than 100 employees (Krackhardt & Kilduff, 1999; Rice & Aydin, 1991), to working teams and task forces with fewer than 10 members (Mayo, 1998). In our model of shared leadership, the term *network* refers to the work team as formally defined by the organization, the *nodes* are the members of the team, and the *links* among them are those interactions of influence related to the leadership process within the team.

## Relational Ties

The link or *tie* is the basic building block of a social network. A link is not the property of any single individual; rather, it is a relational entity that exists only if two individuals are considered together. The content of this relation defines the nature of the network. Some common ties examined in the OB literature are the communication network (Danowski, 1980), friendship and instrumental relations (Ibarra & Andrews, 1993), and help and advice relations (e.g., Krackhardt & Porter, 1986). A task network develops around work-role performance and is directly associated with the prescribed objectives of the task. A friendship network is defined as organizational members' exchanging personal information and developing close friendships. An advice network develops as individuals seek advice from others in the network; it serves to identify the experts in the social system. Because social influence is at the core of the leadership process, our model of shared leadership will focus on influence relations among social actors.

The ties among team members can be described using two dimensions: strength and symmetry. The *strength* or *intensity* of the link refers to the frequency with which the two individuals exchange information or influence. For example, a strong link between Person A and Person B exists if A interacts or exchanges information with B more than five times a week; a weak tie exists if A does so only once a month. The definition of a strong link depends, to a great extent, on the average expectation for that type of exchange in that particular social system. *Symmetry* refers to the extent to which the relationship is bidirectional. This is an important feature of ties in networks of influence, because these relations tend to be asymmetrical. That is, the fact that A influences B does not necessarily mean that B influences A.

## Individual Network Measures

A common way to describe individuals' positions in relation to the whole network is network centrality. Centrality is a proxy for an individual's influence in the social system. *Network centrality* refers to individuals' prominence in the social system. Numerous measures of centrality capture different properties of individuals' position in the overall social structure. The three most popular measures are degree, closeness, and betweenness centrality (see Borgatti, Everett, & Freeman, 1992; Freeman, 1979).

*Degree centrality* refers to the number of links that a person has with other members of the group. The more links, the more central he or she is in the group. Here it is important to distinguish between out-degree links (i.e., those links reported by the focal person) and in-degree links (i.e., those reported by other group members about the focal person). When using reciprocated links, in-degree and out-degree centrality are equivalent. For directed and asymmetric links as in influence networks, however, they take on different meanings. Out-degrees are nominations (*he or she influences me*); in-degrees are choices (*I am selected as someone who influences other team members*).

*Closeness centrality* is a measure of centrality that accounts for both direct and indirect links (those of the actors to whom one has direct ties). Conceptually, it represents ease of access to others. For instance, an individual with five ties to central individuals is "closer" to other members of the group than an individual with five ties to five peripheral members of the group. (In contrast, both actors have the same value of degree centrality: five.)

Finally, *betweenness centrality* refers to the extent to which one individual is between two other individuals who are not connected to each other. A high score in this measure indicates that the person mediates the relationships (following the shortest connecting paths) of a great number of actors. Freeman suggests that this measure indicates how much power a person has in the communication network. If a person is mediating the relationship among several individuals, he or she may withhold or distort the information that is being transmitted. Brass and Burkhardt (1993) point out that although closeness centrality represents independence from others, betweenness centrality is both a measure of control or dependence on others. In a network approach, explanations for regularities in behavior are found in individuals' structural location in the web of relationships, and not just in the inner forces or personal characteristics that impel individuals to act in certain ways (Wellman, 1988).

## Whole Network Measures

Certain concepts are used to describe the whole network. First, *density* refers to the number of links in the network in proportion to the number of possible links. Dense networks imply greater numbers of interactions among members of the network. Second, *centralization* refers to the degree to which all members of the network are unequally central in the network. A highly centralized network is hierarchical with one or few actors very central and the rest connected only to these central actors. By contrast, in a less centralized network, all members participate in and are connected to a similar number of actors in the network.

A social network approach to shared leadership needs the development of two aspects: the nature of the leadership network and the distributional properties that describe the leadership network as a whole system. Next, we discuss the nature of the leadership network using the distinction between transactional and transformational leadership. Later in the chapter, we will discuss the distributional properties of shared leadership using the concept of network centralization.

# The Nature of Shared Leadership

To describe the links among team members as they lead the group, we will use the transactional-transformational theory of leadership (Bass, 1985). Other leadership perspectives could provide valid models for our network model of shared leadership. There are, however, three main reasons why this theory is more suitable for our purposes.

First, Bass's (1985) transactional and transformational leadership theory was developed from a vertical leadership perspective. There is evidence, however, that the transactional and transformational leadership dimensions also apply to shared leadership. Pearce (1997) used a behavioral leadership questionnaire asking team members for their perceptions of vertical and shared leadership. The exploratory factor analysis yielded five behavioral influence strategies of shared leadership (aversive, directive, transactional, transformational, and empowering). A second-order factor analysis of these five dimensions resulted in two factors that closely resembled the transactional (aversive, directive, transactional) and transformational leadership (transformational, empowerment) aspects of leadership.

Second, the transactional and transformational theory of leadership has been successfully applied in different organizational contexts, which adds to its construct validity. Finally, the theory provides a number of leadership dimensions that will allow us to conceptualize shared leadership from a multiple networks perspective.

The transactional and transformational theory of leadership (Bass, 1985, 1990; Burns, 1978) tries to explain the extraordinary effects that certain leaders have on their followers. Whereas transactional leaders obtain expected results from followers, transformational leaders seem to obtain extraordinary effort, motivation, self-sacrificial behavior, and performance from their followers.

Transactional leadership occurs when leader-follower relationships are viewed as exchanges, in which leaders and followers perceive each other as being potentially instrumental to each others' goals and needs, such as accomplishment of a task (Bass, 1990). By contrast, transformational leadership occurs when leader-follower relationships are viewed as transcending their own personal interests to benefit higher-order values and principles (Burns, 1978). During the transformational process, leaders are viewed as visionary, charismatic, sensitive to individuals' needs and feelings, and inspirational (e.g., Bass, 1985; Burns, 1978; Conger, 1989; Conger & Kanungo, 1988).

Charisma has been found to be the major component of transformational leadership (Bass, 1985). Charismatic relationships are characterized by followers' intense emotional feelings about the leader, unquestioning acceptance of leaders' beliefs, and an emotional attachment to the mission. These followers react with devotion, affection, admiration, and extraordinary esteem for their leaders.

These two leadership dimensions have been further described in the literature in terms of specific behaviors. In what follows, we present a brief summary of behaviors that characterize transactional and transformational leadership and how they can be observed among team members in transactional shared leadership and transformational shared leadership. In order to adapt the transactional-transformational leadership model to shared leadership, we will consider the behaviors of team members as they interact with one another in leading the group.

## Transactional Shared Leadership

Transactional leadership occurs through an exchange among team members in which rewards and incentives are offered in exchange for effort and compliance. There are two main categories: contingent reward and management by exception.

### Contingent Reward

Team members clarify goals, talk about expected behaviors and accomplishments, and reward other members for expected performance. Team members assign and get agreements from teammates by clarifying the rewards that will likely be obtained in exchange for satisfactory performance.

### Management by Exception

This is a corrective transaction by which team members arrange to monitor others' performance. They look out for errors in order to correct them. This identification process for mistakes can be passive, waiting for errors to occur, or active, when team members examine work processes so they can be corrected before making mistakes.

## Transformational Shared Leadership

Transformational leadership has an enormous influence on others by paying individualized consideration to each team member, talking about possibilities, and acting self-sacrificially (Bass, 1985). During the shared leadership process, transformational leadership occurs when there is a personal identification with the goals of the team, so that team members are willing to exert high levels of effort and commitment. There are three main dimensions of transformational leadership: charisma, individualized consideration, and intellectual stimulation.

### Charisma

*Charisma* refers to team members' ability to exercise intensive and diffuse influence over other team members' beliefs, attitudes, and behaviors. Charisma here is viewed as a relationship or bond between any two team members in which the behaviors of one of them have a diffuse and intensive influence over the other. Charismatic members articulate overarching goals, communicate high expectations, exhibit confidence in their team members, and establish emotional bonds with the team. Charismatic members project a sense of power, confidence, and dynamism to other team members.

### Individualized Consideration

Team members who provide individualized consideration to other team members show concern for their welfare and engage in conversations. They stress the satisfaction and well-being of their interlocutors and often act as coaches and mentors for other team members. They are perceived as friendly and approachable, and show acceptance of individuals' differences. They show active listening and delegate or involve members in challenging tasks to develop them.

### Intellectual Stimulation

Transformational members provide intellectual stimulation to other team members by questioning assumptions, reframing problems, and approaching old situations in new ways. They stimulate creativity in the team and never criticize individual members' mistakes.

Next, we take these leadership behaviors by team members and translate them into social network concepts and measures. For ease of presentation, first we will present a hypothetical example.

## A Hypothetical Example

This example includes (a) the type of questions needed to collect network data in a team regarding the perceptions of transactional and transformational shared leadership; (b) a hypothetical set of raw data in both transactional and transformational team leadership, resulting in a matrix of transactional leadership and a matrix of transformational leadership; and (c) a sociometric graph of the two leadership networks.

### A Prototypical Questionnaire to Uncover Transactional/Transformational Shared Leadership

The first step in describing leadership networks is to develop questions that uncover the leadership behaviors that team members display. The questions in Table 9.1 can be used as examples of how to uncover these networks.

**Table 9.1** An Example of Items of a Shared Leadership Team Questionnaire

**Question 1a (Transactional-Contingent Reward).** How often does each member of your team acknowledge and reward you for your contributions to the team? Please use the scale below.

| *Never or almost never* | *0* | *1* | *2* | *3* | *4* | *Frequently or almost always* |
|---|---|---|---|---|---|---|
| 1. Charles | 0 | 1 | 2 | 3 | 4 | |
| 2. Frank | 0 | 1 | 2 | 3 | 4 | |
| 3. Debra | 0 | 1 | 2 | 3 | 4 | |
| 4. Donald | 0 | 1 | 2 | 3 | 4 | |
| 5. Gregory | 0 | 1 | 2 | 3 | 4 | |

**Question 1b (Transactional-Contingent Reward).** How often does each member of your team clarify for you the incentives and rewards available to you if the team achieves its goals?

| *Never or almost never* | *0* | *1* | *2* | *3* | *4* | *Frequently or almost always* |
|---|---|---|---|---|---|---|
| 1. Charles | 0 | 1 | 2 | 3 | 4 | |
| 2. Frank | 0 | 1 | 2 | 3 | 4 | |
| 3. Debra | 0 | 1 | 2 | 3 | 4 | |
| 4. Donald | 0 | 1 | 2 | 3 | 4 | |
| 5. Gregory | 0 | 1 | 2 | 3 | 4 | |

**Question 2a (Transformational-Charisma).** How often does each member of your team encourage you to participate in group activities and increase your willingness to cooperate and communicate with other members of the team? Please use the scale below.

| *Never or almost never* | *0* | *1* | *2* | *3* | *4* | *Frequently or almost always* |
|---|---|---|---|---|---|---|
| 1. Charles | 0 | 1 | 2 | 3 | 4 | |
| 2. Frank | 0 | 1 | 2 | 3 | 4 | |
| 3. Debra | 0 | 1 | 2 | 3 | 4 | |
| 4. Donald | 0 | 1 | 2 | 3 | 4 | |
| 5. Gregory | 0 | 1 | 2 | 3 | 4 | |

**Question 2b (Transformational-Charisma).** How often does each member of your team communicate high expectations of performance to you? Please use the scale below.

| *Never or almost never* | *0* | *1* | *2* | *3* | *4* | *Frequently or almost always* |
|---|---|---|---|---|---|---|
| 1. Charles | 0 | 1 | 2 | 3 | 4 | |
| 2. Frank | 0 | 1 | 2 | 3 | 4 | |
| 3. Debra | 0 | 1 | 2 | 3 | 4 | |
| 4. Donald | 0 | 1 | 2 | 3 | 4 | |
| 5. Gregory | 0 | 1 | 2 | 3 | 4 | |

There are two important aspects to the above conceptualization of leadership. First, we consider leadership to be an attribution made about the intentions of an agent of influence. For an influence attempt to be considered part of leadership, it has to be perceived by the receiver of influence as an act of leadership. Second, transactional and transformational leadership are not opposites; rather, they are two aspects of leadership that often coexist in a group. That is, a team member who influences the group can be perceived as transformational and transactional by different team members. The important thing here is how team members perceive each other.

**Table 9.2** Hypothetical Example of Member Responses to the Transactional and Transformational Scales in Table 9.1

| Matrix of Transactional Leadership (Contingent Reward) | | | | | | |
|---|---|---|---|---|---|---|
| | *Charles* | *Frank* | *Debra* | *Donald* | *Gregory* | **TOTAL** |
| Charles | — | 0.5 | 2.5 | 1.5 | 2.5 | *7.0* |
| Frank | 2.0 | — | 0.5 | 2.0 | 1.0 | *5.5* |
| Debra | 2.5 | 1.0 | — | 0.0 | 3.0 | *6.5* |
| Donald | 3.5 | 2.5 | 1.5 | — | 2.5 | *10.0* |
| Gregory | 3.5 | 3.5 | 3.5 | 1.5 | — | *12.0* |

| Matrix of Transformational Leadership (Charisma) | | | | | | |
|---|---|---|---|---|---|---|
| | *Charles* | *Frank* | *Debra* | *Donald* | *Gregory* | **TOTAL** |
| Charles | — | 2.5 | 3.0 | 3.5 | 3.5 | *12.5* |
| Frank | 1.5 | — | 2.5 | 1.0 | 3.0 | *8.0* |
| Debra | 2.0 | 3.5 | — | 2.5 | 3.0 | *11.0* |
| Donald | 0.5 | 0.0 | 1.5 | — | 1.5 | *3.5* |
| Gregory | 0.0 | 1.5 | 2.0 | 1.5 | — | *5.0* |

NOTE: Cell values are the means of the two items included in each scale.

## A Hypothetical Set of Individual Raw Data

The responses from each individual member to the transactional and transformational scales are averaged (in this case with two items) and included in two $5 \times 5$ squared matrices, as shown in Table 9.2.

In this example, each cell represents transactional and transformational leadership attributed to members of the team. The row totals can also be used as a measure of the total amount of leadership influence attributed to each member of the team by his or her peers. For instance, Charles is attributed 7 points in the transactional network and 12.5 points in the transformational network. In contrast, Gregory has 12 and 5 points for the transactional and transformational leadership dimensions respectively.

The diagonal represents self-attributed leadership. It should not be included in the analysis because attributions of leadership have an effect on team members' behaviors to the extent to which the target of influence grants that power and influence to the agent of influence. High degrees of self-attributed leadership have no effect on team members; they merely represent self-perceptions.

## Sociometric Graph of Shared Leadership

The data can be represented in a sociogram or graph, with points representing team members and links representing leadership relations. For ease of presentation, we have dichotomized the data to represent the above network data of shared

**Table 9.3** Dichotomized Matrix of the Transactional and Transformational Leadership Networks

### Matrix of Transactional Leadership (Contingent Reward)

|  | Charles | Frank | Debra | Donald | Gregory | **TOTAL** |
|---|---|---|---|---|---|---|
| 1. Charles | — | 0 | 1 | 0 | 1 | *2* |
| 2. Frank | 0 | — | 0 | 0 | 0 | *0* |
| 3. Debra | 1 | 0 | — | 0 | 1 | *2* |
| 4. Donald | 1 | 1 | 0 | — | 1 | *3* |
| 5. Gregory | 1 | 1 | 1 | 0 | — | *3* |

### Matrix of Transformational Leadership (Charisma)

|  | Charles | Frank | Debra | Donald | Gregory | **TOTAL** |
|---|---|---|---|---|---|---|
| 1. Charles | — | 1 | 1 | 1 | 1 | *3* |
| 2. Frank | 0 | — | 1 | 0 | 1 | *2* |
| 3. Debra | 0 | 1 | — | 1 | 1 | *3* |
| 4. Donald | 0 | 0 | 0 | — | 0 | *0* |
| 5. Gregory | 0 | 0 | 0 | 0 | — | *0* |

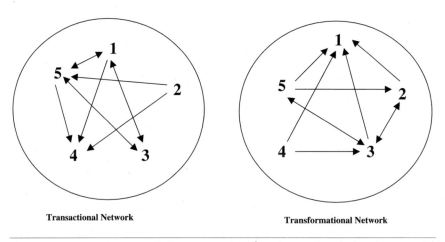

Transactional Network    Transformational Network

**Figure 9.1** Sociogram of the Transactional and Transformational Networks

leadership. Values of 2 or less are considered 0, and values greater than 2 are given the value of 1. In other words, we have moved from a valued network of data down to a binary network of data in which we count only the presence (rather than the strength) of the relationship. Only present links are represented in the sociogram shown in Table 9.3 and Figure 9.1.

# The Topography of Shared Leadership

Once the nature of the leadership network has been identified, the next step in developing a network model of shared leadership involves describing the distributed patterns of leadership within the group and the density of the influence network. This mapping of shared leadership in a network can be described as leadership topography. From a network level of analysis, the degree of shared leadership indicates the distribution and amount of leadership among members of a social unit. As such, it is a compositional construct that describes a social entity rather than one individual.

Work teams vary in terms of how much each member exercises leadership in the group. Thus, one can describe teams in terms of their leadership distribution. For instance, a team with the maximum degree of shared leadership occurs when the transactional and transformational aspects of leadership are distributed evenly among all members of the team. In other words, the maximum degree of shared leadership represents an egalitarian distribution of power and influence among team members along the transactional and transformational leadership dimensions. By contrast, a team with centralized leadership is one in which one or a few members dominate and take on most of the leadership responsibilities in the team. These few members take responsibilities in the group, motivate other team members and correct their actions when necessary.

## Shared Leadership As Team Decentralization

Team centralization is a measure of compactness. It describes the distribution of network ties and whether these links are organized around particular focal points. Team centralization with respect to individuals' centrality in the network can be useful to conceptualize the idea of shared leadership. The degree of shared leadership in a team can be thought of as the degree of team decentralization in the two leadership dimensions: transactional and transformational. If all members of the network participate equally in displaying leadership behaviors, we will have the highest level of shared leadership, but when leadership behaviors revolve around a single individual or few actors, we say the leadership network is highly centralized. That is, one or few individuals are quite central or have emerged as leaders with the remaining group members being in the periphery of the network. The concept of team centralization, then, is a measure of variability and dispersion of individuals' centrality. As such, it could be taken as an indication of leadership differentials within the work team.

The operationalization of team centralization involves two steps. First, one must identify individuals' centrality in the leadership networks; second, the dispersion of these individual centrality indexes is computed. Individual centrality is a structural characteristic of individual members that indicates that the actor is at the center of the social system. For directed relations, as in the case of leadership networks, centrality is also a measure of prestige. Prestigious actors are those with many indegrees or "choices"—that is, prestigious actors are chosen or nominated by many other individual members as displaying leadership. Prestige is a structural attribute of each individual; it refers to his or her level of prominence and importance in a social system (Moreno, 1934/1978; Knoke & Burt, 1983). The prestige of an individual is similar to the more popular term of "star" or being the most "popular." It indicates who stands at the center of attention (Scott, 1991). Prestige is a relational attribute of an individual, and it is taken here as an indication of the individual's contribution to the leadership function in the team.

In our example above, the sum of rows in each of the matrices represents the total leadership influence attributed to each team member in the two leadership dimensions by the rest of the team members. (The cells in the diagonal represent self-attributed influence, and as such are not used to compute total influence.) These values are the in-degrees in network terms, and they are commonly taken as an indication of individual centrality and status within the team. Thus, the individual centrality or prestige of each member of this team in the transactional and transformational networks is Charles (2/4), Frank (0/2), Gregory (2/3), Donald (3/0), and Debra (3/0).

Second, we compute the dispersion of these individual centrality indexes. Team centralization represents the inequality with which group members participate in the leadership process. A team centralization measure expresses how tightly the team is organized around its most central individuals (Scott, 1991). Among all the indices available to measure dispersion of individual prestige (see Wasserman & Faust, 1994, for a review), the variance is the most widely recommended (Coleman, 1964; Hoivik & Gleditsch, 1975; Snijders, 1981). Freeman (1979) provides a convenient formula to operationalize the variance of centrality:

$$S_c^2 = [\sum_{i=1}^{g} (C_D (n^\star) - C_D (n_i))]/max [\sum_{i=1}^{g} (C_D (n^\star) - C_D (n_i))]$$

$\overline{C}_D(ni)$ is the in-degree centrality of individual i, $\overline{C}_D(n^\star)$ is the maximum observed value, and *max* refers to the maximum amount using this formula, which is always the case of a star. This index varies from 0 to 1, with a value of 0 team centralization (or status differentiation) indicating that the status of all individuals in the group is spread equally (condition of maximum shared leadership) and with a value of 1 team centralization indicating that the status in the team is centralized around a single member (condition of minimum shared leadership). When the relation measured is directional, as it is in our case, the denominator equals $(n)^\star - (n-1)$. Therefore, the formula to compute group centralization is

$$S_c^2 = [\sum_{i=1}^{g} (C_D (n^\star) - C_D (n_i))]/ n^\star(n - 1)]$$

The usefulness of the network approach to measuring shared leadership can best be illustrated through our example. In a previous section, we measured individuals' centrality in both the transactional and transformational leadership networks: Charles (2/4), Frank (0/2), Gregory (2/3), Donald (3/0), and Debra (3/0). This still describes each individual member, however, and therefore is not a property of the group.

The next step is to describe the distribution of these individual centrality indices in the network by applying the formula above. In our example, the variance of these centrality values equals 0.31 for the transactional/transformational network and 0.44 for the networks. These values are taken as measures of the degree of shared leadership, which is a property of the group and a group-level measure. The lower the variance, the greater the degree of shared leadership. In our example, the transactional network is more shared than the transformational network. It seems that most team members except Member 2 share responsibilities for rewarding and correcting errors in the group. Only Members 1 and 3, however, seem to take on most activities regarding inspiring, motivating, and paying personal attention to team members.

## Degrees of Shared Leadership

So far we have talked about the dispersion of leadership in a network. Shared leadership occurs when members of the team attribute similar amounts of influence to one another (they are equally central in the attribution of influence network). It is, however, also important to consider the total amount of influence in the group. A dense network represents a group in which members attribute high amounts of influence to its members. For instance, let's think of two teams with five members each. In the first team, all five members are linked to one another with one nomination each, and the team has an index of centralization of "0" (maximum shared leadership). Similarly, a team with five members in which everybody is linked to every other member of the team will also have team centralization of "0." The density of the first team, however, is $5 / (n-1)^*(n-1)^*2 = .16$, whereas the density of the second team is $32 / (n-1)^*(n-1)^*2 = 1.00$. The density of the shared leadership network is taken here as a measure of the amount or degree of leadership (influence) perceived in a team. If we take the density of the leadership network (high or low) and the decentralization of the leadership network (high or low), we obtain a preliminary classification of levels of shared and vertical leadership with four categories (see Figure 9.2).

Quadrant I has low density and high decentralization. It represents a low-moderate level of shared leadership, in which the distribution is egalitarian but with low levels of attributed influence. In these groups, there is low participation in the influence process within the team and members prefer not to take a leadership role as long as things are going OK. This structure may represent long-tenure and production teams with highly structured tasks and environments that reduce the need for influence.

Quadrant II has high decentralization and high density, and it represents the highest degree of shared leadership. Team members attribute high influence to one another in an egalitarian way and perceive high degrees of power and influence in the team. This configuration may be expected in autonomous self-managed and empowered teams working in highly interdependent tasks.

Quadrant III has low levels of decentralization and a low-density influence network. There is domination by the few but with very few connections among group members. There are several isolates with no connections at all to other members. These networks may be typical of traditional teams with hierarchical structures that have been operating for a long time—there is an appointed leader, but familiarity with the task and with one another reduces the need for influence.

Quadrant IV has low decentralization and high density. This quadrant includes cases of strong leadership in a very hierarchical structure. Only one or few members receive attributions of high influence in the team. The network resembles a

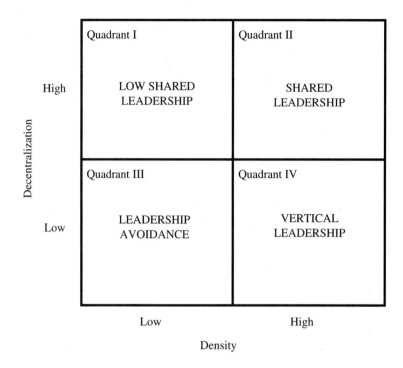

**Figure 9.2**    Degrees of Shared and Vertical Leadership

dense star network with all members connected to one or few individuals that are at the center of the flow of influence. This pattern may be expected from teams with charismatic leadership and strong authority figures.

In the previous sections, we have provided a conceptual framework for analyzing and measuring shared leadership in work teams. The main elements of this framework are conceptualization of work teams as social networks (nodes and relations), development of the two types of shared leadership networks (transactional and transformational networks), and analysis of these networks at the whole-group level with the concept of group centralization and group density. In the next section, we will examine some implications of our model for research in organizations.

## Research Implications

A network conception of shared leadership raises a number of intriguing possibilities for research and theory development. Next, we present a few of these implications in the form of research questions and speculate about some of the implications for a future research agenda on shared leadership.

## What Is the Relation Between, or Interaction of, Vertical and Shared Leadership?

Are vertical and shared leadership substitutes for one another? Are they complementary? Are they redundant systems? How do various forms and amounts of vertical leadership affect the emergence and development of shared leadership among team members? Are certain network characteristics of shared leadership encouraged or discouraged by different vertical leadership styles and approaches? Are certain combinations of vertical leadership (type and amount) and shared leadership (type, amount, and distribution) more or less effective? Let us speculate on some of these questions.

Certain vertical leadership styles may inhibit or facilitate the emergence of shared leadership in a team. Strong vertical leadership styles such as charismatic leadership that involves an intense emotional attachment to the leader (House, 1977) might inhibit the emergence of shared leadership. Subordinates of highly charismatic leaders may find it more rewarding to relate to the formal leader with whom they identify and who shows sensitivity to their individual needs and feelings than to establish connections and emotional ties to their peers. This preference for the figure of the leader will result in a relatively low shared leadership network structure. In contrast, a different relationship could be expected for subordinates who view their interactions with the leader in a transactional mode. Transactional leadership involves the perception of the leader as a mere agent of reinforcement (see Bass, 1990). Transactional leadership does not involve followers' strong emotional attachment to the leader. In this case, it seems reasonable to expect that these subordinates might perceive interacting and communicating with other peers as potentially motivating and as a necessary means to achieve some of their personal goals.

## What Is the Relation Between and Interaction of Different Shared Leadership Concepts?

Within an emergence context, does centralization of one leadership function or type also imply centralization of other leadership types? Shared leadership could imply decentralization (high sharedness) of all leadership functions or types, *or* shared leadership could imply centralized leadership concepts, but not to the same person (similar to different team members' playing different leadership roles). What are the implications of one or the other? For example, the leadership networks for transactional and transformational leadership may operate independently by adopting a centralized/decentralized shape for the transformational aspects of leadership (e.g., inspirational, intellectual stimulation, and charisma) and for the transactional aspects of leadership.

On the one hand, teams with vertical transactional leadership but shared transformational leadership have the strategic vision and idealized influence diffused among team members. Most team members discuss and provide inputs to establish the mission and overall goals of the team. All members may play important efforts in defining the identity of the team and motivating each other to show strong commitment to the group's mission. Once the strategic and overall vision has been developed in a shared way, however, the operational and transactional aspects of leadership such as clarifying how the task has to be done and rewarding people for their efforts are centralized and carried out by one or few individuals. This configuration may be preferred for creative teams and product development teams working on novel tasks. In these cases, the participation of everyone in the strategic direction of the team increases its legitimacy and assures everyone's commitment to the goals.

On the other hand, teams with network characteristics of shared transactional leadership and vertical transformational leadership have a strong charismatic and visionary leader that establishes the overarching goal and mission for the team. Many followers, however, interact to define and clarify what needs to be done to achieve these goals and reward and support each other to accomplish the vision and mission of the leader. This configuration may be expected in production teams and military platoons in which the goals and strategic direction are usually established at higher levels in the organization.

## What Is the Relationship Between and Interaction of the Leadership Network to Other Networks?

Are leadership networks correlated with other networks: friendship, communication, and status? Are some of these networks more or less conducive to the emergence and sustenance of shared leadership? For example, one could speculate that the emergence of shared leadership structures in teams may be negatively correlated with status differentiation. Status theories (Berger, Cohen, & Zelditch, 1972) argue that social categories such as sex, age, and race are indicators of status in our society. These demographic attributes are used as initial markers of status, and therefore status differentiation will likely occur within the team.

Thus, compared with demographically homogeneous teams, demographically heterogeneous teams will be more likely to develop centralized leadership. Furthermore, the centralization of the leadership network will probably develop around individual members regarded as having the highest social status. One familiar type of team that is highly diverse in terms of its members' status is the cross-functional team in a hospital. It is usually composed of doctors, nurses, social workers, and other personnel. Each of these categories is clearly associated with a different relative status in our society. As such, these teams will likely develop less shared leadership than teams whose members are more similar in social status.

## Are Certain Leadership Network Parameters Linked to Team Effectiveness?

Does team effectiveness in certain kinds of tasks depend on the density and centrality of the leadership network? Is there an optimal level of sharedness? There is some empirical evidence suggesting that the amount and sharedness of leadership are significant predictors of effectiveness in change management teams (Pearce & Sims, 2002). They found that high-performing teams exhibited overall greater amount of leadership than low-performing teams. Furthermore, high-performing teams exhibited more shared leadership relative to vertical leadership than low-performing teams in which vertical leadership outweighed shared leadership. Although this study produced a measure of shared leadership based on the aggregation of individual responses, the use of the sociometric parameters of decentralization and density of the leadership network to capture shared leadership will extend these results by providing more fine-grained measures.

Another interesting area for future research is the issue of the conditions under which shared leadership more strongly predicts team effectiveness. One may not assume that a greater degree of shared leadership will always result in greater team effectiveness, but, rather, the importance of shared leadership for team effectiveness will depend on contingency factors such as the nature of the task and the composition of the team. For example, it is reasonable to think that shared leadership will become more useful in teams in which the task is complex and interdependent, as is the case of top management teams. Indeed, these teams may clearly benefit from shared leadership, especially when their members come from diverse backgrounds. There is empirical evidence showing that teams that are diverse with respect to their functional areas of expertise are more innovative (Bantel & Jackson, 1989). Given that the task of a top management team is complex and loaded with information that is often ambiguous (Hambrick & Mason, 1984), shared leadership may increase the probability of the team having key and timely information that may be critical to make decisions that keep the organization aligned with its environment.

The usefulness of shared leadership, however, may not necessarily lead to the existence of it. It is possible that shared leadership may be more useful in cases in which it is also more difficult to develop. For example, functional biases (Hackman, 1990) and political and social dynamics (Lazear, 1989) in top management teams may inhibit the development of shared leadership. Indeed, there is evidence showing that top management teams with heterogeneous experiences tend to prefer more formal communication channels that create psychological distance among team members and inhibit social interaction (Smith et al., 1994). Top managers who feel less psychologically linked with other members of their teams may also be less willing to participate in discussions and to actively provide leadership to the team, making more difficult the development of shared leadership. Thus, research is needed to examine both the conditions that facilitate and inhibit the development of shared leadership in teams.

## How Is the Leadership Network Related to Other Group-Level Processes?

Are characteristics of the leadership network (e.g., density and centrality) correlated to characteristics such as cohesiveness and transactive memory? For example, shared leadership may help to develop transactive memory. As people work together on a task, they develop shared understandings about the task and about who is good at what in the team. In a series of experimental studies (see Moreland, 1999) showed that members who trained together developed better transactive memory systems. That is, they developed more complex and accurate beliefs about the task and the distribution of relevant skills within the team. In a similar vein, these implicit shared understandings of the task and the group members will be facilitated when team members share leadership processes, such as mutual intellectual stimulation, envisioning, and identification with the team.

## How Does the Leadership Network Change or Evolve Over Time?

How does a team evolve from a strictly vertical leadership model to a shared model? How does the leadership network grow and develop over time? Are there typical stages or punctuations in the way leadership becomes increasingly shared? How do external events (e.g., crisis and performance feedback) cause the leadership network to expand or contract? Is the expansion and contraction of the leadership network symmetrical or asymmetrical? There are few studies that have examined longitudinal issues on social network development from a team perspective. For instance, technological changes can influence the degree of sharedness in the network. In a study that examined the effects of introducing a new computer system on the social structure of a federal agency (Burkhardt, 1994; Burkhardt & Brass, 1990), the authors found that previous computer experience, positive attitudes toward computers, computer efficacy, and education level were positively related to early adoption of the system. Early adoption, in turn, put these individuals at the center of the social network as reflected by a sharp increase in their network centrality. As a consequence of becoming more central in the network, they acquired more power and influence in the organization. This newly obtained power remained even after training in how to use the computer system was provided to all employees by the manufacturer. This study shows how changes in the task and technological structure of the team affect the degree of centrality and therefore centralization of the network structure.

There is also evidence to support the idea that the structural characteristics of the team and external events such as crises may affect the emergence of shared leadership. For example, increasing the diversity in a team promotes the centralization of the network since group members will tend to cluster around those similar to themselves. Brass (1985) and Ibarra (1992) found that men and women tend to have segregated networks, and Mayo (1998) found that diverse teams tend to have more hierarchical (vertical) networks. Finally, (Pillai & Meindl, 1998) found a positive relationship between the perceptions of crisis and the emergence of charismatic leadership. Charismatic leadership is characterized by a strong hierarchical structure around the leader (Bradley, 1987). On the other hand, we could expect that team familiarity and cohesion would play an important role in the emergence of shared leadership. Trust emerges in the team as members learn from their successes and failures to rely on one another. When team members are highly qualified and competent, shared leadership may emerge naturally because delegation and participation are easy to transfer among members as the situation changes.

# Concluding Remarks

This chapter contributes to the leadership literature by presenting a novel way to conceptualize and measure shared leadership at the group level by using social network analysis. We have developed a network approach to shared leadership in work teams based on the traditional distinction between transactional and transformational leadership. In particular, the network concept of group centralization applied to these two types of leadership results in two leadership networks: the transactional and transformational leadership networks. The advantage of these leadership networks over aggregated procedures to measure shared leadership is that they capture the distributed patterns that emerge when taking the whole team into account. These patterns are not taken into account with aggregated measures and may be crucial to understanding the different patterns of shared leadership. We then discussed the research implications of this new conceptualization and measurement of shared leadership.

This chapter also advances the social network area by applying whole-network concepts to study team processes. Research in intraorganizational network analysis has often used social network parameters as independent variables. As with those in any other academic field striving for legitimacy, social network researchers have emphasized the predictive power of network-derived measures over more traditional measures. The two network measures that have been used most often to predict individuals' attitudes and behaviors are centrality and the presence or strength of the link. For instance, individuals who are linked by strong ties have been found to have similar attitudes toward technology (Rice & Aydin, 1991), job satisfaction (Roberts & O'Reilly, 1979), and attributions of charisma to the leader (Pastor, Meindl, & Mayo, 2002). Similarly, centrality in the network has been found to be related to power and influence (Krackhardt, 1990; Burkhardt & Brass, 1990) and to high levels of satisfaction (Ibarra & Andrews, 1993).

There have been, however, a few studies that have used social networks as dependent variables and have sought to predict individuals' position in the network based on personal characteristics. We have already mentioned the studies by Brass (1985), Ibarra (1992), and Mayo (1998) showing how team diversity results in segregated networks of contacts in which individuals develop close ties with similar peers. Moreover, education, cognitive complexity, social status, tenure, and communication skills have been associated with centrality in the social network (Albrecht, 1979; Lincoln & Miller, 1979; Monge, Edwards, & Kirste, 1983; Monge & Eisenberg, 1987; Roberts & O'Reilly, 1979). Although there are numerous studies at the individual and dyadic levels of analysis, there seems to be a lack of studies at the whole-network level in intraorganizational research. This chapter is a first step in that direction providing a model of shared leadership using team-level network concepts.

# References

Albrecht, T. L. (1979). The role of communication in perceptions of organizational climate. *Communication Yearbook, 3,* 343-357. New Brunswick, NJ: Transaction.

Astley, W. G., & Sachdeva, P. S. (1984). Structural sources of intra-organizational power: A theoretical synthesis. *Academy of Management Review, 9,* 104-113.

Bantel, K. A., & Jackson, S. E. (1989). Top management and innovations in banking: Does the composition of the top team make a difference? *Strategic Management Journal, 10,* 107-124.

Bass, B. M. (1985). *Leadership and performance beyond expectations.* New York: Free Press.

Bass, B. M. (1990). *Bass and Stogdill's handbook of leadership.* New York: Free Press.

Bennis, W. (2000). *The co-leaders.* New York: Free Press

Berger, J., Cohen, B. P., & Zelditch, M. (1972). Status characteristics and social interaction. *American Sociological Review, 37,* 241-255.

Borgatti, S. P., Everett, M. G., & Freeman, L. C. *UCINET IV* (Version 1.0) (1992). Columbia, SC: Analytic Technologies.

Bradley, R. T. (1987). *Charisma and social structure.* New York: Paragon.

Brass, D. (1984). Being in the right place: A structural analysis of individual influence in an organization. *Administrative Science Quarterly, 29,* 518-539.

Brass, D. J. (1985). Men's and women's networks: A study of interaction patterns and influence in an organization. *Academy of Management Journal, 28,* 327-343.

Brass, D., & Burkhardt, M .E. (1992). Centrality and power in organizations. In N. Nohria & R. Eccles (Eds.), *Networks in organizations: Structure, form, and action* (pp. 191-215). Boston: Harvard Business School Press.

Brass, D., & Burkhardt, M. E. (1993). Potential power and power use: An investigation of structure and behavior. *Academy of Management Journal, 36,* 441-470.

Burkhardt, M. E. (1994). Social interaction effects following a technological change: A longitudinal investigation. *Administrative Science Quarterly, 37*(4), 869-898.

Burkhardt, M. E., & Brass, D. (1990). Changing patterns or patterns of change: The effects of change in technology on network structure and power. *Administrative Science Quarterly, 35,* 104-127.

Burns, J. M. (1978). *Leadership.* New York: Harper & Row.

Cartwright, D, & Harary, F. (1977). A graph-theoretical approach to the investigation of system-environment relationships. *Journal of Mathematical Sociology, 5,* 87-111.

Coleman, J. S. (1964). *Introduction to mathematical sociology.* New York: Free Press.

Conger, J. A. (1989). *The charismatic leader: Beyond the mystique of exceptional leadership.* San Francisco: Jossey-Bass.

Conger, J. A., & Kanungo, R. N. (1988). Behavioral dimensions of charismatic leadership. In J. A. Conger and R. N. Kanungo (Eds.), *Charismatic leadership: The elusive factor in organizational effectiveness* (pp. 78-97). San Francisco: Jossey-Bass.

Danowski, J. A. (1980). Group attitude uniformity and connectivity of organizational communication networks for production, innovation, and maintenance content. *Human Communication Research, 6*(4), 299-307.

Freeman, L. C. (1979). Centrality in social networks: Conceptual clarification. *Social Networks, 1,* 215-239.

Hackman, R. J. (1990). *Groups that work (and those that don't).* San Francisco, CA: Jossey-Bass.

Hambrick, D. C., & Mason, P. A. (1984). Upper echelons: The organization as a reflection of its top managers. *Academy of Management Review, 9,* 193-206.

Hoivik, T., & Gleditsch, N. P. (1975). Structural parameters of graphs: A theoretical investigation. In H. M. Blalock (Ed.), *Quantitative Sociology* (pp. 203-223). New York: Academic Press.

House, R. J. 1977. A 1976 theory of charismatic leadership. In J. G. Hunt & L. L. Larson (Eds.), *Leadership: The cutting edge,* pp. 189-207. Carbondale, IL: Southern Illinois University Press.

Ibarra, H. (1992). Homophily and differential returns: Sex differences in network structure and access in an advertising firm. *Administrative Science Quarterly, 37,* 422-447.

Ibarra, H., & Andrews, S. B. (1993). Power, social influence, and sense making: Effects of network centrality and proximity on employee perceptions. *Administrative Science Quarterly, 38,* 277-303.

Knoke, D., & Burt, R. (1983). Prominence. In R. Burt & M. Minor (Eds.), *Applied Network Analysis* (pp. 195-222). Beverly Hills, CA: Sage.

Krackhardt, D. (1990). Assessing the political landscape: Structure, cognition, and power in organizations. *Administrative Science Quarterly, 35*, 342-369.

Krackhardt, D., & Kilduff, M. (1990). Friendship patterns and culture: The control of organizational diversity. *American Anthropologist, 92*, 142-154.

Krackhardt, D., & Kilduff, M. (1999). Whether close or far: Social distance effects on perceived balance in friendship networks. *Journal of Personality and Social Psychology, 76*(5): 770-782.

Krackhardt, D., & Porter, L. T. (1985). When friends leave: A structural analysis of the relationship between turnover and stayer's attitudes. *Administrative Science Quarterly, 30:* 242-261.

Krackhardt, D., & Porter, L. T. (1986). The snowball effect: Turnover embedded in communication networks. *Journal of Applied Psychology, 71*, 50-55.

Lazear, E. P. (1989). Pay equality and industrial politics. *Journal of Political Economy, 97*(3), 561-580.

Lincoln, J. R., & Miller, J. (1979). Work and friendship ties in organizations: A comparative analysis of relational networks. *Administrative Science Quarterly, 24*,181-199.

Mayo, M. (1998). *Work team diversity: An examination of a process model using artificial intelligence and social network methods.* Unpublished doctoral dissertation, State University of New York, Buffalo.

Meindl, J. R. (1990). On leadership: An alternative to the conventional wisdom. In B. M Staw & L. L. Cummings (eds.), *Research in organizational behavior, Vol. 12,* 159-203. Greenwich, CT: JAI Press.

Monge, P. R., Edwards, J. A., & Kirste, K. (1983). Determinants of communication network involvement: Connectedness and integration. *Group and Organization Studies, 8*, 83-111.

Monge, P. R., & Eisenberg, E. M. (1987). Emergent networks. In Jablin, Putman, L., Roberts, & Porter (Eds.), *Handbook of organizational behavior* (pp. 304-342). Beverly Hills, CA: Sage.

Moreland, R. L. (1999). Transactive memory: Learning who knows what in work groups organizations. In L. L. Thompson, J. L. Levine, & D. Messick (Eds.), *Shared Cognition in Organizations.* (pp. 3-31). Mahwah, NJ: LEA.

Moreno, J. L. (1934/1978). *Who shall survive? Foundations of sociometry, group psychotherapy and sociodrama.* Washington, DC: Nervous and Mental Disease Publishing Co. Reprinted 1978, New York: Beacon House.

Pastor, J. C., Meindl, J., & Mayo, M. (2002). A network effects model of charisma attributions. *Academy of Management Journal, 45*(2), 410-420.

Pearce, C. L. (1997). *The determinants of change management team effectiveness: A longitudinal investigation.* Unpublished doctoral dissertation, University of Maryland.

Pearce, C. L., & Sims, H. P., Jr. (2001). *Vertical vs. shared leadership as predictors of the effectiveness of change management teams.* Unpublished manuscript.

Pearce, C. L., & Sims, H. P., Jr. (2002). Vertical versus shared leadership as predictors of the effectiveness of change management teams: An examination of aversive, directive, transactional, transformational, and empowering leader behaviors. *Group Dynamics: Theory, Research, and Practice, 6*(2), 179-197.

Pearce, C. L., & Sims, H. P., Jr. (in press). Shared leadership: Toward a multi-level theory of leadership. *Advances in Interdisciplinary Studies of Work Teams, 7,* 115-139. Greenwich, CT: JAI Press.

Perry, M. L., Pearce, C. L., & Sims, H. P., Jr. (1999). Empowered selling teams: How shared leadership can contribute to selling team outcomes. *Journal of Personal Selling & Sales Management, 19*(3), 35-51.

Pillai, R., & Meindl, J. R. (1998). Context and charisma: A "meso" level examination of the relationship between of organic structure, collectivism, and crisis to charismatic leadership. *Journal of Management, 24,* 643-671.

Rice, R., & Aydin, C. (1991). Attitudes toward news organizational technology: Network proximity as a mechanism for social information processing. *Administrative Science Quarterly, 9,* 219-244.

Roberts, K. H., & O'Reilly, C. A. (1979). Some correlations of communication roles in organizations. *Academy of Management Journal, 22,* 42-57.

Scott, J. (1991). *Social network analysis: A handbook.* Newbury Park, CA: Sage.

Smith, K. G., Smith, K. A., Olian, J. D., Sims, H. P., Jr., O'Bannon, D. P., & Scully, J. A. (1994). Top management team demography and process: The role of social integration and communication. *Administrative Science Quarterly, 39,* 412-438.

Snijders, T. A. B. (1981). The degree of variance: An index of graph heterogeneity. *Social Networks, 3,* 163-174.

Wasserman, S., & Faust, K. (1994). *Social network analysis: Methods and applications.* New York: Cambridge University Press.

Wellman, B. (1988). Structural analysis: From method and metaphor to theory and substance. In Wellman, B., and Berkowitz, S. D. (Eds.), *Social structures: A network approach* (pp. 130-184). Cambridge, UK: Cambridge University Press.

Yukl, C. A. (1998). *Leadership in organizations* (4th ed.). Englewood Cliff. NJ: Prentice Hall.

PART III

# THE STUDY OF SHARED LEADERSHIP IN APPLIED SETTINGS

# CHAPTER 10

# Flow, Creativity, and Shared Leadership

## Rethinking the Motivation and Structuring of Knowledge Work

*Charles Hooker*

*Mihaly Csikszentmihalyi*

The roots of *shared leadership* can be found in the changing nature of work. Years ago, Peter Drucker (1959) noted the rise of the *knowledge worker* as both symptom and cause in changing patterns of organizational structuring and leadership. According to his mid-century observation, technological advances in industrialized nations and growing interest in innovation spawned a steady increase in the proportion of work requiring a high degree of formal education, training, and knowledge. Instead of performing the repetitive tasks of traditional manual laborers, modern workers have been required to apprehend and apply theoretical and analytical knowledge (Drucker, 1995). In Drucker's estimation, knowledge has become the new currency of work, and the knowledge worker has begun to replace the manual laborer. For Drucker, this has meant that the function of organizations has increasingly become innovation, or "putting knowledge to work"—a new fact that has had a profound impact on philosophies of leadership and the structuring of organizations.

AUTHORS' NOTE: The Transmission of Excellence Study was generously supported by the Spencer Foundation.

Although Drucker's writing has mainly hinted at the changes in leadership structures precipitated by the rise of knowledge work, his contemporaries have been more elaborative. Around the same time that Drucker coined the now-familiar term *knowledge work*, Burns & Stalker (1961) laid the foundations for contingency theory by observing the way in which the rising need for innovation in many economic sectors in Great Britain and Europe had a "flattening," decentralizing effect on corporate hierarchies. In their view, unstable market environments necessitated higher degrees of change and innovation, which in turn tended to produce organizations that structured themselves in a loose, decentralized, "organic" fashion.

Because information and ideas could be shared more directly between relevant members of different departments, these organizations became much more adaptive and innovative than their more conventional counterparts who maintained traditional, "mechanistic," hierarchical forms of leadership. Lawrence and Lorsch (1967) expanded the concepts put forth by Burns & Stalker by adding the idea of "differentiation and integration." They suggested that adequate levels of distinctness between subunits of an organization (differentiation) *and* adequate levels of coordination between subunits (integration) were necessary for the overall success of a decentralized organization. The greater the concern for innovation, the more these conditions were necessary. As this thought caught on, organizations with organic leadership structures began to carry the day in competitive environments where innovation and creativity were crucial to survival.

Recent scholarship and practice in the fields of management and organizational development and change have furthered the trend of structural decentralization in organizations through the increased use of teams and groups in carrying out and leading organizational endeavors (Aldag & Fuller, 1993; Cummings & Worley, 2001; Ilgen, Hollenbeck, Sego, & Major, 1993). One needs only to glance through a recent textbook in the field to see very quickly how the sharing of leadership roles and responsibilities pervades the literature through concepts like *total quality management* (TQM), *employee involvement*, and *self-managed work teams* (Cummings & Worley, 2001). Similarly, differentiation and integration are the dimensions singled out as being the essential components of evolution, as described by the new discipline of complexity studies (Csikszentmihalyi, 1993; Waldrop, 1992).

The implications for the future seem clear. As more work becomes knowledge work, work within organizations will likely become more flexible and varied. This in turn will require teamwork of a new kind, one that is conducive to the expression of creativity and innovation. Decentralized forms of leadership will become more necessary and so will shared forms of leadership.

Pearce and Sims (2000) have documented many of the immediate historical antecedents to what they have coined *shared leadership*, and they have created a useful model of the phenomenon. By their formulation, shared leadership is a process of shared influence between and among individual that can emerge in a group context as an alternate social source of leadership. The notion of shared leadership thus moves out of the traditional transactional-transformational two-factor theory of leadership, which has focused exclusively on the relationship of a solitary leader to a group of followers. But it is not without associated predecessors. Pearce and Sims discuss many lines of previous research related to shared leadership, including *emergent leadership* (Bartol & Martin, 1986), *co-leadership* (Solomon, Loeffer, & Frank, 1953), *empowerment and self-leadership* (Conger & Kanungo, 1988; Manz &

Sims, 1989) and *self-managing work teams* (Manz & Sims, 1987, 1993). To these one might add some of the recent case studies of *great groups* (Bennis & Biederman, 1997) and *hot groups* (Lipman-Blumen & Leavitt, 1999). For Pearce and Sims, the notion of shared leadership unifies these concepts and carries their implications a step further by suggesting relationships to group outcome variables such as group psyche, group behavior, and group effectiveness and by calling for greater empirical research in these areas.

According to Pearce and Sims (2000), when certain group characteristics (such as ability of group members, group size, maturity, and familiarity), task characteristics (such as urgency, complexity, and the need for creativity and interconnectivity), and environment characteristics (such as support systems and rewards) are adequately in place, a form of shared leadership is prone to arise. As the characteristics of the group, the task, and the environment vary, so may the form of shared leadership change from situation to situation. In terms of group outcomes, Pearce and Sims's model shows a reciprocal relationship, or correlation, between shared leadership and group outcomes. That is, as shared leadership takes hold, group psyche, group behavior, and group effectiveness will change, and as they change they in turn affect shared leadership. For example, let's examine elements of group psyche. In order for a form of shared leadership to arise, a certain level of commitment and cohesion among group members must exist. As members of the group lead and influence one another in positive ways, commitment and cohesion will most likely increase also, which in turn will increase the amount of shared leadership within the group. Later, we will return to this dynamic. For now, suffice it to say that the model proposed by Pearce and Sims forms the frame for the outset of this chapter.

The central aim of this chapter is to hone in on the *group psyche* that both shapes and is shaped by an experience of shared leadership. Specifically, we will focus on ways in which shared leadership provides the conditions necessary for *flow* (Csikszentmihalyi, 1990) and intrinsic motivation at the group level, and the way in which these factors can in turn affect shared leadership and organizational outcomes (such as creativity and innovative potential). Put briefly, we hope to show that sharing leadership roles and responsibility has the effect of increasing the opportunities for flow, intrinsic motivation, and optimal experience among group members and for the group as a whole. We believe that by making work more enjoyable, more empowering, and more meaningful to group members, shared leadership increases the creativity and innovative potential of the group.

In light of the rise of knowledge work, the increased drive for innovation in today's economy, and the organizational restructuring that has followed it, we believe our point of view holds particular salience and relevance. As organizations increasingly need innovative and creative ideas (i.e., transformations of knowledge) in the face of rapidly changing market environments (Drucker, 1995), shared leadership may provide useful and timely assistance in boosting innovative potential. As forms of shared leadership gain prominence in contemporary workplaces, we believe that part of their success has been and will be due to the way in which they afford work groups and their members greater opportunities for optimal experience and flow, which then lead to greater creativity and more successful group outcomes.

In what follows, we will introduce and define flow and its components. We will then show how flow operates in groups to augment both motivation and creative outcomes by discussing examples and findings from our recent research on science labs in astrophysics and genetics. Having demonstrated the relationship between shared leadership, flow, and creativity, we will then conclude with broader generalizations and return to our discussion of knowledge work and the future.

# Flow

In order to better understand positive states of being such as happiness, enjoyment, fulfillment, and optimal experience, Csikszentmihalyi began studying people who pursued activities they enjoyed but for which they received no tangible reward. Examining chess players, rock climbers, dancers, and artists, it was easy to see that they loved doing what they were doing. But why were they doing it? Moreover, why were so many of them as devoted as they were despite the absence of extrinsic rewards and the fact that their pursuits often involved painful, risky, or tedious elements? Certainly there were easier, more immediate ways to pursue pleasure on a regular basis such as shopping, watching television or a movie, or simply relaxing.

After interviewing many of these devoted enthusiasts and systematically studying their subjective experience through the experience sampling method (ESM),[1] it became clear that for all of these people the motivating factor was the quality of experience while they were doing their chosen activity. They all described the feeling they got from these pursuits as among the best they experienced in their lives—a state of consciousness that was exhilarating and focused, yet almost automatic and effortless. Many of them used the word *flow* to describe this kind of experience, and so this is how it came to be known.

Flow is a state of consciousness in which people feel completely involved in an activity to the point that they lose track of time and lose awareness of self, place, and all other details irrelevant to the immediate task at hand. It is what the athlete feels at the peak of his game—deep concentration and a vibrant a sense of mastery and coordination. It is how totally involved an artist becomes with what becomes manifest on her canvas—colors, tones, and figures fitting together to give shape to her emerging vision. It is the experience of a chess player mapping out his sequenced strategy even as his opponent moves in against him. It is how a writer feels when she is at last able to articulate her most stimulating ideas. It is any time that any of us become so immersed in what we are doing that we forget about everything else and find that we cannot pull ourselves away from it. In other words, it is deep engagement and pure enjoyment of an activity for its own sake.

Pursuing this research further, Csikszentmihalyi and his colleagues (e.g., Csikszentmihalyi & Csikszentmihalyi, 1988) discovered that the experience of flow is not restricted to avocations, hobbies, and spare time. Although it seems that most people find flow in activities outside of their daily jobs, there are hosts of people who discover this same optimal experience in their work and professional life. Moreover, the fact that more people do not find flow in their work may have more to do with the influence of cultural attitudes toward work than with the actual experience when working (Csikszentmihalyi, 1990, 1997).

Since interviewing artists, dancers, chess players, and other enthusiasts, we have studied physicians, scientists, educators, hourly wage workers, business managers, and assembly-line workers, and found that in all of these professions there are people who can find or create experiences of flow in their day-to-day tasks. So it is useful to think about flow as taking place along a continuum of intensity ranging from slicing salami in a deli to doing surgery. The two ways of making a living may be equally engrossing and enjoyable, although they differ enormously in terms of their complexity, which is the amount of challenges and skills involved in the performance.

Although flow is a subjective phenomenon, it is often triggered and sustained by interpersonal interaction. This is clear in such activities as playing music together or in team sports, improvisational theater, or a good conversation (Csikszentmihalyi & Rich, 1997). It is also true of creative endeavors that, although requiring a great deal of solitude, are also energized by the stimulation of peers. For instance John Bardeen, the only person to have won the Nobel Prize in physics twice, at age 82 was still nostalgic about the "very exciting" years he spent at the Bell Labs constantly talking to fellow physicists about quantum theory (Mockros & Csikszentmihalyi, 1999, p. 206). Most group activities that lead to flow involve interactions among peers. If a leader is necessary for the activity to be successful, he or she is almost always someone who treats the entire team as equally responsible for the direction of the activity.

So, what are the conditions for flow? Among all the people who described moments of deep enjoyment in their lives, whether at work or at play, there were eight key elements mentioned over and over again, and these have come to shape our understanding of the conditions for flow (Csikszentmihalyi, 1996).

## Clear Goals Every Step of the Way

Far from being mired in the uncertainty or ambiguity of typical existence, in flow people have a keen sense of their plan of action. They know what their next move is and are anticipating the next several moves to follow. The rock climber can see which crevice he will grab next and where his foot will follow. The musician knows what note comes next. The executive envisions her next step in implementing a new strategy and knows who she must talk to and what she has to do to make it happen. People in flow have a sense of their next move and of the overall goal of their activity.

## Immediate Feedback to One's Actions

In flow, people are able to interpret their environment clearly in response to their actions. A chess player knows if he has left his rook vulnerable to be overtaken. The musician can detect the slightest disharmony as well as key in on the perfection of a pure note. The surgeon sees clearly if she has caused too much bleeding. The sales person is keen on a customer's verbal and nonverbal cues, and a staff employee in flow has developed an internal sense of how well his performance meets expectation. In many cases, relevant feedback would be obvious to anyone, but in others it is the cultivated expertise of the individual that affords him or her the ability to interpret environmental conditions and responses as useful feedback. Whichever the case, clear feedback allows people to modify their actions and exercise their abilities effectively.

## Balance Between Challenge and Skills

In many life situations, people feel frustrated, anxious, or overwhelmed by challenges they perceive to be too great. Imagine an amateur tennis player finding herself playing in the Wimbledon finals, or a first-year medical student in the throes of open-heart surgery. At other times, people feel bored because their skills far outweigh the demands of a task. An expert mathematician would not be terribly enthused by a class in pre-algebra. An accomplished pianist would probably not feel stimulated by playing "Mary Had a Little Lamb." A person with the ability and wherewithal to work in the top tier of an organization will likely not be satisfied by being relegated to purely menial tasks. By contrast, people in flow sense a balance between the challenges of an activity and the skills they bring to it. They feel challenged but not overwhelmed, and hence walk the fine line between boredom and anxiety that is flow.

## Consciousness Excludes
## Distractions and Irrelevant Information

Another typical element of flow is that people direct their awareness only to relevant information and feedback. A rock climber cannot rethink his grocery list as he lurches for a new hold, nor can a surgeon worry about family difficulties as she slices into precious tissue. Likewise, an employee cannot remain preoccupied with where to spend his vacation time while strategizing in a staff meeting. Flow is the result of intense concentration on the present moment. Attending to unrelated data is sure to distract and disrupt the experience of flow.

## There Is No Worry of Failure

In flow, people's attention is so focused on the activity they are doing that they simply do not have the time or available mental space to worry about failing. The dancer cannot remain in sync with her music and choreography if she is wrought with negative thoughts. The scientist cannot proceed with his investigation if he is consumed by self-doubt and theoretical skepticism. The staff member cannot effectively lead a meeting while she agonizes over all of the ways her ideas could be wrong. The possibility of failure cannot stand in the state of flow because a person's concentration simply excludes it from consciousness and replaces it with a sense of control born out of a certainty for what must be done next.

## Self-Consciousness Disappears

Most of the time we monitor the way we appear to other people. Typically, awareness of the self is a burden. But in flow, people are too involved in what they are doing to worry about how they appear to others. Awareness of the self in flow comes only in the form of relevant feedback. The athlete notices her body as moving either in or out of sync with her immediate goals, but she is not paying attention to how she looks or what impression she is giving others. In the same way, a businessman in the midst of performing in a meeting is not attending to whether or not his clothes match or what kind of aftershave he is wearing. In flow the self forgets itself.

## Sense of Time Becomes Distorted

When time is not an element of the activity itself, people in flow forget about time. For the artist engrossed in his painting, minutes pass as seconds, hours as minutes. On the other hand, a runner or swimmer may be keenly aware of the seconds she is attempting to shave off, and in a strange way each motion may stretch into a seeming eternity. In an organizational context, members may get lost in a challenging and exciting task or maximizing their efficiency to meet a deadline. In flow, when time is relevant feedback it will be lengthened; when it is irrelevant, it will be forgotten.

## The Activity Becomes Autotelic

Whenever the preceding conditions are present, people enjoy what they are doing. They may have initiated a task out of obligation or because they were being paid, but as soon as they begin to enjoy it and experience flow, the task becomes an end in itself, or *autotelic*.[2] By contrast, it seems most endeavors in life are *exotelic*—that is, performed in pursuit of some other end. In these cases, people generally feel motivated only by some type of extrinsic reward such as money or prestige. It is possible, however, for an activity that was begun with exotelic expectations to become enjoyable, intrinsically motivating, and autotelic in character.

In most organizational settings, employees enter their roles and tasks with exotelic expectations. Nonetheless, our research shows it is still possible, and in fact often the case, that people in ordinary jobs find, create, or are given the conditions to transform their time at work into an autotelic experience. It is our thesis that shared forms of leadership are likely to contribute to creating these conditions—to make the experience of flow a more common and consistent one for employees. We further contend that in so doing, organizations are also likely to boost their productive output as well as the creative potential of workers—both individually and collectively. In contrast to vertical, mechanistic forms of leadership in which followers are commonly discouraged to act autonomously or to participate in such things as goal setting and feedback, shared forms of leadership promote worker autonomy, involvement, and engagement—and, in this way, stimulate intrinsic interest, motivation, enjoyment, and flow. In short, shared leadership provides the conditions for a task to become an end in itself, or autotelic. To lend some empirical validity to our thesis, let us now turn briefly to a case study from our recent research on outstanding laboratories in the sciences.

# Sample and Method

The sample presented here came from a larger ongoing study of apprenticeship among multiple professional domains including medical genetics, journalism, business, modern dance, martial arts, and coaching. In both the case to follow and the overall project, the sampling strategy was lab-focused. That is, through expert recommendations and our own research, leading figures were identified within a given field as individuals who pursued creative careers and who became known for training high-caliber successors who in their turn made significant contributions to the field.

The case examined in this chapter came from a particle astrophysics lab at a major midwestern research university. We interviewed five scientists including the generation one (G1) lab head and four generation two (G2) students.[3] All were white males (which was representative of this field), ranging in age from the G1, who was 81 years old, to the youngest G2, who was in his forties. The participants were dispersed across several regions of the United States, including the Midwest, the South, and the East and West coasts.

The primary source of data were in-depth, semistructured interviews, which were designed to take approximately two-and-a-half hours and covered broad as well as specific topics including initial interest in the field; formative experiences; apprenticeship experiences; valued goals, practices, and beliefs; obstacles, pressures, and rewards; training the next generation; and larger vocational vision or purpose. The interviews were recorded, transcribed, and analyzed using a simple coding scheme.

# Shared Leadership in a Space Science Lab

G1 was a supremely successful scientist and leader. A giant in the world of space science, G1 worked on some of the most important ventures of his day including the Manhattan project, where he, as a young scientist with a fresh doctorate, joined the team that achieved the first self-sustaining nuclear reaction on the floor of a squash court that had been turned into a makeshift laboratory at the University of Chicago. G1 was soon thereafter given a faculty position at a major midwestern university, where he remained for his entire career, publicly promoting his peaceful values in relation to science and nuclear technology, teaching undergraduate and graduate students, and managing a premier space science lab that was responsible for the construction and operation of some 35 space missions, including the first missions to Mercury, Jupiter, Mars, and Saturn. He directly advised 34 doctoral students—many of whom are among today's most eminent leaders in space science. He received numerous teaching awards, and he was honored with many of the most prestigious scientific awards, short of the Nobel Prize. One of G1's early apprentices explained, "He was a towering figure in 20th-century science. A large number of his students are research faculty members around the country. His impact has been extremely broad."

Our case, however, only begins with G1 and his achievements. Magnificent as they are, our interest lies in the lab he created and in the way he led it. In reading the transcripts from all of the members of G1's lab, the first and perhaps most striking aspect was G1's conspicuous absence from the daily goings-on of the lab. One G2 explained, "We'd get together for tea and cookies one afternoon for an hour or two every week. We would talk about what we were doing, or maybe someone would give a report or something like that. . . . My PhD thesis, I think I spent a total of 15 minutes discussing with him. He was just basically unavailable. And I was typical." Another G2 corroborated, "[G1 was in the lab] maybe a few hours every week or couple of weeks. Something like that. There was an infrastructure he had with various other staff who were working on the daily analysis and that's where, from these guys, where I really learned most of the techniques."

In fact, all of the G2s we interviewed confirmed this kind of benign neglect on the part of their leader. We say "benign" because in their interviews and in G1's own remarks, we came to discover that this hands-off approach was both intentional and beneficial. It was part of G1's broader philosophy of leadership and teaching—a highly unique way of running a science lab that was nothing short of a form of shared leadership.[4] "I treated them as colleagues," G1 told us, and, indeed, a strong sense of egalitarianism pervaded the lab's atmosphere. For example, whenever lab members collaborated on an article for publication with G1, as they often did, the order of authorship was determined alphabetically by last name.[5] "Almost all papers were written in alphabetical order. So Alfonse Abergale, whoever he would be, was always the first author. I came down the line. . . . This way, the students had the feeling of comfort." G1 continued, "Essentially, I think we were one of the leaders in this style of working with students. But more and more of the laboratories, many of them at least, are going this route. The young people in Germany, for instance, where the German attitude is all 'Herr Director' or 'Herr Professor,' is being broken down by the younger generation as they exert more and more influence."

G1 minimized the "Herr Director" role of leadership for himself in his lab in the way he oriented his students toward discovery and encouraged their creativity. This was accomplished, he said, mainly through a laissez-faire approach to leadership in which he was able to share responsibility and influence over the production in his lab. In setting a research initiative, for instance, G1 said, "I like to present a problem that we want to work on . . . [and then allow] those working with me to come up with a better way to do it." A G2 who continued this same form of leadership and teaching in his own lab explained the process similarly. After providing his lab with a basic problem to work on, he says,

> They would go away and work on this for a while, and they would come back, and as I say, when things really started rolling was when they came back doing things I had not suggested, where they had taken the next steps themselves. Where they said, "Oh, maybe if we look at it this way." . . . They can come back and say, "But we should really look at it this way, this is what. . . ." [And I'd say,] "Okay." And so it was that kind of interaction, developing the ideas, which is really the end point of all the activity. That's where the really creative things are going on.

In this kind of environment, G1's staff members—in this case, primarily students—were trusted enough and given the autonomy to extensively shape the outcome of any given project. They were given the freedom and wherewithal to make a real impact on the ideas and outcomes of the group in which they were working. They were, in a word, *empowered*. In the next section, we will return to the idea of empowerment as a critical enabler of flow in the context of shared leadership. For now, it is perhaps sufficient to emphasize the indispensable value for bestowing group members (e.g., staff members, followers, and students) with trust, autonomy, and real responsibility—that is, with the capability and belief that the work they do and the ideas they conjure can in fact significantly affect the collective project or goal. In the words of the G2 above, that is "really the end point of all the activity. That's where the really creative things are going on." Trust and shared responsibility cultivate creativity and innovation because in the process of experiencing mutuality, workers cease to see their work merely as means to some later reward (e.g., a paycheck, a degree, or a publication) and become interested in the task they are doing for its own sake because the task suddenly takes on new meaning and significance.

Trust bestowed on students or workers in a dramatic fashion can be as invigorating as it is empowering. One G2 recalled the moment he realized G1's lab was a place in which he was as much colleague and collaborator as worker and student.

> I remember my first hint that this was different than anything I'd ever done before was shortly after I was there. We came across a way of improving some of the detectors that we had. . . . This required making some calculations, and then these detectors would be constructed by cutting them out of crystals, and it would cost a lot of money to get it done. Okay. Fine. So, we were building an instrument, and so I did the calculations to find out how these detectors—what shape they should have to go on the instrument. And so I took my results to [G1], fully expecting him to pull out a pencil and paper and check my calculation. But he just ordered them. I thought, "Oh my God!" So I went back and checked them again. I was expecting a sort of tutorial. And that's just not the way things worked. I think that's fun. But it was very interesting— I was horrified. It also showed he was trusting me. He was in essence saying, "Fine. We're going to go off and have these things built at the factory to your specs."

By providing his students with this kind of empowerment, G1 not only shared responsibility and leadership, but he also provided them with experiences to embody their roles as scientists (an idea we'll return to later) and pushed them to exceed even their own expectations in their work.

G1's model of leadership provided a comfortable, collegial, trusting, and challenging environment that encouraged the free expression of ideas and allowed for interactive forms of mutual influence—both between G1 and his students and among the students themselves. G1's lab was designed to cultivate shared leadership. Students felt an uncommon sense of ownership over the outcomes of the group's work, and so they became all the more interested, engaged, and motivated. G2s were able to deeply engage their work, their peers, their colleagues, and other professionals, and, through the process, they collectively forged fascinating new ideas and ways of doing things that kept their lab among the most productive and innovative in the world. One G2 said of the experience, "It was just very interesting. That was the way we worked. You say, 'How did we learn things there?' Well, very easy, because there were research associates working for [G1], there were other students, there were all these engineers. And that's how you worked. You were in this environment and you learned things." One could say the same about how they accomplished things—winning research space for their satellites on NASA launches to far-off planets and the like. They achieved these things because they shared and tapped into one another's deepest interests and abilities, and in the process they became better individually and collectively.

Learning is highly associated with intrinsic motivation and interest, and many organizational theorists have made much of the importance of learning in sustaining innovation and excellence (Senge, 1990). Vygotsky (1978) characterized the optimal conditions for learning as occurring in what he termed "the zone of proximal development." In this zone, the challenge of a given task or activity is just beyond one's level of ability. Similar to the dynamics of flow, overwhelming challenge only causes anxiety and too little challenge results in boredom. In G1's lab, the G2s were challenged by the empowerment they received from G1, but they were not overwhelmed, and in many cases they discovered that as individuals and as a group they were capable of even more than they thought. More importantly, in this zone of learning, of *proximal development* and growth, they found flow and intrinsic motivation. The work they were doing became an end in itself, and all of the G2s characterized their work in G1's lab as among the best and most engaging of their careers—as "happy," "creative," "very interesting," "thoroughly engaging," and "very exciting."

In sum, the circumstances and nature of the work in space science were leveraged by G1 to create a powerful form of shared leadership that produced highly successful outcomes—including a plethora of innovative space missions and top-notch scientists who went on to leading positions in the field. In terms of Pearce and Sims's (2000) model, we can see how the characteristics of G1's lab fulfilled the antecedents, or prerequisites, for shared leadership. The group characteristics of the lab included well-matched ability levels among coworkers, compatible personalities, complementary maturity levels, familiarity among group members, sufficient diversity, and a relatively small group size. The characteristics of their task were also congenial to shared leadership. Their work involved interconnected skills, information, and ideas. It demanded creativity, and it was often critical and urgent. Finally, G1 promoted an environment rich in systems of reward and support for group cooperation that cultivated a general culture of shared responsibility and shared learning. Having established this lab as a case of shared leadership that was unique in its field and yet highly effective, and having begun to establish the connection of shared leadership to flow, let us now turn to the group outcomes of Pearce and Sims's model—in particular, group psyche and flow in the context of shared leadership.

## Finding Flow in Shared Leadership

Isabella Csikszentmihalyi (1988) showed that flow theory could help explain the centuries of success of the Jesuits since their inception by Ignatius of Loyola in 1540. By giving its followers "a unified structure of consciousness whereby psychic energy could be invested in an ordered way" (p. 247). The Jesuit rules for conducting one's life provided a system of intrinsic rewards and deep social meaning that continues to sustain and fulfill its members even in the face of the increasingly pervasive and seductive lures of secular life. Somewhat surprisingly, shared leadership imbues organizational success through flow in much the same way—namely by providing a means to greater intrinsic motivation, interest, and social meaning.

But how does shared leadership promote flow? First, it reduces the salience of extrinsic rewards and replaces them with greater interest for the tasks at hand. One way this was accomplished in G1's lab was through the alphabetizing of authors' names on publications. By reducing competition for social recognition (an extrinsic reward), students were able to turn their attention more completely to the content of their joint work and writing. Shared leadership further encourages intrinsic motivation and interest in the tasks being performed by transforming the nature of work into a meaningful and expressive activity. In the context of G1's lab, younger associates no longer saw their work as merely following their mentor's rote instructions. Instead, they grasped opportunities to significantly affect a collective enterprise—in this case, the designing and building of satellites, space probes, as well as other efforts that go into space research. Understanding their work within a group context, they reported a greater sense of social meaning. Daily activities were no longer mere tasks, but instead marked important opportunities to contribute to a sense of accomplishment they shared with other members of the group.

Second, in shared leadership worry of failure or of being critically supervised is removed. Referred to as *leader solecism* by Pearce and Giacalone (in press), critical supervision of a team from a leader has been shown to lead to various forms of dysfunctional behavior among team members. In G1's lab, both leader solecism and fear of failure were absent. The staff felt challenged by the degree of responsibility they were granted, but they did not feel G1 peering over their shoulder, reprimanding each gaffe. They were given space to learn and to make mistakes, and yet because they took ownership in the final results, they were more vigilant, thorough, and careful than they would have been otherwise.

Furthermore, because their work was made more interesting and enthralling by the responsibility they could claim, fear of failure simply did not significantly enter their thinking. Engrossed in the calculations and ideas they were producing, and excited by the opportunity to have their labor used for practical scientific experiments rather than mere academic exercises in abstraction, G2s' minds were too enraptured to ponder "what ifs."

Third, shared leadership promotes lower self-consciousness among group members. In the absence of strict hierarchical supervision, employees are able to work on their own, to take risks, and to do things their own way without feeling scrutinized. Thus many distractions and much irrelevant information can be removed, and workers can feel freer to engage a task on its own terms and for its own sake. In G1's lab, this dynamic also facilitated greater amounts of interaction and cooperation among students and other staff members. There was a clear sense that, compared with other lab environments they had heard about or known firsthand, employees felt they were much better able to work with and learn from one another in G1's lab. They were able to lose themselves in lab experiences with one another and thus enter what one might call a kind of group flow.

Fourth, shared leadership increases people's sense of autonomy and control over what they are doing. Each of the G2s we interviewed stressed this as a crucial part of their experience in G1's lab. By being handed responsibility for a piece of a project, they gained a sense of control over it—a sense that they were independently in charge of its outcome. Moreover, there was a sense among several of the G2s that having this sense of autonomy and control allowed them to learn and work together better. The same is true on sports teams. Only by feeling in control of where and to whom to throw the football can a quarterback begin to find flow in the heat of a game and effectively play in sync with his teammates. In their work on flow in sports, Jackson and Csikszentmihalyi (1999) noted the importance of control and autonomy. Without it, one cannot take risks, one cannot feel confident; and one cannot continue growing and extending the challenges and skills that eventually lead to top performance and success.

Fifth, in shared leadership group members are able to work in their *zone of proximal development*—in the place where challenge and skill are appropriately balanced for learning and high engagement. Releasing control to group members allows them to work free from constraints that could otherwise impede the delicate balance between challenge and skills. Within a stricter rule of leadership in which subordinates are handed tasks and told how to perform them, employees are likely to either find their jobs not challenging enough or too challenging. That is, they will either be bored or anxious. By having autonomy, creative license, and the sense that their contributions will be taken seriously, however, employees are much more likely to find a balance between their skills and the challenges of the task that will lead to flow. This principle certainly held true in the case of G1's lab.

Finally, and perhaps most importantly, with shared leadership work is transformed into an autotelic activity. When intrinsic interest becomes the emphasis, when fear of failure and self-consciousness are removed, when autonomy and self-control are granted, and when employees can find their own balance between challenge and skills, their work may become an end in itself—something to actually enjoy and find fulfilling. When left on his own to explore his own capabilities in analyzing some data, one scientist we interviewed reported the sort of exhilaration we are talking about. "[It] was not a particularly big paper or anything like that, but it was an idea that I thought was just really, really cool, and nobody had ever thought to look at anything in this way. So that's what I think is the best quality for any of the work that I've done."

When these conditions are provided, and the tasks of work become autotelic—ends in themselves and sources of enjoyment, pride, and intrinsic reward—the remaining characteristics of flow will follow, people will begin to work better together, and discover flow with one another. People's sense of time will become distorted. Their awareness will merge with their action, and their consciousness will exclude all irrelevant information. As more individuals in a group are able to accomplish this experience in their work, the group will find it contagious and their work as a whole is likely to become more innovative and creative. It is to the outcomes of flow in shared leadership that we now turn.

# Motivating Creativity in Knowledge Work

The association between flow and highly creative work has been well-documented (Csikszentmihalyi, 1996; Feldman, 1994). Teresa Amabile (1996) has studied motivation extensively—both in "ordinary" work places and in those requiring higher levels of creativity. According to Amabile, extrinsic factors serve at best as initial motivators for a job or activity. A person might not work if he or she did not need money, just like an artist might not begin a painting without the goal of producing a masterpiece, but Amabile's hypothesis states that people who are intrinsically motivated will be more creative than those who are motivated extrinsically. Extrinsic constraints can contribute to uncreative performance in two ways. They can divert attention away from task-relevant aspects of the environment by directing attention to progress toward the expected extrinsic reward. And they can make the individual reluctant to take risks, since those risks might interfere with achieving the end goal (Amabile, 1996).

Knowledge organizations depend on the creation of new ideas and innovation—the "transformation of knowledge" (Drucker, 1995). Thus, they must find ways to foster intrinsic motivation and flow among their employees. The organization we examined in this chapter was in every way a knowledge organization faced with a fiercely competitive environment and a strong need to behave creatively. Its survival was directly dependent on the quality of ideas and on the knowledge its members discovered.

All of this suggests that a workplace environment is likely to promote flow and creativity if it provides the following six conditions. In the first place, it should be an organization that *values excellence* in performance as much as it values profits, market share, and other results of performance. The leadership must be able to communicate a vision of uncompromising excellence to the rest of the organization. If employees cannot trust that the firm's priority is to do the best possible job regardless of short-term results, instead of focusing on the demands of the task they will be more concerned with cutting corners and looking good on the quarterly balance sheet. If providing shareholders' returns is the only purpose of an organization, it is difficult for people to dedicate themselves fully to it. A self-organizing system works best when its members feel that they are encouraged to give their best effort, and that they are recognized and rewarded for it.

Second, in a creative organization, members have *clear goals*. By this we mean not only long-range, but also day-to-day and even minute-by-minute objectives. The more the employees themselves can set these goals, the more likely it is that creativity will result. One of the main concerns of management in this respect is to define clearly the long-term objectives while leaving as much leeway as possible to groups and individuals to decide how to go about reaching them. A good analogy here is that of climbing Mt. Everest. The ultimate goal is clear and the same for everyone: to reach the top. But there are several main routes among which the expedition must choose. After the ascent party selects a given route, every climber has to decide, each step of the way, where to place his foot, when to take a break, when to retreat, and when to take a risk. Shared leadership has the advantage of being able to remind its members moment to moment about the goals of the task at hand and thereby avoid losing focus and direction.

Third, for a person to concentrate on a task, it is also necessary that he or she gets *constant and timely feedback* on performance. It is easy to get distracted and to fall into a routine performance if we don't know how well we are doing. At first, it is a manager's duty to provide praise and advice on a worker's performance, but a self-organizing group is usually much closer to the action and thus able to give moment-to-moment adjustments to its members' actions. The ideal is to have employees able to learn how to give feedback to themselves. For instance, if my job involves writing weekly reports, I should not have to wait until my supervisor tells me whether the report was good or not (assuming she would take the time to tell me). I should be able to tell whether I had chosen the most effective words in each sentence, the clearest sentences in each paragraph, the most informative paragraphs in the report—and thus whether I had written a report that is the best of its kind. Only if a person can get feedback this detailed—preferably from his or her own inner standards—will he or she enjoy the task and push it to a level where it may make a novel contribution.

The fourth condition that makes a workplace more conducive to flow and creativity is the *matching of challenges and skills*. Organizations can become rapidly dysfunctional if they rely too much on stress to motivate their staff, or if they allow boredom to permeate too many of the jobs. One basic leadership skill is to evaluate the special strengths of each person and then provide opportunities on the job for expressing them. Here again, shared leadership has the advantage: In any self-organizing group, it soon becomes apparent what each member can best contribute to it. Usually, the division of labor in such groups is more organic than in hierarchically organized ones, so that the matching of opportunity and capacity is more easily achieved.

Fifth, in order for a workplace to make flow possible, it is important to find ways to *decrease distractions*. Anything that disturbs a creative or enjoyable train of thought may set back a person hours, if not days, from the pursuit of his or her task. Some of these distractions involve such obvious ambient stimuli as excessive noise, movement, and change in tasks and priorities. In this respect, shared leadership is probably not any better than a hierarchical one, and it may be actually more distracting because agreeing on goals and procedures in an egalitarian setting often involves more negotiations than in a hierarchical milieu—even when the results in the latter case may be less desirable.

Where shared leadership does have a distinct advantage is in removing some of the more subtle obstacles to concentration that are inherent in hierarchical leadership. Every time a boss interacts with a subordinate, the latter becomes involved in thought patterns irrelevant to the task: "Does he like me?" or "Is he likely to give me the promotion I am looking forward to?" are the kind of concerns a subordinate begins to think about after meeting a supervisor. Sometimes, these thoughts occupy the forefront of a person's consciousness for the entire day after even a short meeting, and even if the supervisor has not said anything that could be interpreted as threatening. A few ambiguous words or a scowl are a guarantee that the worker will not focus on his or her job for hours to come. Neither creativity nor enjoyment is likely to survive in that period. In this respect, a self-organizing group with shared leadership is bound to be much more efficient.

Finally, flow and creativity thrive on *freedom* and *control*—not only in choosing goals and selecting means to reach them, but also in such things as having a say in scheduling, in decorating one's workspace, and in developing practices that will define the culture of the firm. If the leadership understands that the most effective organization is one that allows each member to do his or her best and to be most creative, it soon becomes obvious that one can't achieve this goal by forcing people into rigid roles and behaviors. There are still a few firms left that believe it is possible to get a good performance from people by bribing or threatening them. Yet it is quite clear that optimal performance depends on a "buy-in" from each member of the organization. This means relinquishing some of the usual patterns of hierarchical leadership and allowing the organization to develop from the bottom up as well as from the top down.

When these principles are put in practice, one is likely to echo the words of Bennis and Biederman (1997):

> Look how hard people in Great Groups work, without anyone hovering over them. Look how morale soars when intelligent people are asked to do a demanding but worthy task and given the freedom and tools to do it. Imagine how much richer and happier our organizations would be if, like Great Groups, they were filled with people working as hard and as intelligently as they can, too

caught up for pettiness, their sense of self grounded in the bedrock of talent and achievement. (p. 9).

In this chapter, we used qualitative data and previous research to suggest a reciprocal relationship between flow, creativity, and shared leadership. We argued that shared leadership enhances the conditions for flow, and that the experience of flow necessary to the creative process in turn bolsters the effectiveness of groups. The theory also suggests a great number of possible studies to confirm more quantitatively the conclusions drawn here. For example, each of the six conditions specified above could be operationalized and then varied under conditions of both hierarchical and shared leadership. The dependent variables would include the groups' productivity, morale, as well as the enjoyment of the task and the creative output it achieved. The results of such studies will be greatly relevant to understand the dynamics of shared leadership and hence to achieve a competitive advantage for any organization dependent on knowledge work.

# Notes

1. The ESM uses structured response forms, called *experience sampling forms* (ESF), and programmable watches, beepers, or Palm Pilots that participants wear during the day for specified number of days (usually seven). When the beeper goes off at randomly selected times (preprogrammed by the researcher), participants fill out the ESF, which asks questions like what they were doing and where they were, and which incorporates a number of measures of mood, locus of control, self-esteem, and the like. For a more in-depth description of the ESM, see Csikszentmihalyi, 1997, and Csikszentmihalyi & Csikszentmihalyi, 1988.
2. Derived from the Greek *auto* (self) and *telos* (end or goal).
3. Because we promised complete confidentiality, the categorical labels "G1" and "G2" will be used in lieu of respondent names.
4. The style of leadership exemplified in this lab could be classified as co-leadership (Solomon, Loeffer, & Frank, 1953), as empowerment and self-leadership (Manz & Sims, 1989; Conger & Kanungo, 1988), as self-managed work teams (Manz & Sims, 1993), or as emergent leadership (Bartol & Martin, 1986). Although it is beyond the scope of this chapter to work out a specific classification, we hope to demonstrate the way in which this kind of leadership fosters high states of flow, engagement, and motivation and facilitates creative, innovative group outcomes.
5. This marks a significant break from more traditional means for assigning academic authorship in situations like this. Typically, advisors' names appear first, regardless of their level of contribution. It should also be noted that G1's last name fell in the last third of the alphabet.

# References

Aldag, R. J., & Fuller, S. R. (1993). Beyond fiasco: A reappraisal of the groupthink phenomenon and a new model of group decision processes. *Psychological Bulletin, 113*(3), 533-552.

Amabile, T. M. (1996). *Creativity in context.* Boulder, CO: Westview Press.

Amabile, T. M., & Conti, R. (1997). Environmental determinants of work motivation, creativity, and innovation: The case of R&D downsizing. In R. Garud, P. R. Nayyar, & Z. B. Shapira (Eds.), *Technological innovation: Oversights and foresights* New York: Cambridge University Press.

Bartol, K. M., & Martin, D. C. (1986). Women and men in task groups. In R. D. Ashmore & F. K. DelBoca (Eds.), *The social psychology of female-male relationships* (pp. 259-310). New York: Academic Press.

Bennis, W., & Biederman, P. W. (1997). *Organizing genius: The secrets of creative collaboration.* Cambridge, MA: Perseus Books.

Burns, T., & Stalker, G. M. (1961). *The management of innovation.* London: Tavistock.

Conger, J. A., & Kanungo, R. N. (1988). The empowerment process: Integrating theory and practice. *Academy of Management Review, 13*(3), 471-482.

Csikszentmihalyi, I. (1988). Flow in historical context: The case of the Jesuits. In M. Csikszentmihalyi & I. Csikszentmihalyi (Eds.), *Optimal experience: Psychological studies of flow in consciousness.* Cambridge, UK: Cambridge University Press.

Csikszentmihalyi, M. (1990). *Flow: The psychology of optimal experience.* New York: Harper Collins.

Csikszentmihalyi, M. (1993). *The evolving self: A psychology for the third millennium.* New York: HarperCollins.

Csikszentmihalyi, M. (1996). *Creativity: Flow and the psychology of discovery and invention.* New York: Basic Books.

Csikszentmihalyi, M. (1997). *Finding flow.* New York: Basic Books.

Csikszentmihalyi, M. (1999). Implications of a systems perspective for the study of creativity. In R. J. Sternberg (Ed.), *Handbook of creativity* (pp. 313-335). Cambridge, UK: Cambridge University Press.

Csikszentmihalyi, M., & Csikszentmihalyi, I. (Eds.) (1988). *Optimal experienc: Psychological studies of flow in consciousness.* Cambridge: Cambridge University Press.

Csikszentmihalyi, M., & Rich, G. (1997). Musical improvisation: A systems approach. In R. K. Sawyer (Ed.), *Creativity in performance* (pp. 43-66). Greenwich, CT: Ablex.

Cummings, T. G., & Worley, C. G. (2001). *Organization development and change.* Cincinnati, OH: South-Western College.

Drucker, P. F. (1959). *The landmarks of tomorrow.* New York: Harper.

Drucker, P. F. (1995). *Management in a time of great change.* New York: Penguin Putnam.

Feldman, D. H. A framework for the study of creativity. In D. H. Feldman, M. Csikszentmihalyi, & H. Gardner. (1994). *Changing the world: A framework for the study of creativity* (pp. 1-45). Westport, CT: Praeger.

Ilgen, D. R., Hollenbeck, J. R., Sego, D. J., & Major, D. A. (1993). Team research in the 1990's. In M. M. Chemers & R. Ayman (Eds.), *Leadership theory and research.* San Diego, CA: Academic Press.

Jackson, S. A., & Csikszentmihalyi, M. (1999). *Flow in sports.* Champaign, IL: Human Kinetics.

Lawrence, P. R., & Lorsch, J. L. (1967). Differentiation and integration in complex organizations. *Administrative Science Quarterly, 12,* 1-47.

Lipman-Blumen, J., & Leavitt, H. J. (1999). *Hot groups: Seeding them, feeding them, and using them to ignite your organization.* New York: Oxford University Press.

Manz, C. C., & Sims, H. P. (1987). Leading workers to lead themselves: The external leadership of self-managing work teams. *Administrative Science Quarterly, 32,* 106-129.

Manz, C. C., & Sims, H. P. (1989). *Superleadership: Leading others to lead themselves.* New York: Prentice Hall.

Manz, C. C., & Sims, H. P. (1993). *Business without bosses.* New York: Wiley.

Mockros, C., & Csikszentmihalyi, M. (1999). The social construction of creative lives. In A. Montuori & R. E. Purser (Eds.), *Social creativity* (pp. 175-218). Creskill, NJ: Hampton Press.

Morgan, G. (1997). *Images of organization* (2nd ed.). Thousand Oaks, CA: Sage.

Pearce, C. L., & Giacalone, R. A. (in press). Teams behaving badly: Counterproductive behavior at the team level of analysis. *Journal of Applied Social Psychology.*

Pearce, C. L., & Sims, H. P. (2000). Shared leadership: Toward a multi-level theory of leadership. *Advances in interdisciplinary studies of work teams, 7,* 115-139. Greenwich, CT: JAI Press.

Senge, Peter. (1990). *The fifth discipline: The art and practice of the learning organization.* London: Century Business.

Solomon, A., Loeffer, F. J., & Frank, G. H. (1953). An analysis of co-therapist interaction in group psychotherapy. *International Journal of Group Psychotherapy, 3,* 171-180.

Vygotsky, L. S. (1978). *Mind in society.* Cambridge, MA: Harvard University Press.

Waldrop, M. M. (1992). *Complexity: The emergent science at the edge of order and chaos.* New York: Simon & Schuster.

# CHAPTER 11

# Shared Leadership in the Management of Group Boundaries

## A Study of Expulsions From Officers' Training Courses

*Boas Shamir*

*Yael Lapidot*

The following story was told by a team commander in the Officers' Training School of the Israel Defense Forces (IDF). Cadets and commanders in the IDF are required to carry their personal weapons at all times. Failure to do so is considered a serious disciplinary offense.

> During a week of battle training, I had an unpleasant incident. We reached the point where I had to brief the soldiers on the safety regulations and I didn't notice that I'd left my weapon behind with their equipment. As I was giving the briefing, I realized that I'd forgotten it and didn't know what to do. I continued to review the commands as though nothing had happened, and it was only as we were about to go into the dining room to eat, after everyone had gone to bring their equipment, that I told them that I'd forgotten my weapon with their equipment and that I didn't have any excuse. I just ask[ed] everyone to pay attention and to be alert, so that it shouldn't happen to any of us again.

The guys told me that I have an expulsion committee tomorrow morning and laughed. I think that if it weren't for the mutual trust between us and the atmosphere up to that point, they would have taken it differently.

Clearly, the commander in this case trusted his subordinates enough to tell them that he'd forgotten his weapon and to confide in them that he did not have an excuse, and they trusted him enough to "forgive" him and make a joke out of the matter. The joke they chose, however, is revealing. They took the opportunity to reverse the roles jokingly and thus demonstrate that not only are both commander and team bound by the same set of rules and professional standards but both are legitimate guardians of these rules and standards, even if only one has the formal authority to expel the other for a breach of these rules. Because upholding shared values is a leadership function, this case demonstrates the operation of shared leadership. The team commander acknowledged this role sharing when he asked everyone to pay attention "so that it shouldn't happen to any of us again."

The term *shared leadership* can be understood in different ways. From a certain perspective, it is an oxymoron. Many definitions of leadership imply that leadership is a disproportionate social influence process (Rost, 1993). From this perspective, there is no leadership without leaders—namely, individuals who exert more influence on the group than others do. When influence is equally shared among members of the group and there are no individuals who exert disproportionate influence, the group is leaderless and we cannot talk about leadership. Therefore, Shamir (1999) has argued that the term *leadership* should be reserved for cases in which a single individual or a small group of individuals exerts disproportionate influence on a larger group.

Other writers view leadership in terms of certain functions that are important for the survival of the group and the accomplishment of its goals. From this perspective, the leadership functions may be performed by a single individual (vertical leadership) or two individuals (co-leadership), may be divided among group members, or may be performed by the entire team (shared leadership) (Avolio, Jung, Murry, & Suvasubramaniam, 1996; Bowers & Seashore, 1966; Manz & Sims, 1993; Pearce & Sims, 2000). In Yukl's (1998), words, "various leadership functions may be carried out by different people who influence what the group does, how it is done, and the way people in the group relate to each other" (p. 3). Because one of the important functions of leadership is making decisions, participative decision making (e.g., Vroom & Jago, 1988) is an important aspect of shared leadership. To quote Yukl (1998) again, when leadership is shared, "important decisions about what to do and how to do it are made through the use of an interactive process that involves many different people who influence each other, not a single person" (p. 3).

The present chapter adopts the second perspective. Following Yukl (1998), shared leadership is viewed here in terms of reciprocal influence processes among multiple parties (e.g., a designated leader and his or her subordinates) in a systems context (pp. 504-505). This chapter is about shared leadership as it is manifested in the making and execution of decisions regarding an important leadership function: that of managing the boundaries of the group. This function has been neglected by leadership theories and studies, most of which have tended to accept group composition as given and to focus on the leader's behaviors toward the group and relations with the group. Leadership, however, often involves managing the admission of members to the group and the exclusion of members from the group. Admission and exclusion processes determine group membership and therefore indirectly affect group knowledge, skills, culture, and performance. Furthermore, the management of admission and exclusion processes has many symbolic implications because the criteria used for admission and exclusion often carry symbolic meanings regarding the identity of the group, its norms, and its standards. Despite the instrumental and symbolic significance of admission and exclusion processes, these processes and their effects have received little attention in the leadership literature.

The present chapter focuses on one aspect of the management of group boundaries, the dismissal of subordinates from the group. The dismissal of subordinates is seemingly one of the most unilateral acts on the part of the leader in formal organizations. As suggested by Moch and Huff (1983), however, contrary to the common view of terminations as unilateral acts on the part of organizational authorities, in fact they often involve the subordinates in various ways. As an illustration, Moch and Huff (1983) quote a superior who told his immediate subordinates in a staff meeting, "It's the easiest thing in the world to fire someone. All you need is cooperation" (p. 295).

The army is perhaps the most hierarchical organization. In this chapter, we use evidence from a study of expulsions of cadets from officers' training courses to show that even in a hierarchical organization such as the army and even with regard to the dismissal of subordinates, leadership is shared, and when it is not shared, there are considerable negative consequences. We further use this evidence to identify some of the conditions that contribute to the sharing of leadership more generally. In particular, our analysis draws attention to three such conditions: (a) structural arrangements that invite or enable subordinates to play a role in the leadership act, (b) the existence of a shared identity and a shared set of values between the leader and the group, and (c) the vulnerability of the leader to the group.

# Background: Expulsion of Cadets From IDF Officers' Training Courses

A central part of officers' training in the Israel Defense Forces (IDF) is conducted in 3- to 6-month courses in the Officers' Training School. Part of the training in these courses is carried out in teams. Each team consists of 15 to 20 cadets under a lieutenant or second lieutenant, who is the team commander. All cadets and commanders are male. Cadets are typically 19 to 21 years old and the commanders 1 or 2 years older.

On average, the number of expulsions per team is relatively small (two to three). But the sword of expulsion hangs over the heads of the cadets throughout the entire course. There are two types of expulsions. One is a "technical" expulsion due to disciplinary violations, such as sleeping on guard duty, leaving one's weapon unguarded, or behaving dishonestly or unreliably (e.g., cheating on a test). Such expulsions can be initiated at any point in the course. The second type is a "periodic" expulsion. Periodic expulsions occur at specific points in the course. At these points, the cadets are assessed by the commanders, and those whose performance is deemed inadequate are brought before a committee, which the cadets and team commanders often refer to as the "expulsion committee." A team commander's recommendation to expel a cadet does not always result in his expulsion. There are also cadets who are brought up to the committee by persons other than their team commander and against his recommendation. Here, too, the team commander's opinion may be accepted or rejected.

The cadets also play a role in the expulsion process. Prior to the periodic evaluation committee meetings, every cadet fills out an evaluation questionnaire on each of the other cadets in the team, rating his leadership, values, professionalism, and so forth. These questionnaires are referred to as "sociometric" questionnaires. The key question is, Do you think that _____ is suited to being an officer? If over 50% of his peers answer the question in the negative, the cadet is automatically brought before the committee. Even when the cadet is brought up for other reasons, however, the questionnaires are always taken into consideration by the committee and in borderline situations can tip the balance one way or the other.

The issue of expulsions embodies not only personal considerations stemming from the implications of the expulsion for the expellee's social status, self-esteem, and career but also collective or symbolic considerations. The latter stem from the fact that the officer's training course is an organizational "rite of passage" (Trice & Beyer, 1984). It is not only a training course but also a status enhancement mechanism that revolves around the most central status in the military institution, that of an officer. The question of who deserves to be an officer and on whom this status is to be bestowed is of major symbolic significance because the identity of the institution is to a large extent defined by the qualities, character, and values of its officers.

From this point of view, an expulsion from the course can be viewed as a "rite of separation." Clear, justified, and noncontroversial expulsions are necessary to impart the organization's norms, standards, and expectations and to affirm the system values and identity to both its members and external stakeholders. An expulsion from the officers' training course is therefore an event of great symbolic significance. It is a mechanism for defining the limits of the system's core identity. The decision regarding who will not be an officer carries an important message regarding who is an officer. "Just as initiation dramatizes what the group is, so elaborate exclusion rites communicate what the group is not. The definition of the situation is maintained in both ways" (Young, 1965, p. 156).

# The Study

The evidence used in this chapter was collected in the framework of a larger study of subordinates' trust in their leaders (Shamir & Lapidot, in press). As part of this study, critical incidents of trust building and erosion were collected by three methods: (a) a questionnaire administered to 1,100 cadets in 84 teams after two thirds of the course; (b) group interviews with cadets representing 11 teams, which were conducted 2 to 3 weeks before the end of the course; and (c) interviews with the team commanders of the 11 teams selected for the group interviews, which were conducted immediately after the end of the course. A good number of the commanders described the same incidents as the cadets, enabling us to obtain both perspectives.

Expulsions and the way they were handled by the team commander were the most frequently mentioned issues in all three sources of information: written incidents, group interviews, and interviews with team commanders. For the purposes of this chapter, we focus on incidents that demonstrate collaboration or lack of collaboration between the commanders and their teams with respect to the expulsion of cadets. We selected for presentation and analysis those incidents that were independently reported by a number of cadets in the team, and often also by the team commander.

# Some Evidence: Shared Leadership in Expulsion Decisions

Expulsion decisions were potentially controversial. Controversy could take two forms: The first could arise when the team commander recommended the expulsion of a cadet whom the team believed should not be expelled, and the second when the team believed that an individual should be expelled but the team commander did not act to expel him. Both types of controversies concerned not only specific evaluations of cadets but also broader issues of professional judgment and integrity.

## Team Involvement in the Expulsion Process

The cadet teams expected the commanders to involve them in the expulsion decisions. These expectations were often anticipated and acknowledged by the commanders.

For instance, one commander reported that in his opening statement to the team he expressed faith in the team's understanding of the need to weed out those who are not suited to being officers and in their ability to judge each other's suitability even better than he himself can:

> At the beginning of the course, I told them that everyone who's here is suited to the job. And if there's someone who, despite this, doesn't manage, the cadets in the team will be the ones to see it best, and it'll come out in the sociometric.

This statement can be seen as an expression of faith in the team, an acknowledgment of the role of the team in the expulsion process, and an invitation to the team to participate in this process. Another commander conveyed that he saw the team's request for explanation for the leaving of a cadet as natural and legitimate:

> In my team, there were no expellees. One was thrown out on the basis of his sociometric, and another left for health reasons. He missed a lot of the exercises and decided he wouldn't manage to make up what he had missed. A number of cadets asked me why a cadet in another team who was absent for more or less the same period wasn't expelled. I explained that the ability of that cadet was greater than that of the cadet in our team and it was thus believed that he would be able to make up what he had missed. It doesn't strike me that this story made a lot of noise in the team.

Although the commander did not see this incident as an expulsion, it is evident that the team believed the staff played an active role in the cadet's leaving and demanded an explanation. The commander, according to his report, used the phrase "our team" in his explanation, thus clearly including the team in the process.

Sometimes an explanation that legitimizes the role of the team could even increase trust in the leader, even if the decision to expel had been made despite the team's opposition. The following quotation is taken from a case that was reported by cadets as an incident that enhanced their trust in the team commander. In this case, the commander went beyond acknowledging the team's right to have an explanation. He also supported their entitlement to voice their opposition to his decision:

> He expelled a cadet who he believed wasn't suited. He explained the reasons to the team. And in the same breath, he praised the team for standing up for the cadet.

In the following example, the team commander involved the team in a different way. In contrast with the previous examples, in this case it was the team that believed a cadet should be expelled and the commander who tried to protect the cadet. He reacted to the team's view that a cadet should be expelled by trying to recruit the team to help the cadet overcome his difficulties:

> One of the cadets was brought up to the expulsion committee because of his sociometric. I believed that he didn't deserve to be kicked out, because I felt that he had a social problem and was thus somewhat distant from the team. I fought to get him a second chance. I spoke to the team without the knowledge of the cadet to get them to help him, and in tandem advised the cadet to speak with the guys. Things seemed to be working out better. Later on in the course, when we were on the Golan Heights, I told this cadet that I was going to bring him up to the committee on professionalism. After I talked to him, I went into a tent and went to sleep. He came into this tent with a few other cadets—they didn't know I was there—and told them that I intended to bring him up to the committee, and that he fully deserved it. After he was expelled, he came to visit the team one Saturday and brought them candies. I know that he and the rest of the team saw this expulsion as fair. They realized that I did everything I could to keep him in the course but that sometimes there's no choice.

In this incident, the commander emphasizes how he worked cooperatively with the team despite their differences in opinion, explained his position, and got them to help the cadet they believed was unsuited to being an officer. According to his account, the result of involving the team was a feeling of mutual trust.

In contrast, when a commander failed to involve the team, the result was reduced trust, as the following incident indicates:

> During the mid-course committees, three cadets were brought up without the team knowing about it directly or indirectly until the committees met. The team commander didn't talk to the team about his decision and caused the

team not to value him, since the team felt that he was insulting them by doing everything behind their backs.

The sense of collective insult reported in this incident can be interpreted as resulting from the perception that the commander's failure to involve the team reflected mistrust on his part of their ability or inclination to apply the same professional standards to the three cases of expulsion concerned.

## Consequences of Failure to Exercise Shared Leadership

Failure to involve the team in expulsion decisions and processes could result in more than insult or erosion of trust. This was exemplified in one complex and rather extreme case in which the differences of opinion concerning an expulsion decision deteriorated to an open power struggle between the commander and his team. The interviewed team commander gave the richest description of this incident:

When we got back from Lebanon, it was a week of the periodic expulsion committee meetings. It was then that one of the crises of trust occurred. Up to this week, several cadets had been expelled. In general, I would tell them in advance that they were at risk and that they should try to improve. I would also involve the team and speak to them about the expulsion to see whether they agreed or did not agree with it—not to get their permission but to involve them. In the first two committees, the team agreed with me. In this one, I wanted to bring up a cadet that the team liked very much but whom I thought wasn't suited to being an officer from the point of view of his character. It was certainly not a classic expulsion. I had the feeling that in light of the atmosphere that had been created after the mid-course exercise, the team would see it as a war. Who would win—them or me? After I brought him up to the committee, the team sent a number of representatives to speak with the company commander about the expulsion. It bothered me a lot that they went straight to the company commander and didn't come to me first or at least speak to the company commander in my presence. The company commander threw them out of the room and wouldn't speak with them. I know that not all the team agreed to go straight to the company commander. But this really broke me. I felt I was no longer interested in trying to improve the relationship with the team. The expulsion turned into a power struggle. The next day, two cadets came up to me to apologize for the team. From what they said, I gathered that they were talking more for themselves than for the team. And so for me, the conversation with them wasn't a team apology. They asked me for permission to send a letter about the expulsion to the base commander. Even though it bothered me a lot that they were fighting me, I gave them permission. In the end, the cadet was expelled. It may have been a victory, because the company commander and I were very concerned that the cadet might return because of pressure from the team. They give their opinion in the sociometrics they write about one another. But all in all, the rift with the team only deepened.

This incident shows that a failure to exercise shared leadership with regard to expulsion decisions could develop into a power struggle between the team and the commander, in which the team engaged in collective action by trying to mobilize support from the commander's superiors. It reveals the awareness of the commander of the importance of getting team support for his decisions, as evident from his report that in previous occasions he talked with the team about the expulsions before making his decisions "not to get their permission but to involve them." It also indicates the potential power of the team, especially through the commander's remark that both he and his superior, the company commander, were very concerned that the cadet might return to the team because of the team's pressure.

This commander's description of the case and its negative implication for his leadership were supported by the cadets' accounts of the same incident. Here is an example:

> Trust really declined at the expulsion committees toward the end of the course. The team commander brought a cadet up for expulsion without any compelling reason. The team presented a petition against the expulsion straight to the company commander, and the team commander saw this going above his head as a major crisis in our trust of him. A mutual crisis of trust was created. I told him in one of our last conversations that there was an explosion between him and the team, and that I was ending the course with the feeling that I didn't want to have any more contact with him.

The development of the conflict into an open power struggle involving a team petition to higher authorities was exceptional. The failure to exercise shared leadership with respect to expulsion decisions and the erosion of trust between the team and the leader, however, did not have to reach such proportions in order to have serious implications. For instance, one commander reported that his career was negatively affected by his unilateral approach to expulsions:

> I also saw my job as selecting out those who weren't suited and kept a close eye on some of the cadets. For example, in the first week, I realized that one of them was a slacker, and by the third week I managed to catch him shirking one time after another and even lying. . . . The situation just got worse. They [the team] felt that I was picking on them, wanted to expel, and was arrogant, and I felt that they would try to get back at me in every way they could. And the fact is that they managed. Because their evaluations screwed up my promotion.

Another possible manifestation of failure to exercise shared leadership with respect to expulsion decisions was that the cadets gained too much power and the commander was excluded from the process. In the following case, a commander yielded to his subordinates' pressure and refrained from expelling cadets that in his opinion should have been expelled, to avoid the potential negative consequences of an anticipated controversy with the team.

> Two people were expelled from my team. I feel that there were a few others that I should have expelled and didn't because of my naïveté. For instance, there

was a cadet who wasn't mature enough to cope with military orders that he didn't agree with. This is a big minus in a military system. In the end, I decided not to expel him. Part of the reason may have been that I didn't have the energy to fight with the team. This cadet was one of the better liked cadets in the team, and I have no doubt that some of the conflicts that he and I had undermined my leadership and the team's trust in me.

## Disputed Decisions Not to Expel a Cadet

Most of the controversies about expulsions between the commander and the team, reflected in the previous examples, concerned incidents in which the commander wanted to expel a cadet who the team thought did not deserve expulsion. Such differences of opinion could be attributed to team solidarity and the desire of the team to protect its members. From a shared leadership perspective, however, perhaps more important are the cases in which the differences of opinion and their leadership implications stemmed from the opposite situation, in which the cadets believed that one of their number should be expelled but the team commander took no action to expel him. These cases clearly do not reflect team solidarity or power struggles for defensive reasons. They must be seen as reflecting the cadets' wish to play an active leadership role in managing the team's boundaries.

One such example was already reported in a previous section. Here is another. The following incident was cited by most of the team members as an event that destroyed their trust in their team commander. A cadet used a map in a blind navigation exercise in which the cadets were required to navigate by memory without a map. The cadet tried to hide what he did and didn't report that he'd opened a map. Opening a map, and especially not reporting it, is considered a very serious violation both of the disciplinary code and the honor code of the officers' course. The cadets were surprised and disappointed that the team commander tried to downplay the event and did not bring the cadet up to an expulsion committee. The gist of the next statement was repeated in one form or another in another 10 accounts of the same incident:

> That he didn't bring the cadet up to the committee for opening a map was really stinky. I still don't understand why he didn't do it.

The team commander provided a fuller account of this incident from his point of view:

> I don't know how, but the company commander and I allowed him to return to the course. In retrospect, it turned out that this very much bothered his partner in the exercise and the entire team. . . . A situation was created where the staff expelled a cadet that the team did not want to be expelled and opposed the expulsion of a cadet that the team did want to be expelled. In truth, I didn't know what stand to take in this matter. On the one hand, I believed the cadet that this was a one-time slip in veracity; on the other hand, it's a really serious violation. I preferred to transfer this decision to the base commander and not to take a clear position. I think they saw my fumbling and

got very angry and rightfully so. In the end, this cadet was expelled too. From the point of view of trust between me and the team, it was one of the hardest weeks.

This type of "positive" discrimination eroded the team's trust in the commander not only because it reflected indecisiveness or weakness, as implied in the team commander's account, but also because it raised a great deal of doubt about his professional integrity. The team detected lack of sufficient leadership on the part of the commander and exerted pressure on the commander to expel the cadet in an attempt to fill this gap, not to protect a cadet but on behalf of the system, its values, and its professional standards.

# Discussion: Conditions for Shared Leadership

Although our study was conducted in a particular and perhaps not very typical situation, we believe it allows us to identify some conditions that enable or invite the sharing of leadership that may apply to formal organizations more generally.

## Structural Arrangements

As mentioned, the cadets were given by the organization a formal role in the expulsion process. Their sociometric evaluations of each other were taken into consideration by the expulsion committees, and in extreme cases could even be the reason for bringing a cadet before such a committee in the first place. In addition, at the end of the course, team members were requested to complete performance evaluation forms on their commander. These forms were reviewed by the commander's superiors and entered his file. When these evaluations were negative, they could harm the military career of the commander, and in extreme cases even lead to the termination of his military career.

Such formal arrangements are by no means unique to the situation we studied. New methods of performance evaluation in organizations tend to increasingly rely on peer evaluations and even on subordinate evaluations of their superiors. Such evaluation methods assume that, at least collectively, peers and subordinates share certain professional and organizational standards with their superiors, and can be relied on to use them in their evaluations. Such a manifestation of the organization's trust in its members is therefore not unique to the organization we studied. Indeed, some of the more generalizable implications of our study may concern the effects of inviting subordinates to play a collective role in peer and superior's evaluations on the exercise of shared leadership in organizations.

## Shared Values and a Shared Identity

Clearly, the teams' actions in relation to expulsion decisions involved more than automatic manifestations of solidarity. They focused on the content of the decisions and their justification. To understand these team responses, we have to remember that the officer's training course is an organizational rite of passage, and an expulsion from the course can be viewed as a rite of separation. As a consequence of its symbolic relevance, the expulsion issue becomes an arena for negotiating the values and norms of the system. This is particularly evident from the substantial amount of controversies between teams and their commanders around expulsion decisions that concerned not the prevention of expulsion but, rather, cases in which the commander did not act to expel a cadet that the team thought should be expelled. In such cases, the cadets clearly acted as guardians of collective values and standards and sometimes even perceived themselves as better guardians of these values and standards than their commanders were.

The cadets are relatively veteran soldiers who have already been socialized to the military system. By the time they reach the officers' course, they perceive themselves, and are perceived by others, as legitimate stakeholders in the system, and as members of an "occupational community" that includes both officers and aspiring officers who share a set of values, norms, and perspectives that apply to the job (Van Maanen & Barley, 1984). This is nicely illustrated in the story that opens this chapter about the commander who left his weapon behind. It is also recognized by the organization, which gives the cadets an official role in the expulsion process by taking their evaluations of each other into consideration in the expulsion decisions.

Given the aforementioned considerations and arrangements, no wonder the teams we studied felt they have a right to a say in the expulsion process or at least to a satisfactory explanation for decisions regarding expulsion-related matters, and most of the commanders acknowledged these rights. As legitimate stakeholders and custodians of system values and norms, the cadets passed a collegial judgment on the expulsion-related actions of the team commander and based their collective trust in him on this judgment. Their membership in the same organizational community both with other cadets and with their formal leaders, and the shared identity and values that this membership implies, provided the basis for their exertion of influence in the expulsion process, whether in collaboration with the team commander or in opposition to him.

The application of collective standards and values to shared leadership actions and the grounding of such standards and values in a shared collective identity do not depend on the particular features of the organization or the officer identity. In many organizational situations, subordinates share with each other and with their superiors a collective identity, be it organizational, departmental, or professional, and a set values and standards associated with that identity (Pratt, 1998). Whenever they share such collective standards and values, they may feel obliged to apply them and participate in the leadership process, and such participation may be justified from an organizational point of view.

The application of such standards and values should not be limited to sensitive rites of separation such as expulsions from the course. Many superiors' decisions have symbolic implications with regard to an organizational or professional identity and the values associated with it. These decisions may be directly related to the subordinates, such as recruitment and promotion decisions, or to the application of sanctions and rewards, but they may also concern areas that implicate the subordinates' values and identity only indirectly, such as relationships with customers or other stakeholders. Whenever a superior and subordinates share a cherished identity and a set of collective values, and the leadership actions or decisions implicate these identity and values, there is a basis for the exercise of shared leadership.

Even more broadly, shared values and a shared identity are aspects of the group or organizational culture. One of the most important functions of leadership is the development and maintenance of a group or an organizational culture. Leading through culture implies leading through shared perceptions, assumptions, values, norms, and practices and therefore in a sense is always shared leadership. Furthermore, although leaders can influence organizational cultures (Schein, 1992; Trice & Beyer, 1991), they cannot perform the functions of cultural development and maintenance on their own. Cultures are also influenced by the background and prior socialization of organizational members and by social influence and construction processes that occur among organizational members without the influence of the leader. Therefore, the more the culture is shared among members of the group and between them and their designated leaders, the more leadership is likely to be shared among them.

## Leader Vulnerability and Teams' Collective Power

In several ways, the incidents collected for this study indicate the power of the team vis-à-vis the commander and the vulnerability of the commander to the team. As individuals, subordinates may often be highly vulnerable to the actions of their superiors. Our study suggests, however, that as a group they may have much greater power to influence the behaviors of their superiors. This is not merely a question of numbers. It is also easier and more acceptable for a group than for an individual to speak and act in the name of common interests, common values, and a common identity.

Indeed, although we requested each participant in the study to provide incidents that affected his own level of trust in the superior, one of the most salient features of the reported incidents was participants' extensive use of the plural: *"He spoke with us." In the opinion of the team, . . . ," "We realized . . . " "As the team saw it, . . . "* and so forth. Similarly, when leaders were interviewed in the same study about the same incidents and others, they often referred not to individual subordinates but to the group of subordinates as the party that affected their actions and was affected by them. Typical statements were these: *I spoke with the team, It doesn't strike me that this story made a lot of noise in the team,* and *From the point of view of trust between me and the team, it was one of the hardest weeks.*

In addition, some sources of the commanders' vulnerability to their teams emanated from their own position. Some of these sources may be particular to the setting we have studied (for instance, the small age difference between the cadets and the commanders), but others may be found in other organizational situations as well. First, the vulnerability of the commander to the cadets was enhanced by the fact that, as mentioned, the latter performed a formal evaluation role with respect to their commanders.

Second, and more important, perhaps the main source of vulnerability of the team commanders stemmed from the obvious yet often neglected fact that ultimately their leadership, like that of all leaders, depended on their subordinates' trust (Hollander, 1992). Even in a clearly hierarchical organization like the army, leaders depend on followers no less than followers on their leaders. In our case, the way the team commander handled the expulsions was a major arena in which his leadership was tested. As we saw, the cadets could collectively withdraw their trust and support from the team commander if they disputed his actions and decisions, thus "punishing" him for what they perceived to be suspect motives, wrong decisions, or manifestation of mistrust on his part. Thus, even if other sources of commander vulnerability did not exist, the commanders would still be vulnerable to their teams due to the essential relationship between subordinates' trust and superiors' ability to lead. In other words, all leaders depend on their subordinates and hence are vulnerable to them, at least as a group. If this is true in a military organization, which places a particularly high value on subordinates' "blind" obedience of superiors' orders, it should certainly be true in civilian and less bureaucratic organizations.

Theories and studies of subordinates' trust in their leaders have emphasized the impact of superiors' behaviors on subordinates' trust (e.g., Butler, 1990; Conger & Kanungo, 1998; Mayer & Davis, 1999). For instance, Conger and Kanungo (1998) suggest that "leading implies fostering changes in followers through the building of trust and credibility" (p. 46). These studies tend to emphasize the dependence of subordinates on their superiors and to place the power to determine the level of trust chiefly in the superiors' hands. In contrast with these studies, the study described in the present chapter demonstrates that trust in the leader does not depend only on the leader's characteristics and behaviors but is jointly produced by the leader and the followers. Therefore, to the extent that trust is an important characteristic of leadership, it is also a key aspect of shared leadership.

Our study contributes to a more realistic and less "leader-centered" conception of the relationship between leadership and trust. Our evidence and interpretation suggest that leaders are often vulnerable to their subordinates, leadership is a cooperative task, and leader-team relations are often characterized by mutual interdependence. In such relations, neither side has full "fate control" (Kelley & Thibaut, 1978) over the other, yet each side has some control over the fate of the other. This mutual vulnerability and interdependence, in addition to the sharing of values and identities mentioned above, create the conditions for shared leadership. Shared leadership has been presented as a special type of leadership and contrasted with vertical leadership (Pearce & Sims, 2000, 2002). It is important to remember, however, that because leadership relations are typically characterized by mutual interdependence and vulnerability, and because leadership includes elements like trust that are jointly produced by leaders and followers, in some respects all leadership, even vertical leadership, is always shared.

# Conclusion

The phenomenon of shared leadership raises three major issues for future research: Under what conditions does shared leadership emerge? What forms does it take? What are its effects? The study described in this chapter focused on a single manifestation of shared leadership in a unique military context and with respect to the single issue of expulsions from officers' training courses. Furthermore, it employed a qualitative methodology, which is prone to biases in data selection and interpretation. Therefore, it cannot serve as a basis for developing a model of shared leadership to guide future research, although we have tried to draw from the study some tentative propositions regarding the conditions under which shared leadership is likely to emerge.

Before proceeding with further studies to address the three questions presented above, some conceptual issues that have been raised and exemplified in this chapter need to be resolved. Currently, the term shared leadership is applied too broadly, because it has several meanings and refers to very different situations. First, our discussion of leader vulnerability and followers' trust implies that the term may be used to refer to the role of followers in the creation and maintenance of vertical leadership—namely, their role in selecting, accepting, supporting, and empowering the leader. Second, the term may be used to refer to the division of leadership roles and functions among members of a group, a topic that was not discussed in this chapter.

Third, it may refer to the performance of leadership functions by entire teams. With respect to this possibility, a further distinction should be made between situations of leaderless collective action (e.g., Barker, 1993), in which normative control fully substitutes for vertical leadership, and the more common situations such as the one studied here, in which there is a designated leader and a coexistence of vertical leadership and team leadership. In the latter type of situations, one could study the relative effects of vertical leadership and team leadership (Pearce & Sims, 2002) or focus on the sharing of leadership between the leader and his or her subordinates, as we did in this study.

In such situations, researchers should address the differences and commonalities between shared leadership and the more traditional constructs of democratic leadership and participative leadership. Shared leadership has been contrasted with "heroic" leadership (Yukl, 1998), but this is an artificial and misleading contrast because vertical leadership can take various nonheroic forms, including (but not limited to) participative leadership. Much has been learned about participative decision making (e.g., Sagi, 1997; Vroom & Jago, 1988), which is relevant to the sharing of leadership between a leader and his or her subordinates but which may be less relevant to other forms of shared leadership. In conclusion, although all forms of shared leadership have something in common—namely, that not all leadership is performed by a single person—various forms of shared leadership should be more clearly distinguished form each other before studying their emergence and effects.

# References

Avolio, B. J., Jung, D. I., Murry, W., & Sivasubramaniam, N. (1996). Building highly developed teams: Focusing on shared leadership processes, efficacy, trust, and performance. *Advances in Interdisciplinary Studies of Work Teams, 3,* 173-209.

Barker, J. R. (1993). Tightening the iron cage: Concertive control in self-managing teams. *Administrative Science Quarterly, 38,* 408-437.

Bowers, D. G., & Seashore, S. E. (1966). Predicting organizational effectiveness with a four-factor theory of leadership. *Administrative Science Quarterly, 11,* 238-263.

Butler, J. K. (1990). Toward understanding and measuring conditions of trust: Evolution of a conditions of trust inventory. *Journal of Management, 17*(3), 643-663.

Conger, J. A., & Kanungo, R. N. (1998). *Charismatic leadership in organizations.* Thousand Oaks, CA: Sage.

Hollander, E. P. (1992). Leadership, followership, self, and others. *Leadership Quarterly, 3*(1), 43-54.

Kelley, H. H., & Thibaut, J. W. (1978). *Interpersonal relations: A theory of interdependence.* New York: Wiley.

Manz, C. C., & Sims, H. P., Jr. (1993). *Business without bosses.* New York: Wiley.

Mayer, R. C., & Davis, J. H. (1999). The effect of the performance appraisal system on trust for management: A field quasi-experiment. *Journal of Applied Psychology, 84*(1), 123-136.

Moch, M. K., & Huff, A. S. (1983). Power enactment through language and ritual. *Journal of Business Research, 11,* 293-316.

Pearce, C. L., & Sims, H. P., Jr. (2000). Shared leadership: Toward a multi-level theory of leadership. In M. M. Beyerlein, D. A. Johnson, & S. T. Beyerlein (Eds.), *Advances in interdisciplinary studies of work teams: Vol. 7. Team development* (pp. 115-139). New York: Elsevier Science.

Pearce, C. L., & Sims, H. P., Jr. (2002). Vertical vs. shared leadership as predictors of the effectiveness of change management teams: An examination of aversive, directive, transactional, transformational and empowering leader behaviors. *Group Dynamics: Theory, Research, and Practice, 6*(2), 172-197.

Pratt, M. G. (1998). To be or not to be: Central questions in organizational identification. In D. A. Whetten & P. C. Godfrey (Eds.), *Identity in organizations: Building theory through conversation* (pp. 171-207). Thousand Oaks, CA: Sage.

Rost, J. C. (1993). *Leadership in the twenty first century.* Westport, CT: Praeger.

Sagi, A. (1997). Leader direction and employee participation in decision making: Contradictory or compatible practices? *Applied Psychology: An International Review, 46,* 387-452.

Schein, E. H. (1992). *Organizational culture and leadership* (2nd ed.). San Francisco: Jossey-Bass.

Shamir, B. (1999). Leadership in boundary less organizations: Disposable or indispensable? *European Journal of Work and Organizational Psychology, 8*(1), 49-72.

Shamir, B., & Lapidot, Y. (in press). Trust in organizational superiors: Systemic and collective considerations. *Organization Studies.*

Trice, H. M., & Beyer, J. M. (1984). Studying organizational culture through rites and ceremonials. *Academy of Management Review, 9*(4), 653-669.

Trice, H. M., & Beyer, J. M. (1991). Cultural leadership in organizations. *Organization Science, 2,* 149-169.

Van Maanen, J., & Barley, S. (1984). Occupational communities. In B. M. Staw & L. L. Cumminges (Eds.), *Research in Organizational Behavior: Vol. 6* (pp. 287-366). Greenwich, CT: JAI Press.

Vroom, V. H., & Jago, A. G. (1988). *The new leadership: Managing participation in organizations.* Englewood Cliffs, NJ: Prentice Hall.

Young, F. W. (1965). *Initiating ceremonies: A cross-cultural study of status dramatization.* New York: Bobbs-Merrill.

Yukl, G. A. (1998). *Leadership in organizations* (4th ed.). Englewood Cliffs, NJ: Prentice Hall.

# CHAPTER 12

# The Promise and Pitfalls of Shared Leadership

## When Two (or More) Heads Are Better Than One

*James O'Toole*

*Jay Galbraith*

*Edward E. Lawler, III*

What is the most effective way to lead a large organization? In 1999, the publication of *Co-Leaders: The Power of Great Partnerships* seemed to presage a new way of thinking about corporate leadership (Heenan & Bennis, 1999). This iconoclastic book broke with the traditional concept of leadership as an individual endeavor and instead treated the activity as a shared effort. At the time the book was published, our research at the Center for Effective Organizations was leading us to the conclusion that leadership is as much an *institutional* as it is an *individual* trait (O'Toole, 2001). Hence, we concluded that "great minds were converging" on a new model in which leadership soon would come to be thought of as a team sport (or, at least, as "doubles"). In fact, nothing of the sort has happened.

AUTHORS' NOTE: A later version of this chapter appears in the summer 2002 issue of the *California Management Review*.

Without creating a ripple, *Co-Leaders* disappeared into that vast sea of unread leadership tomes. Our own research received a hearing in 2000 at the World Economic Forum in Davos, Switzerland, but the findings were received with indifference. Despite some recent attention by a few scholars (Avolio, Jung, Murry, & Sivasubramaniam, 1996; Pearce & Sims, 2000, 2002; Seers, 1996), shared leadership is also a topic that is largely ignored in the research literature. Despite this, we believe the topic warrants additional theoretical and empirical attention.

As we see it, resistance to the notion of shared leadership stems from thousands of years of cultural conditioning. Four hundred years before the birth of Christ, Plato wrote that leadership is a rare trait typically possessed by only one person in any society, an individual who has a unique lock on wisdom and truth. Later efforts by Plato's pupil, Aristotle, to demonstrate that truth is not singular—and wisdom never the sole province of one person—fell on deaf ears. The die had been cast, and, besides, Plato's view coincided with the nature of the only kind of leadership people ever saw in practice: one-man rule.

Shared leadership for most people is simply counterintuitive: Leadership is obviously and manifestly an individual trait and activity. When we speak of leadership, the likes of Mohandas Gandhi and Martin Luther King, Jr., spring to mind. We don't immediately remember that, during the struggle for Indian independence, Gandhi was surrounded and supported by dozens of other great Indian leaders, including Nehru, Patel, and Jinnah, without whose joint efforts Gandhi clearly would have failed. We also forget that, far from doing it all himself, King's disciples included such impressive leaders in their own right as Jesse Jackson, Andrew Young, Julian Bond, Coretta Scott King, and Ralph Abernathy. Ditto Winston Churchill, Franklin Roosevelt, Thomas Jefferson, George Washington, and almost every other great leader. When the facts are fully assembled, even the most fabled "solitary" leaders relied on the support of a team of other effective leaders (O'Toole, 1999).

Moving to the business world, the identities of American corporations are often viewed as mere reflections of the personalities of their leaders: Entire organizations are portrayed as shadows of the "Great Men" who sit in the chief executive chairs. *Fortune* and *BusinessWeek* cover stories are more likely to be about Jack Welch, Bill Gates, William Clay Ford, or Larry Ellison than about GE, Microsoft, Ford, or Oracle. Moreover, investors join journalists in the personification of corporations, focusing on the characters, biographies, and "charisma" of a single leader. In the most extreme case, for all intents and purposes the Berkshire Hathaway Corporation *is* Warren Buffett.

Business schools dutifully conform to the common wisdom: Leadership is studied and taught in the singular. Corporations are assumed to have one leader who is clearly in charge—the CEO; MBA students are schooled to behave as solo operators in that role (over the last decade, the dominant model has been Jack Welch). If team concepts are taught at all, it is not generally in leadership courses. Of course, this individual focus is often appropriate—for example, when studying the role of an entrepreneur who is running a small company that he or she has founded. Moreover, there is the widely held belief in Western cultures that in the final analysis, a single person must be held accountable for performance of a group or corporation (Hollander, 1978; Mack & Konetzni, 1982).

# Change at the Top

Nonetheless, the trend over the last half century has been to expand the capacity for leadership at the top of business organizations. In the early days of publicly traded corporations, businesses were run by a president and a vice president (whose primary role was to step in if the president became incapacitated). Since the end of World War II, countless combinations and permutations of such roles as chairman (or woman), president, CEO, vice chairman (or woman), COO, and CFO have been created and proliferated. The reasons for this increase of shared leadership are relatively obvious. History shows that businesses dependent on a single leader run a considerable risk: If that individual retires, leaves, or dies in office, the organization may well lose its continuing capacity to succeed—witness the performance of General Motors after Alfred Sloan, ITT after Harold Geneen, Polaroid after Edwin Land, and Coca-Cola after Roberto Goizueta.

Frequently, organizations learn the hard way that no one individual can save a company from mediocre performance—and no one individual, no matter how gifted a leader, can be "right" all the time. As the CEO of Champion Paper, Richard Olson, explains, "None of us is as smart as all of us" (O'Toole, 1999, p. 160). Most simply, in large corporations there is just too much work for one person to do, and no one individual is likely to have all the skills needed to do it all (Pearce, Perry, & Sims, 2001; Perry, Pearce, & Sims, 1999). Since leadership is, by definition, doing things through the efforts of others, it is obvious that there is little that a business leader—acting alone—can do to affect company performance (other than try to "look good" to investors).

Amana Corporation chief executive Paul Staman recently explained to author Joe Tye (2002) the benefits of shared leadership: "It allows more time for leaders to spend in the field; it creates an internal dynamic in which the leaders constantly challenge each other to higher levels of performance; it encourages a shared leadership mindset at all levels of the company; it prevents the trauma of transition that occurs in organizations when a strong CEO suddenly leaves" (Tye, 2002). Significantly, Staman is *one of four co-leaders* at Amana. The company has not had a single CEO since 1995, when leadership of the complex organization (with business units in farming, forestry, utilities, construction, manufacturing, retail, and tourist services) was divided among a team of four co-equals along industry lines. Until that restructuring of leadership, Amana had not made money since it sold its famous refrigerator line years earlier. Now, the company is making steady profits even though it is involved in cyclically volatile businesses. When Amana's "Gang of Four" is asked what is most important in making their unusual arrangement work, according to Tye they identify "a shared set of guiding principles, and a team in which each member is able to set aside ego and 'what's in it for me' thinking" (Tye, 2002).

# Partnership at the Top

The first thing one must understand about shared leadership is that the practice is neither new nor unusual. As is shown in Table 12.1, there are many past and present examples of shared leadership at the top of major American corporations. Most of the examples are of co-leaders, but shared leadership may involve more

**Table 12.1**    Evaluating Shared Leadership (Some Selected Examples)

| Company (Approximate Years) | Co-Leaders | | Effectiveness of Team Over Time (+ or −) |
|---|---|---|---|
| ABB (1980s) | Percy Barnevik | Goran Lindhal | + |
| Apple (1980s) | Steve Jobs | Steve Wozniak | − |
| Apple (1990s) | John Sculley | Steve Jobs | − |
| Arco (1980s) | R. O. Anderson | Thornton Bradshaw | + |
| Asda (1990s) | Archie Norman | Allan Leighton | + |
| Berkshire Hathaway (1980s-1990s) | Warren Buffett | Charlie Munger | + |
| Boeing (current) | Phil Condit | Harry Stonecipher | + |
| Citigroup (1990s) | Sanford Weill | John Reed | − |
| Disney (1980s) | Michael Eisner | Frank Wells | + |
| Disney (1990s) | Michael Eisner | Michael Ovitz | − |
| Ford (1980s) | Donald Peterson | Red Poling | + |
| Goldman Sachs (1970s) | John Whitehead | John Weinberg | + |
| Goldman Sachs (1980s) | Steven Friedman | Robert Rubin | + |
| Goldman Sachs (90s) | Hank Paulson | John Corzine | − |
| HP (1950s-1980s) | Bill Hewlett | David Packard | + |
| Intel (1970s) | Bob Noyce | Gordon Moore | + |
| Intel (1980s) | Gordon Moore | Andy Grove | + |
| Intel (1990s) | Andy Grove | Craig Barrett | + |
| Microsoft (current) | Bill Gates | Steve Ballmer | + |
| Morgan Stanley (1990s) | Phil Purcell | Jack Mack | − |
| Motorola (1960s-1980s) | Bob Galvin | Mitchell/Weitz/Fisher | + |
| Oracle (1990s) | Larry Ellison | Ray Lane | − |
| Patagonia | Yvon Chounard | Tom Frost | − |
| Schwab (1990s) | Charles Schwab | David Pottruck | + |
| TIAA-CREF (current) | John Biggs | Martin Liebowitz | + |

than two individuals. Because the aura (or public relations) of great, high-profile solo operators like Jack Welch, Henry Ford, and Harold Geneen has caused the general public to believe that leadership is an aria sung by one prima donna, we need to remind ourselves from time to time of the famous duos of the business world: HP's Hewlett and Packard, Berkshire Hathaway's Buffett and Munger, and ABB's Barnevik and Lindhal. Then there is Intel, which has been run by leadership teams from day one: various combinations of leaders Bob Noyce, Gordon Moore, Andy Grove, and Craig Barrett (see Appendix A, below). We tend to overlook these counterexamples because we are misled by the fact that shared leadership is seldom identified as such. Instead, the members of leadership teams usually carry differentiated titles (CEO, chair, president, COO, vice chair, and the like) to make it easier for outsiders—and particularly those in the investment community—whose traditional views of leadership cause them to insist on the order of formal hierarchy and who drive firms toward isomorphic organizational structures and practices (Abzug & Mezias, 1993; Tolbert & Zucker, 1983).

The fact that shared leadership exists doesn't make it a good practice or necessarily better than the solo variety. Indeed, as is indicated in Table 12.1, some of the most visible examples of shared leadership have ended in failure. So, when are two (or more) leadership heads better than one? The simple answer is *when the challenges a corporation faces are so complex that they require a set of skills too broad to be possessed by any one individual.* That was recognized as true as early as the 1940s, when strategist Charles Merrill teamed up with implementer Winthrop Smith to make Merrill Lynch, Pierce, Fenner, and Smith the longest household name recognizable in the U.S. (Heenan & Bennis, 1999). Avis CEO Robert Townsend's (1970) bestseller *Up the Organization* touted the advantages of what he termed *joint leadership* and outlined how two executives can divide the tasks of the CEO. Townsend explained that the best duos are like yin and yang: Both say, "Neither of us is very good, but our weaknesses (and strengths) may be compensating" (p. 220). The trick, Townsend said, was for joint leaders to "split up the chores, check in advance on strategic matters, and keep each other informed after the fact on the daily disasters" (p. 220).

During the mid-1970s, there were several American companies with two leaders. The most visible was Atlantic Richfield, headed by the entrepreneurial oilman Robert O. Anderson (who directed the company's acquisitions, growth strategy, and board) and the scholarly, inspiring Thornton Bradshaw (a former Harvard Business School professor who oversaw internal operations and external stakeholder relations).

In the 1980s, a nearly bankrupt Ford was saved by the dynamic duo of "finance whiz" Red Poling and "car guy" Donald Petersen. This joint leadership effort was nearly a failure. Poling and Petersen had been bitter rivals in pursuit of Ford's top rung. It wasn't until they put aside their personal competition that had characterized their long careers at Ford—and publicly acknowledged their complementary contributions—that positive change started to occur in the organization. Eventually, after much counseling and effort, Poling and Petersen's public truce grew into genuine mutual respect for each other's skills. Only then did the silo-based conflict that had characterized Ford's culture finally recede. As one Ford executive explained to Richard Pascale (1990), once Ford's leaders got over worrying about, "Are we winning against each other?" they were ready to focus on "Are we winning against the Japanese?" (p. 5).

The Ford experience highlights both the promise of shared leadership and the obstacles that stand in the way of its success. It is commonly assumed, as Townsend did in the 1970s, that the biggest problem is "dividing up the work." In fact, experience has proved that to be just one determinant of success. That is why there are as many examples of failure of shared leadership (Sanford Weill and John Reed at Citigroup) as there are examples of success (Steve Ballmer and Bill Gates at Microsoft). Below, we identify the factors that frequently explain why the shared leadership model works in some cases and not in others. Based on our observations, that success depends on how shared leadership roles originate; how complementary the skills, emotional orientations, and roles of the leaders are; whether they are selected as a team or as individuals; how they work together; and how they involve others on the management team.

# Origins of Shared Leadership

Shared leadership can originate in different ways and for different reasons: Shared leadership can arise from corporate mergers of equals, from co-founders, from the practice of individuals sharing jobs, and from invitations from sitting CEOs to share power. The first of these—creation of shared leadership from the merger of equal companies—is seldom successful because, in truth, there is no such thing as a merger in the real world: There are only acquisitions. Hence, to pretend, for example, that two former CEOs are going to be equals in a newly formed company is the triumph of public relations over reality.

Another source of difficulty arises from the fact that merger-created co-CEOs have no history of working together (except in closing the deal). The relationship between such relative strangers doesn't have a basis of trust to build on (a rare quality that needs to be created slowly from scratch, decision by decision). Worse, mergers of any kind require win-lose decisions to be made quickly—which usually means laying off people and closing facilities. Tough issues include (a) which merger partner gets the CFO job, (b) which HR policies are to be followed. and (c) whose branches are to be closed. Trust is an unlikely by-product of such a rushed and high-stakes decision-making process. The negative examples of Reed and Weill at Citigroup and Purcell and Mack at Morgan Stanley are the unfortunate results of such *mergers of equals*. Moreover, the CEOs of the merged companies rarely have a history of working in a shared leadership structure and often don't have the skills or desire to work in one. Often, they see the merger as just one more challenge in their lifelong pursuit of becoming the sole CEO of a major corporation.

Not all merger-originated forms of shared leadership are doomed to fail. At Boeing, CEO Phil Condit (originally from Boeing) and Harry Stonecipher (ex-CEO of McDonnell Douglas) have managed to work together seamlessly after the merger of their two giant companies (that is, after Boeing's *acquisition* of McDonnell Douglas). One might expect to find that these two powerful individuals had divided their responsibilities along the lines of the company's two main businesses, commercial and defense. Although that is partly true, the full story is more complex. The two have a relationship that is often described as symbiotic. Insiders say they work in tandem, each picking up different parts of a problem.

Condit is described as the visionary who provides spiritual and long-range leadership because he is seen as embodying the ideals of Boeing (he was, after all, the father of the 757, 767, and 777 projects). In contrast, Stonecipher, coming from the hard-nosed culture of GE (by way of McDonnell Douglas), watches the numbers and holds people accountable. Yet, it is Stonecipher who has taken the lead in the "soft" area of executive development. But even there, Condit plays a supportive role as well. Apparently, they have each learned to take a step back in the areas in which the other takes the lead. The secret here may be that, because Stonecipher is much older than Condit (and about to retire), there is no competition between them for power or acclaim.

The creation of shared leadership from co-founders has a better track record because the individuals involved have typically chosen each other as partners. Although they may start with a good working entrepreneurial relationship because of their success as entrepreneurs, this doesn't mean they can learn to become co-CEOs of a large business. Often, these relationships end amicably as one partner develops other interests. When Steve Wozniak left Apple in the hands of Steve Jobs, he did so after having learned that he wanted no part of running a big company (he left to finance rock concerts). When Paul Allen let his start-up partner Bill Gates have full managerial control of Microsoft, he did so because of his health problems. Although Allen has remained on the company's board of directors, it is extremely rare for a founder of a company to remain as a content and productive member of the board after stepping down from a leadership position. More typically—at Patagonia, for example—co-founders end up going their separate ways because irreconcilable differences about the future of a company often develop shortly after an initial public offering (IPO). Sometimes, such partings are voluntary but, more often, one of the founders dominates the board and forces the other out.

Just like individual founders, co-founders often fail at shared leadership because the skills needed to start a company are not the same as those needed to run it. The late Bob Noyce, co-founder and first chairman of Intel, was a rarity among successful entrepreneurs; he understood his strengths and weaknesses (see Appendix A, below). Early on, he fired himself and became vice chairman of the company. Fellow co-founder Gordon Moore became the chairman (later, he turned over the reins to another co-founder, Andy Grove). Noyce was fortunate to have a co-leader with complementary skills whom he trusted and with whom he could work. Most entrepreneurs, in contrast, are loners (Ensley, Carland, & Carland, 2000) who end up getting the boot from the board when it discovers they haven't got what it takes to be CEOs.

The most visible example of co-founders becoming successful co-CEOs is Bill Hewlett and David Packard. They both focused on strategy, but they differentiated their other leadership roles. Bill Hewlett became the heart of the company (to this day, he is the patron saint of HP's engineers). In contrast, David Packard was the guts of the organization, the hard-nosed businessman who made the tough calls. It was Packard who removed the nonperformers. Together, "Bill and Dave" were a great combination, yet HP's board did not replace them with another set of co-leaders. Instead, they were succeeded by John Young, a man very much in the same mold as Bill Hewlett, warm, caring, and respected by all. But Young could not manage the conflict that occurred as a matter of course in HP's highly decentralized structure. Packard was forced to come out of retirement and run the company while a new CEO was groomed for the job (who also failed to live up to the high standard set by the co-founders). The lesson at HP seems to be that failure to replace all of the many and diverse skills of the founders has led to continual turmoil in the executive suite. HP may be one company that requires more than two heads to run.

Some companies have a tradition of shared leadership. Investment banks in general, and Goldman Sachs in particular, use shared leadership as a matter of course, in part as a residue of their historical partnership structures (most of which have now been abandoned). In 1976, when the CEO of Goldman Sachs died, senior partners John Whitehead and John Weinberg put together a succession plan identifying themselves as co-CEOs. The partnership's management committee quickly approved the shared leadership construct, and collaboration became the name of the game at Goldman for the next 25 years. Typically, one of the company's CEOs has come from the sales and trading side of the house, and the other from investment banking.

In 1984, when Whitehead retired to join the Reagan administration, Weinberg appointed Steven Friedman and Robert Rubin to serve as co-COOs. In 1990, they became co-CEOs and served until Rubin joined the Clinton administration. They were succeeded in 1994 by another set of co-CEOs, Hank Paulson and John Corzine. Even though Goldman's shared leadership model has lasted for a long time, it has had its rough moments. In 1999, when Corzine left the firm, there was great controversy and debate over whether Goldman should give up its partnership structure and go public, which it did. Yet, in general, the shared leadership model has worked well in investment banking, in which it is often extended down the line to co-heads of major business units, like investment banking and equities.

The shared leadership approach seems to work best when an existing CEO creates it. For example, Charles Schwab invited his long-time collaborator, David Pottruck, to become his co-CEO, and Bill Gates invited his collaborator, Steve Ballmer, to join with him in various joint leadership relationships before finally turning over the CEO job to him. Significantly, Gates remains co-leader of Microsoft as chairman of the board and head of software research. At both Schwab and Microsoft, long histories of working together built trust and rapport between the principals. The Schwab-Pottruck relationship showed some signs of unraveling in the 2001 recession when Schwab took back some of the authority he had ceded to Pottruck and began more directive, personal leadership of the company. Nonetheless, this partnership still appeared strong as this chapter went to press in mid-2002.

# Different Roles

The odds on the success of shared leadership appear to go up when the individuals involved play different and complementary roles: HP's "heart" was Bill Hewlett and its "guts" David Packard. Charles Schwab is often described as the "voice of the customer" and the "company conscience," whereas David Pottruck provides task leadership. Steve Ballmer provides emotional leadership at Microsoft, ditto John Weinberg at Goldman Sachs and Phil Condit at Boeing. These *emotional leaders* are (or were) matched by *task leaders* Gates, Whitehead, and Stonecipher in their respective companies. In the 1980s, ABB became a world-class corporation under the economist and strategist, Percy Barnevik, and a leadership team that included a people person (Goran Lindhal) and a computer guy (Jurgen Centerman)—both of whom, significantly, would eventually take their turns as CEO of ABB. By having shared leadership at ABB, it was easy to switch the focus at the top to meet changing business conditions. Similarly, Motorola succeeded in the 1970-1990 era under two- and three-man leadership. CEO Bob Galvin was the glue at the top, the stabilizing force, whereas such technical whiz kids as John Mitchell, George Fischer, and William Weisz ran operations.

Power at the top can be distributed in many ways: In the 1970s, Simon Ramo (the "R" in TRW) worked as team leader with several different chairmen, CEOs, and presidents (his highest title: vice chairman in charge of innovation, a position much like the one Bill Gates occupies today at Microsoft). Galvin, a people manager, and Ramo, a technologist, each compensated for his respective weaknesses by sharing power with others whose skills could help them to achieve their goals. Similarly, the charismatic and entrepreneurial Larry Ellison finally made a real go of Oracle in the 1990s when he brought in the analytical and managerial Ray Lane. Then Ellison fired Lane in 1999, taking back the power he had shared, much as (but far less gracefully than) Charles Schwab reclaimed power from David Pottruck. If nothing else, these two examples illustrate the fragility of shared leadership and the fact that one member of every team of two is usually more equal than the other!

Because of the increasing complexity of most businesses, shared leadership has become almost a necessity when it comes to leading change in large organizations. For example, the successful transformation of England's giant Asda supermarket chain in the late 1980s was led by two individuals who both admit they couldn't have accomplished the feat as a solo act. The analytical Harvard MBA, Archie Norman, provided the strategic framework and financial acumen, whereas the more open and accessible Allen Leighton brought the people and marketing skills needed for the tasks at hand.

Intel exemplifies the combining of different roles into a total leadership package: Bob Noyce was Mr. Outside, Intel's face to the world; Gordon Moore was the long-term strategist and thinker; and Andy Grove was the short-term, hands-on, "make your numbers guy." Grove was volatile, whereas Noyce and Moore were calm and rational.

The situation at the top of GE has been more fluid with respect to membership and roles(see Appendix B, below). The office of the chairman at GE was created when Reg Jones selected Jack Welch as chairman along with two vice chairmen to work with him. They were selected as a complementary team both in terms of skills and chemistry. In due course, Welch brought Larry Bossidy to the office to gain oversight of GE Capital. When Bossidy later left the company, Welch added Dennis Dammerman, the former CFO, to fill the same role. Finally, Paolo Fresca was put on the team to bring international experience when GE was expanding into Europe and Asia. The office of the chairman varied from between three and four members during Welch's tenure, and people came and went as Welch needed their skills (and needed to free up their positions down the line to test young talent).

## Selecting a Leadership Team

It is often forgotten that, in the process that led to the selection of Jack Welch as GE's CEO, Reg Jones (the retiring CEO) vowed to choose a team of leaders—and not just an individual. The process Jones used became a Harvard Business School case study, and it is worth going back to it to see how he conducted thorough interviews with all of the CEO candidates, their peers, and others (Bartlett, Aguilar, & Elderkin, 1991). Jones was primarily interested in issues of trust and chemistry. He knew the skill profiles of the various candidates, but the interpersonal relationships between them were hidden from him in his role as chairman. The lesson of the case is that it is better to select a team of co-leaders who have rapport and complementary skills than to choose a group of talented individuals. Goldman Sachs appears to use this same process of joint selection, stressing, as Jones did, the importance of a combination of talent and chemistry.

Chemistry, like leadership ability, is often overlooked in executive searches (Bennis & O'Toole, 2000). The late Frank Wells succeeded as Michael Eisner's co-leader at Disney, whereas Michael Ovitz would later fail in the same role. Why? Not because the earlier team had done a better job of divvying up power and authority, but because members of the latter team competed for time "in front of the mirror" (attention and credit in the press). Frank Wells was satisfied that Disney's executives and board knew he was the cerebral leader of Disney (whereas Eisner was the public and emotional leader of the company). In contrast, Ovitz needed *everybody*'s love and adulation and quickly began to compete with Eisner.

Who should choose co-leaders? Jack Welch, Bob Galvin, and Bill Gates selected their own co-leaders; hence, there is some evidence and theoretical rationale (Ensley, Pearson, & Pearce, in press; Pearce et al., 2001; Pearce & Sims, 2002) that it is wise to involve the current leader in the selection of his or her complements. But it doesn't always work: Since the death of Frank Wells, Eisner has been unable to select someone with whom to share the leadership of Disney. Having the current leader make the selection is, however, most likely a necessary, but not sufficient, condition for success.

# Working Together

Once selected, co-leaders need to learn to work together (Pearce et al., 2001; Pearce & Sims, 2000; Seers, 1996). Role ambiguity has long been linked to dysfunction in groups. Thus, for the sake of accountability, tasks must be divided. Perhaps more important than the division of tasks is that co-leaders need to learn how to handle the division of credit (Ensley et al., in press). The hardest thing for individuals considering joint governance to understand is that their biggest challenge is not practical or technical. Instead, it is managing their egos: Can one of them step back and let the other take the bows? Can they come onstage and take their bows together? In the final analysis, shared leadership has worked at Intel and TIAA-CREF because executives at those companies are able to share credit, and it has failed at Disney and Citigroup because of the egos that were rampant in the executive suites of those companies.

In addition to managing the allocation of credit, the success of shared leadership depends on how effectively the individuals involved communicate, handle crises, allocate and reallocate joint tasks and decision making, and develop common positions on key issues (Ensley & Pearce, 2001; Pearce & Sims, 2000). The roles and tasks at the top can be divided in various ways: (a) Mr. Inside and Ms. Outside, (b) Mr. Business Line A and Ms. Business Line B, or (c) Mr. Operations and Ms. Acquisitions. Tasks can be also divided by interests (innovation versus operations), skills (technology versus people), or personality bent (strategy versus implementation). Indeed, roles and tasks can be divided along as many lines as there are individual skills and interests on one axis and organizational needs and opportunities on the other.

In some cases, the most effective approach to task division is to have a fluid approach to who takes responsibility for leadership tasks. For example, at TIAA-CREF (managers of over $600 billion in pension assets), CEO John Biggs once had the investments function reporting to him when he shared leadership with a president who ran operations (who has since left the company). But now Biggs manages strategy, new businesses, and external affairs while his co-leader, Vice Chairman Martin Liebowitz, runs investments (which handles most of the risk in the business). What is important to understand is that titles and turf are meaningless to the two leaders of TIAA-CREF—everyone knows that Biggs and Liebowitz are co-leaders who share equally in the credit and blame that attach to the executive suite.

In the final analysis, it doesn't matter so much how responsibilities are divided as it matters that the individuals involved are clear about their roles and honest with themselves and each other about their respective contributions and needs for acknowledgement and power. So the questions individuals in shared leadership situations should ask when starting out are these: (a) What are we each good at doing? (b) What areas in the organization need our direct leadership in order for the corporation to succeed? (c) How are we going to coordinate and communicate with each other so we don't step on each other's toes? and (d) How can we make sure we send the same message?

Coordination and alignment begin with communication (Locke & Latham, 1990). When there are only two co-leaders, communication often takes place spontaneously and constantly. Our colleague Jay Conger reports that Schwab and Pottruck were in touch continually throughout the day. But some sharing of thoughts and ideas needs to be formalized. In the case of the Midwest Manufacturing Company (see Appendix C, below), the co-CEOs have a monthly dinner scheduled indelibly on their calendars. Very few co-leaders are as well coordinated and aligned as was the team of Noyce, Moore, and Grove at Intel (see Appendix A, below). The opposite was true at Citigroup, where insufficient communication among the co-leaders led to an irreparable divergence of views and opinions. It was reported in the press that Reed and Weill actually avoided each other. Subordinates accentuated the rift by "shopping ideas" with the two leaders, which led to further conflict and a resulting decay in the level of trust.

# Working With Others

The division of tasks between people involved in shared leadership often affects their subordinates' work. For example, questions arise concerning attendance at executive team forums: Whose meeting is it? Who should attend what meeting? Such questions are relatively easy to answer at companies organized like Amana, where the four co-leaders each head a relatively independent business unit. At the other extreme is the Midwest Manufacturing Company (see Appendix C, below), where the co-leaders have divided responsibility based on their interests and skills. Because co-CEO Sue looks after all sales and distribution activities, including those in the businesses run by her co-leader, this makes everyone else's work highly interdependent. Issues of responsibility for inventory, prices, and customer priorities constantly need to be resolved. Because the co-CEOs did not involve others in their decisions concerning the allocation of their tasks, the responsibilities of others had to be worked out in the heat of day-to-day issues. This was clearly the wrong way to go. Co-leaders need to discuss these issues and resolve the ambiguities themselves, rather than leaving them to their subordinates. Managers should be spending their time dealing with business issues, not with political issues caused by the co-leaders' role ambiguities. The lesson is this: The more interdependent the work of co-leaders, the more input they should solicit from affected others and the more they need to coordinate between themselves.

# Leadership Institutionalized

Shared leadership is not just an issue at the top of corporations. We have surveyed over 3,000 managers in a dozen global corporations, and, in a few of these companies, we discovered that *many of the key tasks and responsibilities of leadership were institutionalized in the systems, practices, and cultures of the organization* (O'Toole, 2001). Without the presence of a high-profile leader (or "superiors" goading or exhorting them on), we observed that people at all levels in these organizations

> acted more like owners and entrepreneurs than employees or hired hands; they assumed owner-like responsibility for financial performance and managing risk.
>
> took initiative to solve problems and to act, in general, with a sense of urgency.
>
> willingly accepted accountability for meeting commitments and for living the values of the organization.
>
> created, maintained, and adhered to systems and procedures designed to measure and reward the above behaviors.

Among other things, this discovery helps to explain some persistent contradictions to the dominant model of leadership: If leadership were solely an individual trait, why is it that some companies are able to renew their strategies and products and outperform competition in their industries *over the tenures of several different chief executives?* Moreover, why is it that some CEOs who have succeeded in one organization often turn in so-so performances in the next? It is our conclusion that the reason is found in such key organizational variables as systems, structures, and policies—factors that are not included in research based on a solo leadership model.

# Conclusion

Despite continued assertions that shared leadership does not work, we believe there are enough examples of such successful combinations that we can reject that conventional wisdom with some confidence. See, for example, Pearce and Sims (2002), who found shared leadership to be a significant predictor of team effectiveness. Thus, we believe that the issue is to identify the factors that improve the odds that a particular combination of leaders will succeed. As we have shown, it seems that joint selection, complementary skills and emotional orientations, and mechanisms for coordination are among those key factors. Although these may seem to be common-sense indicators, our point is that they are not common practice. Research and analysis should continue to test these factors and others. It is important to do so because shared leadership is here to stay.

# Appendix A

## The Intel Office Model

The Intel office differs from the one at GE in two respects. First, the members of the office were founders of the company. All three owned sizeable stakes in the company. Second, the office is used to groom successors. The particular office that I will describe is the one that contained Bob Noyce, Gordon Moore, and Andy Grove, all of whom became the CEO.

The original office had Bob Noyce as CEO and chairman, Gordon Moore as president, and Andy Grove as executive vice president. This office lasted only a couple of years. Bob Noyce was proud of having fired himself as CEO and for taking the position of vice chairman. Noyce, the co-inventor of the integrated circuit, knew he was not a manager, so after the company achieved a certain size and its financing was stable, he turned the CEO role over to others. In this case, Gordon Moore became chairman and CEO and Andy Grove became the president and COO. Noyce said he would fire himself the day that he walked down the hall, saw a new employee, and did not take the time to introduce himself. That day was the day the organization had so many people that he could not know everyone's name. It was also a time when the company was of a size that it needed to be run by formal systems, plans, and budgets. Noyce knew he was not the person to build and run these processes.

In the office that took shape, Bob Noyce became Mr. Outside. He was Intel's face to the world. An attractive and articulate man, he testified before Congress on the Japanese threat in semiconductors. He represented Intel to the customer and to the Semi-conductor Industry Association. When Intel was having a tough competition over an attractive job candidate, it was Noyce who did the last interview and made the offer. Few could resist.

Gordon Moore was the CEO and the long-term thinker. The originator of Moore's Law (double computing power every eighteen months), Moore thought about the evolution of technology. He took care of technology and finance. He was a quiet and introverted man. But he was always at home with a young engineer with a new idea. Andy Grove was on the opposite ends of the time, emotional, and management spectrums relative to the other two. Grove was short-term and hands-on. He held people accountable. Everyone had quarterly goals called Q-ones or Q-twos. He was, in fact, the COO. Whereas Bob Noyce hated formal systems, Grove loved them. He built and ran the strategic long range planning process, the council system, the performance management process, the practice of one-on-ones, and the matrix organization. He was the organization designer and wrote books about the Intel way.

Whereas Moore and Noyce were quiet and calm, Grove was volatile. During a business review, Grove would explode, "That's nonsense!" A heated discussion would ensue. The episode would typically end with a thoughtful summary and proposed solution from Moore. The review would then proceed until Grove erupted again. Grove would surface the issues (albeit not very diplomatically) that required discussion and could profit from the insights of Moore and Noyce. Although no pushovers, Moore and Noyce's styles would not necessarily have surfaced the tough issues.

The three members of the office were opposites. Yet they were able to convert their differences into complements rather than conflicts. Indeed, the group regarded conflict to be healthy. Grove wrote about "constructive confrontation" as a means to surface tough issues and discuss them from all sides. The three met together every Friday morning, probably at Grove's initiative. They shared information, developed their shared positions, and decided on the agenda for the Tuesday executive staff meeting. No one really knew what took place on Fridays, but they probably worked through their differences. In the end, all three got their chance to be chairman and CEO.

There are two main lessons from the founders of Intel. They were able to combine their different skills into a combination of complementary skills. Each one had a specialty and did not compete for credit. A lot of the credit goes to Bob Noyce and his low ego needs and realistic assessment of his own skills; plus, after two successful startups, he became a mentor. The second lesson is that they worked hard and talked together to maintain a unified position on major issues. If there were differences, the Friday meeting was the appropriate forum for discussion and resolution.

—Jay Galbraith

# Appendix B

## The General Electric Model

The GE model has a chairperson and CEO and two or three vice chairpeople. They do not use a chief operating officer (COO). The model has been shaped by Jack Welch, the CEO for the last 20 years. Initially, however, it was shaped by Reginald Jones, the CEO before Jack Welch.

When Reg Jones was selected as CEO, his two competitors for the chairman's role became his vice chairmen. These two competitors stayed on in their roles and the office was characterized by a great deal of discontent. So when Jones was choosing Welch, he did a great deal of interviewing of the candidates, their peers, and the corporate staff. He wanted to know the chemistry and trust between the candidates. Then, when he selected Jack Welch as chairman and CEO, he simultaneously selected the vice chairmen with whom Jack could work. He selected a team of three to move into the office.

Every discussion of co-leaders of corporate offices always emphasizes trust and chemistry between the members. In this case, Reg Jones chose the office based on trust and chemistry in addition to competence. So if trust and chemistry matter, why not select for it rather than let it emerge on its own? When selecting people simultaneously, the board can do this. Otherwise, the members of the office can select new members based on trust and chemistry.

The office of three worked fairly well at GE. One of the members, John Burlingame, took on some projects like selling Utah International and then left. He was replaced by one of Jack's favorites, Larry Bossidy, who built GE Capital. The trio of Ed Hood, Jack, and Larry worked quite effectively until Ed retired and Larry became CEO of Allied Signal. Jack has since selected a series of people to work with him in the office. On all occasions, these are people who can work with Jack and the other office members. The new members are also selected in part on the needs of the office and in part to free up development opportunities for young talent. When GE was promoting international growth, Paolo Fresca, the head of the international division, became a vice chairman. Jack had little international experience and wanted the skills of the office to be rounded out. Paolo is now the CEO of Fiat.

The office before the appointment of Jeffrey Imelt as the new CEO consisted of Dennis Dammerman and Robert Wright. Dennis was brought in because Jack wanted some oversight of GE Capital after his falling out with the former GE

Capital chairman. Dennis, the former GE CFO, became the chairman of GE Capital and vice chairman of GE. The move freed up the CFO role, which went to a talented young 40-year-old. Robert Wright moved to the vice chairman role and freed up the leadership of NBC to some new talent.

The office concept works at GE because the members are selected to contribute needed skills but also can become a member of Jack's office team. I am sure that they have their rough days, but the office works well. In part, the members of the office know that they will never be the CEO of GE. Robert Wright left GE to become the CEO of Cox Communications. When Cox was taken over, he came back to GE to run NBC. They have no agenda to make the CEO look bad. They are often elder diplomats. They are probably more interested in leaving a legacy than getting to be CEO.

The office under Welch worked in a fluid manner. In addition to new members, the work was constantly reshuffled. Typically, Jack took a couple of businesses that were undergoing the most strategic change. The other members then took the other businesses and functions. Jack typically took the strategy function and human resources. For example, if Aircraft Engines was undergoing a big change, Jack wanted the business to report to him with no filters in between. Since Aircraft Engine and Power Generation share turbine technology, Power Generation and R&D would also report to Jack. He would be CEO and COO for those parts of the company undergoing the most change. He wanted those businesses to be able to make decisions quickly. If this meant another $100 million for R&D and capital, so be it. After eighteen months had passed and Aircraft Engine was clear on its development, Jack would take Lighting and Major Appliances. The other members of the office would then sort out their portfolios in turn.

There are two major lessons from GE's office experience. First, if chemistry and trust are important, do not leave them to chance. GE selects for chemistry and trust. They also managed for them under Jack Welch. Second, when you became a member of the office with Jack, you were a valued person but you were no longer a candidate for the CEO of GE. Candidates ran businesses. Vice chairpeople were valued elder diplomats.

—Jay Galbraith

# Appendix C

## Midwest Manufacturing Company

Midwest Manufacturing Company is a 5,000-employee equipment manufacturer. It sells its products through distributors and, at the time of the study, had seven different product lines. It also has the typical functions of sales, marketing, R&D, finance, HR, IS, and legal. The company is an old one and is family owned. At the time of this study, Midwest Manufacturing had recently shifted its organization design. In the old structure, the co-CEOs John and Sue (children of the founder) were in a two-in-a-box arrangement. They virtually did nothing separately and all reporting relationships were to both of them. There were some differences in how they spent their time, since Sue seemed to be particularly skilled at dealing with distributors and enjoyed meeting customers more than John. This led them to change from their two-in-a-box structure to one in which they had separate reporting relationships.

Rather than go to a COO-CEO reporting structure, each of them took certain lines of businesses and certain support functions. The ones they took seemed largely to be dictated by their preferences and knowledge about certain areas rather than the interdependency that might exist among the functions and business units. In essence, they decided to take primary responsibility for things they knew the most about and most wanted to manage. When the change occurred, little input was sought from other members of the organization, but in essence Sue and John were the major owners of the company and little resistance occurred. Through all the changes and different structures, John and Sue have maintained a good personal relationship. Indeed, once a month they meet with their respective spouses to talk about how well they are working together and the impact of their working together on their spouses.

## Positive Results of the New Structure

The most important reason for the change was efficient use of time. Both Sue and John felt that they were simply extra wheels at certain meetings and that they could collectively have more influence and provide more expertise to the organization if they operated independently in certain situations. This, of course, is also consistent with their having different skills and different interests. Furthermore, there were some members of their direct report group that preferred working with one of them, so the new structure was seen as a positive by them.

The major advantage of moving to the new structure was better use of both John and Sue's time and skills. They simply could do more and could be more comfortable with the new structure. In general, their direct reports preferred the new relationship because it gave them more opportunity to get guidance and discuss issues with one of the leaders of the organization.

## Weaknesses of the New Structure

Perhaps the major weakness of the new structure was the tendency of subordinates to shop decisions. Even though there was a clear reporting relationship, there often was enough ambiguity so that individuals could take it to either John or Sue. Not surprisingly, they preferred to take it to the one they thought was most likely to give them the decision they wanted. In some cases, they took it to both if they didn't like the answer from the other.

The second problem for the direct reports concerned communication between Sue and John. Because John and Sue were not always together in meetings, subordinates always had the question of whether Sue (or John) explained to John (or Sue) what decision had been made. Because of ambiguity in this area, subordinates often felt like they had to explain Sue's decisions to John and vice versa when only one of them was present at the meeting where a decision was made.

Finally, the situation led to some increased competition between John and Sue. Both wanted to perform their jobs well, so, as a result, they tended to push their divisions and their functions particularly hard. They also more often felt left out of issues and decisions and raised issues about whether they should have been included in a particular meeting that might have some implications for the areas for which they were responsible.

*Conclusion*

When Sue and John changed to the new structure, they did little work in the area of group process and communication. Because of this, their subordinates were often unclear as to how John and Sue planned to work together and indeed how they should treat them in terms of decision making and communication. It was often not clear what was a group activity and what was a one-on-one activity, particularly given the history of Sue and John working together and dealing with virtually every issue. Much of this could have been resolved if the top management team had spent some time talking about their decision process and communication.

The structure made coordination between John and Sue particularly critical. By making different assignments of reporting relationships to both Sue and John, it would have been possible to reduce the importance of their activity coordinators; in essence, the reporting relationships to them would need to be based on the degree to which functions and business units are interdependent. The objective would be to identify the groups of relatively independent functions and business units.

As John and Sue developed the new reporting relationships, they tended to speak less and less frequently as united leaders. This began to cause problems and certainly contributed to the tendency of their subordinates to decision shop. The critical learning is that when leadership takes the form that it does in Midwestern Manufacturing, the two leaders need to be sure that they frequently make joint presentations and representations of what the company is about, what its basic strategy is, and what it stands for.

Overall, the structure that Midwestern Manufacturing used was judged to be effective. Moving to different reporting relationships for John and Sue did seem to represent an improvement over the earlier structure. An important note of caution is appropriate here, however. The success of any co-leader approach very much depends on the relationship between the two individuals and how it is received by the others in the organization. In the case of John and Sue, it was perceived that they were fundamentally on the same page with respect to the direction of the company and that they had different skills, so that them having different reporting relationships passed the credibility test.

—Edward E. Lawler, III

# References

Abzug, R., & Mezias, S. J. (1993). The fragmented state and due process protections in organizations: The case of comparable worth. *Organization Science, 4,* 433-453

Avolio, B. J., Jung, D. I., Murry, W., & Suvasubramaniam, N. (1996). Building highly developed teams: Focusing on shared leadership processes, efficacy, trust, and performance. *Advances in Interdisciplinary Studies of Work Teams, 3,* 173-209.

Bartlett, C. A., Aguilar, F. J., & Elderkin, K. W. (1991). *General Electric: Reg Jones and Jack Welch* (Case 9-391-144). Cambridge, MA: Harvard Business School.

Bennis, W., & O'Toole, J. (2000). Don't hire the wrong CEO. *Harvard Business Review, 78*(3), 170-176.

Ensley, M. D., Carland, J. W., & Carland, J. C. (2000). Investigating the existence of the lead entrepreneur. *Journal of Small Business Management. 38*(4), 59-77.

Ensley, M. D., & Pearce, C. L. (2001). Shared cognition as a process and an outcome in top management teams: Implications for new venture performance. *Journal of Organizational Behavior, 22,* 145-160.

Ensley, M. D., Pearson A., & Pearce, C. L. (in press). Top management team process, shared leadership and new venture performance: A theoretical model and research agenda. *Human Resource Management Review.*

Heenan, D., & Bennis, W. (1999). *Co-leaders: The power of great partnerships.* New York: Wiley.

Hollander, E. P. (1978). *Leadership dynamics: A practical guide to effective relationships.* New York: Free Press.

Locke, E. A., & Latham, G. P. (1990). *A theory of goal setting and task performance.* Englewood Cliffs, NJ: Prentice Hall.

Mack, W. P., & Konetzni, A. H., Jr. (1982). *Command at sea* (4th ed.). Annapolis, MD: Naval Institute Press.

O'Toole, J. (1999). *Leadership A to Z: A guide for the appropriately ambitious.* San Francisco: Jossey-Bass.

O'Toole, J. (2001). When leadership is an organizational trait. In W. Bennis, G. M. Spreitzer, & T. G. Cummings (Eds.), *The future of leadership* (pp. 158-175). San Francisco: Jossey-Bass.

Pascale, R. (1990). *Managing on the edge: How the smartest companies use conflict to stay ahead.* New York: Simon & Schuster.

Pearce, C. L., Perry, M. L., & Sims, H. P., Jr. (2001). Shared leadership: Relationship management to improve NPO effectiveness. In T. D. Connors (Ed.), *The nonprofit handbook: Management.* (pp. 624-641). New York: Wiley.

Pearce, C. L., & Sims, H. P., Jr. (2000). Shared leadership: Toward a multi-level theory of leadership. *Advances in the Interdisciplinary Studies of Work Teams, 7,* 115-139. Greenwich, CT: JAI Press.

Pearce, C. L., & Sims, H. P., Jr. (2002). Vertical versus shared leadership as predictors of the effectiveness of change management teams: An examination of aversive, directive, transactional, transformational, and empowering leader behaviors. *Group Dynamics: Theory, Research, and Practice,* 6(2), 179-197.

Perry, M. L., Pearce, C. L., & Sims, H. P., Jr. (1999). Empowered selling teams: How shared leadership can contribute to selling team outcomes. *Journal of Personal Selling and Sales Management,* 19(3), 35-52.

Seers, A. (1996). Better leadership through chemistry: Toward a model of emergent shared team leadership. *Advances in Interdisciplinary Studies of Work Teams, 3,* 145-172.

Tolbert, P., & Zucker, L. (1983). Institutional sources of change in the formal structure of organizations: The diffusion of civil service reforms, 1880-1935. *Administrative Science Quarterly, 23,* 22-39.

Townsend, R. (1970). *Up the organization.* New York: Knopf.

Tye, Joe. (2002). Retrieved August 21, 2002, from http://www.joetye.com.

# PART IV

# CRITIQUE OF SHARED LEADERSHIP THEORY

# CHAPTER 13

# Leadership

## *Starting at the Top*

*Edwin A. Locke*

Since the focus of this book is the topic of shared leadership, let me begin with the definition of it given by Cox, Pearce, and Perry (see Chapter 3, this volume): "Shared leadership relies on a dynamic exchange of lateral influence among peers rather than vertical downward influence by an appointed leader" (p. 48). Mayo, Meindl, and Pastor (see Chapter 9) appear to agree with this definition. Presumably, this conceptualization would preclude upward influence by subordinates as well as downward influence by a leader.

The wider leadership issue, however, is this: Where does shared leadership fall in the grand scheme of things? More specifically, what is it that should be shared, by whom and with whom? To answer these questions, it is necessary to look at leadership in the context of the organization as a whole. I will focus here on profit-making organizations. In this chapter, I will describe different models of leadership, identify what I believe are the core tasks of the leader at the top, specify what tasks the top leader should and should not share, and present an integrated model showing the recommended directions of influence.

## Top-Down Model

Let me begin by specifying what leadership is. Most people view leadership as a top-down process. My definition of leadership (Locke & Associates, 1991), "the process of inducing others to take action toward a common goal" (p. 2), does not

L = Leader     S = Subordinate

*1a:  Top Down*

*1b:  Bottom Up*

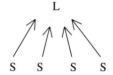

*1c:  Shared Leadership*

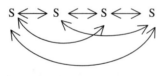

*1d:  Integrated Model*

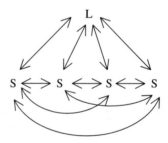

**Figure 13.1**   Four Leadership Models

preclude lateral influence, but most people would interpret it to mean that the leader persuades subordinates. The top-down model is shown in Figure 13.1a.

The top-down leader is described in many ways in the literature—almost always pejoratively. He is typically a male. He is said to be a prima donna. He thinks he knows everything. He wants only obedience, not disagreement, from subordinates. He is a tough, masculine guy who likes to throw his weight around. He is a loner who works only as an individual and disparages the idea of teamwork. He has technical skills but no people skills. He does not listen to others or give them any useful information. He has no respect for the abilities of his subordinates. He makes all the decisions himself. He does not grow; he is static and unchanging. Even seemingly desirable leadership attributes, such as independence, are treated as undesirable on the grounds, for instance, that independence precludes working with others.

Leaders who consistently acted as described above would certainly be very poor leaders. Such leaders would clearly be irrational and would be doomed to failure in the long run, especially if they did not value and use the talents of capable subordinates. But it does not follow from this that leaders should never make any unilateral decisions. To know when this is appropriate or not appropriate, one would have to specify clearly what leadership involves—an issue I will come back to later.

Underneath the attack on top-down leadership is another premise: an assault on the importance of the individual. Fletcher and Käufer (see Chapter 2) favor "a significant shift from the focus on individual achievement and meritocracy to a focus on collective achievement, empowerment and the importance of teamwork" (p. 2). The implicit package deal here is that respect for individual achievement is incompatible with the promotion of teamwork. These authors do not consider the possibility that teams are most effective when they have outstanding individuals leading them and comprising them—and sometimes avoiding them (Locke et al., 2001)! To quote Ayn Rand (1993),

> Men have been taught that it is a virtue to agree with others. But the creator is the man who disagrees. Men have been taught that it is a virtue to swim with the current. But the creator is the man who goes against the current. Men have been taught that it is a virtue to stand together. But the creator us the man who stands alone. (pp. 680-681). . . . The creator denied, opposed, persecuted, exploited—went on, moved forward and carried all humanity along on his energy (p. 682).

## Bottom-Up Model

The opposite of the top-down leader model would be the bottom-up model shown in Figure 13.1b. In this model, leaders simply reflect what those below want, do not have independent views of their own, and do not impose their wishes on others. It is almost pure egalitarianism. The leader is a leader in name only. This neo-Marxist model was popular back in the 1960s but was clearly so wildly impractical that it dropped out of favor. On the other hand, it does not follow from this that upward influence is inappropriate. Again, it would depend on one's view of what leadership involves.

## Shared Leadership Model

Figure 13.1c is shared leadership. Everything that the top-down leader allegedly lacks is said to be found here. There is constant teamwork. The focus is on the group and not on the individual. People listen to one another and share information. The team members are all equal and interdependent. Independence is frowned on. Each person influences the others equally. They participate in joint decision making. The team is empowered and dynamic. The members have social skills. The style is more feminine that masculine.

But there are problems with this model too. First, and most fundamentally, what happens to the top leader? No successful, profit-making company that I know of has ever been run by a team. Cox et al. as well as Mayo et al. indicate that they would combine shared leadership with vertical leadership (Figure 13.1a)—a smart move—for reasons that I will make clear. A critical question that must be answered here is *what should be the responsibilities of the team versus those of the leader?*

Second, it is not the case that shared leadership will always occur in an empowered team, and, if it does occur, it is not always the case that the team will be effective. Here, one needs a theory of group effectiveness. For example, if the group is to make a good decision, this requires at least four things: (a) The relevant knowledge must be contained within the group or at least the group must have the ability to discover it; (b) relevant knowledge must be communicated or shared among the members; (c) the members have to have the ability to distinguish between relevant and irrelevant or better and worse ideas; and (d) the members have to accept the correct, or at least the best, ideas to implement. The chapter by Burke, Fiore, and Salas (see Chapter 5) puts great stress on the importance of team agreement in the form of shared mental models and the like, but team agreement is not useful unless the team has valid knowledge.

The group effectiveness issue harks back to the long studied issue of participation in decision making (PDM). It was originally assumed that PDM would automatically make for greater group effectiveness, mainly due to its supposedly beneficial motivational effects, but the research did not support this assumption. Rather, PDM seems to be most useful when it promotes the sharing of relevant information between peers and between supervisor and subordinate (Locke, Alavi, & Wagner, 1997). In this context, it becomes critical for the parties to discover who knows what.

Equal influence among team members is not necessarily desirable, even if it could be attained—which it often cannot, as Seers, Keller, and Wilkerson (see Chapter 4) observe. Ideally, the most influential member or members will be the one or ones with the best ideas. This may or may not actually occur. Seers et al. note that "individuals who verbalize more most often emerge as leaders" (p. 81). This means that the most talkative and assertive member or members may have undue influence—which is all right, providing they have the most knowledge. If they do not, those with relevant knowledge may not get heard and the decision will be suboptimal. People differ not only in their knowledge but also in their willingness to speak up in a group setting. Others are sorely lacking in social skills and alienate the other members through tactless or obnoxious behaviors.

Seers et al. also note that group influence also can be based on status, a category in which they lump both skill and knowledge along with demographic characteristics. If skill and knowledge do not correlate as expected with hierarchical position or demographic characteristics, then, again, this could undermine the group's ability to make a high-quality decision. The leader, if there is one, can help here by trying to develop norms that focus on facts and arguments rather than on other factors. The leader may have to play an active role in urging people who might feel intimidated to speak out.

Given all these contingencies, I agree with Seibert, Sparrowe, and Liden (see Chapter 8), that overall "we should expect shared leadership to benefit group performance only under certain conditions" (p. 175). One of their concerns is whether all team members share the organization's goals. This is a valid and important point, but, as I have shown, it is not the only relevant contingency.

Seibert et al. also point to the importance of the particular influence tactics used by group members. In an effective group, I believe that the main influence tactic would be an appeal to reason based on the pertinent facts, rather than tactics involving social exchange. Seers et al. distinguish between restricted (one-on-one, quid pro quo) versus generalized social exchange, with the latter involving more indirect exchanges with multiple people spread out across time. They give an example from Ekeh (1974) of A calling the fire department when he sees B's house burning; he is not necessarily expecting B to reciprocate but rather hopes that other people in the neighborhood will reciprocate if they see his house burning. I do not, however, believe that everything that happens in a group necessarily involves a social exchange in the sense of a specific or general quid pro quo expectation. People may call the fire department simply out of good will. Beliefs about what others might do for them at a later date might never enter their minds when they decide to make the call. They call because they believe it is the right thing to do. Nor does the motivation have to involve altruism (self-sacrifice); it may simply reflect good will and empathy. This good will, of course, may dissipate later, if one discovers that one's neighbors, or coworkers, are morally corrupt people.

As Seibert et al. imply, many things can get in the way of group effectiveness and lead to various types of conflict. I would suggest that effective groups need to have at least the following explicit or implicit group norms: (a) doing a good job on the assignment is important (commitment), (b) truth counts (facts are to be taken seriously), (c) you have to give the reasons behind your arguments (respect for reason), and (d) disagreeing with others' ideas is permitted and even encouraged but no personal attacks or hidden agendas are allowed (focus on the task at hand).

This assumes that the group's goal or task or mission is clear; without that, nothing can be accomplished. Hooker and Csikszentmihalyi (see Chapter 10) note that clear, challenging goals accompanied by feedback on progress are a prerequisite of the experience of flow. Assigning a goal does not impede the flow experience so long as people have freedom in determining the means. Hooker and Csikszentmihalyi write, "One of the main concerns of management in this respect is to define clearly the long-term objectives while leaving as much leeway as possible to groups and individuals to decide how to go about reaching them" (p. 230).

Many successful CEOs have followed the practice of assigning goals and then delegating full responsibility, within the limits of the company's core values, for deciding how to achieve them to trusted, skilled subordinates (Locke, 2000). A theory of shared leadership would have to start by identifying what the proper functions of leaders at the team level are, regardless of whether leadership is shared within the team or not. Burke et al. made a start at this by pointing to the importance of such team leader functions as clarifying the mission, developing group norms and skills, and efficacy building. Whether it is practical to shift these various functions to different people over time, as they suggest, remains to be seen.

In sum, I agree with Seibert et al. that the concept of shared influence by itself is too broad an abstraction to be a useful guide to action. What would be necessary would be to specify the conditions that make a group effective.

O'Toole, Galbraith, and Lawler (see Chapter 12) have tried to simplify the issue by discussing shared influence in one specific context, that of co-CEO's. Their Table 12.1 does not, however, inspire confidence that this is a viable, generalizable leadership strategy. Let's consider some of their examples. The Stanford Weill, John Reed team at Citibank failed when Reed was forced out. Steve Jobs took over at

Apple from Steve Wozniak, who did not want to run a company. John Scully got Steve Jobs fired and then was pushed out himself after a lackluster term as CEO. Charles Schwab took back some of David Pottruck's responsibilities. At Morgan Stanley, the Phil Purcell and Jack Mack partnership failed.

Bill Gates was clearly the boss at Microsoft; Steve Ballmer was better described as Gates' right-hand man (Locke, 2000) than as his coequal. Right-hand employees are not literally coequals, as valuable as they may be to CEOs. Michael Eisner was always the boss at Disney even when Frank Wells was there, just as Warren Buffett, despite his modesty, was always the top man at Berkshire Hathaway as was Larry Ellison at Oracle. Right-hand men have played critical roles in many companies, but this does not mean that they have equal power with the CEO. O'Toole et al. describe Jack Welch as having co-leaders, but this is misleading. Welch was a very strong CEO who also used extensive delegation on many *but not all* matters to people he trusted. He spent years getting rid of top executives he did not think could do the job and replacing them with ones he thought were better. The CEO chooses the top managers and can just as easily get rid of them if things do not work out. Rational CEOs will cede responsibility directly in accordance with the capabilities of their direct reports but not to the degree that they will take over the CEO's own job.

I am not familiar with the other companies in their Table 12.1. Successful co-leadership examples such as Noyce and Moore at Intel and Hewlett and Packard at HP may be exceptions. I think successful long-term co-CEOs are just that—exceptions—and I do not think they could be anything more than that. It is almost inevitable that the people at the top will disagree on some, if not many, issues, and it would paralyze decision making if neither had the final say. I would agree with O'Toole et al. that any genuine co-CEO relationship will usually be a very fragile one.

# The Tasks of the Top Leader

Is there a model, then, that is better than the three I have just described? I believe so. But before presenting it, it is necessary to identify what the key tasks of leadership are. I am referring here to the top person in a company, such as its CEO. I will draw here from a previous chapter (Locke, in press).

The core leadership tasks, as I see them, are these:

1. *Vision*—formulating the vision of what the company should be (Locke, 2000). This includes deciding what business or businesses the company should be in and the competitive strategy it will use.

2. *Core values*—deciding what the company will stand for including its basic moral principles (e.g., honesty). Shamir and Lapidot, in the context of Israeli officers' training courses (see Chapter 12), documented the role of shared values in affecting leader-member relationships. Shared values are also important in business organizations, but it is critical that the values that are shared be the right ones. For example, sharing the value of dishonesty will not work. Sometimes, a leader has to change dysfunctional organizational values, which is not very easy to do without strong allies.

3. *Structuring*—making sure the organization's structure supports its strategy.

4. *Selection and training*—hiring good people based on what the company needs and ensuring that they develop any further skills that they need.

5. *Motivating the employees*—There are many aspects involved here, including the use of formal authority, role-modeling, building subordinate confidence, empowerment, goal setting, performance appraisal, recognition, reward, and morale building.

Role-modeling and confidence building are key elements in social-cognitive theory (Bandura, 1986, 1997). Role-modeling refers to learning through observing others, though the effect is not just a matter of rote copying but the product of several cognitive processes (Bandura, 1986). Self-efficacy or task specific confidence is a powerful motivator and operates both at the individual and group levels (Bandura, 1997). Pearce, Gallagher, and Ensley (2002) found that team efficacy, which they labeled potency, was significantly associated with the effectiveness of change management teams. The relevant measurement at the group level would involve either asking each individual member to rate group efficacy and averaging the results or having the group reach a consensus estimate. The former method may be less prone to social biases (Bandura, 1997). Goal setting too operates at both the individual and group levels (Locke & Latham, 1990; O'Leary-Kelly, Martocchio, & Frink, 1994). Self-efficacy or group efficacy promotes the setting of higher goals (Durham, Locke, Poon, & McLeod, 2000). The effects of empowerment (Conger, 2000), recognition (Luthans & Stajkovic, 2000), and rewards (Durham & Bartol, 2000) are well-known.

6. *Communicating*, or fostering communication in every direction throughout the organization.

7. *Team building*, including and especially the top management team.

8. *Promoting change*, which under capitalism is a continually ongoing process.

A full-fledged leadership questionnaire would have to measure all of these facets and more (see Locke & Associates, 1991). Avolio, Sivasubramaniam, Murry, Jung, and Garger (see Chapter 7) developed measures of five facets pertaining to shared (horizontal) leadership: inspiring leadership, intellectual stimulation, individual consideration, contingent reward, and management by exception. Inspiring leadership seems to be a combination of vision, core values, and motivation. It might be desirable to separate these. Intellectual stimulation is not specifically in Locke (in press) and probably should be. Ideally, such stimulation would operate in many different directions in an effective organization (up-down, sideways, and diagonally). The downward part of stimulation would stem, in part, from leaders communicating their vision. Individual consideration seems to be focused mainly on good communication. Management by exception is a negative facet that involves focusing on errors and failures. It would have been helpful for Avolio et al. to include information regarding how these facets were related to group effectiveness. I believe that more facets should be included in any future studies.

Mayo et al. focus on measurement also, including some of the same dimensions as Avolio et al., in order to show how to quantitatively calculate influence networks.

Such quantitative information may be useful in some contexts, but would probably best be supplemented by information regarding the content or substance of what was communicated. By *content*, I do not mean just the topic communicated but what was actually said.

## What Should Not Be Shared

Now let us consider which of these tasks can be properly shared and to what degree. I am not talking here about who has input but rather who has the final say. My view is that great companies (with very few exceptions) cannot function unless led by a single vision. If there were multiple visions with each person having equal influence, as would be the case if there were leadership by a team, then the result would be anarchy. Imagine seven oarsmen in a boat, each rowing in a different direction. The boat would never go anywhere. I do not believe that vision can or should be delegated.

O'Toole, Galbraith, and Lawler claim that "resistance to the notion of shared leadership stems from thousands of years of cultural conditioning" (p. 251). I disagree. I think the resistance stems from reality and the laws of logic. It simply does not work for a ship to have two—or more—captains. You cannot go in more than one direction at a time. It might be argued that the team would rule by consensus, but this is naïve. Groups do not always come to agreement, which means they will accomplish nothing unless one person takes charge. Furthermore, the requirements of consensus may lead to a vision that is so watered down that it means nothing. All people are not equally visionary and team management would simply cripple the best mind in the group.

I also believe that core values must be pushed from the top down. They must be reflected not only in CEOs' words but also in their daily behavior, including the actions the leaders takes to reward and punish those who foster or reject those values. Since people differ in their values, leaving this up to the group, again, would lead to chaos. For example, one person might put a high priority on honesty and another might let it slide and even promote a less than honest person. This could motivate others to conclude, "I had better be dishonest too if I want to get ahead." The recent Enron scandal points to the need for moral leadership at the top of corporations. The failure to set firm moral standards at the top can lead to a poisoning of the whole organization. The CEO has to have the willingness and authority to fire those who breach core values.

CEOs must also choose the members of their top management team. Hooker and Csikszentmihalyi observe, "One basic leadership skill is to evaluate the special strengths of each person" (p. 231). As Houghton, Neck, and Manz note (see Chapter 6), leaders must pick people with the skills that the company needs to implement the strategy, especially in cases in which the leader personally lacks those skills (e.g., finance or marketing). Leaders also have to ensure that they choose team members with whom they can work effectively and who can work smoothly with each other. If team members were to choose each other, they could easily form a cabal to undermine the CEO and might also choose peers who do not have the breadth of outlook or skills that the CEO needs.

Appraising top managers should be done by the CEO, especially to ensure that core values are being put into action and that the kinds of people needed to make the core strategy succeed are being properly rewarded through promotions and bonuses. The CEO also needs to ensure consistency of practices between people and over time.

CEOs must also play at least a major role in structuring and restructuring the organization. Their vision needs to encompass the whole organization; they must figure out how the parts are best fitted together.

Let me emphasize that none of this precludes the CEO from getting ideas from below—an issue I will have more to say about shortly. The critical point is that even though leaders may have input from many different people on many different issues, they must have the final say—especially because the input from others may be contradictory and at odds with the needs of the organization.

## What Can Be, At Least in Part, Shared

Selection and training at the lower levels can be delegated, although if training is to be company-wide to support a new strategic initiative, as in Work Out or Six Sigma at GE (Slater, 1999), then this must be led and mandated by the CEO. Otherwise, some managers, having many other tasks to perform, will just neglect it.

Motivation must occur at all levels, with the CEO focusing mainly on motivating the top management team. The CEO's vision can be a motivator if it inspires people. The CEO, as noted, must always be a role model but so must those below. Goal setting, empowerment, confidence building, and recognition should be practiced throughout the organization. The CEO may set the goals at the top but can properly delegate the rest.

Morale building is complex. If the company is doing well and the CEO is perceived as knowledgeable and honest, and if a good top management team has been picked, morale will usually be high. When the company is in a crisis, however, the CEO may have to step in and appear before the troops at every level to explain what the company will do to resolve the crisis and to quash false rumors.

CEOs may need to play some role in motivating information sharing. They can do this directly within the top management team. Jack Welch spent a lot of his time in meetings encouraging members of the Corporate Excellence Council to share their knowledge and discoveries with each other. CEOs should encourage information sharing throughout the company, including, among other means, by purchasing technology that facilitates it.

Team building below the level of the top management team can be delegated. Organizational change can occur at all different levels in an organization. The CEO will need to lead it, as noted, if it is a company-wide change program. Jack Welch even tied managers' bonuses to their involvement in the Six Sigma program designed to improve quality.

The critical point here is that delegation or empowerment, though a very valuable tool for motivating and fully using the skills of subordinates, must be circumscribed. It is not open-ended or unlimited. Houghton et al. argue that "the vertical leader should empower team members by providing the team with the full authority to make decisions, solve problems, set objectives, and develop and pursue appropriate courses of action" (p. 125). The critical word here is "appropriate." In the context of my model of leadership, appropriate would mean consonant with the CEO's vision, the company's core values, and the goals of the organization. I support Hooker and Csikszentmihalyi's view that the leader "must be able to communicate a vision of uncompromising excellence to the rest of the organization" (p. 230). This needs to precede empowerment.

Houghton et al. argue that the vertical leader's main function should be "to serve as a facilitator of the shared leadership process" (p. 133). In my view, this view of leadership is far too narrow and would put the organization in real danger because critical decisions that need to be made at the top would not be successfully addressed. The same principle holds for self-leadership (Manz & Sims, 2001), which Houghton et al. also recommend. This is a form of delegation or empowerment, but to individuals. Like team empowerment, self-leadership only makes sense if the individual is committed to the organization's vision, core values, and goals. Outside of this context, it could only lead to organizational anarchy. Passive leadership can be just as dangerous as authoritarian leadership. But one does not have to choose between Scylla and Charybdis. The real alternative to the false alternatives of mindless obedience versus leaderless chaos is *empowerment within a context.*

A good example of this is AES Corporation, a maker of power plants. The company uses extreme delegation at the plant level, which has served them well over the years, but this did not save them from the consequences of a failed company strategy, mainly involving their plants in South America, which has almost destroyed the value of their stock. Empowerment does not make up for lack of vision.

Self-leadership is supposed to be accompanied by self-rewards. I agree, but I would not restrict these just to tangible rewards like a restaurant meal. Personal pride is also very important and the leader can encourage this. Self-rewards alone, however, simply will not do. People need justice from their organizations. Distributive and procedural justice have very powerful motivational effects (Greenberg, 2000). If people keep performing well and are told to keep rewarding themselves but get no organizational rewards like raises and promotions, they will feel treated unjustly and will probably look for work elsewhere, especially if they are highly competent.

Houghton et al. also stress the idea of encouraging thought self-leadership. Their examples include altering erroneous beliefs, positive as opposed to negative self-talk (i.e., thinking), opportunity thinking, and overcoming obstacles thinking. Such thinking processes could surely be trained (e.g., see Millman & Latham, 2001). This is an excellent idea, but I think the scope of such training could be expanded. Other aspects of thinking that could be taught at all levels of the organization include independent thinking (using one's own judgment and not blindly agreeing with what others say), reality-focused thinking (taking facts seriously and not evading what is true or acting just on emotion—also note that positive thinking must not blind one to real problems that need addressing), long-range thinking (not looking only at the short-range consequences of decisions but also long-range effects), and moral thinking (considering moral principles when taking actions).

## The CEO As Listener and Information Seeker

The question may be asked, *Should CEOs listen to others' opinions regarding any of the above issues, including those that are their sole prerogative?* My answer is a strong yes, even with respect to formulating the vision, choosing core values, and choosing the top management team. *CEOs should listen to anybody—inside or outside the company—who has a potentially good idea about any subject relevant to the company's mission.* To fail to do this carries the implication that the leader is omniscient, a very irrational premise. In fact, CEOs should go way beyond just listening, which implies passivity. They should have active minds (Locke, 2000) and proactively seek out knowledge from other people. If CEOs choose very capable people to work for them, then inevitably they are going to know things that CEOs do not know. To hire smart people and then fail to listen to their ideas is a contradiction and also self-destructive.

As noted earlier, however, in the end the CEO has to make the final decision about critical matters like vision, core values, appraising top managers, and structure. This is why independence is an important CEO trait (Locke, 2000). Independence in this context does not mean functioning as a loner—this accusation is just a red herring; rather, it means using their own rational judgment after considering all the relevant information that is available. Critical decisions cannot be made by just using majority opinion; the majority is often wrong. CEOs have to look at the reasoning behind others' opinions and decide if that is commensurate their own observations.

Fletcher and Käufer's assault on independence goes so far as to stress the desirability of dissolving the boundaries between self and other; but this a metaphysical impossibility. Each person is separate from every other and there are no direct connections between the bodies or brains of different people. Denying this, even metaphorically, is to revolt against reality. Focusing solely on relationships between people, even if done rationally, omits the fact that organizations have to make real products or services and have to compete in the real world against other real companies and make real profits. Relationships in the business context are a means to an end, not an end in themselves.

If trust in competence and morality is high and if it is not an area of CEO prerogative, then they can properly delegate entire projects to people and teams without even asking their opinion. In fact, no CEO could succeed without delegating thousands of decisions to others because one person simply would not have the time or the knowledge to do everything in any but a very small organization. This fact is sometimes offered as some kind of profound insight, but it seems like an almost self-evident truth.

# The Integrated Model

So what, then, would be the ideal leadership model? This is shown in Figure 13.1d. Note that it is a combination of the first three models. Observe first that there is real leadership. Some things do go from the top down. Second, there is upward influence; the CEO can seek and get ideas from those below. Normally, the upward direction of influence would be weaker than the top-down influence because of the nature of hierarchical relationships. Third, there is teamwork and the top management team members influence each other.

This preserves the potential benefits of the other three models without their disadvantages. There is still leadership, but it is focused mainly on certain core issues that need to be the product, however much consultation precedes the final decision, of one mind. I, therefore, agree with Cox, Pearce, and Perry that shared leadership supplements but does not replace hierarchical leadership. This model allows capable subordinates to influence the CEO. For example, Jack Welch, who was a very strong leader, got the idea of pushing ahead with the Six Sigma initiative mainly from his own subordinates. But he had to make the decision that it would be a company-wide program and that dedication to the program in action would become part of the top managers' performance appraisals.

In actuality, there should be additional arrows going downwards and upwards to people below the level of the top management team. CEOs should not be so isolated that their only communications are with that team. E-mail technology allows a CEO to communicate with anyone in the organization, though in a large organization the volume of mail would require some screening. The model allows for delegation to the team when appropriate, although this cannot be shown graphically. The model also shows mutual influence among the top management team members, although, as noted, such influence by itself does not guarantee team effectiveness. Again, I agree with Cox et al. who argue that leaders need to play a role in fostering shared leadership among top management team members. For example, they need to establish group norms that encourage information sharing and the legitimacy of disagreement.

The model could be extended to lower levels so that members of the team lead their own units and, in turn, have a subordinate management team. The details here are, however, a bit different. Unit leaders can have their own vision for a unit, but it should reinforce and not contradict the company vision or strategy. Nor should unit leaders promote core values that contradict company values. They may have reward authority for those several layers below them, but not necessarily for direct reports if the CEO has chosen to make those decisions. Here, the unit manager would have only input to the CEO.

Not everything, however, needs to be or should be done in teams (Locke et al., 2001). Very smart, creative, driven people, as Cox et al. astutely observe, may be stifled in a team setting and may also overwhelm the other team members. It is often best to let such people work alone and then present their ideas to those who need to approve of them before implementation.

I do not want to imply that this model has now solved the problem of effective leadership. It has not. It has only laid out directions of influence, the core tasks of leadership, and a suggested allocation of authority for these tasks. Leadership is an art more than a science. The role of the CEO is to orchestrate everything with the help of competent, trustworthy subordinates so that, in the end, the company makes a profit.

It is very incomplete to imply that all the leader has to do is delegate authority and encourage everyone to influence everyone else and then everything is solved. Real leadership is much more difficult than that. People are not equal in their intelligence, reasoning ability, drive, and knowledge. Fletcher and Käufer deny the importance of any individual characteristics in leaders, arguing instead that it is "a social process." What is missing in this formulation is the fact that some people are much better at carrying out the processes involved in successful leadership than others (Locke, 2000). Especially critical is the leader's ability to think inductively (Locke, in press)—to examine thousands of facts and numerous context factors and tie them together into a viable competitive strategy. This is just plain hard mental work. Subordinates and outsiders can help, but they cannot do the leader's own thinking.

It should not be assumed that the requirements of leadership in different domains are the same. Corporate leadership is very different from military leadership and both are very different from political leadership, even though they all may have some elements in common. My focus here has been on corporate (profit-making) leadership.

Obviously, there are many interesting research questions implied in the model I have proposed. Most interesting would be studies of what types of decisions more effective leaders (versus less effective ones) actually share and the form in which the sharing occurs (e.g., consultation versus group consensus). This would include the actual content of the decisions. This approach would involve a more sophisticated type of study than simply asking about the degree of participation or delegation in general. Obviously, I would predict that the integrated model (Figure 13.1d) would generally be more effective than the other models. The directions of influence alone, however, do not tell the whole story, because some leaders have more intelligence, skill, and energy than others do. Leaders who are not visionary, who do not see what's happening in the market, and who do not lead their companies in the right direction will not succeed no matter what model they use.

I strongly disagree with those that say the leader is no longer important on the grounds that this is now the age of groupism (Locke et al., 2001). I think that the leader is more important that ever. The high turnover among CEO's is one indication of how hard it is to find great leaders in our very complex and fast-moving economy. Shared leadership is not, by itself, a solution to this problem but rather a tool that an able leader will use, among others, to accomplish the tasks that leadership requires.

# References

Bandura, A. (1986). *Social foundational of thought and action: A social-cognitive theory.* Englewood Cliffs, NJ: Prentice Hall.

Bandura, A. (1997). *Self-efficacy: The exercise of control.* New York: Freeman.

Conger, J. (2000). Motivate performance through empowerment. In E. A. Locke (Ed.), *Handbook of principles of organizational behavior.* New York: Blackwell.

Durham C. C., & Bartol, K. M. (2000). Pay for performance. In E. A. Locke (Ed.), *Handbook of principles of organizational behavior.* New York: Blackwell.

Durham, C. C., Locke, E. A., Poon, J., & McLeod, P. L. (2000). Effects of group goals and time pressure on group efficacy, information seeking strategy and performance. *Human Performance, 13,* 115-138.

Ekeh, P. P. (1974). *Social exchange theory: The two traditions.* Cambridge, MA: Harvard University Press.

Greenberg, J. (2000). Promote procedural justice to enhance worker acceptance of outcomes. In E. A. Locke (Ed.), *Handbook of principles of organizational behavior.* New York: Blackwell.

Locke, E. A. (2000). *The prime movers: Traits of the great wealth creators.* New York: AMACOM.

Locke, E. A. (in press). Foundations for a theory of leadership in profit-making organizations. In S. Murphy (Ed.), *The future of leadership development.* Mahwah, NJ: Lawrence Erlbaum.

Locke, E. A., Alavi, M., & Wagner, J. (1997). Participation in decision-making: An information exchange perspective. In G. Ferris (Ed.), *Research in personnel and human resources management: Vol. 15* (pp. 293-331). Greenwich, CT: JAI Press.

Locke, E. A., & Associates (1991). *The essence of leadership.* New York: Lexington Books.

Locke, E. A., & Latham, G. P. (1990). *A theory of goal setting and task performance.* Englewood Cliffs, NJ: Prentice Hall.

Locke, E. A., Tirnauer, D., Roberson, Q., Goldman, B., Latham, M., & Weldon, E. (2001). The importance of the individual in an age of groupism. In M. Turner (Ed.), *Groups at work: Theory and research.* Mahwah, NJ: Lawrence Erlbaum.

Luthans, F., & Stajkovic, A. D. (2000). Provide recognition for performance improvement. In E. A. Locke (Ed.), *Handbook of principles of organizational behavior.* New York: Blackwell.

Manz, C. C., & Sims, H. P. (2001). *The new superleadership: Leading others to lead themselves.* San Francisco, CA: Berret-Koehler.

Millman, Z., & Latham, G. P. (2001). Increasing re-employment through training in verbal self-guidance. In M. Erez, U. Kleinbeck, & H. K. Thierry (Eds.), *Work motivation in the context of a globalizing economy.* Mahwah, NJ: Lawrence Erlbaum.

O'Leary-Kelly, A., Martocchio, J., & Frink, D. (1994). A review of the influence of group goals on group performance. *Academy of Management Journal, 37,* 1285-1301.

Pearce, C. L., Gallagher, C., & Ensley, M. (2002). Confidence at the group level of analysis: A longitudinal investigation of the relationship between potency and team effectiveness. *Journal of Occupational and Organizational Psychology, 75,* 30.

Rand, A. (1993). *The fountainhead.* New York: Signet.

Slater, R. (1999). *Jack Welch and the GE way.* New York: McGraw-Hill.

# CHAPTER 14

# A Landscape of Opportunities

## Future Research on Shared Leadership

*Jay A. Conger*

*Craig L. Pearce*

Though this volume conveys the impression of significant progress in our understanding of the dynamics of shared leadership, we would argue that the field is still in its infancy. Like other fledgling fields, the initial research on shared leadership was shaped by a pioneering but small group of individuals curious about the phenomenon (Avolio, Jung, Murry, & Sivasubramaniam, 1996; Ensley & Pearce, 2000; Ensley, Pearson, & Pearce, in press; Pearce, 1997; Pearce, Perry, & Sims, 2001; Pearce & Sims, 2000, 2002; Perry, Pearce, & Sims, 1999; Seers, 1996). These initial "scholar entrepreneurs" and the widening circle of scholars who have joined them in this volume will continue to have a profound influence on the field. After all, they have established the first models, developed the first survey instruments, and laid the groundwork for what must be studied in the future. At the same time, their efforts may paradoxically narrow the focus of where and how research on shared leadership is conducted in the future. There is a strong tendency for later generations of researchers to build on existing models rather than to reinvent or challenge them (Kuhn, 1970). In this chapter, our aim is to counteract such a tendency at this formative stage in the field's life. We believe that this can best be accomplished by highlighting the critical gaps in our knowledge. This exercise will hopefully broaden the agenda for future research rather than narrow it. For example, it will already be apparent to readers that numerous dimensions of the phenomenon have received little or no attention. There has been no real inquiry into the liabilities of shared leadership or into the impact of cross-cultural factors. We have only a rudimentary understanding of the "fine-grained" dynamics of shared leadership. Our knowledge about the process of implementing shared leadership is at best simplistic. In other words, the shared leadership field remains a mother lode of research opportunities.

Our task in this closing chapter, therefore, is to survey the landscape for where the future research opportunities reside. At this stage, we feel that there are at least seven domains of opportunity. They include (a) the relationship between shared leadership and vertical leadership, (b) the fine-grained dynamics of how leadership is shared in group and organizational settings, (c) the steps required to effectively implement shared leadership, (d) the outcomes associated with shared leadership settings, (e) measurement of the phenomenon, (f) cross-cultural influences, and (g) the liabilities and limits of shared leadership. What follows is our description of the research opportunities in each of these domains.

Before we begin, it is instructive to reiterate the definition of shared leadership that we articulated in our opening chapter. We define shared leadership as a dynamic, interactive influence process among individuals in work groups in which the objective is to lead one another to the achievement of group goals. This influence process often involves peer, or lateral, influence and at other times involves upward or downward hierarchical influence. The key distinction between shared leadership and traditional models of leadership is that the influence process involves more than just downward influence on subordinates by an appointed or elected leader (see Pearce & Sims, 2000).

# The Relationship Between Shared and Vertical Leadership

Although researchers in social and organizational psychology have long accepted leadership as a group or organizational phenomenon, their focus has been on the behaviors of a single individual who is either the formally appointed leader or else the most influential member of the group. The relationship between this individual and group members is typically a vertical one—superior versus subordinates—hence the term "vertical leadership." Although some have suggested that vertical and shared leadership are mutually exclusive, several authors in this volume have raised the intriguing question of whether vertical leadership and shared leadership might be dependent on one another. For example, to what extent are the actions of the vertical leader critical catalysts in the promotion of shared leadership? Houghton, Neck, and Manz would argue that an enlightened vertical leader—one oriented toward the development of self-leadership in team members—is indeed the primary catalyst. Without this individual, shared leadership is less likely to occur. Does the absence, therefore, of an enlightened vertical leader preclude the possibility of shared leadership from occurring in traditional team and organization settings? Alternately, might it be possible to develop shared leadership without a vertical leader to initiate the process under certain conditions? Questions such as these require extensive research to be adequately answered. In essence, there are at least three areas to be investigated: (a) what roles vertical leaders can play as catalysts or facilitators of shared leadership, (b) in what ways does vertical leadership act as a barrier to expressions of shared leadership?, and (c) in what ways can vertical leadership and shared leadership complement one another to enhance the effectiveness of a group or organization?

Another issue concerning the two forms of leadership is the question of suitable contexts. Are there certain settings that are more conducive to the coexistence of the two forms? Are there settings that by their very nature preclude one form over the other? For example, in team settings in need of strong direction setting, might vertical leadership be the more effective form, assuming that the vertical leader is well-informed? In situations requiring high levels of consensus and ownership, is shared leadership the more effective form? Are self-managing teams unlikely to see enduring expressions of vertical leadership given their mandate and norms? From research examining questions like these, it is quite conceivable that contingency models of vertical versus shared leadership could be developed. In addition, research needs to examine shared leadership in a wider range of settings. For example, O'Toole, Galbraith, and Lawler explore shared leadership at the very top of the organization and argue that it is quite feasible. Locke, on the other hand, has argued to the contrary. In general, the empirical research to date has been limited in examining samples up and down the hierarchy, among different industries, and in specialized team settings such as strategic alliances.

Finally, there is a set of interesting research issues surrounding the life cycle dynamics of groups. For example, are we more likely to see expressions of vertical leadership at the start of a group's life? Are we more likely to observe shared leadership at later stages? Are crises likely to cause a shift from one form to another in the group? Will shared leadership assume different forms at the various life stages of a working group? For instance, the display of shared leadership would seem to be qualitatively different at Tuckman's (1965) "performing" stage than it would be at his "forming" stage. Questions such as these need to be answered.

## The Dynamics of Shared Leadership

It is clear that we need a far more fine-grained understanding of how shared leadership unfolds within group and organizational settings. At this stage, our knowledge is still fairly simplistic. There are at least five areas surrounding the process of shared leadership that are in need of significant investigation by researchers. These include (a) the roles or bases of leadership that can be shared by members of a group; (b) the demands, events, or processes that trigger the sharing of leadership among members of a group; (c) the factors that facilitate the display of shared leadership; (d) the influence approaches that are most conducive within a context of shared leadership; and (e) the life cycle or evolutionary stages that occur in settings where leadership is shared. We begin our discussion by focusing on the first area.

*The Bases or Roles of Leadership.* It is apparent that most of the authors in this volume see the process of shared leadership as dependent on certain bases of leadership. For example, in a given team and organizational setting, there is a broad range of leadership roles demanded over time to successfully address organizational challenges. A single individual—the formally appointed leader—is unlikely to possess great strength in all the necessary competences. In addition, a formally appointed leader may have strong preferences for playing certain roles and not others. Finally, teams are increasingly composed of individuals who are multifunctional, highly skilled, and possess leadership competences themselves. It therefore makes sense to take advantage of individual members' strengths to complement the formally appointed leader. Given these conditions, leadership is optimized when it is distributed among group members. Shared leadership is therefore an effective solution to a fundamental dilemma: No single individual possesses the capacity to effectively play all possible leadership roles within a group or organizational setting.

Although both the leadership and team literature have proposed a broad range of leadership roles, we might ask whether all of these roles are relevant under shared leadership and instead whether certain ones are more salient especially in facilitating leadership transitions. For example, Hackman (1987) describes a range of leadership roles such as processing information, decision making, coordinating and monitoring performance, developing and enforcing group norms, and planning task performance strategies. Kozlowski and colleagues (Kozlowski, Gully, Salas, & Cannon-Bowers, 1996) identify four leadership functions: mentor, instructor, coach, and facilitator. The charismatic/transformational leadership literature (Bass, 1985; Conger & Kanungo, 1998) offers additional competences. Locke offers a list of eight in his chapter. Pearce and Sims (2002) identify twenty leader behaviors that they group into five overarching types of leadership: aversive, directive, transactional, transformational, and empowering. We suspect that not all of these leadership roles have a similar level of importance in shared leadership situations. Some seem more likely to facilitate transitions. Some may take on greater significance depending on specific task demands or life cycle stages. At this early stage in the field's development, it would be extremely useful to have a comprehensive, well-defined set of leadership bases on which to explore and test hypotheses.

*Influence Tactics Under Shared Leadership.* In this volume, Locke as well as Seibert, Sparrowe, and Liden raise the question of whether certain influence tactics may be more appropriate than others in shared leadership settings. For example, Locke argues that the main influence tactic should be "an appeal to reason based on the pertinent facts" rather than tactics involving social exchange (p. 275). In contrast, Seibert and his colleagues believe that tactics involving social exchange are appropriate in shared leadership settings. They also argue that one should not expect a simple and direct relationship between the behavioral influence strategies used in a group and aspects of the group's effectiveness. In addition, the patterns of influence within a shared leadership setting may be shaped by coalition dynamics or minority influence.

The issue of influence tactics is an especially critical one deserving extensive investigation. Pearce and Sims (2002) offer some interesting insights here. They found several significant effects of their five specific types of shared leadership. For example, they found shared aversive leadership to be negatively related to team self-ratings of team effectiveness. They also found shared directive leadership to be negatively related to manager and internal customer ratings of team effectiveness. In contrast, they found shared transformational leadership to be positively related to manager, internal customer, and team self-ratings of team effectiveness. Finally, they found shared empowering leadership to be positively related to team self-ratings of team effectiveness. Pearce and Sims's results not withstanding, our knowledge at this stage in the field's life remains still incomplete and would benefit from further extensive investigations.

*Triggers for Sharing Leadership.* Our understanding of the transition triggers for the sharing of leadership is particularly important area for future research. Pearce (1997) has raised the possibility of a process of "serial emergence." In other words, individuals will assume a leadership role as attention turns from one task to another. Individuals possessing the greater capability of leading others to address that particular demand assume the leadership role. Shared leadership, therefore, becomes a pattern of rotations in which the triggers for one to lead are based on *task or demand transitions.* This seems like a simplistic conceptualization of what is most likely a very complex process.

We expect that managing these transitions is a particularly difficult challenge in developing shared leadership. For example, we know that cognitive schema are resistant to change (see Sims & Gioia, 1986). Thus, when one member of a team has been categorized as the "leader" and the other members have been categorized as "followers," it seems likely that the followers may unintentionally continue to defer to the initially identified leader simply due to the inertial effects of their cognitive schema. Research in the emergent leadership literature also suggests that the transition may be difficult to manage. We could find no study in the emergent leadership literature that identified a leadership transition from one person to another. Given these challenges, how and why do certain situations trigger a transition to shared leadership? One might also ask: Is there a special class of triggers that *initiate* shared leadership? After initiation of a state of shared leadership, are there additional types of triggers that facilitate ongoing transitions? We may also be able to classify transition triggers around time frames. There may be short time-frame triggers that have to do with stages in a specific task facing a group. On the other hand, there may be triggers tied to longer-term, developmental stages in the life of the group itself. In the latter case, the developmental stage model offered by Kozlowski and his colleagues (1996), in which the four functional roles of leaders—mentor, instructor, coach, and facilitator—come into play by life stages, is one possible model.

Beyond the possibility of classes of triggers, it is conceivable that there is a broad range of supporting factors that facilitate leadership transition triggers. Are there ways that teams could enhance the effectiveness of triggers? What might these be? For example, do trigger points need to be clearly articulated by the team to be effective or is it a more emergent process? Do certain norms need to be in place for triggers to work consistently?

The domain of transition triggers is rich with research opportunities. On the agenda for future research, therefore, should be work that teases out the following: (a) what are typical triggers to the sharing of leadership?, (b) are certain triggers more influential than others?, (c) how do situational determinants shape specific triggers?, and (d) can triggers be classified by typologies such as time frames tied to phases in tactical challenges versus developmental or life cycles of a group?

*Facilitating Factors.* Another set of research questions concerns the *facilitators* of shared leadership—in other words, those factors that encourage its display or expression. A broad range of factors have been proposed in this volume and in the literature—most of which have been poorly explored. Among the more important factors are the following: (a) task competence of members; (b) task complexity; (c) shared knowledge and mental models of group members; (d) leadership proto- types; (e) power, influence, and status of individual members; (f) familiarity; (g) membership turnover; (h) group diversity; (i) member proximity; and (j) group size. A discussion of each factor follows.

*Task Competence.* It has been suggested that task competence is a critical facilitator of shared leadership. For example, when group members become highly skilled at their task requirements, one would expect group members to more actively engage in shared leadership. Similarly, wide differences in individual task competence among group members should hinder the emergence of shared leadership. A lack of task competence presumably makes it difficult for individual members to take on additional and demanding roles such as leading the group. The most immediate demand becomes task mastery and not the demonstration of leadership. In addi- tion, a self-perception that one has limited task competence may undermine the sense of self-efficacy needed to assert oneself in a leadership role. Team members may also be reluctant to accept someone in a leadership role who has not yet demonstrated strong task competence. Such hypotheses have yet to be adequately confirmed and therefore are fertile ground for exploration. An intriguing research question is whether task competence and leadership competence are one and the same in the perceptions of group members. Conversely, if they are perceived as separate competences, are leadership competences more influential than actual task competences?

*Task Complexity.* The level of complexity in tasks confronting the group may also play a critical role in the successful implementation of shared leadership. Unfortunately, much of the research to date that is related to this issue has been conducted in laboratory studies with often a single shared goal. As Seers, Keller, and Wilkerson point out in Chapter 4, rarely do organizational groups work with a single shared goal. Multiple and complex tasks may facilitate shared leadership given that no one individual is likely to possess all the skills necessary to address all task demands. Therefore, it has been suggested that greater task complexity facili- tates shared leadership especially under conditions involving interdependencies that require complementary skills and abilities (Cox, Pearce, & Perry, this volume; Pearce & Sims, 2000). For example, Steiner's (1976) typology of tasks reveals that groups tend to outperform individuals under conditions in which tasks are highly integrative. On the surface, this is a very appealing hypothesis, but it requires validation.

*Shared Knowledge and Mental Models.* Burke, Fiore, and Salas argue that before leadership roles can be shared by group members, there must be certain knowledge or mental models that are shared among team members. This knowledge gives rise to the development of a shared situation assessment among team members. But it is not enough that team members have a common understanding of the situation and its demands. There must also be a shared recognition among members that, due to environmental demands, the leadership function needs to or is about to change. A climate must therefore be created, such that team members feel that it is acceptable to have fluid leadership roles. This involves not only accepting the fact that some ambiguity is to be expected, but also that members are comfortable with taking guidance and cues from different people, dependent on who is currently leading the team. The confluence of these enabling factors is a smooth transference of leadership from one member to another and the facilitation of adaptive team behaviors. Given that this hypothesis presented by Burke et al. is theoretical and speculative, there is a significant amount of research to be done to empirically test their ideas. One of the first challenges facing researchers, however, will be the issue of how best to operationalize their concepts for study. These mental models seem likely to be built to some extent around tacit knowledge that is difficult for researchers to access. In addition, there are a number of related research issues. For example, how are these shared mental models developed in a manner that is most supportive of shared leadership? Are there specific domains of knowledge that are particularly important in the case of shared leadership? Are there interventions that can accelerate the development of the appropriate shared mental models? What experiences lead a group to form mental models such that they know the leadership function needs to change and to whom it needs to change? Similarly, what experiences shape mental models in which team members are comfortable with the ambiguity associated with the constant shifting of leadership among the group? These research questions would most likely require in-depth and longitudinal qualitative studies to find satisfactory answers.

*Leadership Prototypes.* The extent to which leadership can be shared within a group or organizational setting may be strongly influenced by individual biases around what constitutes leadership. As several researchers (e.g. Lord, Foti, & De Vader, 1984; Lord & Maher, 1993; Phillips & Lord, 1982) have noted, individuals are classified as leaders when they resemble cognitive prototypes (e.g., implicit leadership theory). In other words, group members expect individuals who fit their leadership prototypes to act as leaders whether these individuals have the capacity to do so or not. In contrast, group members will discount other members as leaders if they do not fit these prototypes. As such, shared leadership may not emerge in groups in which a large number of the individual members have strong cognitive biases about what constitutes leadership—especially if their prototypes are built around a narrow range of behaviors and dispositions. On the other hand, prototypes that include dimensions of shared leadership behavior would presumably be more favorable. Future research that examines the presence, extent, and nature (e.g., narrowness of the schema comprising the prototypes) of leadership prototypes and their impact on the expression of shared leadership would be valuable. Equally useful would be investigations around interventions that aim at altering leadership prototypes so that shared leadership can be more effectively promoted.

*Power, Influence, and Status.* One of the issues raised by Seers, Keller, and Wilkerson in their chapter is the question of a group's dispersion of power and influence and its influence on shared leadership. Their argument is straightforward: Greater dispersion of power and influence enhances the likelihood of shared leadership. Although the research to date has confirmed that distributed influence does facilitate the sharing of tasks, consideration, and activity roles, no one has looked at this issue specifically in terms of shared leadership. This is an important area for future investigations.

Tied to power is the notion of status differentials. As Seers and his colleagues point out, status differentials within groups are inevitable (Bales, 1958; Carter, 1954; Slater, 1955). Moreover, it is usually the leadership positions that are reserved for the highest status individuals. As such, this tendency should undermine expressions of shared leadership. Therefore, in the cases in which shared leadership does occur, how are status differentials perceived and treated? Other questions raised by this issue include the following: Is there a threshold level of status differentials that makes shared leadership impossible? Can groups simply impose norms around status that minimize or downplay the influence of status and in turn facilitate shared leadership?

Pearce and Sims (2002) also raise the question of what happens in groups when all members possess very high needs for personalized power. Under such a scenario, it seems unlikely that individuals would pull together and subjugate their individual agendas to the higher purpose of the group. It would be interesting to test group members in organizational settings in which membership is commonly associated with high needs for personal power, such as investment banking, to see if indeed their hypothesis is correct.

*Personal Attraction and Familiarity.* Another potential facilitator worthy of investigation is the extent to which team members perceive each other as likable and rate each other's abilities favorably (Feldman, 1973). Team members' appreciation for one another may open individual members to greater influence by one another. As Seers and his coauthors note, interpersonal attraction often results in a greater dispersion of power—a prerequisite of environments conducive to shared leadership.

*Member Turnover.* Turnover may play a role in shared leadership. The findings in the chapter by Avolio, Sivasubramaniam, Murry, Jung, and Garger suggest that high turnover appears to affect the development of a collective identity and in turn perceptions of shared leadership. In other words, some settings may encourage rapid turnover in membership or short life spans for working groups that in turn hinder shared leadership. Special project teams or rotational assignments would be examples. Under conditions as these, how stable and effective will shared leadership be?

*Diversity.* Mayo, Meindl, and Pastor discuss team heterogeneity and homogeneity along the lines of social versus informational diversity. They suggest that these two dimensions of diversity may have important consequences for shared leadership. Specifically, they hypothesize that social diversity may encourage more vertical or centralized leadership whereas informational diversity will likely promote greater shared leadership. This is an intriguing question and one deserving of serious exploration. Knight et al. (1999) found that decision-making style mediates the relationship between diversity in top management teams and consensus on organizational strategy. Since decision-making style is highly related to shared leadership, it follows that group diversity characteristics will influence both the form and display of shared leadership. In addition to these forms of diversity, what other dimensions of diversity might play a role in either facilitating or hindering expressions of shared leadership? This is a particularly rich area for future explorations.

*Proximity.* The physical distance between team or organizational members may influence expressions of shared leadership. On the one hand, geographic dispersion should make shared leadership more difficult. For example, from the standpoint of coordination and clearing of information, it is far easier to have a central individual as the leader. On the other hand, as Cox, Pearce, and Perry argue in this volume, shared leadership may be particularly valuable in such situations. After all, shared leadership may allow the team to be more responsive since leadership is distributed. For example, individuals in the group may be exposed to opportunities or dilemmas that they can quickly address if they have the freedom to assume a leadership role. Therefore, it is important that we begin to investigate shared leadership in settings where members are geographically dispersed (little proximity) such as in virtual teams or in teams built around organizational alliances or in multicountry teams. In addition, factors such as technologies that enable location transparency, the role of legal or contractual barriers, and organizational support systems such as knowledge management processes would need to be examined in these investigations.

*Group Size.* Cox et al. suggest that the number of team members plays a role in shared leadership. As the size of the group increases, the ability of a group to sustain shared leadership diminishes in large part due to problems with building close working relationships. In essence, a large number of members in a group create a proximity barrier. Conversely, one might ask whether a group could be too small to effectively sustain shared leadership. In other words, there may not be enough individuals present in the group who possess the requisite range of leadership skills beyond the formal leader. Research questions that follow include these: Is there an ideal size of group members to sustain shared leadership? What is the threshold range at which the sheer number of members hinders the expression of shared leadership? Can a group be too small if its membership is missing an adequate dispersion of leadership competences?

*Life-Cycle Issues.* The reliability and stability of shared leadership over time is an issue demanding serious investigation. Most of the research to date has not been longitudinal in nature. We have little knowledge about whether shared leadership can be a long term, stable phenomena within a group. Consider, for example, situations in which teams remain intact over periods of several years and are composed of complementary others in terms of functional background or expertise. It could be argued that shared leadership is more likely to appear in such situations. The argument is a simple one: The leadership skills of team members have had an opportunity to develop, and team members have developed an understanding and appreciation for one another's capabilities to lead under differing conditions. On the other hand, as the group evolves, one or a few individuals in a group may consistently demonstrate greater leadership capability within the group. In return, they will be awarded with more formal leadership status by group members—in essence, fostering a vertical leadership model in the group over time. Which of these scenarios is the more common case? Are there certain situational variables that can mitigate against the trajectory toward vertical leadership? Longitudinal research will be needed to answer these thorny questions.

# Implementing Shared Leadership

How does a team successfully migrate from a vertical leadership model toward a shared one? How does a team establish a shared leadership approach from its initiation? Are there "best practices" and interventions that can facilitate the effective implementation of shared leadership? From the standpoint of managerial practice, these are a number of the more intriguing research questions. From the chapters by Cox et al., Hooker and Csikszentmihalyi, Fletcher and Käufer, Houghton et al., and O'Toole et al., we have some sense of what leaders and team members can do to facilitate and sustain shared leadership. But little research has been conducted that directly examines issues of implementation. In addition, researchers have tended to focus at the group level rather than the organizational level of analysis. As a result, we know little about the influence of organizational culture, design, and politics on the expression of shared leadership. For example, can shared leadership be successfully implemented in organizational settings where the culture values top-down and vertical forms of leadership? Hooker and Csikszentmihalyi's chapter would suggest not. They would also argue that organizations that do not value excellence or those that do not possess clear goals are equally problematic for shared leadership. Is this the case, or could organizational mavericks or remote operations still promote shared leadership in spite of organizational barriers?

What role must organizational design play in the facilitation of shared leadership? For example, what types of performance measurements, rewards, and selection systems are necessary to promote shared leadership? Are team-based metrics more conducive than individual metrics? Are team-based rewards the answer? Research by O'Bannon and Pearce (1999) would suggest that team-based rewards are indeed at least a part of the answer. Conversely, in an environment based on individual rewards and competition, are we less likely to see the expression of shared leadership? Could training and 360-degree assessments play facilitative roles? Work by Conger (1998), Cox, Pearce, and Sims (in press) Forsyth (1999), Giacalone, Knouse, and Pearce (1998) and McCauley, Moxley, and Van Velsor (1998) would suggest it does. Clearly in the Shamir and Lapidot chapter, the subordinate evaluations of the leader played an important role. Questions such as these are of great interest to practitioners who find the concept of shared leadership appealing yet find themselves in environments where the demonstration of shared leadership is a relatively rare phenomenon.

From our earlier discussion of vertical versus shared leadership, there is the issue of how an individual, a working group, or an organization can initiate shared leadership. Houghton and his colleagues suggest that the vertical leader's actions are critical to the implementation process. Specifically, they identify the following: (a) selecting the appropriate team members, (b) establishing group norms supportive of shared leadership, (c) coaching and developing team members' leadership skills, (d) empowering team members to self-lead, (e) role modeling self-leadership behaviors, and (f) encouraging team problem solving and decision making. It would be important to test over a variety of settings whether indeed these behaviors facilitate shared leadership. In addition, might there be other behaviors and actions? Are certain actions more influential than others? The chapter by Shamir and Lapidot would suggest, however, that leader actions in themselves may not be sufficient. What, then, is required from individual team members themselves?

In conclusion, we suspect it is a much broader range of contributing factors—all the way from the organizational culture to rewards to performance management systems to organizational structure to job assignments to senior management attitudes about leadership.

# Cross-Cultural Factors

Cultural values shape perceptions, cognitions, and preferences in teams (Gibson, 2001). Given wide differences in behavioral norms across cultures, it is a natural question to ask whether shared leadership could be found across all cultural settings or whether it is likely to be restricted to certain settings. For example, one key cultural characteristic, power distance, may indeed limit the effective functioning of shared leadership across all cultures.

Power distance represents the degree to which members of a culture accept and expect that power in society be distributed unequally (Hofstede, 1980; House et al. 1999; Pearce, in press; Pearce & Osmond, 1999). People in cultures low in power distance will try to minimize inequalities, favor less autocratic leadership, and favor less centralization of authority. On the other hand, people in cultures high in power distance will be characterized by greater acceptance of inequalities, more autocratic leadership, and greater centralization of authority. For example, Hofstede (1991) found that in high power distance cultures, managers were more often satisfied with a directive leadership style from their supervisors whereas managers in low power distance cultures preferred a participative supervisor. Smith, Peterson, and Misumi (1994) have shown that managers in high power distance countries employ a greater use of rules and procedures than managers in low power distance cultures. Although House et al. (1999) found that several aspects of leadership were universally endorsed (i.e., charismatic and value-based leadership behaviors), they also obtained preliminary evidence that collective value orientations are positively related to team-oriented leadership endorsement, and that power distance is negatively related to participative leadership. The authors (1999) concluded that "societal cultural variables have non-trivial influences on culturally endorsed leadership theories and explain, in part, why there is variance across cultures with respect to what is expected of leaders" (p. 218). It would appear from these findings that shared leadership may be extremely rare in high power distance cultures and more prevalent in low power distance cultures.

Finally, in perhaps the most comprehensive investigation of a cultural contingency model of team effectiveness, Gibson and Zellmer-Bruhn (2001) explored a sample of 52 teams across four countries that varied based on power distance and collectivism. Using qualitative analyses of team members' language about teamwork, referred to as teamwork metaphors, the researchers demonstrated that power distance and collectivism affect the meaning that members ascribe to teamwork and to their expectations of team leadership. For example, in the high power distance cultures, team members tended to use teamwork metaphors containing information about hierarchy such as the family and military. In the low power distance cultures, team members used teamwork metaphors such as a sports metaphor that contained very little information about status and hierarchy. Stated another way, the meaning team members ascribed to teamwork in high power distance cultures included prescriptions for status relationships and in turn shaped members' expectations regarding hierarchical relationships in teams. Based on their interview results, the authors argue that teams in a high power distance culture will be more effective when managed in a way that recognizes status relationships and incorporates these into the team structure. Teams in a low power distance culture will be more effective when status relations are equal within teams—in other words, when leadership is more peer-based and shared.

# Outcomes of Shared Leadership

To date, very few studies of shared leadership have been implemented. Nonetheless, the initial evidence suggests that shared leadership can have a powerful effect on *group behavior, attitudes, cognition,* and *performance.* Below, we discuss each of these potential outcomes in greater detail.

*Shared Leadership and Group Behavior.* Avolio et al. (1996), in a study of undergraduate teams, found shared leadership to be significantly related to the amount of extra effort team members exerted on their projects. Similarly, Pearce (1997), in a study of change management teams, found shared leadership to be significantly related to citizenship behavior within the teams and networking behavior by team members. In a study of virtual teams, Pearce, Yoo, and Alavi (in press) found shared leadership to be a better predictor of problem-solving quality than measures of vertical leadership. Thus, the initial evidence seems to suggest that shared leadership is an important predictor of group behavior. Now what is needed are more studies that test the link between shared leadership and group behavior in a wide variety of contexts. We also recommend longitudinal research to examine any potential patterns between specific types of shared leadership and specific types of behavioral responses. Prior studies have examined group level behavior, so it would also be useful to examine the potential behavioral responses of individuals to shared leadership.

*Shared Leadership and Attitudes.* Avolio et al. (1996) found shared leadership to be significantly related to team member satisfaction. Pearce et al. (in press) found shared leadership to be a better predictor of social integration between the members of the team than measures of vertical leadership. The Shamir and Lapidot study reported in this volume also links shared leadership to important group attitudes such as trust in and satisfaction with the vertical leader. Clearly, more work needs to be done in this area. For example, future research might develop a typology of attitudinal effects of shared leadership. As part of this process, researchers might examine the efficacy of vertical leadership versus shared leadership as antecedents of important group member attitudes. On the one hand, we might expect shared leadership to be more efficacious since it is closer to the target of influence. On the other hand, the symbolic value of the vertical leader might mean that the words of the vertical leader are a more powerful source for attitude change. It would also be interesting to examine these potential effects on both positive and negative attitude change. As with the examination of the effects of shared leadership on team member behavior, we recommend broadening the scope of studies to examine teams in a wide variety of contexts.

*Shared Leadership and Cognition.* Avolio et al. found shared leadership to be significantly related to collective efficacy and potency. Pearce (1997) found shared leadership to be significantly related to potency. Pearce et al. (in press) found shared leadership to be a better predictor of potency than measures of vertical leadership. Finally, Hooker and Csikszentmihalyi's chapter in this volume suggests that there is a reciprocal relationship between creativity and shared leadership. Their case study reveals that shared leadership, under certain conditions, can enhance the conditions for flow (Csikszentmihalyi, 1988), which in turn bolsters the creative process. Thus, one area for future research would be to empirically test their conclusions. Other fruitful avenues would include the empirical investigation of the model forwarded by Burke et al. in this volume. As with behavior and attitudes, we recommend generally broadening the contexts under which the potential relationship between shared leadership and cognitive events within the group are examined.

*Shared Leadership and Effectiveness.* Avolio et al. found shared leadership to be significantly related to self-ratings of effectiveness. Ensley and Pearce (2000) studied entrepreneurial firms and found shared leadership to be a more important predictor than vertical leadership of both revenue and new venture growth rates. In a longitudinal study of change management teams, Pearce and Sims (2002) found shared leadership to account for more unique variance in manager, customer, and team self-ratings of effectiveness than did vertical leadership. Pearce et al. (in press) also found shared leadership to be a more important predictor than vertical leadership of self-rated perceived effectiveness. Finally, the studies in this volume by Hooker and Csikszentmihalyi and by Shamir and Lapidot suggest that shared leadership is related to the effectiveness of groups. As with the previous outcome variables, we would suggest more research in a wide variety of contexts. More fine-grained analyses would also prove useful.

# Measuring Shared Leadership

There has been little research to date examining the effective measurement of shared leadership. Given the complexity of the phenomenon and the youth of the field, it is not surprising that research on methods is lagging. We would argue, however, that we are now at a juncture where sophisticated methods are critical to advancing our understanding. To date, there have been five alternate methods articulated for examining shared leadership (Pearce, 2002). Three of these are quantitative survey-based, and two are qualitative observation-based.

Using modified traditional leadership items (e.g., MLQ), the three quantitative survey-based approaches to the study of shared leadership have involved the study of the group as (a) a whole, (b) a sum of its parts, and (c) a social network. For example, the approach examining the "group as a whole" uses items with the group as an entity as the source of influence and the group as a whole as the target of the influence. Using variables created at the group level of analysis, one can conduct analyses like those done with individual leader data (e.g., regression and SEM). This approach has been successfully demonstrated in this volume and by Avolio and colleagues, as well as by Avolio et al. (1996), Pearce (1997, 1999), Ensley and Pearce

(2000), Pearce and Sims (2002) and Pearce et al. (in press). The strength of this approach is that the data collection process is relatively nonburdensome to research participants. This approach, however, may smooth over differences in contributions by individual members of the group.

The second approach—the "group as a sum of its parts"—uses items with each of the team members measured separately as the sources of influence and the group as a whole as the target of influence. This approach involves three options for the creation of group level variables. First, shared leadership may be assessed using the weakest link option, in other words, using the scores of the individual rated lowest on leadership. Second, shared leadership may be assessed using the dominant member option, in other words, using the scores of the highest rated individual. Third, shared leadership may be assessed using the behavioral average option, which is similar to the group as a whole approach. Pearce and colleagues have begun research on these options but more data need to be collected before meaningful results can be discussed. These group level variables may then be used to conduct analyses much like those done with individual leader data. The primary strength of this approach is that it provides the ability to examine the influence of individuals to the overall leadership of the group. The primary weakness is that this method requires a great deal of effort from research participants because the respondent must respond to the same item multiple times (once for each member of the group), potentially resulting in problems associated with respondent fatigue.

The third quantitative method—the group as a social network—has been advocated by Mayo et al. and Seibert et al. in this volume. This approach uses items that measure each of the individuals as the sources of influence and each of the individuals as the targets of influence. The group level variable of interest in this approach is the degree to which the leadership behaviors are centralized and controlled by one or a few individuals or are dispersed and shared across the members of the group. Much of social network research has been concerned with predicting who, among a group, will be the "central" member(s). It is, however, possible to use the opposite of the centrality score as an indicator of shared leadership and use it to conduct analyses much like those done with individual leader data. The strengths of this approach are that it permits examination of the following: (a) the degree to which all members are involved in the leadership of the team; (b) the extent of dispersion of leadership in the team; and (c) the pattern of interaction between individuals, or who influences whom and how influence "travels" through the group. The primary weakness of this method is that it is quite burdensome on participants. It also does not assess influence that comes from the group as a whole or influence that is targeted at the group as a whole. Finally, the methods are somewhat complex.

In terms of qualitative approaches, the two approaches to date include: (a) leadership sociograms (Pearce, 2002) and (b) ethnographic methods. The leadership sociogram method involves the observation of group meeting(s) and recording of interaction patterns. The strengths of this approach include the following: (a) it permits a richer understanding of ongoing group dynamics than questionnaire-based methods, and (b) it is possible to quantify the analysis as input into a social network analysis. As for weaknesses, it requires a researcher to be onsite, and it does not capture the influence that occurs outside of the specific meeting(s) observed.

The ethnographic approach involves extensive, long-term observation of the group in their natural setting(s). It is not solely focused on the group when it is in a meeting and thereby provides a more naturalistic feel for the group in its various tasks. The strength of this approach is that it provides the richest possible understanding of ongoing group dynamics. The weakness is that it requires an extensive time commitment on the part of the researcher onsite for data collection on a single group.

We have illuminated five promising methodological avenues to the study of shared leadership. Each has its own strengths and weaknesses. Thus, important future research might compare and contrast these methods to determine the relative efficacy of each in the examination of shared leadership. Moreover, although we have identified five methodological approaches, we do not suggest that this is an exhaustive list of potential methodologies that might be employed in the study of shared leadership. As such, we encourage future research into alternative methodologies.

## The Limits and Liabilities of Shared Leadership

We do not advocate shared leadership as a new panacea for all organizational woes. Clearly, there are limitations regarding the efficacy of shared leadership. As Locke has argued, there are certain leadership tasks that are more effectively carried out by individuals rather than by groups. In fact, we believe there are situations in which shared leadership is actually harmful and should be discouraged. Limitations to shared leadership include the following: (a) lack of knowledge, skills, and abilities necessary for shared leadership; (b) lack of goal alignment between members of the team; (c) lack of goal alignment between the team and the organization; (d) lack of time to develop shared leadership; and (e) lack of receptivity to shared leadership. Below, we describe these limitations and liabilities in more detail.

*Lack of Knowledge, Skills, and Abilities.* If members of a team do not possess the requisite knowledge, skills, and abilities (KSAs) required to lead one another to successful task achievements, it seems unlikely that shared leadership would result in positive outcomes. This could easily be the case in situations where teams are required to take a big-picture strategic or company-wide perspective. If the team members' career paths have been in highly siloed, functional assignments that demand tactical rather than strategic thinking, the team may not be able to successfully accomplish its mandate due to a simple lack or breadth of experience. It would seem likely that this type of scenario would result in the team leading itself into directions that would prove counterproductive and ineffectual. Furthermore, we would argue that possession of the requisite KSAs for their task is a necessary but not sufficient condition for the effective development and display of shared leadership in the team. More significantly, it seems likely that team member attempts at influence would be far less successful when a critical number of members lack the appropriate *leadership* competences. In the worst case scenario, one can envision a case in which clumsy attempts at influence could result in affective conflict, which in turn could spiral out of control and ultimately lead to the demise of any form of teamwork. Thus, a major limitation to the potential for effective shared leadership would be poorly distributed task and leadership KSAs among the team members.

*Lack of Goal Alignment Between Team Members.* One implicit assumption all of the writings in this volume have made, with the exception of Locke, Seibert, et al. and Cox et al., is that the team members are implicitly working toward similar ends. We know, however, that this is not always the case in organizational settings. For example, temporary cross-functional teams are often plagued with problems when members bring into the group ongoing interdepartmental feuds. Consider the situation of teams at the top. Although O'Toole, Lawler, and Galbraith suggest that leadership can be shared by senior executives, Lazear (1989) argues that the tops of organizations are occupied by "hawks" that have a natural proclivity toward politicking and conflict. Others have made the observation that members of the tops of organizations are engaged in a tournament with one another (Main, O'Reilly, & Wade, 1993) in which the short-term-prize is compensation and the long-term prize is ascension to the position of CEO. If the goals of the individual members of the team are not aligned, it seems unlikely that shared leadership would flourish.

*Lack of Goal Alignment Between the Team and the Organization.* Another implicit assumption of the thinking presented in this volume is that the goals of teams are aligned with the overarching organizational goals. Clearly, this is not always the case. Thus, although shared leadership may make a team effective in the pursuit of its own goals, this is no guarantee that the overall organization will benefit. This can even be true of teams at the top. For example, one only need look at the increased level of shareholder activism in response to top management teams driving the organization toward the pursuit of their own objectives and personal enrichment. In addition, maverick teams might arise whose activities undermine the overall organization's goals. Thus, the positive contribution of shared leadership is limited by the extent to which the goals of the team are aligned with the overarching organizational goals.

*Lack of Time to Develop Shared Leadership.* We believe that shared leadership generally requires time to develop. Thus, early in the life of a team, it seems less likely that shared leadership will produce positive benefits. For example, transactive memory is something that enhances the ability of the team members to engage in constructive team leadership. Yet transactive memory requires time to develop, and so it seems likely that shared leadership in early team life will likely be less effective. In this case, it may be best to rely more heavily on the appointed leader. It follows that in temporary teams of extremely short duration, effective shared leadership may not even have the opportunity to develop and flower and perhaps should even be avoided all together.

*Lack of Receptivity to Shared Leadership.* At its most basic level, we can define leadership by whether or not someone has followers. It is certainly conceivable that some members may not be willing to accept influence attempts from other members. This would be especially true of individuals with high power needs and high levels of narcissism who may wish to dominate the group. In an extreme case, one might observe all team members trying to be the leader at all times. For shared leadership to be effective, all team members must be open to the possibility of both engaging in leadership as well as following the appropriate leadership of other members. Thus, a reluctance to share leadership with other individuals is another limiting factor in its potential success.

# Conclusion

As readers will have realized by now, the field of shared leadership holds remarkable opportunities for researchers in the future. There is so little that we actually know—to use an old truism, "We have only scratched the surface." We hope that this survey will provide a starting point for other scholars to join with the existing small band of explorers in charting how and why shared leadership can make a significant contribution to the world of organizations. We deeply believe that we are in an era that is demanding far more leadership that is truly shared among a greater number of individuals as well as up and down the hierarchy. Only when we have achieved a greater appreciation for the positive outcomes associated with shared leadership and a real understanding of how it works effectively will we be able to harness its full potential to contribute to organizational performance. Only then will shared leadership also stand as an equal to traditional notions of leadership, the solitary individual in a position of authority.

# References

Avolio, B. J., Jung, D. I., Murry, W., & Sivasubramaniam, N. (1996). Building highly developed teams: Focusing on shared leadership processes, efficacy, trust, and performance. In M. Beyerlein, D. Johnson, & S. Beyerlein (Eds.), *Advances in interdisciplinary studies of work teams: Team leadership* (pp. 173-209). Greenwich, CT: JAI Press.

Bales, R. F. (1958). Task roles and social roles in problem-solving groups. In E. E. Maccoby, T. M. Newcomb, & E. L. Hartley (Eds.), *Readings in social psychology* (pp. 437-447). New York: Henry Holt.

Bass, B. M. (1985). *Leadership and performance beyond expectations.* New York: Free Press.

Carter, L. F. (1954). Recording and evaluating the performance of individuals as members of small groups. *Personnel Psychology, 7,* 477-484.

Conger, J. A., (1998). Education for leaders: Current practices, new directions, *Journal of Management Systems, 10*(2), 81-90.

Conger, J. A., & Kanungo, R. N. (1998). *Charismatic Leadership in Organizations.* Thousand Oaks, CA: Sage.

Cox, J. F., Pearce, C. L., & Sims, H. P., Jr. (in press). Toward a broader agenda for leadership development: Extending the transactional-transformational duality by development directive, empowering *and shared leadership skills.* In R. E. Riggio & S. Murphy (Eds.), *The Future of Leadership Development.* Mahwah, NJ: Lawrence Erlbaum.

Csikszentmihalyi, I. (1988). Flow in historical context: The case of the Jesuits. In M. Csikszentmihalyi & I. Csikszentmihalyi (Eds.), *Optimal experience: Psychological studies of flow in consciousness.* Cambridge, UK: Cambridge University Press.

Ensley, M. D., & Pearce, C. L. (2000, June). *Assessing the influence of leadership behaviors on new venture TMT processes and new venture performance.* Paper presented at the 20th Annual Entrepreneurship Research Conference, Babson Park, MA.

Ensley, M. D., Pearson, A., & Pearce, C. L. (in press). Top management team process, shared leadership, and new venture performance: A theoretical model and research agenda. *Human Resource Management Review.*

Feldman, R. A. (1973). Power distribution, integration, and conformity in small groups. *American Journal of Sociology, 79,* 639-665.

Forsyth, D. R. (1999). *Group dynamics* (3rd ed.). Belmont, CA: Wadsworth.

Giacalone, R. A., Knouse, S. B., & Pearce, C. L. (1998). The education of leaders: Impression management as a functional competence. *Journal of Management Systems, 10*(2), 67-80.

Gibson, C. B. (2001). From accumulation to accommodation: The chemistry of collective cognition in work groups. *Journal of Organizational Behavior, 22*(2): 121-134.

Gibson, C. B., & Zellmer-Bruhn, M. (2001). Metaphor and meaning: An intercultural analysis of the concept of teamwork. *Administrative Science Quarterly, 46,* 274-303.

Hackman, J. R. (1987). The design of work teams. In J. W. Lorsch (Ed.), *Handbook of organizational behavior* (pp. 315-342). Englewood Cliffs, NJ: Prentice Hall.

Hofstede, G. (1991). *Cultures and organizations: Software of the mind.* New York: McGraw-Hill.

House, R. J., Hanges, P. J., Ruiz-Quintanilla, S. A., Dorfman, P. W., Javidan, M., Dickson, M., et al. (1999). Cultural influences on leadership in organizations: Project globe. In W. H. Mobley, M. J. Gessner, & V. Arnold (Eds.), *Advances in Global Leadership* (Vol. 1, pp. 171-234). Stamford, CT: JAI Press.

Knight, D., Pearce, C. L., Smith, K. G., Sims, H. P., Jr., Olian, J. D., Smith, K. A., & Flood, P. (1999). Top management team diversity, group dynamics, and strategic consensus: An empirical investigation. *Strategic Management Journal, 20*(5), 445-466.

Kozlowski, S. W. J., Gully, S. M., Salas, E., & Cannon-Bowers, J. A. (1996). Team leadership and development: Theory, principles, and guidelines for training leaders and teams. In M. Beyerlein, D. Johnson, & S. Beyerlein (Eds.), *Advances in interdisciplinary studies of work teams* (Vol. 3, pp. 253-291). Greenwich, CT: JAI Press.

Kuhn, T. S. (1970). *The structure of scientific revolutions.* Chicago: Chicago University Press.

Lazear, E. P. (1989). Pay equality and industrial politics. *Journal of Political Economy, 97,* 561-580.

Lord, R. G., Foti, R. J., & De Vader, C. L. (1984). A test of leadership categorization theory: Internal structure, information processing, and leadership perceptions. *Organizational Behavior and Human Performance, 34,* 343-378.

Lord, R. G., & Maher, K. J. (1993). *Leadership and information processing: Linking perceptions and performance.* Boston, MA: Rutledge.

Main, B. G. M., O'Reilly, C. A., & Wade, J. 1993. Top executive pay: Tournament or teamwork? *Journal of Labor Economics, 11*(4): 606-628.

McCauley, C. D., Moxley, R. S., & Van Velsor, E. (Eds.). (1998). *The Center for Creative Leadership handbook of leadership development.* San Francisco: Jossey-Bass.

O'Bannon, D. P., & Pearce, C. L. (1999). A quasi-experiment of gainsharing in service organizations: Implications for organizational citizenship behavior and pay satisfaction. *Journal of Managerial Issues, 11*(3), 363-378.

Pearce, C. L. (1997). *The determinants of change management team effectiveness: A longitudinal investigation.* Unpublished doctoral dissertation, University of Maryland, College Park.

Pearce, C. L. (1999, August). *The relative influence of vertical vs. shared leadership on the longitudinal effectiveness of change management teams.* Paper presented at the to the Annual Conference of the Academy of Management, Chicago.

Pearce, C. L. (2002, August). Quantitative and qualitative approaches to the study of shared leadership. In C. L. Pearce (symposium chair), *Shared leadership: Reframing the hows and whys of leadership.* Presented to the annual conference of the Academy of Management, Denver, CO.

Pearce, C. L. (in press). *Mas allá del liderazco heroico: Como el buen vino, el liderazco es algo para ser compartido.* Revista de empresa.

Pearce, C. L., & Gallagher, C., & Ensley, M. (2002). Confidence at the group level of analysis: A longitudinal investigation of the relationship between potency and team effectiveness. *Journal of Occupational and Organizational Psychology, 75,* 115-119.

Pearce, C. L., & Osmond, C. P. (1999). From workplace attitudes and values to a global pattern of nations: An application of latent class modeling. *Journal of Management, 25*(5), 759-778.

Pearce, C. L., Perry, M. L., & Sims, H. P., Jr. (2001). Shared leadership: Relationship management to improve NPO effectiveness. In T. D. Connors (Ed.), *The nonprofit handbook: Management* (pp. 624-641). New York: Wiley.

Pearce, C., & Sims, H. P., Jr. (2000). Shared leadership: Toward a multi-level theory of leadership. In M. Beyerlein, D. Johnson, & S. Beyerlein (Eds.), *Advances in the interdisciplinary studies of work teams* (Vol. 7, pp. 115-139). New York: JAI Press.

Pearce, C. L., & Sims, H. P., Jr. (2002). The relative influence of vertical vs. shared leadership on the longitudinal effectiveness of change management teams. *Group Dynamics: Theory, Research, and Practice, 6(2),* 172-197.

Pearce, C. L. (in press). *Mas allá del liderazco heroico: Como el buen vino, el liderazco es algo para ser compartido.* Revista de empresa.

Pearce, C. L., Yoo, Y., & Alavi, M. (in press). Leadership, social work and virtual teams: The relative influence of vertical vs. shared leadership in the nonprofit section. In R. E. Riggio and S. Smith Orr (Eds.), *Improving leadership in nonprofit organizations.* San Francisco: Jossey-Bass.

Perry, M. L., Pearce, C. L., & Sims, H. P., Jr. (1999, Summer). Empowered selling teams: How shared leadership can contribute to selling team outcomes. *Journal of Personal Selling and Sales Management, 3,* 35-51.

Phillips, J. S., & Lord, R. G. (1982). Schematic information processing and perception of leadership in problem solving groups. *Journal of Applied Psychology, 67,* 486-492.

Seers, A. (1996). Better leadership through chemistry: Toward a model of emergent shared team leadership. *Advances in Interdisciplinary Studies of Work Teams, 3,* 145-172.

Sims, H., & Gioia, D. (Eds.). (1986). *The thinking organization: Dynamics of organizational social cognition.* San Francisco: Jossey-Bass.

Slater, P. E. (1955). Role differentiation in small groups. *American Sociology Journal, 20,* 300-310.

Smith, P. B., Peterson, M. F., & Misumi, J. (1994). Event management and work team effectiveness in Japan, Britain and USA. *Journal of Occupational and Organizational Psychology, 67,* 33-43.

Steiner, I. D. (1976). Task-performing groups. In J. W. Thibaut & R. C. Carson (Eds.), *Contemporary topics in social psychology* (pp. 393-422). Morristown, NJ: General Learning Press.

Tuckman, B. W. (1965, December). Developmental sequences in small groups. *Psychological Bulletin, 63,* 384-399.

# Author Index

# Subject Index

# About the Contributors

**Craig L. Pearce** is Assistant Professor of Management at the Peter F. Drucker Graduate School of Management at Claremont Graduate University. His areas of expertise include leadership, teamwork, and change management. He has won several awards for his research, including an award from the Center for Creative Leadership for his research on shared leadership. His research has appeared in *Organizational Dynamics, Journal of Management, Strategic Management Journal, Journal of Organizational Behavior, Journal of Occupational and Organizational Psychology, Group Dynamics: Theory, Research, and Practice, Journal of Managerial Issues, Advances in Interdisciplinary Studies of Work Teams, Journal of Personal Selling and Sales Management, Journal of Applied Social Psychology, Human Resource Management Review, Journal of Management Systems, The Future of Leadership Development,* and *Improving Leaderhip in Nonprofit Organizations* as well as other publications. He serves on the board of directors of Small Potatoes, Inc., an agricultural biotech company. He is also the co-founder of the Risk Assessment Institute, an organization that works primarily with venture capital firms in conducting due diligence work on start-up organizations, as well as on mergers and acquisitions. One of the primary tools of the Risk Assessment Institute is the Top Management Team Evaluator, which can be viewed online at www.tmtevaluator.com.

Prior to beginning an academic career, he worked as an international management consultant in the area of process reengineering, organizational development, and turnaround management. His clients have included AAI, ACNielsen, American Express, British Bakeries, GEICO Insurance, Land Rover, Mack Trucks, Manor Bakeries, Pickering Foods, Rayovac, The Rouse Company, Rover Cars, and Serono. He received his Ph.D. from the University of Maryland, his M.B.A. from the University of Wisconsin-Madison, and his B.S. (hons.) from Pennsylvania State University.

**Jay A. Conger** is Professor of Organizational Behavior at the London Business School and Senior Research Scientist at the Center for Effective Organizations at the University of Southern California in Los Angeles. Formerly the executive director of the Leadership Institute at the University of Southern California, he is an expert on leadership. *Business Week* named him as number five on its list of the world's top ten management gurus. He has also been selected by *Business Week* as the best business school professor to teach leadership to executives. In 2001, he was awarded by the Center for Creative Leadership their H. Smith Richardson Fellowship for his research on leadership. Author of over 90 articles and book chapters and 10 books, he researches leadership, innovation, boards of directors, organizational change, and the training and development of leaders and managers. His articles have appeared in the *Academy of Management Review, Harvard Business Review,* the *Journal of Organizational Behavior,* the *Leadership Quarterly,* and *Organizational Dynamics.* His books include *Corporate Boards: New Strategies for Adding Value at the Top* (2001), *Building Leaders* (1999), and *Charismatic Leadership in Organizations* (1998). His book *Charismatic Leadership in Organizations* (1998) received the Choice Book Award in 1999. He received his B.A. from Dartmouth College, his M.B.A. from the University of Virginia, and his D.B.A. from the Harvard Business School.

**Bruce J. Avolio** (Ph.D., University of Akron) is the Donald and Shirley Clifton Chair in Leadership at the University of Nebraska in the College of Business Administration. Previously, he was codirector of the Global Center for Leadership Studies, State University of New York at Binghamton. He has an international reputation as a researcher in leadership, having published over 80 articles and book chapters. He consults with a large number of organizations in North America, South America, Africa, Europe, Southeast Asia, Australia, New Zealand, and Israel. His research and consulting includes work with the militaries of the United States of America, Singapore, Sweden, Finland, Israel, South Africa, and Europe. His latest book is titled *Full Leadership Development: Building the Vital Forces in Organizations* (Sage, 1999). His forthcoming book is *Leadership Development in Balance: Made/Born.*

**C. Shawn Burke**, Ph.D., is Research Associate at the University of Central Florida, Institute for Simulation and Training. Her primary research interests include teams, team leadership, team training and measurement, and team effectiveness. She has presented at numerous conferences, has published in several scientific journals on the topics of teams and team training, and serves as an ad hoc reviewer for the *Human Factors* journal. She earned her doctorate degree in 2000 from George Mason University in industrial and organizational psychology.

**Jonathan F. Cox** is a program manager with Dell Computer Corporation. Before joining Dell, he was a manager with the Change Leadership practice of Deloitte Consulting L.C. and an associate with the Center for the Study of Work Teams at the University of North Texas. His areas of expertise include change management, leadership, teamwork, and sociotechnical design. His work has appeared in *Journal of Applied Psychology, Group and Organization Management, Advances in the Interdisciplinary Studies of Work Teams,* and other publications. He has worked with a range of private- and public-sector clients representing telecommunications, insurance, industrial manufacturing, aerospace and defense, utilities, health care, law enforcement, and education. Representative clients include AT&T, IXC (now Broadwing), GEICO, Group NCH, Raytheon, Lockheed-Martin, Westinghouse, and Conectiv. He received his Ph.D. and M.A. in industrial and organizational psychology from the University of Maryland and his B.A. from Grinnell College.

**Mihaly Csikszentmihalyi** is C. S. and D. J. Davidson Professor of Psychology at the Peter F. Drucker Graduate School of Management at Claremont Graduate University and Director of the Quality of Life Research Center. He is also Emeritus Professor of Human Development at the University of Chicago, where he chaired the department of psychology. In addition to the influential *Flow: The Psychology of Optimal Experience* (1990), which was translated into 15 languages, he is the author of 13 other books and some 210 research articles. His latest volume (with Howard Gardner and William Damon) is titled *Good Work: When Excellence and Ethics Meet.*

**Stephen M. Fiore**, Ph.D., is Research Scientist at the University of Central Florida, Team Performance Laboratory. His research interests incorporate aspects of cognitive, social, and organizational psychology to investigate learning and problem solving. He is currently investigating the processes and products emerging from distributed learning environments and how advanced training technologies can accelerate perceptual learning processes. He serves as an ad hoc reviewer for journals such as *Applied Cognitive Psychology*, *Human Factors*, *Group Processes*, and *Intergroup Relations*.

**Joyce K. Fletcher** is Professor of Management at the Center for Gender in Organizations, Simmons Graduate School of Management in Boston, and a Senior Research Scholar at the Jean Baker Miller Training Institute at the Wellesley College Centers for Women. She is the coauthor of a widely read Harvard Business Review article titled "A Modest Manifesto for Shattering the Glass Ceiling" and is a frequent speaker on the topics of women, power, and leadership. She is author of *Disappearing Acts: Gender, Power and Relational Practice at Work* (1999) and coauthor of a book on leading change titled *Beyond Work Family Balance: Advancing Gender Equity and Workplace Performance* (2002).

**Jay Galbraith** is Professor Emeritus at the International Institute for Management Development (IMD) in Lausanne, Switzerland. He is also Senior Research Scientist at the Center for Effective Organizations at the University of Southern California. Prior to joining the faculty at USC, he directed his own management consulting firm. He has served on the faculties of the Wharton School at the University of Pennsylvania and the Sloan School of Management at MIT. His work focuses on the areas of organizational design, change, and development; strategy and organization at the corporate, business unit, and international levels; and international partnering arrangements including joint ventures and network-type organizations. His most recent book, *Designing the Global Corporation*, describes how leading multinational corporations address the demands of their increasingly global customers to provide solutions, not just products. Other books include *Designing Organizations* and *Competing With Flexible Lateral Organizations*. Edited volumes include *Tomorrow's Organization* and *Organizing for the Future*.

**John W. Garger** is a doctoral candidate in the School of Management at State University of New York at Binghamton. He is pursuing his degree in management with a concentration in organizational behavior. His research interests include distance leadership, e-leadership, virtual teams, e-commerce, and the impacts of technology on the individual. His working papers include leader-member exchange in virtual teams, factors influencing individual adoption and use of web-based communication systems, and levels of analysis in e-leadership.

**Charles Hooker** is a doctoral candidate in Emory University's joint J.D./Ph.D. program in Law and Religion. He holds an A.M. in Religious Studies from the University of Chicago, where he ventured into human development and began assisting Mihaly Csikszentmihalyi on the "Good Work" project. Following his time at Chicago, he worked for a year (2000-2001) as a Research Associate at the Quality of Life Research Center at the Peter F. Drucker School of Management at Claremont Graduate University. In conjunction with his doctoral work, he continues to research and write in the areas of mentorship, ethics in the professions, and cultural evolution.

**Jeffery D. Houghton**, Ph.D., is Associate Professor of Management at Abilene Christian University. His research specialties include the self-regulation of behavior and cognition, personality and individual differences, team performance and sustainability, and leadership. He has presented his research at various professional meetings and has published articles in a variety of respected journals. In addition to his research activities, he has given presentations and conducted training seminars for a number of organizations including the Bruce Hardwood Floors Company of Nashville, Tennessee.

**Don Jung** (Ph.D., State University of New York at Binghamton) is Associate Professor of Management at San Diego State University, where he teaches courses in organizational behavior, international management, and international negotiations. His research interests include transformational/charismatic leadership, cross-cultural leadership, team dynamics, and international management. His publications have appeared in many scholarly journals such as the *Academy of Management Journal, Leadership Quarterly, Group and Organization Management, Group Dynamics, Journal of Applied Behavioral Science, Journal of Organizational Behavior,* and *Journal of Occupational Psychology.*

**Katrin Käufer** is a visiting scholar at the MIT Sloan School of Management and a founding research member at the Society for Organizational Learning. Her current research focuses on methods for leading profound change processes in organizations and on distributed forms of leadership. She won an innovation award (Stiftung für Industrieforschung, Germany) for the development of an integrated study program at 12 universities around the world. She has consulted with a global pharmaceutical company, the World Bank, a learning network of small- and mid-sized companies, and nonprofit organizations, and is currently working with the United Nations Development Program (UNDP) on civic dialogue.

**Tiffany Keller** is Director of the Brain Leadership Program at Baldwin-Wallace College. Her research focuses on leader-follower relationships, implicit theories of leadership, and levels of analysis issues, and appears in *Human Relations, Leadership Quarterly,* and *Organizational Research Methods.* She is a member of the Academy of Management, American Psychological Association, International Leadership Association, and Society for Industrial and Organizational Psychology. She received her Ph.D. from the State University of New York at Buffalo in organizational behavior.

**Yael Lapidot** is an organizational consultant and Lecturer at the College of Management, Tel-Aviv University. She holds an M.A. in organizational behavior from Tel-Aviv University and is currently completing her doctorate at the School of Business Administration, Hebrew University of Jerusalem. Her work has been published in the *Journal of Applied Psychology.* Her research interests are leadership and trust in organizations.

**Edward E. Lawler, III** is Distinguished Professor of Business and Director of the Center for Effective Organizations in the Marshall School of Business at the University of Southern California. He joined USC in 1978 and, during 1979, founded and became director of the University's Center for Effective Organizations. He has consulted with over 100 organizations on employee involvement, organizational change, and compensation and has been honored as a top contributor to the fields of organizational development, organizational behavior, and compensation. The author of over 300 articles and 30 books, his works have been translated into seven languages. His most recent books include *The Ultimate Advantage* (1992), *Organizing for the Future* (1993), *From the Ground Up: Six Principles for*

*Creating the New Logic Corporation* (1996), *Tomorrow's Organization* (1998), *Strategies for High Performance Organizations—The CEO Report* (1998), *The Leadership Change Handbook* (1999), *Rewarding Excellence* (2000), and *Corporate Boards: New Strategies for Adding Value at the Top* (2001). His most recent book is *Organizing for High Performance* (2001).

**Robert C. Liden** is Synovus Chair of Servant Leadership in the Institute for Leadership Advancement and Professor of Management in the Terry College of Business at the University of Georgia. His research focuses on interpersonal processes as they relate to such topics as leadership, groups, career progression, and employment interviews. In 2000, he was inducted into the Academy of Management Journal's Hall of Fame. He has served on the editorial boards of the *Journal of Management* and the *Academy of Management Journal.* In 2000-2001, he served as division chair of the Academy of Management's Organizational Behavior Division.

**Edwin A. Locke** is Dean's Professor of Leadership and Motivation (Emeritus) at the R. H. Smith School of Business at the University of Maryland, College Park. He has published over 220 chapters, notes, and articles in professional journals on such subjects as work motivation, job satisfaction, incentives, and the philosophy of science. He is also the author or editor of 9 books, including *Study Methods and Study Motivation* (1998), *Goal Setting: A Motivational Technique that Works* (1984, with G. Latham), *A Theory of Goal Setting and Task Performance* (1990, with G. Latham), *Handbook of Principles of Organizational Behavior* (2000), and *The Prime Movers: Traits of the Great Wealth Creators* (*AMACOM*, 2000). He is internationally known for his research on goal setting. A survey of over 100 scholars in industrial-organizational psychology and organizational behavior ranked Locke's goal setting theory as one of the two most valid and useful theories in the field. He was a winner of the Outstanding Teacher-Scholar Award at the University of Maryland, the Distinguished Scientific Contribution Award of the Society for Industrial and Organizational Psychology, and the Career Contribution Award from the Academy of Management (Human Resource Division). He is a member of the board of advisors of the Ayn Rand Institute, and is interested in the application of the philosophy of objectivism to the behavioral sciences. He received a Ph.D. in industrial psychology from Cornell University in 1964.

**Charles C. Manz**, Ph.D., is Charles and Janet Nirenberg Professor of Business Leadership in the Isenberg School of Management at the University of Massachusetts. He is the author of over 100 articles and book chapters and 12 books including the bestsellers *Business Without Bosses, SuperLeadership* (which won the Stybel-Peabody Prize), and *The Leadership Wisdom of Jesus.* His publications have especially focused on empowering leadership, self-leadership, and work teams and have been translated into several foreign languages. He has also served as a consultant and executive trainer to numerous organizations including many Fortune 500 companies.

**Margarita Mayo** is Professor in Organizational Behavior at the Instituto de Empresa, Spain. Her current research interests include leadership, self-directed work teams, social network theory, and diversity. Her research has been published in professional journals such as *The Academy of Management Journal* and *The Leadership Quarterly* and she has received an award from the Center for Creative Leadership. She earned a Ph.D. in organizational behavior from the State University of New York at Buffalo and a M.A. in social psychology from Clark University. She was a Visiting Fulbright Scholar at Harvard University.

**James R. Meindl** is the Carmichael Professor of Organization and Human Resources at the State University of New York at Buffalo. He is broadly interested in the interplay between microprocesses and macrostructures. He has published numerous articles and book chapters in such areas as leadership and decision making, power and influence, justice and cooperative behavior, information processing, and group relations. He has served on the editorial boards of the *Academy of Management Journal*, *Administrative Science Quarterly*, and *Academy of Management Review*. He is also coeditor of an annual series titled *Advances in Managerial Cognition and Organizational Information Processing*. He is the recipient of the Chancellor's Teaching Excellence Award. He is an active member of the Academy of Management, where he is an executive member of the Organizational Behavior Division. He received his Ph.D. in social psychology from the University of Waterloo.

**William D. Murry** (Ph.D., Virginia Polytechnic Institute) is Assistant Professor of Management at the A. J. Palumbo School of Business Administration at Duquesne University, where he teaches leadership, strategy, organizational behavior, and human resource management classes at both the undergraduate and graduate levels. Previously, he has taught at the State University of New York at Binghamton, Virginia Polytechnic Institute (VPI), and Roanoke College. His research and publications include the areas of leadership, team building, organizational cultures, affirmative action, sexual harassment, personality, and genetic testing in the workplace. His publications have appeared in *Leadership Quarterly*, *Group and Organization Management*, *Journal of Business Ethics*, *Journal of Personality Assessment*, *Education and Psychological Measurement*, and in such books as *Leadership: The Multiple Level Approaches*, *The Impact of Management*, and *Advances in Interdisciplinary Studies of Work Teams*. He has also presented numerous symposia and papers at multiple professional conferences.

**Christopher P. Neck**, Ph.D., is Associate Professor of Management at Virginia Polytechnic Institute and State University. He has published over 50 journal articles and book chapters and 3 books, including *Mastering Self-Leadership: Empowering Yourself For Personal Excellence* and *Medicine for the Mind: Healing Words to Help You Soar*. He has been cited in numerous national publications including the *Wall Street Journal*, the *Washington Post*, the *Los Angeles Times*, *Entrepreneur Magazine*, *Runner's World*, and *New Woman Magazine*. Organizations he has worked with include the United States Army, America West Airlines, American Electric Power, and Prudential Life Insurance. An avid runner, he has completed 12 marathons, including the Boston Marathon.

**James O'Toole** is Research Professor in the Center for Effective Organizations in the Marshall School of Business at the University of Southern California. In 1994, he retired after a career of over 20 years on the faculty of USC's Graduate School of Business, where he held the University Associates' Chair of Management. At USC, he served as executive director of the Leadership Institute, editor of *New Management* magazine, and director of the Twenty-Year Forecast Project, where from 1974-1983 he interpreted social, political, and economic change for the top management of 30 of the largest American corporations. His research and writings have been in the areas of planning, corporate culture, and leadership. He has addressed dozens of major corporations and professional organizations and has published over 70 articles. One of his thirteen books, *Vanguard Management*, was named among the best business and economics books of 1985 by the editors of *Business Week*. *Leading Change* was published in the spring of 1995, and his latest book, *Leadership A to Z*, was published in 1999. He has served as a special assistant to the Secretary of Health, Education, and Welfare, Elliot Richardson; as chairman of the Secretary's Task Force on Work in America; and as director of Field Investigations for President Nixon's Commission on Campus Unrest. Most recently, he has been managing director of the Booz-Allen & Hamilton Strategic Leadership Center. He received his doctorate in social anthropology from Oxford University, where he was a Rhodes Scholar.

**Juan-Carlos Pastor** is Professor and Chair of Organizational Behavior and Human Resources at the Instituto de Empresa, Spain. Before, he taught management behavior in the Richard Ivey School of Business at the University of Western Ontario. He teaches courses on organizational behavior, leadership, and managing people skills. His research interests include a social psychological approach to leadership that emphasizes the cognitions and social environments of both leaders and followers. His research on leadership has been published in *The Academy of Management Journal, Leadership Quarterly, Journal of Environment and Behavior, Best Paper Proceedings of the Academy of Management, The Diffusion and Consumption of Business Knowledge*, and *Diversity in Work Teams: Selected Research*. His work has received a competitive award from the Center for Creative Leadership. He earned a Ph.D. in organizational behavior from the State University of New York at Buffalo and an M.A. in social psychology from Clark University. He was a Visiting Fulbright Scholar at Harvard University.

**Monica L. Perry** is Associate Professor of Marketing at California State University, Fullerton, and has taught at the University of North Carolina at Charlotte, the Richard Ivey School of Business in London, Ontario, and the Peter F. Drucker School of Management in Claremont, California. Her teaching and research focus on relationship marketing and technology. Her work has appeared in the *Nonprofit Handbook, Journal of International Marketing, Industrial Marketing Management*, and the *Journal of Personal Selling and Sales Management*. She has consulted profit and nonprofit organizations and has worked in business-to-business marketing at Nortel, marketing research at 3M, and product management at CBS Educational and Professional Publishing. She earned her Ph.D. in marketing from the University of Maryland and her M.B.A. from Pennsylvania State University.

**Eduardo Salas,** Ph.D., is Professor of Psychology at the University of Central Florida and Program Director for the Human-Systems Integration Department at the Institute for Simulation & Training at UCF. He has coauthored over 200 journal articles and chapters, edited 11 books, serves on 10 editorial boards, and is currently editor of *Human Factors*. He is a fellow of Division 14 and 21 of the APA and a fellow of the Human Factors and Ergonomics Society.

**Anson Seers** (Ph.D., University of Cincinnati) is Professor of Management at Virginia Commonwealth University. His major research interests have centered on work roles and working relationships, encompassing topics such as leader-member exchange relationships, team-member exchange relationships, emergent leadership, role conflict and role ambiguity, team and organizational commitment, work team effectiveness, and task force pacing. Prior to joining VCU, he held the Frank Anthony Rose Professorship in Leadership at the University of Alabama and was a visiting professor at Edith Cowan University in Perth, Western Australia.

**Scott E. Seibert**, Ph.D., is Assistant Professor in the Department of Managerial Studies at the University of Illinois at Chicago. His interest in personality and interpersonal processes informs his work on careers, empowerment, organizational climate, leadership, and group processes. His work has been published in the *Academy of Management Journal*, the *Journal of Applied Psychology*, and *Personnel Psychology*. He received his doctorate from the School of Industrial and Labor Relations at Cornell University.

**Boas Shamir** is Professor at the Department of Sociology and Anthropology, Hebrew University of Jerusalem, and held visiting positions at Suffolk University, Boston; Binghamton University; the Institute of Rural Management, Anand, India; and the National University of Singapore. He holds a Ph.D. in social psychology from the London School of Economics and Political Science. He has published over 70 journal articles and book chapters. His work has appeared in the *Academy of Management Journal*, *Academy of Management Review*, and the *Journal of Applied Psychology*. His main research interest is leadership in organizations.

**Nagaraj Sivasubramaniam** (Ph.D., Florida International University) is Assistant Professor of Management in the A. J. Palumbo School of Business Administration at Duquesne University where he teaches courses in strategic management at the undergraduate and graduate levels. He previously taught at the State University of New York at Binghamton and at Southwestern University in Georgetown, Texas. His research interests include the effects of technology on business-to-business relationships, leadership roles and their impact in the virtual world, and the use of computer-mediated communications in organizations. His prior work has appeared in several scholarly journals including *Leadership Quarterly*, *Group and Organization Management*, *Omega*, and *Advances in Interdisciplinary Studies of Work Teams*. He has also presented his work at several national and international conferences.

**Raymond T. Sparrowe**, Ph.D., is on the faculty of the John M. Olin School of Business at Washington University in St. Louis. His research interests include leadership, social networks, and group processes. His work has been published in the *Academy of Management Journal*, the *Academy of Management Review*, and the *Journal of Applied Psychology*. His doctorate is from the University of Illinois at Chicago.

**James M. Wilkerson** is Assistant Professor of Management at Southern Illinois University Edwardsville. His research interests include employee deviance, leader-member exchange relationships, work groups' effectiveness, and corporate social performance. In his earlier career, he was a human resource management professional in a variety of managerial, executive, and consultant roles with several manufacturing and service companies. He is a lifetime certified Senior Professional in Human Resources (SPHR) and also served in the U. S. Air Force as an ICBM combat crew commander, evaluator, and trainer. He earned his doctorate in organizational behavior at the Georgia Institute of Technology.